Philosophy

The Pursuit of Wisdom

THIRD EDITION

LOUIS P. POJMAN
UNITED STATES MILITARY ACADEMY

D0024035

WADSWORTH

™

THOMSON LEARNING

Australia • Canada • Mexico • Singapore • Spain
United Kingdom • United States

Philosophy Editor: Peter Adams
Assistant Editor: Kara Kindstrom
Editorial Assistant: Mark Andrews
Marketing Manager: Dave Garrison
Print Buyer: Tandra Jorgenson
Permissions Editor: Bob Kauser

Production Service: Gustafson Graphics
Copy Editor: Linda Ireland
Cover Designer: Laurie Anderson
Cover Printer: Webcom Limited
Compositor: Gustafson Graphics
Printer/Binder: Webcom Limited

Printed in Canada
1 2 3 4 5 6 7 03 02 01

For permission to use material from this text, contact us by:
  Web: http://www.thomsonrights.com
  Fax: 1-800-730-2215
  Phone: 1-800-730-2214

**Library of Congress
Cataloging-in-Publication Data**

Pojman, Louis P.
    Philosophy: the pursuit of wisdom /
Louis Pojman.—3rd ed.
        p. cm.
    Includes bibliographical references
and index.
    ISBN 0-534-55818-6
    1. Philosophy—Introductions.
  I. Title.
BD21 .P57 2000
100—dc21   00-040806

For information about our products, contact us:
Thomson Learning Academic Resource Center
1-800-423-0563
http://wadsworth.com

International Headquarters
Thomson Learning
International Division
290 Harbor Drive, 2nd Floor
Stamford, CT 06902-7477
USA

UK/Europe/Middle East/South Africa
Thomson Learning
Berkshire House
168-173 High Holborn
London WC1V 7AA
United Kingdom

Asia
Thomson Learning
60 Albert Street, #15-01
Albert Complex
Singapore 189969

Canada
Nelson Thomson Learning
1120 Birchmount Road
Scarborough, Ontario M1K 5G4
Canada

Dedicated to my students, some of whom have become friends, who for twenty years have taught me so much about philosophy and have made teaching a wonderful experience. How fortunate to be paid for doing exactly what I would choose to do if I didn't have to work.

Contents

      and Immortality**   208

     Box: Reincarnation   213

**PART V   FREEDOM OF THE WILL
           AND DETERMINISM**   **217**

18   **Determinism**   219

     Universal Causality   220

     Teleological Determinism   223

19   **Libertarianism**   225

     The Argument from Deliberation   225

     The Argument from Moral Responsibility   230

20   **Compatibilism: How to Have Your Cake
      and Eat It Too**   233

     A Reconciling Project   233

     A Critique of Compatibilism: A "Quagmire of Evasion"?   236

     The Argument Against Compatibilism

     from Moral Responsibility   236

     The Compatibilist Response   240

PART VI ETHICS   **245**

21   **What Is Morality?**   246

     Why Do We Need Morality?   249

     The Purposes of Morality   251

22   **Ethical Relativism versus Ethical Objectivism**   255

     An Analysis of Ethical Relativism   257

     Subjective Ethical Relativism (Subjectivism)   258

     Conventional Ethical Relativism (Conventionalism) 259

     The Case for Ethical Objectivism   262

23   **Egoism, Self-Love, and Altruism**   268

     Arguments for Ethical Egoism   271

     Arguments Against Ethical Egoism   273

     Evolution and Altruism   275

Preface

Having used a number of introductions to philosophy and having examined several others, I have tried to combine the strengths of the available texts (eliminating what I perceived as the weaknesses) into a book that might serve students and teachers in learning about philosophy. I wanted a book that would, first of all, consider philosophy seriously and convey the wonder and importance of the subject as it so richly deserves—hence the historical emphasis—especially at the beginning of this work. Philosophy was not invented yesterday. It has a rich heritage without which one cannot fully understand the discipline.

Second, I wanted a book that was written clearly and presented the major problems and arguments in a cogent manner. I hope the reader will find the discussion level a little deeper than that usually contained in introductory texts, while finding the style clear and free from unnecessary jargon. Of course, there is a minimal vocabulary and use of terms necessary to any discipline, and philosophy is no exception.

Third, I wanted a single-authored text that could be used as both the sole text for a course and as a supplement for anthologies containing classical and contemporary readings, such as Joel Feinberg's *Reason and Responsibility* and my two introductory anthologies, *Philosophy: The Quest for Truth* and *An Introduction to Philosophy: Classical and Contemporary Readings,* all published by Wadsworth.

Seven major subjects are covered in this text:

- **Part I Introduction to Philosophy,** which includes a little logic and something about the origins of philosophy in Ancient Greece, including the Presocratics, Sophists, and Socrates.

- **Part II Philosophy of Religion,** including the major arguments for and against theism.
- **Part III The Theory of Knowledge,** which includes chapters on skepticism, perception, and the definition of knowledge.
- **Part IV Philosophy of Mind,** which includes the problem of dualism versus monism, functionalism, cognitive naturalism, as well as personal identity and survival after death.
- **Part V Freedom of the Will and Determinism,** including discussions on Compatibilism and Moral Responsibility.
- **Part VI Ethics,** including chapters on relativism, objectivism, egoism, religion and ethics, utilitarianism, and deontological ethics.
- **Part VII Existentialism and the Meaning of Life,** dealing with the work of Kierkegaard, Nietzsche, Sartre, and Camus.

Although the order of the table of contents is the order I generally follow, there is nothing sacred about it. I vary the order from semester to semester and never cover all the material in the text. I always begin with Part I, **Introduction to Philosophy** (which orients the students and initiates them to logic and the origins of philosophy in ancient Greece), but after that I've used three different strategies:

1. *Normal Introductory Classes* With normal intelligent college students, I go straight to Part II (**Philosophy of Religion**) and cover most of this. Occasionally, I skip Chapter 7 (The Ontological Argument). Next, I do the first two chapters of Part III (**Theory of Knowledge**): What Can We Know? and Skepticism. Sometimes I do Chapters 13 and 14, but Chapter 15 may be difficult. Then I turn to Part IV (**The Mind-Body Problem**) and cover Chapters 16, 17, 19, and 20 (the dualism/materialism debate, personal identity, and immortality). Chapter 18 may be too difficult for the average class. Next, I do the whole of Part V (**Freedom of the Will and Determinism**. After this, I finish up the course with a section on **Ethics,** Part VI, doing as much as possible.

   On occasions I have taught Part VII (**Existentialism and the Meaning of Life**), sometimes introducing it early in the course right after Chapter 4 (**Sophists and Socrates**), sometimes right after Chapter 1 (**What Is Philosophy?**), skipping the rest of Part I.

   I often use an anthology with primary texts in these courses.
2. *Honors Course.* With superior students, I go more thoroughly into fewer chapters, emphasizing Parts III and IV, after spending ample time on Part I. I generally thoroughly cover only one other topic, either Part II or VI, in addition to a brief look at Part V on free will and determinism. In these classes I always use an anthology of primary sources along with this text.
3. *Large Classes.* On occasion, I've taught large sections which I define as more than 40 students with very mixed abilities. Here I spend a good deal of time covering Parts I, II, VI, and VII. I'm usually able to cover either part of Part IV (excluding Chapter 18) or the whole of Part V.

The process works well for me and others report similar experiences. But there are other ways to use this material, which you will discover for yourself.

I have provided some aids for students reading the text. Each chapter has a summary at its end, questions for discussion, as well as a short annotated bibliography. An appendix, "How to Read and Write a Philosophy Paper," and a glossary follow the main text.

On the Third Edition I'm grateful for the success of the earlier editions of this book. In response to comments of users and reviewers, I have made several changes in this edition. I have revised several chapters, especially Chapters 1, 3, 4, 5, 6, 10, 11, 12, 20, 23, and 27. I have added a section on fallacies in Chapter 2, developed the work of the Presocratics in Chapter 3, a very important but difficult subject (since we have only fragments), added material on the empiricist/rationalist debate in Chapter 11, and added a discussion of free will, compatibilism, and moral responsibility in Chapter 20. I have made several improvements throughout Part VI on ethics, especially on egoism in Chapter 23 and deontological ethics in Chapter 25.

In addition, my friend and former colleague, William Lawhead of the University of Mississippi, has prepared an excellent instructor's manual to aid you in teaching this material.

I hope this book will help you teach philosophy (if you are an instructor) or learn to do philosophy (if you are a student). I would be delighted to hear from you on your experience with it and to receive your suggestions for improvement. A card for comments is provided with this book.

ACKNOWLEDGMENTS

Many people have helped me make this book a reality: my teachers who first taught me philosophy and my students who challenged me and forced me to become a better and clearer philosopher (of special mention are John Ates, Tim Atkins, Billy Berryhill, Bob Boyd, Chris Bradford, Chris Carlson, Brendan Engen, Julie Grimes, LeAnne Habib, Patrick Hopkins, Glenn Hutchinson, Richard Howe, David Ley, Scott Morris, Segun Ogungbemi, Karen Schmersahl and Joe Van Roy). This book is dedicated to all my students.

Peter Adams, senior editor at Wadsworth Publishing Company, was most supportive. Reviewers for this work—David Beck, Liberty University; Steven W. Godby, Broward Community College; David Haugen, Western Illinois University; Paul Herrick, Shoreline Community College; Richard Lee, University of Arkansas; John L. Longeway, University of Wisconsin-Parkside; Gary Ortega, Santa Monica College; Michael Potts, Methodist College; Terry J. Sader, Westark College; Frances Schneiter, Jefferson Community College; Robert Sweet, University of Dayton—made important criticisms and suggestions that greatly improved this work. Frank Dilley, Michael Levin, and Bill Lawhead read through the entire work and offered wise advice. Scott Rohr and his associates at Gustafson Graphics did a splendid job in bringing this edition into production. Most of all, my gratitude goes to my wife Trudy, who read through my manuscript in several forms. Her love and support have wonderfully enriched my life. To her I owe more than words can tell.

Louis P. Pojman
English and Philosophy Department
United States Military Academy
West Point, NY 10996

A Personal Word
to the Student

Nothing worthwhile was ever accomplished without great difficulty.

—PLATO

Just about everyone who comes to philosophy—usually in college—feels a sinking sensation in his or her stomach when first encountering this very strange material, involving a different sort of style and method from anything else with which they have ever dealt. It was certainly my first reaction as a student. Lured by questions such as Is there a God? What can I truly know? What is the meaning of life? Is there life after death? How will I live my life? I began to read philosophy on my own.

My first books were Søren Kierkegaard's *Fear and Trembling,* a book part poetry and part philosophy, about the nature of religious belief, and Bertrand Russell's *History of Western Philosophy,* which is much more than a history of the subject but Russell's own analysis and evaluation of major themes in the history of Western philosophy. Kierkegaard's book had a devastating effect on me, forcing me to become totally dissatisfied with the mediocre life I had been living in college and drove me to depths of intensity and seriousness from which I have still not recovered.

Regarding Russell's tome, although not a terribly difficult text, most of the ideas and arguments were new to me. Since he opposed many of the beliefs I had held all my life, I was angry with him. But since he seemed to argue so persuasively, my anger gave way to confusion and then to a sense of defeat and despair. For a while, Kierkegaard and Russell were juxtaposed in my mind as positing two opposing philosophies of life, both attractive. When I read a work of Kierkegaard, I'd conclude, "That's exactly right. What a persuasive case he makes!" But then I'd read some more of Russell and reluctantly say the same thing about his work. Why couldn't I figure out what I believed and how to settle the conflicting viewpoints?

I was perplexed, dissatisfied with my lack of ability to outargue these masters, and a bit angry at these philosophers for the state they left me in. Yet I felt compelled to go on with this "forbidden fruit," finishing Russell's long work and going on to read Plato's *Republic,* René Descartes's *Meditations,* David Hume's *Dialogues on Natural Religion,* selected writing of Immanuel Kant, John Stuart Mill's *Utilitarianism,* William James's *Will to Believe,* and finally contemporary readings by Albert Camus, Jean-Paul Sartre, Anthony Flew, R. M. Hare, John Hick, and Ludwig Wittgenstein. Gradually, I became aware that on every issue on which I disagreed with Hume or Russell, someone else, perhaps it was Kant or James or Hick, had a plausible counterargument. Eventually, I struggled to the place where I could see weaknesses in arguments (sometimes of those philosophers with whom I had agreed), and finally I came to the point where I could write my own arguments. The pain of the process slowly gave way to joy—addictive joy, let me warn you—so that I decided to pursue an advanced degree in philosophy.

As I mentioned, it was a gnawing worry about fundamental questions of existence that drew me to philosophy. Is there a God? What can I know for sure? What is the relationship of the mind to the body? Do I have a soul that will live forever? Am I truly free or simply determined by my heredity and environment? What is it to live a moral life? Are there objective moral truths, or is everything relative either to culture or the individual? If you have asked these questions and pondered alternative responses, this book will make sense to you. If you haven't spent much time thinking about these issues, you might ask yourself whether these are important questions and outline your own present responses to them. For unless you have asked the questions, the proposed answers may sound like one end of a telephone conversation.

The present text is meant to suggest responses to stimulate you to work out your own position on the questions addressed herein. Ideally, this text should be used along with original sources, such as an anthology, where opposing viewpoints are juxtaposed. However, it can be used alone, for I have endeavored to set forth the arguments on both sides of each issue as fairly as possible. I hope that you, with your teacher's help, will be able to use this work as a guide, leading you to develop your own ideas and arguments so that you might work out your own philosophy of life.

Good luck, and I hope you enjoy your philosophical pursuit of wisdom and truth as much as I have. I would be glad to hear from you on any thoughts you might have on philosophical problems or on the material in this book. Please write to me at English and Philosophy Department, United States Military Academy, West Point, NY 10996.

PART I

Introduction to Philosophy

RAPHAEL
The School of Athens

The Vatican Museum

He that would seriously set upon the search of truth ought in the first place to prepare his mind with a love of it. . . . How a man may know whether he be [a lover of truth] in earnest, is worth inquiry; and I think there is one unerring mark of it, viz. the not entertaining any proposition with greater assurance than the proofs it is built upon will warrant. Whoever goes beyond this measure of assent, it is plain receives not the truth in the love of it; loves not truth for truth's sake, but for some other bye-end.

—JOHN LOCKE, *AN ESSAY CONCERNING HUMAN UNDERSTANDING*

1

What Is Philosophy?

PHILOSOPHY BEGINS WITH WONDER

Philosophy begins with wonder, and even now it is wonder that causes philosophers to philosophize. At first they wondered about the obvious difficulties and then they gradually progressed to puzzle about the greater ones, for example, the behavior of the moon and sun and stars and the coming to be of the universe. Whoever is puzzled and in a state of wonder believes he is ignorant (this is why the lover of myths is also in a way a philosopher, since myths are made up of wonders). And so, if indeed they pursued philosophy to escape ignorance, they were obviously pursuing scientific knowledge in order to know and not for the sake of any practical need.[1]

The first philosophers looked into the heavens and wondered how the universe had come about. They pondered the structure of the world. Is there one fundamental substance that underlies all of reality or are there many substances? What is the really *real,* and not just a matter of appearance? What is the ultimate explanation of reality?

The first philosophers were Greeks of the sixth century B.C. Other people in other cultures had wondered about these questions, but usually myth or religious authority had imposed an answer. Typically, as in the Hebrews' Genesis 1 or the Greek Hesiod's *Theogony,* the world order was said to have arisen from the gods or God. Now a break occurred. Here for the first time a pure philosophical and scientific inquiry was allowed to flourish. The great civilizations of Egypt, China, Assyria, Babylon, Israel, India, Persia, and the Incas and Mayans had produced art and artifacts and governments of advanced sorts, but nowhere, with the possible exception of India, had anything like philosophy or science been developed.

The first Greek philosophers were materialists and naturalists, for they sought naturalistic explanations of reality. The standard date for the beginning of philosophy is May 23, 585 B.C., when **Thales** of Miletus (625–545 B.C.) on the coast of Asia Minor (then called Ionia, now Turkey), predicted a solar eclipse that ended a war. (The invaders reasoned, if our opponents have such magic, we'd better not mess with them.) What has the prediction of an eclipse to do with philosophy? Thales used mathematical and astronomical investigations to make his prediction. In this sense he may have been the first scientist, and since at this early stage of development science cannot be separated from philosophy, the prediction of the solar eclipse serves as a clothespin holding one end of the long sheet of the history of philosophy to the clothesline of world history.

Thales, who was an engineer by training, asked, "What is the nature of reality? What is the ultimate explanation of all that is?" and speculated and experimented in order to come up with the answer. What was his answer? "Water." Water is necessary for the production and sustenance of life. Water is everywhere: look past the coastline and you'll find a sea of water; dig under the ground and you're bound to find water. It rises as mist from the sea and falls down to earth as rain. Heat water and it becomes a gas like air; freeze it and it becomes solid. So Thales concluded that the earth was just especially solid water, a hard flat cork that floated in a sea of liquid of the same substance. It is the first recorded attempt to give a naturalistic answer to the question "What is reality?"

A simple beginning? No doubt, but it is worth quoting Friedrich Nietzsche (1844–1900) here:

> Greek philosophy seems to begin with a preposterous fancy, with the proposition that water is the origin and mother-womb of all things. Is it really necessary to stop there and become serious? Yes, and for three reasons: Firstly, because the proposition does enunciate something about the origin of things; secondly, because it does so without figure and fable; thirdly, because in it is contained, although only in the chrysalis state, the idea—Everything is one. The first-mentioned reason leaves Thales still in the company of religious and superstitious people; the second, however, takes him out of this company and shows him to us as a natural philosopher; but by virtue of the third, Thales becomes the first Greek philosopher.[2]

After Thales, his fellow Ionian **Anaximander** (ca. 612–545 B.C.) rejected the idea that water was the root substance. He hypothesized that ultimate reality could not be equated with any one material substance but was neutral between them, yet underlying all matter. It was an unknown boundless material substance, the *Infinite*.

> The source and elements of existing things is the *Infinite*. He was the first to introduce this name for the source. He says that it is neither water nor any of the other so-called "elements," but of another nature which is infinite, from which all the heavens and the world-order in them arise. No mention of the gods, nor of a beginning nor end of reality. The Infinite is eternally in motion and the source of time, space, matter and mind.

Anaximander rejected Thales' notion of a flat earth and suggested that the earth was a revolving, cylindrical body, whose flat top was our home. Rejecting the anthropocentric notions of the religious and mythological explanations and anticipating Darwin by 2,500 years, Anaximander put forth a theory of evolution based on the need for species to adapt to their environment. Human beings evolved from fish who had to adapt to land and so developed the characteristics we now have.

PYTHAGORAS

The first philosopher of which we have substantial information is **Pythagoras** of Samos (580–496 B.C.), who settled in Croton in southern Italy, where he found-ed the first community of philosophers. It could be argued that Pythagoras, not Thales, is the father of philosophy, for with him a comprehensive study of the fun-damental questions of philosophy first takes place: What is reality? How does one come to know the truth? How shall I live my life? Here is an early document on what he taught:

> First he said that the soul is immortal; second, that it migrates into other kinds of animals; third, that the same events are repeated in cycles, nothing being new in the strict sense; and finally, that all things with souls should be regarded as related to each other. Pythagoras seems to have been the first to introduce these ideas into Greece.

Pythagoras rejected the materialism of Thales and the other early Greek philosophers and opted for a refined spiritualism, a mathematical mysticism, aim-ing at the purification of the whole person, body and soul. Knowledge (or Science) and Music would purify the soul and Gymnastics and Medicine the body. All living things (including plant life) had souls and were related to one another and involved in the transmigration of souls. Pythagoreans were vegetari-ans, eating neither meat, nor eggs, nor beans (lest they should eat their brothers and sisters whose souls had migrated there), nor drinking wine. The Pythagorean Milo was renowned as the strongest man in Greece, proving to the ancient world that meat was not necessary for strength. But in spite of Milo's musculature, Pythagoreans generally despised the body as inferior to the soul, which they sought to purify by ascetic practices.

Pythagoras related morality to the harmony of the soul. A good soul has a proper order of standards and impulses within itself like beautiful music and the sublime system of the heavens. Pythagoreans were renowned for their mutual friendship, altruism, integrity, and devotion to duty. At the end of each day they asked themselves what wrongs they had committed, what duties they had ne-glected, what good they had done.

Pythagoras is the first person on record to hold the doctrine of universal brotherhood, which led him to provide equal opportunity for men and women. Two centuries before Plato's famous declaration of this doctrine in the *Republic,* Pythagoras accepted women on an equal basis with men, admitting them into his school and exalting them to positions of authority.

Nevertheless, the Pythagoreans were not egilatarians, but held to a social order that resembled nature itself, based on intrinsic merit and having different levels. Just as animals have a higher quality of life than plants, and humans than animals, some humans have attained a higher degree of worth than others and should be regarded as having higher souls.

Pythagoras's fundamental doctrine was that the world is really not material but made up of numbers. Numbers are things and constitute the essence of reality.

> The Pythagoreans construct the whole heaven out of numbers. Not, however, out of numbers considered as abstract units; for they suppose the units to have magnitude. But how the first "one" was constructed so as to have magnitude, they seem unable to say.

The original "one," being fire, sets the surrounding cold air in motion, drawing it upon itself and limiting it. From numbers the world is created: Aristotle reports their doctrine this way:

> From numbers points, from points lines, from lines plane figures, from plane figures solid figures, from these sensible bodies, of which the elements are four: fire, water, earth, and air. These change and are wholly transformed; and from them arises a cosmos animate, intelligent, and spherical, embracing earth (itself spherical and inhabited all around) as its center.

Pythagoras was led to this doctrine by his musical studies. He recognized that the pitch of tones depends on the length of the strings on musical instruments and that musical harmony is determined by definite mathematical propositions. This recognition led him to believe in a soul that was suprasensual and separate from the body. From there he hypothesized a Cosmic Soul, similar to Anaximander's *Infinite,* as responsible for everything that exists. The Pythagoreans developed an elaborate number mysticism.

You have, no doubt, encountered Pythagoras in high school via his *Pythagorean theorem* (the sum of the squares of the sides of a right triangle are equal to the square of the hypotenuse). Theophrastus tells us that the Pythagoreans were the first to speak of the spherical shape of the earth, the harmony of the spheres, and planetary motion. Pythagoras supposed there to be a central fire around which the round earth evolved.

THE ELEATICS

With **Parmenides** (540–470 B.C.), a further advance in philosophical discourse took place. Parmenides observed that nature is constantly changing and noted that such flux was inimical to the idea of knowledge. In order to have knowledge there must be permanence, something that is unchanging. From this he theorized that the real world was unchanging on the order of Pythagoras's number, whereas the apparent, illusory world was the world of change. The senses grasped the changing world of unreality or *Nonbeing,* whereas reason alone could grasp the real world of *Being.* Being never comes into existence, nor does it cease to be, for it always is. It cannot be divided or added onto, for it is whole and complete in itself, one. It is unmoved and undisturbed, for motion and disturbance are forms of becoming. Being is. It doesn't become. It is self-identical and uncaused. This view is sometimes called *Absolute Idealism:* An Absolute Idea makes up all there is, and all change is illusory. All is One and Permanently at Rest. Here is a portion of Parmenides' philosophical poem, "The Way of Truth":

Come now I will tell thee
What are the only ways of inquiry
That can be thought.
The one is the way of how it is,
And how it is impossible
For it not to be;
It attends the truth.
The other is the way of how it is not,
And how it is necessary for it not to be.
This is a way wholly unknowable.
Since you cannot know what is not.
Nor could you speak of it,
For thought and being are the same.
It makes no difference
At what point I begin,
For I shall always come back again to this.
Thinking and the thought that it is are the same;
For you will not find thought apart from what is,
In relation to which it is uttered.[3]

Three theses can be identified in Parmenides' work.

1. That which-is, is and cannot not-be; that which-is-not, is not and cannot be. The real is and cannot be nonexistent.
2. That which-is can be thought or known and truly named. That which-is-not, cannot. Thinking and the thought that it is are the same thing.
3. That which-is, is one and cannot be many. The real is unique. There is no second thing besides it. It is also indivisible. It does not contain a plurality of distinct parts.

Being or reality is one: immaterial, continuous, indivisible, motionless, beginningless, imperishable, and everywhere. It is wholly indeterminate and can only be described in negative terms. It cannot be created, for if it were, it would have to be created from nothing, which is impossible. It cannot be destroyed, for if it could, then something could become nothing, which is also impossible. When thought has negated all that can be negated, it is Being that remains, the unique, godlike One.

Common sense tells us, as it did Parmenides' contemporaries, that he is mistaken in his rejection of time, change, and diversity. His views were attacked in his own time, especially by **Heracleitus** (ca. 540–480 B.C.). At this point, one of the most ingenious logicians of all time, **Zeno** of Elea (ca. 489–430 B.C.), arose to defend Parmenides' doctrines.

Zeno is the first philosopher we know of who self-consciously makes use of the law of noncontradiction to argue against his opponents. Using universally acceptable premises, he developed a series of paradoxes that lead to the conclusion that there is no motion or multiplicity:

1. The Line The Eleatics held that a line was one unit, whereas their opponents held that it was divisible into parts, discrete units. Zeno argued that if it was divisible into units, it must be divisible into an infinite number of discrete units, so that each unit must be infinitely small. But if there were an infinite number of these units, then if we multiplied them, we would get a line that was infinitely large, for the smallest magnitude multiplied by infinity becomes an infinite magnitude. So what started out as a finite line turns out to be infinitely long, which is a contradiction.

2. Motion Zeno put forth a second argument against the possibility of motion. To traverse distance *A* to *B*, a body must first travel half of the distance (*A* to *C*):

A   E D   C   B

But before it can get from *A* to *C*, it must get from *A* to *D*, but before that it must get from *A* to *E*, and so on to infinity. So if there is motion, one will never be able to get to one's destination, for one will always have to traverse an infinite set of points before one gets there.

3. Achilles and the Tortoise This argument is aimed specifically at the Pythagoreans who held that a line is made up of an infinite number of points. As Achilles starts from point *A* toward point *B*, the tortoise, already at *B*, moves ahead to *C*. But by the time Achilles reaches *C*, the tortoise has moved on to *D*.

A   B   C   D
Achilles   Tortoise

No matter how fast he runs, it takes him some finite amount of time to reach the place where the tortoise has been. During that time, the tortoise will have moved some distance forward. Thus, Achilles is always coming nearer to the tortoise but never actually overtakes it and can never do so, on the supposition that a line is made up of an infinite number of points, for then Achilles would have to traverse an infinite distance. Thus, it follows that on the Pythagorean doctrine, the slower runs as fast as the faster, which shows that motion is an illusion.

4. The Arrow and the Argument Against Movement Consider an arrow flying from one place to another. Does it really move? No, movement is only an illusion:

1. The arrow could not move in the place in which it is not.
2. But neither could it move in the place where it is.
3. For this is "a place equal to itself."
4. Everything is always at rest when it is "at a place equal to itself."
5. But the flying arrow is always at the place where it is.
6. ∴ The flying arrow is always at rest and cannot move. A body must either be moving in a place where it is or where it is not. It can't be moving in a place where it is not, for it is not there. The arrow is at rest at any point in the trajectory, and what is at rest at every point cannot move. Therefore, the flying arrow cannot be moving.

All the paradoxes have the same form. Any quantity of space must either be indivisible or divisible ad infinitum. If it is composed of indivisible units, these must have a magnitude that can't be divided. If it is composed of divisible units, it must be divisible ad infinitum, and we are faced with the contradiction of supposing that an infinite number of parts can be summed to make a finite total. Thus did he defend the Eleatic doctrine that Reality was One, immovable, eternal, and uncreated against the commonsense ideas of plurality and motion.

If you, like Zeno's contemporaries, believe in change, time, and diversity, the challenge before you is to show what is wrong with Zeno's paradoxes.

HERACLEITUS

Heracleitus of Ephesus (535–475 B.C.) a cynical, aloof, solitary aristocrat, sometimes called "the weeping philosopher," was scornful of the Pythagorean Idealism and set forth an opposing philosophy. Rejecting the notion that only Being is, he posited that only Becoming is. All things are in perpetual flux (Greek, *panta rei*), and permanence is an illusion. There is a single principle at work in the universe. It is fire. Fire, an infinite mass of substance, uncreated and eternal, is identical with the universe.

> The world order was not made by a god or a man, but always was and is and will be an ever-living fire.

Fire consumes fuel, thus changing all, but itself is in constant flux. Transforming all that it comes in contact with, fire replaces Anaximander's Infinite.

Reality is like a stream of fire in constant motion. Nothing is stable. Heracleitus uses the metaphor of a river to signify that the world is in a dynamic equilibrium of opposites:

> All things come into being through opposition, and all are in flux like a river. You cannot step into the same river twice, for other and yet another waters are ever flowing on. Wisdom is at once the unity of all things, the measure and harmony, but it is pure as well. . . . Mind is fire.

At the same time, Heracleitus posited *logos* (reason) as the lawlike process that governed the world. This would make him the father of the doctrine of natural law. The world follows an orderly process, though one of conflict and survival of the fittest.

> War is natural, justice is conflict, and everything that is is created through conflict, according to how things must be. For fire lives through the death of earth, and air lives through the death of fire; and water lives through the death of air, and earth that of water. War is the father and king over all.
>
> Though the *logos* is eternal, as I have said, men always fail to comprehend it, both before they hear it and when they hear it for the first time. For though all things come into being in accordance with this logos, they seem like men without experience, though in fact they do have experience both of words and deeds such as I have set forth, distinguishing each thing in accordance with its nature and declaring what it is. But other men are as unaware of what they do when awake as they are when they are asleep.
>
> Though they are in daily contact with the *logos,* they are at variance with it, and what they meet with appears alien to them.
>
> Listen not to me but to the *logos,* it is wise to acknowledge that all things are one.

The logos, as the rational principle of the universe, has independent existence and according to it, all things come into existence. It perpetually confronts people, calling on them to awake from their sleep of illusion. "To those who are awake the world-order is one, common to all, but the sleeping turn aside each into a world of his own."

The logos is hidden in humanity. We become intelligent "by drawing in the divine logos when we breathe." In sleep we are separated from the source of our being and forget. Further, Heraclitus said that the laws of the city were but a reflection of the logos that runs through all things.

> It is necessary for men who speak with common sense to place reliance on what is common to all, as a city relies upon law, and even more firmly. For all human laws are nourished by the one divine law. For it governs as far as it will, and it is sufficient for all things and outlasts them.

Heraclitus sets forth the two moral principles of antiquity: "Know theyself" and "In nothing too much."

> It is hard to contend with passion; for whatever it desires to get it buys at the cost of soul. It is part of all men to know themselves and to be temperate. To be temperate is the greatest virtue; and it is wisdom to speak the truth and to act according to nature with understanding.

OTHER SIGNIFICANT PHILOSOPHERS

Socrates (470–399 B.C.), who we will study in Chapter 3, brought philosophy down from the heavens and forced it to contend in the home and in the marketplace. He raised the Ethical Question, How should we live?, holding that this is the only important question in life. His disciple **Plato** (427–347 B.C.) systematized philosophy into the first comprehensive philosophical system, concentrating on metaphysical and epistemological questions: What is the really *Real* as opposed to Appearance? What can I truly know? and How may I come to know the truth? Plato's student **Aristotle** (385–322 B.C.) broke with his teacher and set forth a more naturalistic philosophy, developing a virtue theory of ethics and setting forth the first system of logic—which was not substantially improved on for over two millennia. After Aristotle came the Stoics, with their idea of resignation to life's fortunes, the medieval Christian philosophy of Boethius, St. Augustine, and Thomas Aquinas. Modern philosophy begins with the French Rationalist René Descartes, who doubted all in order to discover the indubitable truth. Then came the British Empiricists: John Locke, Bishop George Berkeley, and David Hume, culminating in the transcendental philosophy of the German Immanuel Kant, all of whom we will study in this work. In the nineteenth century, John Stuart Mill, Søren Kierkegaard, Friedrich Nietzsche, and Karl Marx were the leading philosophers, and in the twentieth century, Bertrand Russell, Martin Heidegger, and Ludwig Wittgenstein. All of these thinkers give us a sense of wonder at the mysteries of life and the enigmas of the universe.

The Questions they ask are, among others, Who am I? Where did I come from? Why am I here? Where am I going? Why is there Something and not just nothing? What is time and space? Is the Universe essentially friendly, personal—or is it indifferent to our welfare? That is, is it the work of a benevolent intelligence or simply an intricate and complicated machine that accidentally cranked out a freak entity (humans) endowed with consciousness and reason in this tiny corner of the universe? Is there a God?

Who am I? What am I made of? Simply matter, a material brain in a material body—or do I have a soul, a spiritual core within? Am I free, possessed of a free will, or am I completely determined by antecedent causes? What can I know?

PHILOSOPHY: THE LOVE OF WISDOM

If Philosophy begins in *Wonder,* it ends in *Wisdom.* The word *Philosophy* means love of wisdom. It is for those who would be not rich in material possessions or necessarily famous, but rich in understanding, wise and content in comprehending the depths of existence.

Philosophy is the love of wisdom (etymologically from the Greek *philos,* meaning "love," and *Sophia,* meaning "wisdom"). It is the contemplation or study of the most important questions in existence with the end of promoting illumination and understanding, a vision of the whole. It uses reason, sense perception, imagination, and intuitions in its activities of clarifying concepts and analyzing and constructing arguments and theories as possible answers to these perennial questions. It is revolutionary because its deliverances often disturb our common sense or our received tradition. Philosophy usually goes "against the stream" or the majority, since the majority is often a composite of past intellectual struggles or "useful" biases. There is often deeper truth, better and new evidence that disturbs the status quo and forces us to revise or reject some of our beliefs. This experience can be as painful as it is exciting.

The pain may lead us to give up philosophical inquiry, and a great deal of emotional health may be required to persevere in this pursuit. We may retreat into unreason and obey the commandment of Ignorance: "Think not, lest thou be confounded!" Truth (or what we seem justified in believing) may not always be edifying. But in the end, the philosopher's faith is that the Truth is good and worth pursuing for its own sake and for its secondary benefits. Intelligent inquiry, which philosophy promotes, is liberating, freeing us from prejudice, self-deceptive notions, and half-truths. As Bertrand Russell (1872–1970) put it,

> The [person] who has no tincture of philosophy goes through life imprisoned in the prejudices derived from common sense, from the habitual beliefs of his age or his nation, and from convictions which have grown up in his mind without the co-operation or consent of his deliberate reason. . . . While diminishing our feeling of certainty as to what things are, [philosophy] greatly increases our knowledge as to what they may be; it removes the somewhat arrogant dogmatism of those who have never travelled into the region of liberating doubt, and it keeps alive the sense of wonder by showing familiar things in an unfamiliar light.[4]

Philosophy should result in a wider vision of life in which the impartial use of reason results in an appreciation of other viewpoints and other people's rights and needs. It typically engenders an attitude of philosophical modesty or *fallibilism* in the inquirer—an awareness that, since in the past many of my firmest beliefs have been found to be false, the probability is that some of my present convictions are false. But different people react differently to philosophical inquiry. Some become radical skeptics, doubting what most accept as common-sense beliefs. Some become even more dogmatic, finding in philosophical method an instrument for certainty. Some nasty people seem to be able to do philosophy quite well without being transformed by it. But for the most part, those who have had the vision of a better life and have worked through arguments on substantive issues relating to human nature and destiny have been positively affected by the perennial pilgrimage. They march to a different drummer and show in their lives the fruits of their travail. This ability to live by reflective principle in spite of and in the midst of the noise of the masses is a hallmark of philosophy. This is illustrated by one of its heroes, Socrates, who we encounter in Chapter 3 and then throughout this book.

We mentioned that one of the tasks of philosophy is clarifying concepts. Let me illustrate how this works with two different examples. The American philosopher and psychologist William James (1842–1910), brother to the novelist Henry James, was vacationing with friends in New England one summer. On returning from a walk, he found his friends engaged in a fierce dispute. The problem in question was this: Suppose a squirrel is clinging to the side of a tree and you are trying to see the back of the squirrel. But as you walk around the tree, the clever squirrel moves edgewise around the tree on its other side so that you never get a look at the squirrel. The question was, Did you go around the squirrel? Half the group contended that you did go around, and half contended that you did not. What do you think is the answer?

Here is what William James said:

> Which party is right depends on what you *practically mean* by "going around" the squirrel. If you mean passing from north of him to the east, then to the south, then to the west, and then to the north of him again, obviously the man does go around him, for he occupies these successive positions. But if on the contrary you mean being first in front of him, then on the right of him, then behind him, then on his left, and finally in front again, it is quite obvious that the man fails to go round him, for by the compensating movements the squirrel makes, he keeps his belly turned towards the man all the time, and his back turned away. Make the distinction, and there is no occasion for any further dispute.[5]

Here was a dispute over the concept of "going around something." The philosopher is trained to look at the frame of reference of the phrase, to note its inherent ambiguity, and to unravel it, making things clearer. In this case, once James had pointed out the equivocation in the idea of "going around," all dispute ceased. The first step in philosophy is to make your ideas (concepts, notions) as clear as possible.

A second illustration has to do with the difficult matter of whether abortion is morally permissible. Often it is alleged that abortion is morally wrong because it is the killing of innocent human beings. Putting this in syllogistic form, we get the following:

1. It is morally wrong to kill innocent human beings.
2. Abortion is an act of killing an innocent human being.
3. ∴ Abortion is morally wrong.

On the face of it, this looks like a good argument, and it is often used in opposition to abortion. There may be good arguments against abortion, but this is not one of them. Early on in the debate over abortion, philosophers like Michael

Tooley and Mary Anne Warren pointed out that the argument contained an equivocation over the phrase *human being.*[6] We use the term *human being* ambiguously, sometimes meaning a biological concept, the species *Homo sapiens,* and other times meaning a psychological–moral concept, *someone who has the characteristics that make humans of special moral worth,* such as rationality or rational self-consciousness. We sometimes refer to this second concept by the term *person.* It is human beings as *persons,* as having requisite psychological qualities and not merely our membership in a biological group, that gives us a serious moral right to life. But other beings may also have the required psychological qualities. Perhaps apes, dolphins, and Galacticans are also rationally self-conscious beings; then they would be persons. And there are no doubt some *Homo sapiens* who are not minimally rationally self-conscious; they would not be persons. Applying this insight to our argument, we need to change the premises to read:

1. It is morally wrong to kill innocent persons.
2. Abortion is an act of killing an innocent member of the species *Homo sapiens.*
3. ∴ Abortion is morally wrong.

If the attempt at clarification has succeeded, this argument is not sound, for the original term *human beings* is being used differently in the two premises. In the first premise, it refers to beings with intrinsic moral status, but in the second, to the biological species *Homo sapiens.*

 The hallmark of philosophical method is *argument.* Philosophers clarify concepts and analyze and test propositions and beliefs, but their major task is analyzing and constructing arguments. Bertrand Russell said that one aim of philosophy is to begin with assumptions that no one would ever think of doubting and proceed through a careful process of valid reasoning to conclusions so preposterous to common sense that no one could help doubting. Indeed, in philosophy there is no "political correctness." No hypothesis, however outrageous to common sense or conventional thinking, is ruled out of court, *provided* only that you endeavor to support your claim with arguments, with good reasons. Otherwise, anything goes.

 Philosophical reasoning is closely allied to scientific reasoning in that both look for evidence and build hypotheses that are tested with the hope of coming closer to the truth. However, scientific experiments take place in laboratories and have testing procedures through which to record objective or empirically verifiable results. The laboratory of the philosopher is his or her mind, where imaginative thought experiments take place; the study, where ideas are written down and examined; and wherever conversation about the perennial questions takes place, where thesis and counterexample or counterthesis are considered. We will look more closely at this aspect in Chapter 2. The persistent quest for truth does not mean that progress is impossible in philosophy. On the contrary, I think that we can make progress in solving perennial philosophical problems, as the discussion of various problems in this book should indicate. However, a consensus that a problem has been solved still permits the dissenters to offer counterexamples, and among those who deem the consensus correct, problems arise at a new level of discourse—on how best to interpret the solution. For example, while the majority of moral philosophers are convinced that the thesis of moral **objectivism** (that is, there are universally valid moral norms) is correct, the debate continues on a new level, related to the limited truth of relativism (see Chapters 19 and 20).

Those who hold to moral objectivism disagree among themselves about whether the grounds of moral objectivity are some form of intuitionism, utilitarianism, contractualism, or practical reason. Thus, the debate goes on, expanding the issue, refining the distinctions, and contributing to an understanding of the further implications of the debate.

Furthermore, the relationship of philosophy to science is more complicated than the differences between them suggest, for much of what theoretical scientists do could with justice be called philosophy. The term *prove* is best left to mathematics and logic, for scientists do not prove their theories either. They do confirm them, however, with evidence. They make predictions on what will occur under certain conditions in case their hypotheses are true. In general, the sciences have one-by-one made their way out of the family fold of philosophy to independence as they systematized their decision-making procedures. In the words of Jeffrey Olen,

> The history of philosophy reads like a long family saga. In the beginning there were the great patriarch and matriarch, the searchers for knowledge and wisdom, who bore a large number of children. Mathematics, physics, ethics, psychology, logic, political thought, metaphysics, . . . and epistemology . . .—all belonged to the same family. Philosophers were not *just* philosophers, but mathematicians and physicists and psychologists as well. Indeed, in the beginning of the family's history, no distinction was made between philosophy and these other disciplines. . . .[7]

In the beginning, then, all systematic search for knowledge was philosophy. This fact is still reflected in the modern university, where the highest degree granted in all of the sciences and humanities is the Ph.D.—the doctor of philosophy.

> But the children gradually began to leave home. First to leave were physics and astronomy, as they began to develop experimental techniques of their own. This exodus, led by Galileo (1564–1642), Isaac Newton (1642–1727), and Johannes Kepler (1571–1630), created the first of many great family crises. . . . Eventually, psychology left home.[8]

The four major areas of philosophy and some of the questions they raise are the following:

1. *Metaphysics (concerned with such issues as the nature of ultimate reality)*
   - What is ultimate reality?
   - Is there one ultimate substance (e.g., matter) or more (e.g., ideas, mind, and/or spirit)?
   - *Is there a God (or gods) who created us, to whom we owe our allegiance?*
   - What is mind?
   - How is the mind related to the body?
   - Is there life after death, or is this life all there is?
   - Am I free, or is *every* act determined by antecedent conditions?
   - What is a self or person, and under what conditions can I be said to be the same self or person through change over time?

2. *Epistemology (regarding the nature of knowledge)*
   - What is knowledge?
   - What can I know? Anything at all? Or must I remain skeptical about reality? Could I be mistaken about most of my beliefs?

- How reliable is sense perception? Does it give me the truth about the world?
- What is truth?
- How can I justify my beliefs?
- What, if any, are the limits of reason?
- Are there other ways to attain the truth besides rational inquiry, for example, through faith?

3. *Axiology (the study of values, including aesthetics, ethics, and political philosophy)*
   - *What is value?*
   - Are values intrinsic in things or states of affairs, or are they simply a product of sentient desire?
   - What is beauty?
   - Is art intrinsically good or bad, or is aesthetic beauty simply in the eye of the beholder?
   - What makes an action right or wrong? Good or bad?
   - Are moral principles objectively valid, or are they relative to culture?
   - Does morality depend on religion?
   - Which is the correct moral theory?
   - What is the correct political theory? How should society be organized?
   - What justifies government? This is, why isn't anarchy justified? Or is it?
   - Is civil disobedience ever justified and under what circumstances?
   - Are there natural rights, rights we have in virtue of our humanity?
   - Are all men equal, or is human equality a myth?

4. *Logic (having to do with the laws of thought and forms of argument)*
   - What is a valid and sound argument?
   - How can our belief in induction be justified?
   - How does logic contribute to our knowledge and belief justification?
   - What is a logical fallacy, and what are some of the ways we go wrong in our thinking?

Besides these central topics, secondary areas of philosophy work on conceptual or theoretical problems (or both) arising within first-order nonphilosophical disciplines. Examples of these are philosophy of science, philosophy of psychology, philosophy of mathematics, philosophy of language, and philosophy of law. Wherever conceptual analysis or justification of a theoretical schema is needed, philosophical expertise is appropriate. More recently, as technology creates new possibilities and problems, applied ethics (e.g., biomedical ethics, business ethics, environmental ethics, and legal ethics) has arisen. History plays a dialectical role with regard to philosophy, for not only do philosophers do philosophy while teaching the history of philosophy, but they also involve themselves in the critical examination of the principles that underlie historical investigation itself, creating a philosophy of history.

We will touch on many of these areas in this work: a little logic and history of philosophy; philosophy of religion; epistemology; metaphysics, including the mind–body problem, personal identity, immortality, and free will and determinism; ethics; and the problem of the meaning of life. We will also spend a little time with the question of whether there is meaning to life. These are more than enough for an *introduction* to philosophy.

Philosophical study is dialectic, proceeding as an intellectual conversation in which thesis/counterthesis and hypothesis/counterexample continue in a way that shows up the weaknesses of proposed solutions to the puzzles of existence and leaves some answers as more or less plausible. In this conversation, all sides of an issue should receive a fair hearing, and the reader is left to make up his or her own mind on the issue. Hence, in this work, at least two opposing views are set forth on almost every issue.

Philosophy, we noted, is centered in argument. It is a rational activity. You may have questions about just what this means. Sometimes students, especially in introductory classes, get annoyed, even angry, that their views are subjected to sharp critical scrutiny or that the views of philosophers of the past, who cannot defend themselves, get torn to pieces by their teacher. So they ask, "So what if [so and so's] argument is unsound. Why do we always have to follow the best reasons? Why don't philosophers respect leaps of faith or our nonrational beliefs?"

The initial response to this query is to ask whether the questioner wants a *rational* answer or a nonrational one: "Do you want a reason for justifying philosophical practice or just my own emotional prejudice?" Presumably, the former is wanted. Indeed, the question "Why?" implies that a reason is called for, so even a question about the appropriateness of reason must be addressed by reason. If reason has limits, it is reason that discovers them and explains this fact.

The teacher may go on and point out that reason does recognize the limits of reason. Immanuel Kant (1724–1804) tried to show these limits in order to make room for religious faith, and, more problematically, Søren Kierkegaard (1813–1855) used rational argument to show that sometimes it is rational even to go against reason. What does this mean?

Here we have to distinguish two kinds of reason: practical reason from theoretical reason. Practical reason has to do with *acting* in order to realize a goal. For example, you desire to be healthy and so carry out a regimen of exercise, good nutrition, and general moderation. You have a goal (something you desire), you ask what are the necessary or best means of reaching that goal, and then, if you are rational in the practical sense, you act on your judgment. Theoretical reason, on the other hand, has to do with *beliefs*. It asks, What is the evidence for such and such a proposition or belief? What does reason lead us to believe about such matters as the best way to stay healthy, the existence of God, the existence of ghosts, or life after death?

Thus, we have two types of rationality: practical and theoretical, having to do with actions and beliefs. Sometimes, however, these two types of reasons may conflict. For instance, I may have evidence that my friend has committed a crime. My evidence is substantial but perhaps not decisive. For practical reasons, I may ignore or dismiss the evidence against him or her, reasoning that to believe my friend is guilty would be an act of disloyalty or greatly damage our relationship (for I cannot hide my feelings very well). Or I may use theoretical reason to conclude that I should not use reason to analyze the best way to make baskets while I am playing basketball, for the act of shooting is more likely to succeed if I don't think too much about what I am doing, but just do it. Or when reading literature, I may want to turn off my critical faculties to more fully enjoy the story.

If all this is accurate, it is sometimes rational not to be rational. Paradoxical? Yes, but explainable and not contradictory. We are *practically* rational in not always using *theoretical* rationality when engaged in some activities. On one level, theoretical reason judges that we are justified in not using theoretical reason when engaged in practical activities but that we are practically rational in acting spontaneously, following our feelings, making leaps of faith.

There are cases, however, where theoretical reason is simply not an issue, where practical reasons are justified by theoretical reasoning. The more difficult question is, Is it ever right to allow ourselves to believe propositions where there is insufficient reason? Should practical reason sometimes *override* theoretical rationality? The British philosopher W.K. Clifford (1845–1879) said, "No, it is wrong always, everywhere, and for anyone, to believe anything upon insufficient evidence."

One problem with Clifford's absolute prohibition is that there seems to be insufficient evidence to support it, and if so, it is self-referentially incoherent (or self-refuting). Other philosophers—such as Blaise Pascal (1623–1662), Søren Kierkegaard, and William James—argue the reverse. Sometimes we are (practically) justified in getting ourselves to believe against the conclusions of (theoretical) reason, against the preponderance of evidence. We will examine some of these philosophers and arguments in Chapter 10. Here we need only point out that it is a live philosophical issue whether practical reason should override theoretical reason.

Thus, philosophy is a practice of giving reasons in support of one's beliefs and actions. Its ultimate goal is to arrive at a rationally justified position on one's beliefs about the important issues of life, including what is the best way to live one's life and organize society. Philosophy consists in the rational examination of worldviews, metaphysical theories, ethical systems, and even the limits of reason.

SUMMARY

Philosophy, as its etymology suggests, is the love of wisdom. It begins with wonder at the world, aims at truth and wisdom, and hopefully results in a life filled with meaning and moral goodness. It is centered in clarifying concepts and analyzing and constructing arguments regarding life's perennial and perplexing questions. In general, it involves hard thinking about the important issues in life. There is no subject or issue necessarily beyond its domain. Whatever seems vital to humankind is a candidate for philosophical examination. Virtually all the sciences arose from philosophy, which continues to ask questions wherever an empirical process is inadequate for a definitive answer. It gives the following advice:

> Nondogmatically, pursue truth and wisdom, harken to the voice of wisdom, and aim at letting the fruits of philosophy transform your life. This is what Socrates meant when he said, "The unexamined life is not worth living." My hope is that philosophy will add a vital dimension to your life. Let's be on our way, then, with a brief look, in Chapter 2, at the central method of philosophical discourse, logic.

QUESTIONS FOR DISCUSSION

1. Consider the quotation by John Locke at the beginning of this book:

   > He that would seriously set upon the search of truth ought in the first place to pre-pare his mind with a love of it. . . . How a man may know whether he be [a lover of truth] in earnest, is worth inquiry; and I think there is one unerring mark of it, viz. the not entertaining any proposition with greater assurance than the proofs it is built upon will warrant. Whoever goes beyond this measure of assent, it is plain receives not the truth in the love of it; loves not truth for truth's sake, but for some other bye-end.

   Many people believe that philosophy, as reflected in this quotation, overempha-sizes reason. "The heart has its reasons that the mind knows nothing of," said Pascal, and Kierkegaard echoes his refrain (see Part VII). Reason has limits, they both contend. Do you agree? Discuss the matter. Ask yourself as you discuss it, "Am I using *reason* even in inquiring about the limits of reason?" That is, is even the contention that reason is limited a thesis that reason must adjudicate?

2. Consider Zeno's paradoxes. What were they supposed to prove? Are they successful? Can you solve them?

3. Examine Nietzsche's assessment of these early Greek philosophers (p. 3). What is significant about these philosophers according to Nietzsche? Do you agree with this assessment? Explain your answer.

4. Why do you think philosophy began in Greek culture and not elsewhere?

5. A man in one of Molière's plays discovered one day that he had been speak-ing prose all his life without knowing it. Similarly, all of us have been doing amateur philosophy all our lives. In a sense, philosphy is just hard thinking about the important issues of life. Mark Woodhouse illustrates how virtually every human activity has philosophical implications:

   1. A neurophysiologist, while establishing correlations between certain brain func-tions and the feeling of pain, begins to wonder whether the "mind" is distinct from the brain.

   2. A nuclear physicist, having determined that matter is mostly empty space con-taining colorless energy transformations, begins to wonder to what extent the solid, extended, colored world we perceive corresponds to what actually exists, and which world is the more "real."

   3. A behavioral psychologist, having increasing success in predicting human behav-ior, questions whether any human actions can be called "free."

   4. Supreme Court justices, when framing a law to distinguish obscene and non-obscene art forms, are drawn into questions about the nature and function of art.

   5. A theologian, in a losing battle with science over literal descriptions of the uni-verse (or "reality"), is forced to redefine the whole purpose and scope of tradi-tional theology.

   6. An anthropologist, noting that all societies have some conception of a moral code, begins to wonder just what distinguishes a moral from a nonmoral point of view.

   7. A linguist, in examining the various ways language shapes our view of the world, declares that there is no one "true reality" because all views of reality are conditioned and qualified by the language in which they are expressed.

8. A perennial skeptic, accustomed to demanding and not receiving absolute proof for every view encountered, declares that it is impossible to know anything.

9. A county commissioner, while developing new zoning ordinances, begins to wonder whether the *effect* or the *intent* (or both) of zoning laws makes them discriminatory.

10. An IRS director, in determining which (religious) organizations should be exempted from tax, is forced to define what counts as a "religion" or "religious group."

11. A concerned mother, having decided to convert her Communist son, is forced to read the *Communist Manifesto* and to do some thinking about Marxist and capitalist ideologies.

We could continue this list of examples indefinitely. But already you can see that given a particularly relevant problem, even the nonphilosopher is lured into a modest amount of philosophical thinking. If the nonphilosopher fails to see any purpose in the discipline, try raising a philosophical problem of special relevance to his or her interests. In examining possible responses, that person will probably discover a commitment to certain philosophical theses.[9]

Find some examples in your life or in the newspaper that illustrate philosophical inquiry and discuss them.

6. As you read and work your way through this book, it will help if you can think of some puzzling philosophical problems that you would like to make progress in solving for yourself. Pick out a few and try to think about them every day. Ask your friends for their ideas on them and keep a journal on your own insights.

NOTES

1. This and other quotations on the Pre-Socratics in this chapter, unless otherwise noted, are from the first book of Aristotle's *Metaphysics.*

2. Friedrich Nietzsche, quoted in Ed. L. Miller, *Questions That Matter* (New York: McGraw-Hill, 1987), 61.

3. Quoted in G. S. Kirk and J. E. Raven, The Presocratic Philosophers (Cambridge, Eng.: Cambridge University Press, 1957), 269–279.

4. Bertrand Russell, *The Problems of Philosophy* (Oxford: Oxford University Press, 1912), 156.

5. William James, *The Writings of William James* (New York: Random House, 1967), 367.

6. Michael Tooley, "Abortion and Infanticide," *Philosophy and Public Affairs* 2,

no. 1 (1972); Mary Anne Warren, "On the Moral and Legal Status of Abortion," *The Monist* 57, no. 1 (1973). In my discussion, I do not mean to imply that the equation of "rational self-consciousness" with being a person with a serious right to life is the correct answer to the personhood problem. This is controversial and needs a defense. I use it simply as a more plausible alternative to the biological equation of specieshood with personhood.

7. Jeffrey Olen, *Persons and Their World* (New York: Random House, 1983), 3.

8. Ibid.

9. Mark Woodhouse, *A Preface to Philosophy* (Belmont, CA: Wadsworth, 1984).

FOR FURTHER READING

Audi, Robert, ed. *The Cambridge Dictionary of Philosophy.* Cambridge, Eng.: Cambridge University Press, 1996. The best dictionary of philosophy available.

Copleston, F. C. *History of Philosophy,* 8 vol. New York: Doubleday, 1966. The most comprehensive work in the history of philosophy in English.

Edwards, Paul, ed. *Encyclopedia of Philosophy,* 8 vol. New York: Macmillan, 1967. Contains a rich and comprehensive set of essays on virtually every problem in philosophy. A supplementary, updated volume was published in 1996.

Jones, W. T. *A History of Western Philosophy,* 5 vol. New York: Harper & Row, 1976. A lucid, accessible, reliable work.

Lawhead, William. *The Voyage of Discovery: A History of Western Philosophy.* Belmont, CA: Wadsworth, 1996. A realiable, user-friendly introduction to the history of philosophy.

Matson, Wallace. *A New History of Philosophy,* 2 vol. New York: Harcourt Brace Jovanovich, 1987. An insightful, acute, short introduction to the history of philosophy.

Nagel, Thomas. *What Does It All Mean?* Oxford: Oxford University Press, 1990. A succinct, thoughtful invitation to philosophical reflection.

Pojman, Louis. *Philosophy: The Quest for Truth,* 4th ed. Belmont, CA: Wadsworth, 1998.

Rosenberg, Jay. *The Practice of Philosophy,* 2d ed. Englewood Cliffs, NJ: Prentice Hall, 1984. An excellent handbook to philosophy for beginners: concise, witty, and philosophically rich.

Russell, Bertrand. *The Problems of Philosophy.* Oxford: Oxford University Press, 1912. Although a little dated, this marvelously lucid book, reputedly written in ten days, is a gold mine of ideas and pressing argument.

Woodhouse, Mark. *A Preface to Philosophy.* Belmont, CA: Wadsworth, 1984. This little gem is useful in discussing the purposes and methods of philosophical inquiry. It contains lively discussions of informal logic, reading philosophy, and writing philosophical papers.

2

A Little Bit of Logic

Philosophy is centered in the analysis and construction of **arguments.** We call the study of arguments **logic.** Let us devote a little time to the rudiments of logic. By argument we do not mean a verbal fight but a process of supporting a thesis (called the *conclusion*) with reasons (called *premises*). An argument consists of at least two declarative sentences (sometimes called **propositions**), one of which (the conclusion) follows from the others (the premises). The premises are intended to support the conclusion. The connection by which the conclusion follows from the premises is called an **inference:**

Premise 1
Premise 2   (Inference)
Conclusion

DEDUCTIVE AND INDUCTIVE REASONING

Deductive Arguments A **valid deductive argument** is one that follows a correct logical form, so that if the premises are true, the conclusion must also be true. If the form is not a good one, the argument is invalid. We say that a valid deductive argument *preserves truth*. It does so in much the same way as a good refrigerator preserves food. If the food is good, a good refrigerator will preserve it; but if the food is already spoiled, the refrigerator will not make it good. Similarly, the same is true with premises of a valid argument. If the statements are true and the form is correct, the conclusion will be true; but if the premises are not true, a valid argument will not guarantee a true conclusion.

A classic example of a valid argument is the following:

1. Socrates is a man.
2. All men are mortal.
3. ∴ Socrates is mortal.

To identify the form, let us look at conclusion 3 and identify the two major components: a subject (S) and a predicate (P). *Socrates* is the subject term, and *mortal* is the predicate term. Now return to the two premises and identify these two terms in them. We discover that the two terms are connected by a third term, *man* (or the plural *men*). We call this the *middle term* (M).

The form of the argument is as follows:

1. S is M.
2. All M are P.
3. ∴ S is P.

This is an example of a valid deductive form. If premises 1 and 2 are true, we will always get a true conclusion by using this form. But notice how easy it would be to get an invalid form. Change the order of the second premise to read "All P are M." Let the first premise read "My roommate is a mammal" and the second premise read "All dogs are mammals." What do you get?

1. My roommate, Sam Smith, is a mammal. (Premise)
2. Dogs are mammals. (Premise)
3. ∴ My roommate is a dog. (Conclusion)

Regardless of how badly you might treat your roommate, the argument has improper form and cannot yield a valid conclusion; it is *invalid*. Every deductive argument is either valid or invalid. Like a woman who cannot be a little pregnant, an argument cannot be partly valid or invalid but must be completely one or the other. By seeking to find counterexamples for argument forms, we can discover which are the correct forms. (A full study of this would have to wait for a course in logic.)

Validity is not the only concept we need to examine; **soundness** is also important. An argument can be valid but still unsound. An argument is *sound* if it has a valid form and all its premises are true. If at least one premise is false, the argument is *unsound*. Here is an example of a sound argument:

1. If Mary is a mother, she must be a woman.
2. Mary is a mother (for she has just given birth to a baby).
3. ∴ Mary is a woman.

If Mary hasn't given birth, then premise 2 is false, and the argument is unsound.

You should be aware of four other deductive argument forms: *modus ponens, modus tollens, disjunctive syllogism,* and *reductio ad absurdum.* Here are their forms:

Modus Ponens (MP)
(Affirming the Antecedent)
1. If P, then Q.
2. P.
3. ∴ Q.

Modus Tollens (MT)
(Denying the Consequent)
1. If P, then Q.
2. Not-Q.
3. ∴ Not-P.

Note in a hypothetical proposition (if P, then Q) the first term (the proposition P) is called the antecedent and the second term (Q) the consequent. Both affirming the antecedent and denying the consequent yield valid forms:

Disjunctive Syllogism (DS)
(Denying the Disjunct)

1. Either P or Q.
2. Not-Q.
3. ∴ P.

Reductio ad Absurdum (RAA)
(Reducing to a Contradiction)

1. Assume A. (A is the logical opposite of the conclusion you seek to prove.)
2. Logically deduce a contradiction from A. (This shows that A implies a contradiction.)
3. This proves A is false, since a contradiction cannot be true. So not-A must be true.

We have already given an example of a modus ponens:

1. If Mary is a mother, she must be a woman.
2. Mary is a mother.
3. ∴ Mary is a woman.

Here is an example of a modus tollens:

1. If Leslie is a mother, she is a woman.
2. Leslie is not a woman (but a man).
3. ∴ Leslie is not a mother.

Here is an example of a disjunctive syllogism (sometimes called "denying the disjunct"—the whole proposition "P or Q" is a disjunction of which each component "P" and "Q" is a disjunct).

1. John is either a bachelor or a married man.
2. We know for certain that John is not married.
3. ∴ John is a bachelor.

We turn to reductio ad absurdum (RAA). This is an indirect method of proving or establishing a thesis. You assume the opposite of what you wish to prove and show that it produces an absurd conclusion. Therefore, your thesis must be true. Here is an example of an RAA; a little more complicated than the other forms, it is important especially in reference to the ontological argument (see Chapter 6). Suppose someone denies that there is such a thing as a self and you wish to refute the assertion. You might argue in the following manner:

1. Suppose you're correct and there is no such thing as a self (not-A).
2. But if there is no such thing as a self, then no one ever acts (if not-A, then not-B).
3. But if no one ever acts, then no one can utter meaningful statements (if not-B, then not-C).
4. But you have purported to utter a meaningful statement in saying that there is no such thing as a self, so there is at least one meaningful statement (C).
5. According to your argument, there is and there is not at least one meaningful statement (C and not-C).

6.   ∴ It must be false that there is no such thing as a self (not, not-A—which by double negation yields A). Thus, we have proved by reductio ad absurdum that there is such a thing as a self.

Before we leave the realm of deductive argument, we must point out two invalid forms that often give students trouble. To understand them, look back at forms MP and MT (p. 21), which respectively argue by affirming the antecedent and denying the consequent. But notice that there are two other possible forms. You can also deny the antecedent and affirm the consequent in the following manner:

Denying the Antecedent (DA)
1. If P, then Q.
2. Not-P.
3. ∴ Not-Q.

Affirming the Consequent (AC)
1. If P, then Q.
2. Q.
3. ∴ P.

Are these valid forms? Remember a valid form must always yield true conclusions if the premises are true. Try to find a counterexample that will show that these two forms are invalid. You might let proposition 1 (if P, then Q) be represented by the previous proposition, "If Mary is a mother, then she is a woman." First, deny the antecedent. Does it necessarily yield a true conclusion? Not necessarily. The conclusion says that Mary is not a woman, but there are many women who are not mothers. So DA is an invalid form:

1. If Mary is a mother, she is a woman.
2. Mary is not a mother.
3. ∴ Mary is not a woman.

Take the same initial proposition and affirm the consequent "Mary is a woman." Does this in itself yield the conclusion that she is a mother? Of course not. She could be a woman without being a mother:

1. If Mary is a mother, she is a woman.
2. She is a woman.
3. ∴ Mary is a mother.

Thus, whereas MP and MT are valid forms, DA and AC are not. Be careful here. Many students slur over these distinctions. Work out your own examples of each form of argument.

These are just simple examples of deductive argument forms. Often, alas, it is difficult to state exactly what the author's premises are.

Inductive Arguments   Let us turn our attention to inductive arguments. Unlike their counterpart, valid deductive arguments, **inductive arguments** are not truth-preserving—that is, they do not guarantee that if we have true premises, we will obtain a true conclusion. They bring only *probability;* but in most of life, that is the best we can hope for. David Hume (1711–1776) said that "probability is the guide of life." The wise person guides his or her life by the best evidence available, always realizing that one could be mistaken. We usually do not speak of inductive arguments as valid/invalid or sound/unsound but as strong/weak or cogent/implausible. In inductive arguments, the premises are *evidence* for the conclusion or hypothesis. If the evidence for the conclusion is substantial, we call the argument a strong inductive argument; but if the evidence is weak, so is the argument as a whole. An inductive argument has the following form:

1. A_1 is a B.
2. A_2 is a B.
3. A_3 is a B.
4. So probably the next A we encounter (A_4) will also be a B.

For example, suppose you are surrounded by four islands somewhere in the Pacific Ocean. You examine all trees on three of the islands but cannot get to the fourth. Nevertheless, you might make some predictions on the basis of your experience on the first three islands. For example, you note that all trees on islands A, B, and C are coconut trees. From this you predict that coconut trees will be on island D and that coconut is probably the only tree found there.

We learn from experience, that is, by induction. We observe resemblances and regularities in life and generalize from them. After a few experiences of getting burned by fire (or after a few experiences with people of a certain type), we learn to avoid fire (or people of a certain type). The human race has learned by inductive experience that cooperation generally produces more benefits than non-cooperation, so we advocate cooperative ventures.

Naturally, the greater the sample size of our observation, the greater the probability of our generalization. Asking 1000 representative Americans whom they will vote for is likely to yield a more accurate prediction of who will be elected than asking only 100 Americans. Sometimes, when we should know better, we generalize or make predictions from an inadequate sample; we call this *prejudice,* a type of malformed induction. If a child infers from his only six bad experiences with people from Podunkville that all people in Podunkville are bad, that might be acceptable. However, if an adult, who could easily have evidence that many good people live in Podunkville, still generalizes about the people of Podunkville and acts accordingly, we label this an irrational bias, a prejudice.

Inductive reasoning can lead us astray—it can be dangerous. The chicken who innately reasons that the farmer will feed her again today because he has done so twice a day for a long time is in for a cruel shock when he wrings her neck in preparation for his meal.

A special kind of induction reasoning is called *reasoning by analogy* (see Chapter 5 for its use). Reasoning by analogy allows us to reason from the similarity of two things in some relevant respects to their similarity in an unexpected respect. For example, suppose I am lost in the forest and I want to determine whether to eat a certain mushroom, which my hungry stomach craves. I note that it is similar in shape, color, and consistency to other mushrooms that turned out to be edible. Thus, I infer that probably this mushroom will be edible too.

ABDUCTIVE REASONING

Abductive reasoning, or reasoning to the best explanation, was first formulated by the American philosopher Charles S. Peirce (1839–1914). Like inductive reasoning, **abduction** yields only probable truth. Whereas induction typically establishes general conclusions or probabilities about future occurrences, abduction provides explanatory hypotheses. It answers the question, Why is such and such the case? We can illustrate abductive reasoning with the following example of Sherlock Holmes's reasoning:

> The portly client puffed out his chest with an appearance of some little pride and pulled a dirty and wrinkled newspaper from the inside pocket of his greatcoat. As he glanced down the advertisement column with his head thrust forward and the paper flattened out upon his knee, I took a good look at the man and endeavored, after the fashion of my companion, to read the indications which might be presented by his dress or appearance.
>
> I did not gain very much, however, by my inspection. Our visitor bore every mark of being an average commonplace British tradesman, obese, pompous, and slow. He wore rather baggy gray shepherd's check trousers, a not over-clean black frock-coat, unbuttoned in the front, and a drab waistcoat with a heavy brassy Albert chain, and a square pierced bit of metal dangling down as an ornament. A frayed top-hat and a faded brown overcoat with a wrinkled velvet collar lay upon a chair beside him. Altogether, look as I would, there was nothing remarkable about the man save his blazing red head and the expression of extreme chagrin and discontent upon his features.
>
> Sherlock Holmes's quick eye took in my occupation, and he shook his head with a smile as he noticed my questioning glances. "Beyond the obvious facts that he has at some time done manual labour, that he takes snuff, that he is a Freemason, that he has been in China, and that he has done a considerable amount of writing lately, I can *deduce* nothing else." Mr. Jabez Wilson started up in his chair, with his forefinger upon the paper, but his eyes upon my companion.
>
> "How, in the name of good-fortune did you know all that, Mr. Holmes?" he asked. "How did you know, for example, that I did manual labour? It's as true as gospel, for I began as a ship's carpenter."
>
> "Your hands, my dear sir. Your right hand is quite a size larger than your left. You have worked with it, and the muscles are more developed."
>
> "Well, the snuff, then, and the Freemasonry?"
>
> "I won't insult your intelligence by telling you how I read that, especially as, rather against the strict rules of your order, you use an arc-and-compass breastpin."
>
> "Ah, of course, I forgot that. But the writing?"
>
> "What else can be indicated by that right cuff so very shiny for five inches, and the left one with the smooth patch near the elbow where you rest it upon the desk?"
>
> "Well, but China?"
>
> "The fish which you have tattooed immediately above your right wrist could only have been done in China. I have made a small study of tattoo marks and have even contributed to the literature of the subject. That trick of staining the fishes' scales of a delicate pink is quite peculiar to China. When, in addition, I see a Chinese coin hanging from your watchchain, the matter becomes even more simple."
>
> Mr. Jabez Wilson laughed heavily. "Well, I never!" said he. "I thought at first that you had done something clever, but I see that there was nothing in it, after all."[1]

Philosophers appreciate Mr. Wilson's final remark, that Holmes's explanation makes so much sense that one wonders why one didn't think of it oneself. Holmes often chided Watson: "You see, but you do not observe." A good philosopher, like a good detective or scientist, observes while he or she sees.

There is a significant inaccuracy, however, in Holmes's description of what he does. He claims to be deducing the conclusions about Mr. Wilson from the telltale signs. Strictly speaking, he is doing no such thing. In deductive reasoning, if the form is correct and the premises are true, one cannot help but obtain a true conclusion, but such is *not* the case with Mr. Holmes's reasoning. For example, consider Wilson's arc-and-compass breastpin, which leads Holmes to conclude that Wilson is a Freemason. If the reasoning were deductive, the argument would go something like this:

1. Everyone wearing an arc-and-compass breastpin is a Freemason.
2. Mr. Wilson is wearing an arc-and-compass breastpin.
3. ∴ Mr. Wilson is a Freemason.

Is this a sound argument? Of course not. Imagine that Mr. Wilson, who is not a Freemason, bought a similar arc-and-compass breastpin at a pawnshop and wore it, thinking it was a beautiful bit of Muslim design. In that case, premise 1 would be false. Not everyone wearing an arc-and-compass breastpin is a Freemason. Because it is possible that non-Freemasons wear that pin, the above deductive argument is not sound.

What Holmes has really done is reason abductively, that is, reason to the best explanation of the facts. Like inductive reasoning, abduction does not guarantee the truth of the conclusions. Unlike induction, it is not simply about the probability of such and such being the case based on the evidence. Abductive reasoning attempts to offer explanations of the facts, why things are the way they are. The best explanation of Mr. Wilson's wearing the arc-and-compass breastpin is his belonging to the Freemasons. The best explanation of a child's having a fever and red spots is that she has the measles. The best explanation of the puddles outside is that it has recently rained.

The notion of the best explanation is fascinating in its own right. How do we discover the best explanation? What characteristics does it have? How do we rank various virtues of a good explanation? There are no definite answers to these questions, but it is generally agreed that such traits as predictability, coherence, simplicity, and fruitfulness are among the main characteristics. If a theory helps us predict future events, that is a powerful weapon. If it coheres well with everything or nearly everything else that we hold true in the field, that lends support to it. If it is simpler than its rivals, if it demands fewer **ad hoc,** or auxiliary, hypotheses, that is a virtue. If it leads to new insight and discoveries, that is also a point in its favor. But what if explanatory theory A has more of one of these features and theory B more of another? Which should we prefer? There is no decision-making procedure to decide the matter with any finality. In a sense, abduction is educated guesswork or intuition. Counterevidence counts strongly against a hypothesis, so that if we can falsify our thesis, we have good reason to drop it; however, sometimes we can make adjustments in our hypothesis to accommodate the counterevidence.

Abduction has been neglected in philosophy, but it really is of the utmost importance. Consider the following questions: Why do you believe in God? Why do you believe in evolutionary theory? Why do you believe that there are universal moral principles? Why do you believe that all events are caused? In one way or another, the answer will probably be abductive: What you believe seems to you to be the best explanation among all the competitors of certain phenomena. We will have opportunity to use abductive reasoning at several points during our course of study.

SOME APPLICATIONS

Let's apply these brief lessons of logic to reading philosophy. Because the key to philosophy is the argument, you will want to concentrate and even outline the author's reasoning. Find his or her thesis or conclusion. Usually, it is stated early on. After this, identify the premises that support or lead to the conclusion. For example, Thomas Aquinas (1224–1274) holds the conclusion that God exists. He argues for this conclusion in five different ways. In the second argument, he uses the following premises to reach his conclusion: There is motion, and there cannot be motion without something initiating the motion.

It helps to outline the premises of the argument. For example, here's how we might set forth Aquinas's second argument:

1. Some things are in motion. (Premise)
2. Nothing in the world can move itself but must be moved by another. (Premise)
3. There cannot be an infinite regress of motions. (Premise)
4. There must be a First Mover who is responsible for all other motion. (Conclusion of premises 1–3, which in turn becomes a premise for the rest of the argument)
5. This First Mover is what we call God (explanation of the meaning of God). (Premise)
6. ∴ God exists. (Conclusion of second part of the argument, premises 4 and 5)

After you have identified the premises and conclusion, analyze them, looking for mistakes in the reasoning process. Sometimes arguments are weak or unsound, but not obviously so. Then stretch your imagination and think of possible counterexamples to the claims of the author. I found this process almost impossible at first, but gradually it became second nature.

Because philosophical arguments are often complex and subtle (and because philosophers do not always write as clearly as they should), a full understanding of an essay is not readily available after a single reading. So read it twice or even thrice. The first time I read a philosophy essay, I read it for understanding. I want to know where the author is coming from and what he or she is trying to establish. After the first reading, I leave the essay for some time, ruminating on it. Sometimes objections to the arguments awaken me at night or while I am working at something else. Then I go back a day or so later and read the essay a second time, this time trying to determine its soundness.

A few pointers should be mentioned along the way. Some students find it helpful to keep a notebook on their reflections on the readings. If you own the book, I suggest that you make notes in the margins—initially in pencil because you may want to revise your impressions after a second reading. Finally, practice charity. Give the author the best possible interpretation in order to see if the argument has merit. Always try to deal with the most generous version of the argument, especially if you don't agree with its conclusion. A position has not been seriously challenged unless the best arguments for it have been refuted. That's why it is necessary to construe all arguments, including those of your opponents, as charitably as possible. The exercise will broaden your horizons and help you develop sharper reasoning skills.

FALLACIES OF REASONING

Before we sum up this chapter, I would like to identify a number of common fallacies of reasoning. Good reasoning depends on justified beliefs (acceptable premises) and valid logical form. Many arguments, however, fail to satisfy these conditions. I have listed some of the main fallacies of reasoning. See if you can illustrate them with examples of your own.

- *Ad Hominem Argument*   This is an argument "against the man." This argument attacks the person instead of the position—for example, "You can't trust what Joan says about abortion, for she is an immoral person." Her argument for or against abortion, however, may be sound on independent grounds. Even the devil has true beliefs. The character of the person is irrelevant to the soundness of the argument.

- *Argument from Authority*   Suppose we are arguing about the death penalty, and I tell you that we should believe in the death penalty because Plato believed in it. Since you don't know Plato's reasons (I may not either), it is not sufficient grounds for either of us to believe in the death penalty. We need positive arguments, not simply authority. Advertisements are notorious for subtly and sometimes not so subtly using this device. In a beer commercial, a famous athlete (nicely remunerated for the exercise) may be seen gratifying his thirst, proclaiming the ecstasy of the beverage, as if that were proof of its quality.

  Of course, authority may sometimes be the best we can get and sufficient for justified belief, as when a physicist tells us the conclusions of a complicated physics research or a friend from Australia gives you pertinent information for your upcoming visit to that country. We sometimes do need to trust authority, but often it is an improper substitute for good reasoning.

- *Arguing in a Circle*   This is sometimes referred to as "begging the question." Suppose I argue that you should believe that God exists. You ask why. I say, "Because the Bible says so." You ask, "Why should I believe what the Bible says?" I reply, "Because it's the Word of God." That is, I argue in a circle, using my conclusion as a premise to prove the conclusion. Note that all valid deductive arguments can appear as arguing in a circle, since the conclusion of such an argument is contained in the premises. The difference is that in a cogent argument the conclusion brings out a nontrivial feature of the premises. Essentially, arguing in a circle is not invalid, just trivial and unconvincing, having no power to convince an opponent.

- *Argument from Ignorance*   This kind of argument occurs when I claim that, because you cannot prove a proposition is false, I am justified in believing it to be true. For example, because you can't prove God doesn't exist, I am free to believe that He does exist. Or because you can't prove that we do not have a soul, I am free to believe that we do.

- *False Dilemma*   This happens when we reduce several possibilities to two alternatives. I once read of two travelers facing a swamp in which traveler A said to traveler B, "Since you admit you don't know the way through the swamp and there must be a way, follow me. I must know the way." Of course, neither may know the way. Similarly, someone may argue that since your answer to a problem isn't correct, his or hers must be. But, of course, both may be wrong.

- *Slippery Slope*   This is sometimes called the "edge-of-the-wedge" argument (once you let the camel nose under the wedge of the tent, it will capsize the entire tent). Similarly, it will be argued, once we allow act A to occur, event B, which is evil, will occur. Robert Wright has argued that "once you buy the premise that animals can experience pain and pleasure, and that their welfare therefore deserves *some* consideration, you're on the road to comparing yourself with a lobster. There may be some exit ramps along the way—plausible places to separate welfare from rights—but I can't find any." Others have argued that if we allow voluntary euthanasia, we are on the slippery slope to involuntary euthanasia, even eventually to a holocaust. Still others have argued that if we pass a national health care bill, it will inevitably lead to socialism and communism. The slippery slope fallacy ignores the truth that, very often, wise policy is a moderate stance between two extremes and that rational people can hold to a rational position without going to an extreme.

- *Straw Man Argument*   This is an instance of misrepresenting an opponent's position. It occurs when someone ignores the evidence for a position and instead attacks an inferior version of the position. In the heat of debate on whether our nation should reduce its military spending, a militarist may argue that his opponent wants to leave our nation defenseless or a willing prey to communism. I once heard of a Russian tourist guide who claimed that she knew that God didn't exist, because if he did, he would announce his presence from heaven. The straw man argument is often a distortion of the other person's position. There is a tendency in all of us to attack a weaker—less plausible—version of our opponent's position. The *principle of charity* is the opposite of the straw man argument. It instructs us to give our opponent's position the very best form we can find—and then try to show it is unsound.

- *Genetic Fallacy*   This is arguing against a position or argument because its origins are suspect. Suppose I tell you not to believe in the principles of chemistry because they originated in superstitious alchemy or not to believe in an astronomical theory because it arose from astrological sources. The fact that a theory or position originated in discredited circumstances is irrelevant if the theory is supported by the evidence. For their theories, chemistry and astronomy can produce impressive evidence that is independent of the authority of alchemy and astrology. It doesn't matter where the truth comes from, as long as it is true.

- *Inconsistency*   When we argue inconsistently, we argue from contradictory premises. When trying to win votes from one constituency, politicians sometimes contradict what they have said to other constituencies. To illustrate this, consider some statements made by former President Ronald Reagan at different periods of his political career:

On Civil Rights

1. "I favor the Civil Rights Act of 1964 and it must be enforced at the point of a bayonet, if necessary" (October 19, 1965).
2. "I would have voted against the Civil Rights Act of 1964" (June 16, 1966).

On Redwood National Park

1. "I believe our country can and should have a Redwood National Park in California" (April 17, 1967).
2. "There can be no proof given that a national park is necessary to preserve the redwoods. The state of California has already maintained a great conservation program" (April 18, 1967—the next day).

On the Soviet Grain Embargo

1. "I just don't believe the farmers should be made to pay a special price for our diplomacy, and I'm opposed to [the Soviet grain embargo]" (January 7, 1980).
2. "If we are going to do such a thing to the Soviet Union as a full grain embargo, which I support, first we have to be sure our own allies would join us on this" (January 8, 1980—the next day).[2]

Of course, people change their minds and come to believe the opposite of what they formerly believed. That may show progress, but many of us are not aware of the inconsistencies in our own belief systems. For example, Fred may believe that morality entails universalizing principles ("what's good for the goose is good for the gander") but fail to note that his view on premarital sex—morally permissible for men but not for women—is inconsistent with that principle.

NECESSARY AND SUFFICIENT CONDITIONS

One logical relationship that will appear throughout this book deserves to be highlighted now. Sometimes we speak of A being a *necessary* condition for B, or of B being a *sufficient* condition for A, or of A and C being *necessary and sufficient* conditions for B. Sometimes these terms refer to causal relationships. For example:

1. Cutting off a person's head is sufficient to kill him. Cutting off someone's head is not a necessary condition for killing someone (there are other equally effective ways), but it will get the job done.

   On the other hand, we might read that:

2. Grandma's will states that her death is necessary for the grandchildren to inherit her estate. That is, the grandchildren will inherit Grandma's estate only if she dies. But Grandma's death may not be a sufficient condition for such an inheritance, for her will may stipulate other conditions that must be fulfilled, such as that all outstanding bills be paid, that the grandchildren remain Southern Baptists, and that the grandchildren refrain from drinking alcoholic beverages. If these are the only conditions for inheriting her estate, we might formulate the complete necessary and sufficient conditions in terms of a statement containing the phrase "if and only if": The grandchildren will inherit Grandma's estate if and only if (a) Grandma dies, (b) all outstanding bills are paid from the estate and funds are left, (c) the grandchildren remain members of the Southern Baptist Church, and (d) they refrain from drinking alcoholic beverages. Conditions a–d are necessary and jointly sufficient for inheriting Grandma's estate. If only some of the conditions obtain (are realized), this is not sufficient for inheriting the estate, but if we discover that the estate has been inherited, we can infer that all conditions have obtained. That the estate was passed down to the grandchildren is *sufficient* for us to know that the four conditions were fulfilled.

3. The idea of necessary and sufficient conditions is sometimes applied to definitions, as in "A means B." Suppose we define a mother as a female who has given birth to a child. We may spell this out this way:

   mother = a female who has given birth to an offspring

We may also say of any person X, "X is a mother if and only if X is a female and has given birth to an offspring." Breaking this down, we find:

a. *A is a necessary condition for B* means that if B is true, then A is true: Being a female and having given birth are two necessary conditions for being a mother.

b. *A is a sufficient condition for B* means that if A is true, then B is true: Being a mother is a sufficient condition for being a woman who has given birth to an offspring.

Putting the two together, we get:

c. *A is a necessary and sufficient condition for B* means that if A is true, B is and if B is true, A is: If Mary is a mother, then she is a woman who has given birth, and if she is a woman who has given birth, she is a mother.

Philosophers use the idea of necessary and sufficient conditions to state the conditions that must be fulfilled for a state of affairs to be realized. In Part III, we will see that one recommendation for a definition of *knowledge* is that of justified true belief. That is,

4. Some person X knows that p (where p stands for a proposition) if and only if

a. X believes p.

b. p is true.

c. X's belief that p is justified.

Conditions a–c are necessary and jointly sufficient conditions for knowledge. Similarly, the truth of the first part of the conditional "X knows that p" is *sufficient* for us to know that conditions a–c have been fulfilled. However, proposition 4 may not be a completely adequate definition of the term "knowledge." It's a disputed matter.

SUMMARY

In a valid deductive argument, if the premises are true, the conclusion must be true by virtue of a logically necessary form. In a strong inductive argument, the premises, if true, make the conclusion probable but do not guarantee the truth of the conclusion. In a good abductive argument, the conclusion or hypothesis offers the best explanation of the data.

QUESTIONS FOR DISCUSSION

1. Using the argument forms discussed in this chapter, construct an argument of your own for each form shown.

2. Explain the difference between deductive, inductive, and abductive reasoning.

3. Get a copy of your student or local newspaper and analyze two arguments therein. Begin to look at the claims of others in argument form.

4. Philosophy can be seen as an attempt to solve life's perennial puzzles. Taking the material at hand, it tries to unravel enigmas by thought alone. See what you can do with the puzzles and paradoxes included here.

   a. There is a barber in Barberville who shaves all and only those barbers who do not shave themselves. Does this barber shave himself? (Who does shave him?)

b. You are the sole survivor of a shipwreck and are drifting in a small raft parallel to the coast of an island. You know that on this island there are only two tribes of natives: Nobles, kind folk who always tell the truth, and Savages, cannibals who always lie. Naturally, you want to find refuge with the Nobles. You see a man standing on the shore and call out, "Are you a Noble or a Savage?" The man answers the question, but a wave breaks on the beach at that very moment, so you don't hear the reply. The boat drifts farther down along the shore when you see another man. You ask him the same question, and he replies, pointing to the first man, "He said he was a Noble." Then he continues, "I am a Noble." Your boat drifts farther down the shore where you see a third man. You ask him the same question. The man seems very friendly as he calls out, "They are both liars. I am a Noble. They are Savages."

The puzzle: Is the data given sufficient to tell you any man's tribe? Is it sufficient to tell you each man's tribe?

c. Mrs. Smith, a schoolteacher, announces to her class on Friday that there will be a surprise test during the following week. She defines "surprise test" as one that no one could reasonably predict on the day of the test. Johnny, one of her students, responds that she may not give the test on pain of contradicting herself. Mrs. Smith asks, "Why not?" Johnny replies, "You cannot give the test on Friday because on Friday everyone would know that the test would take place on that day, and so it would not be a surprise. So the test must take place on a day between Monday and Thursday. But it cannot take place on Thursday, for if it hasn't taken place by then, it would not be a surprise on Thursday. So the test must take place between Monday and Wednesday. But it cannot take place on Wednesday for the same reason that we rejected Friday and Thursday. Similarly, we can use the same reason to exclude Tuesday and Monday. On no day of the week can a surprise test be given. So the test cannot be given next week."

Mrs. Smith heard Johnny's argument and wondered what the solution was. She gave the test on Tuesday, and everyone was surprised, including Johnny. How was this possible?

d. What follows from this puzzle?

It is sometimes said that space is empty, which means presumably, that there is *nothing* between two stars. But if there is nothing between stars, then they are not separated by anything, and, thus, they must be right up against one another, perhaps forming some peculiar sort of double star. We know this not to be the case, of course.[3]

5. A good reason to be a critical thinker is to avoid getting cheated. Occasionally, you may be in danger of being duped by an unscrupulous salesperson. Thinking clearly may save you. Here is an example of such a situation that occurred after the Loma Prieta earthquake in the San Francisco Bay Area in 1989.

Last week the 55-year-old [Eva] Davis was evicted from her . . . home of 22 years by San Francisco sheriff's deputies. Her troubles began in 1990 when a contractor offered to repair front steps damaged in the Loma Prieta earthquake. Two hours later came a disaster worse than an earthquake, a disaster with a smile, a representative of Congress Mortgage Co. of San Jose. Convinced that she was getting a federal loan that didn't have to be repaid until the house was sold, Davis signed a 15 percent loan with a 15 percent origination fee. The 15 points meant a $23,000 fee, instead of a usual $4,000 or so. Suddenly, Davis had $1,800 monthly payments instead of $459. It was only a matter of time before the house belonged to Congress Mortgage.

Congress Mortgage sold the home, valued at $225,000. The company makes some 400 loans a year and has scheduled 51 foreclosure sales in the next month alone. The bust business is booming.[4]

Think of other examples of how critical thinking can save people from evil.

NOTES

1. Arthur Conan Doyle, *The Red-Headed League* (New York: Harper & Bros., 1892).

2. Marc Green and Gail MacCall, *There He Goes Again: Ronald Reagan's Reign of Error* (New York: Pantheon, 1982).

3. Jay Rosenberg, *The Practice of Philosophy* (Englewood Cliffs, NJ: Prentice Hall, 1978), 99.

4. Rob Morse, *San Francisco Chronicle* (Feb. 20, 1994).

FOR FURTHER READING

Copi, Irving. *Introduction to Logic,* 6th ed. New York: Macmillan, 1982. A widely used text, clear and concise.

Hurley, Patrick. *A Concise Introduction to Logic,* 4th ed. Belmont, CA: Wadsworth, 1991. An excellent work, clear and accessible.

Kahane, Howard. *Logic and Contemporary Rhetoric,* 7th ed. Belmont, CA: Wadsworth, 1995. An accessible introduction to critical thinking. Filled with interesting illustrations and examples.

More, Brooke, and Richard Parker. *Critical Thinking.* Mountain View, CA: Mayfield, 1992. A very good introduction to logical thinking.

Scriven, Michael. *Reasoning.* New York: McGraw-Hill, 1976. A rich presentation of the major topics in philosophical reasoning.

3

The Rise of the Sophists
and Socrates

THE RISE OF THE SOPHISTS

In the middle of the fifth century B.C., Athens flourished materially and culturally. Partly due to an unexpected and resounding victory over the Persians and
partly due to exceptional leadership of the likes of Solon and Pericles, the
founders of democracy, Athens became a prosperous economic force. In the arts,
it produced such geniuses as the playwrights Euripides, Sophocles, Aeschylus, and
Aristophanes. The Parthenon was built, and sculpture and the plastic arts reached
their pinnacle. Because the city's prosperity depended on a large number of slaves,
citizens enjoyed an unprecedented amount of leisure time to think and converse.
The state religion, which was based on the Homeric gods, was scrutinized, tried,
and found wanting by the brightest citizens, and secularism increased. Political
speech making and rhetoric to persuade citizens grew in importance. Litigation
also increased because the rising entrepreneurial class found it could tap into the
wealth of the conservative aristocracy through the courts.

Into this world, a new profession arose, one bent on teaching citizens how
to win cases in court: the Sophists. The Sophists were secular relativists, skeptical, even cynical, about religious and idealistic pretensions, aiming at material
and political success in democratic society by using rhetoric and oratory in
persuading people. They rejected the quest of the pre-Socratic philosophers as
useless speculation. The big question of the pre-Socratics was, What is the
nature of reality? The Sophists' question, however, was more mundane: How
can I succeed in the practical affairs of life, or how can I play the game of life
and win? These are always appealing questions. Some Sophists made enormous

sums of money selling their services to rich young men, teaching them how to win at litigation and use debating tricks to defeat their opponents.

The Sophists were prominent between 460 and 380 B.C. The older generation, Protagoras of Abdera in Thrace (ca. 490–420 B.C.), Gorgias of Leontini in Sicily (485–380? B.C.), Prodicus (460–399? B.C.) of Ceos, and Hippias of Elis (fifth century B.C.), were urbane, socially responsible, professional teachers, who even held political offices. Protagoras greatly influenced Pericles, the developer of Athenian democracy, and Gorgias was his friend. They took a pragmatic view toward social conventions and religious worship. Although they were skeptical about religion, they advised worship of the gods for socially prudent reasons. Laws and religious beliefs and rituals are the "glue" that holds society together. So even though they are probably human inventions, they are useful and should be valued for that reason.

The younger generation, consisting of men like Callicles, Critias (Plato's uncle [480–403? B.C.]), Antiphon, and Thrasymachus, were much more hardened, not merely skeptical but cynical about religion, law, and moral conventions. For them, religion was a fraud, and conventional justice was simply a way of keeping the naturally superior from exercising their ability. Breaking with the older Sophists on attitude, it can be argued that they simply took the ideas of the older generation and developed their logical implications. Some philosophers, however, believe that this view is incorrect. The views of the early Sophists, they would argue, do not entail the more cynical ones of the later group. Perhaps the hardening of the position is due to the violence and destructive character of the Peloponnesian War (431–404 B.C.), in which Sparta and her Peloponnesian allies defeated Athens. Whatever the cause, there was a change toward radical cynicism to the point where Thrasymachus calls immorality a virtue and morality a vice. While recognizing these differences in attitude and the fact that the Sophists sometimes disagreed among themselves, it will, nevertheless, be useful to set forth a rough composite of their main ideas.

General Features of the Sophists   1. The Sophists were secularists—skeptical or atheistic on religious belief, often cynical of the use of religion as a mechanism for social control. The gods were invented to function as an invisible, all-seeing police force. The Sophist Critias wrote:

> There was once a time when human life was chaotic,
> Brutal and subservient to force,
> When there was neither a reward for being decent
> Or any restraint on evil men.
> In consequence human beings
> Have enacted laws to be avengers
> So that justice might be ruler
> And keep violence in subjection;
> And if anybody did wrong he would be punished.
> After this, since the laws prevented people
> From doing violent deeds that could be seen,
> They committed them in secret, and it was then
> I think some man of clever well-compacted intellect
> Invented fear of the gods for mortal men so that

It might be a kind of terror for wrongdoers
Even if in secret they did or said or thought
Some wrongful thing:
Further to this he introduced the divine principle
That there exists a spirit flourishing in life that
Is free from decay,
Hearing and seeing with its intelligence with supreme
Power of thought, applying its vast faculties and
Bearing a god-like nature, that will
Hear everything said amongst mankind and see their
Every act.[1]

Thus, the institution of religion can be explained as an invention by those who would provide incentive for obeying the laws. But, as noted above, Sophists like Protagoras, who were not quite as cynical, advocated worship of the gods for social reasons.

2. The Sophists developed the art of *rhetoric,* the process of using language to persuade. Their chief tool was *eristics,* argument used to win debates, not to pursue truth, and aimed at defeat rather than enlightenment. Aristotle called eristics "dirty fighting in argument."[2] What was needed was cleverness and ready speech, whereby to sway the passions of the mob and citizens. They were justly accused of "making the worse argument seem better."

Another rhetorical tool was *antilogic*—arguing by means of contradictory propositions, leading to an *aporia,* or dead end. They taught their disciples to argue both sides of the case and showed that, regarding any act, it could be seen as good, bad, or indifferent.

3. The Sophists made education into a business; they were the first teachers to get paid for their services, charging fees for teaching "wisdom" and "virtue." Their key question was, Can virtue be taught? They answered that it could be taught and they were the ones skilled to teach it. Holding that virtue was relative to the culture, Protagoras taught that teachers and enlightened parents could train children to be good, law-abiding citizens. The laws and sanctions of society could also play a role.

4. The Sophists were pragmatists. They were not speculative, systematic, or concerned with cosmology as the pre-Socratic philosophers were. However, they took the joint, mutually exclusive conclusions of the pre-Socratic to show that the best minds could know virtually nothing of the nature of ultimate reality. Because knowledge is impossible, they embraced **skepticism** about ultimate reality and concentrated on that which is certain: Success in business, politics, and the practical life is very satisfying. Use common sense on a social and individual scale.

The Sophist Gorgias exemplifies this pragmatic attitude better than anyone. He said,

1. Nothing exists.
2. But if something does exist, it can't be known.
3. But even if it can, it can't be communicated.
4. ∴ Live by appearances. Practice prudence. Be practical. Avoid idle speculation. Seek practical education—that which has an optimum payoff.

As you might expect, Gorgias taught rhetoric to the wealthy young men so that they might win political offices and court cases (which they could now confi-dently create; "Sue Your Opponent if He Is Rich" might have been their motto).

5. The Sophists believed that **egoism** was proper or natural. Each of us must look out for himself. Hence, manipulation of others is permitted. Callicles argues that Socrates is either being naive or disingenuous in holding that laws (*nomos*) are objectively true. Essentially, nature teaches that the superior should exploit and rule the weaker:

> You, Socrates, who pretend to be engaging in the pursuit of truth, are appealing to the popular and vulgar notions of right, which are admirable by convention, not by nature. Social convention and nature are generally opposed to one another. . . . The reason is that the makers of laws are the majority who are weak; and they make laws and distribute praise and censure with a view to themselves and to their own inter-ests; and they terrify the stronger sort of men, and those who are able to get the bet-ter of them, in order that they may not get the better of them; and they say, that self-interested ambition is shameful and unjust, meaning, by the word injustice, the desire of a man to have more than his neighbors; for knowing their own inferiority, I sus-pect that they are only too glad of equality. And therefore the endeavor to have more than the many is conventionally said to be shameful and unjust, and is called injustice, whereas nature herself intimates that it is just for the better to have more than the worse, the more powerful than the weaker; and in many ways she shows, among men as well as among animals, and indeed among whole cities and races, that justice consists in the superior ruling over and having more than the inferior. For on what principle of justice did [the Persian King] Xerxes invade Greece, or his father the Scythians? Nay, but these men, I suggest, act in this way according to the nature of justice; yes, by Heaven, according to the law of nature, though not, perhaps, according to that law which we enact. We take the best and strongest of our fellows from their youth upwards, and tame them like young lions,—enslaving them with spells and incantations, and saying to them that with equality they must be content, and that the equal is the honorable and the just. But if there were a man born with enough ability, he would shake off and break through, and escape from all this. He would trample under foot all our formulas and spells and charms, and all our laws which are against nature. The slave would rise in rebellion and be lord over us, and the light of natural justice would shine forth.[3]

At its worst, the Sophists' ethics degenerated to a sinister doctrine of "might makes right," as advocated by Thrasymachus in Book 1 of Plato's *Republic*. They defined justice as promoting the interest of the stronger or superior—the tyrant. Most people are sheep waiting to be manipulated by the clever and stronger egoist.

These ideas were deemed obvious or plausible by the Athenians when it came to war. In 416 B.C., when invaded by the Athenians, the people of the Isle of Melos refused to give up their independence to the Athenians and argued that the Athenians were unjust to force them to become subservient to them. To this hero-ic celebration of freedom, the Athenian general responds:

> This is not a law that was made by us nor were we the first to use it when it had been made. We are merely acting in accordance with it after finding it already in existence, and we shall leave it to exist for ever in the future. We know that you or anyone else with the same power as us would act in the same way.

Justice is only applicable to equals, those with roughly equal power; otherwise, might makes right! In other words, the big fish eat the little fish.

The Sophists applied the logic of international relations to all of life. Isn't all of nature a struggle for survival and power?

6. The Sophists were relativists, even subjectivists, contending that each person is his or her own measure of truth, thus abandoning the notion of an independent reality apart from our consciousness. Truth is whatever you take it to be.

Perhaps the greatest Sophist of all was Protagoras of Abdera, an exceptional man, who was renowned for arguing either side of a legal case successfully. He gave us the "Hymn to Relativism":

> Man is the measure of all things:
> Both of things that are,
> Man is the measure that they are,
> And of the things that are not,
> Man is the measure that they are not.

Protagoras was reacting against the distinction between sensation and thought, which was held by the Eleatics as well as Heracleitus. Sensations are private, but thought is public. Your experience of the color green cannot be had by me, but we can both understand the concept (idea) of green and can assent to the proposition that nothing green can be red. According to the Eleatics, the senses are untrustworthy, whereas thought, via reason, leads to truth, which is universal and public. Protagoras denied the objectivity of reason as well as the universality and public nature of truth. He subordinated thought under the same private world as is appropriate to sensation. Each person is his own measure or standard of what is true and false. What seems true to me is true. What seems true to you, though it contradicts what I believe, is true relative to you. In the same way, your pain is true for you, and my pain is truly painful for me. *All* opinions are true.

Similarly, in ethics, whatever I deem morally right for me is right for me, and whatever seems right for you is morally right to you. Actually, there are two types of ethical **relativism:** conventional and subjective ethical relativism. Some Sophists held conventionalism, and still others held subjectivism. Conventionalism states that the validity of moral principles depends on cultural approval. The conventionalist relativists were influenced by the diversity of customs in the ancient world. One such example is found in the Greek historian Herodotus's *Histories,* where Herodotus (ca. 485–430 B.C.) tells the story of how Darius, the king of Persia, once brought together some Callatians (Asian tribal people) and some Greeks. He asked the **Callatians** how they disposed of their deceased parents. They told how they ate the bodies of their dead parents. The Greeks, who cremated their parents, were horrified at such barbarous behavior. No amount of money could tempt them to do such an irreverent thing. Then Darius asked the Callatians, "What should I give you to burn the bodies of your fathers at their decease?" The Callatians were utterly horrified at such barbarous behavior and begged Darius to cease from such irreverent discourse. Herodotus concludes that "custom is the king o'er all."[4]

Sophists like Protagoras and Gorgias seem to have generally held this conventional sense of moral relativism, but sometimes the Sophists seem to be subjectivists, holding that virtue or the moral good is relative to individual perception.

Like beauty, virtue is in the eye of the beholder. In this way, the Sophists anticipated contemporary moral relativists and subjectivists like Ernest Hemingway,
who once said, "What is moral is what you feel good after and what is immoral
is what you feel bad after."

There is a story that Protagoras once offered to give a student lessons, defer-
ring payment until he had won his first suit. After the first lesson, Protagoras sued
his student for payment, arguing: (1) If the student wins, he must pay according
to the agreement; (2) if I win, the student must pay according to the law. But the
student counterargued: (1) If I lose, the agreement hasn't been fulfilled, so I don't
have to pay; (2) but if I win, I shouldn't have to pay according to law, which now
overrides the agreement. The jury ruled in favor of the student.[5]

The Sophists challenged the traditional values and opinions of Greek society.
They undermined both religion in general and the specific Greek myths. They
asserted that the state is founded on power, custom, and conventions, not eternal
truth. They argued that there was no objective truth or right or wrong, unless it
be the realistic adage that might makes right. Most important, they caused one of
the major events in the history of philosophy: To challenge the Sophists' reliance
on rhetoric, their businesslike pragmatism, their cynicism and relativism about values and morality, and their egoism, Socrates came forth and declared war against
the panoply of their ideas.

SOCRATES: THE FATHER OF ETHICS

> Ancient philosophy up to Socrates, who was taught by Archelaus the pupil of
> Anaxagoras, dealt with number and movement, and the source from which all
> things arise and to which they return; and these early thinkers inquired zealously
> into the magnitude, intervals and courses of the stars, and all celestial matters. But
> it was Socrates who first called philosophy down from the sky, set it in the cities
> and even introduced it into homes, and compelled it to consider life and morals,
> good and evil.[6]

Life and Influence A dramatic turn occurs in philosophical inquiry under the
influence of Socrates (ca. 470–399 B.C.). Before him, as we have seen, two intellectual groups dominated the Greek world, the cynical and egoistic Sophists and
the speculative Cosmologists, discussed in Chapter 1. The main question asked by
the Hylicists and other early Cosmologists was, What is the nature of reality?
Thales (585 B.C.) had taught that the ultimate stuff of the universe was water;
Anaximander (547 B.C.), an infinite mixture; Anaximenes (536 B.C.), air; and
Heracleitus (480 B.C.), fire. Parmenides (480 B.C.) and Zeno of Elea (460 B.C.)
taught that the universe was a single, unmoving oneness, that all change was an
illusion. Anaxagoras (460 B.C.) posited a pluralistic universe with four essential elements (fire, air, water, and earth) under the direction of a great universal Mind
(*Nous*). Socrates rejected both the cynicism, relativism, and entrepreneurial pragmatism of the Sophists and the ethereal speculation of the Cosmologists. As
Cicero said, he was the first to call "philosophy down from the sky, set it in the
cities and even introduced it into homes, and compelled it to consider life and
morals, good and evil."

Socrates was born around 470 B.C. in Athens. His father was a stonecutter and his mother a midwife. A stonecutter himself by profession, who also served his city as a soldier, Socrates was captivated by the philosophical quest. He spent his youth studying the philosophy of nature under the tutelage of Archelaus, the disciple of Anaxagoras. He abandoned the pursuit, however, for a more pressing concern, the philosophy of human nature, specifically a concern for how we ought to live. Perhaps he was spurred on to this study by the Sophists who claimed to make people wise or virtuous through their instruction. Perhaps Socrates saw that the problems with which the Sophists were concerned were the important issues, only they misunderstood them. They asked the right questions—How should I live? What is virtue? How can I succeed in life?—but they lacked the passionate and disinterested use of reason in the pursuit of truth, which was necessary to answer these questions. They seemed to accept an unexamined cynicism about higher truth in settling for shallow, relativist answers to these questions, substituting rhetoric for reason, oratory for logic. Socrates's genius was to transfer the rigorous truth-centered methods of scientific inquiry to questions of human nature and ethics. With him, ethical inquiry became a discipline worthy of regard. He is the father of moral philosophy.

What makes Socrates especially interesting with regard to ethics is that he apparently was an extraordinarily good person, one who was modest, wise, self-controlled, courageous, honest, and concerned about the true well-being of others. The renowned hero Alcibiades confessed that Socrates defended his life on the battlefield and deserved the distinguished medal that he, Alcibiades, won. During the Peloponnesian War, after the disastrous battle of Arginusae, in which Athens paid for a naval victory by losing twenty-five ships and 4000 men, the eight naval officers involved in the battle were tried for culpable negligence. Rather than being tried one-by-one in the presence of their accusers, they were condemned to death in absentia by a bloc vote. Socrates, at that time a member of the Senate, risked his life by rendering a lone, courageous protest against this illegal verdict. A few years later (403 B.C.), after Athens had lost the Peloponnesian War and surrendered to Sparta, a violent, reactionary Commission of Thirty under the leadership of Critias, Plato's uncle, came to power in Athens. They forced the leading democrats to leave the city, executed some enemies, and confiscated their property. The oligarchy tried to implicate Socrates in their dealings and sent him with four others to arrest one of the wealthy democrats, Leon of Salamis, whose property they planned to confiscate. Although the other men obeyed, Socrates exercised civil disobedience and refused to be a part of these nefarious proceedings. He would probably have been executed as a traitor for this act had not a democratic revolution overthrown the oligarchy.[7]

This is how he made powerful enemies, which eventually led to his being put on trial for his life. His friend Chaerephon went to the sacred shrine of Delphi and asked the god Apollo whether there was anyone wiser than Socrates. The god answered through the priestess that no one was wiser than Socrates. When Chaerephon returned to Athens and reported this story, Socrates thought that there must be some mistake, so he proceeded to attempt to disprove the god's assertion. He went into the marketplace and began to quiz those citizens who had a reputation for wisdom, the civic leaders and politicians. Through a process of intense questioning, in which the answer to one question is followed up by questions about the implications of that answer (a method he immortalized as the Socratic method), he discovered that although these notables made great pretensions to wisdom, they possessed very little of it. Having exposed the ignorance of the leading citizens in front of the youth of the city, Socrates went to the poets and quizzed them on the meaning of their poetry. He discovered that although the poets were very gifted individuals, their own interpretations of their work were banal, not especially superior to the common man's insights. Leaving the poets enraged, he turned to the skilled artisans and questioned them on the nature of wisdom, only to discover that they pretended to have but really lacked wisdom. Perturbed by results of his investigation, he reluctantly concluded that he was indeed wiser than any of these others, for although both he and they lacked wisdom, he had one advantage over them: They knew nothing but didn't know that they knew nothing, whereas he knew nothing, except that he knew that he didn't know anything:

> Neither of us knows anything of beauty or of goodness, but he thinks he knows something when he knows nothing, and I, if I know nothing, at least never suppose that I do. So it looks as though I really am a little wiser than he, just in so far as I do not imagine myself to know things about which I know nothing at all.[8]

One may detect the renowned "Socratic irony" in the narration of his ignorance, for Socrates certainly did think he knew something of the meaning of virtue: Virtue is knowledge and can be attained. Socrates tells his jury at his trial that the goal of life is really to perfect one's soul by becoming wise, so it is the quest for truth and understanding that should preoccupy us, not the quest for success, fame, or fortune. Really, the unexamined life is not worth living, implying that the examined life constitutes a worthwhile life.

We learn a great deal about his character and professional activity in Plato's report of one of the most famous trials of all history (399 B.C.). Socrates is accused of religious heresy—that is, of not believing in the Olympian gods—and corrupting the youth. These are trumped-up charges. Although Socrates, like most of the educated, did not believe in the Olympian pantheon but was a monotheist, there was no law mandating such orthodoxy. What was important was the observing of the religious rituals and festivals of the city, and there is no evidence that Socrates went out of his way to disrupt these. With regard to the charge of corrupting the youth, Socrates was unfairly blamed for the bad behavior of his students, especially the betrayal by Alcibiades. It is closer to the truth that many of the leading citizens "lost face" before the youth of the city due to Socrates's relentless probing into their value system.

Socrates was found guilty by a vote of 280 to 220. He was now expected to offer a penalty for his crime to match the prosecution's proposal of the death penalty. It was normal for the accused, at this point, to grovel before the jury, display his wife and children, and plead for mercy, lest the jury leave his children fatherless. Instead, Socrates refused to admit guilt and proposed as a fitting "penalty" that he be given free, deluxe meals at the Prytaneum, the dining hall of the Olympian and military heroes:

> And so the prosecution proposes death as the penalty. And what shall I propose on my part, O men of Athens? Clearly that which is my due. And what is my due? I who neglected my own affairs in order to persuade every man among you that he must seek virtue and wisdom before he looks to his private interests. What should be

done to such a one? Surely some good thing. What would be a suitable reward for a poor man who is your benefactor? There can be no reward so fitting as maintenance in the Prytaneum, O men of Athens, a reward which he deserves far more than the citizen who won the prize at Olympia in the horse or chariot race.[9]

At this display of insolence, the jury became infuriated and voted for the death penalty, 360 to 140; 80 jurors who voted that he was innocent now voted to execute him. Upon receiving the sentence, Socrates forgave his accusers: "I am not angry with my condemners, or with my accusers; they have done me no harm, although they did not mean to do me any good; and for this I may gently blame them."[10]

When condemned to death and awaiting his execution, instead of taking a safe opportunity to escape, he engaged in a discussion of civil disobedience and argued that it was proper for him to accept the decision of the court. Before his grieving, agonizing disciples, he dutifully drank the hemlock without a trace of repugnance and thus became the first philosophical martyr. A witness summed up the consensus of his followers: "Such was the end, Echecrates, of our friend, who was, I think, of all the men of our time, the best, the wisest, and the most just."[11]

Socrates's life was deeply committed to the pursuit of truth and moral goodness. Unlike the Sophists, he refused to take money for his services and carried on his pilgrimage at great personal material sacrifice. The effect he had on others was phenomenal. The brilliant idol of Greek society, Alcibiades, put it this way:

> When I listen to him, my heart leaps up much more than in a corybantic dance, his words move me to tears. I see this happening to many others too. When I listened to Pericles and other fine orators, I thought: they speak well. But nothing like this happened to me, my soul was not thrown into turmoil. I was not enraged at myself for living so like a slave. But this Marsyas[12] has often put me into a state where I felt that the life I lived was not worth living. . . . He is the only man who ever made me feel ashamed.[13]

Socrates's Moral Philosophy: Knowledge Is Virtue What were the distinguishing features of Socrates's ethics? What exactly did he believe about the good life? We can set forth five theses that he held:

1. Care for the soul is all that matters.
2. Self-knowledge is a prerequisite for the good life.
3. Virtue is knowledge (there is no place for weakness of will, and evil is ignorance).
4. You cannot harm the good person, but in trying to harm the other, you harm yourself. The Good is good for you, and the Bad is bad for you.
5. The autonomy of ethics: To the dilemma set forth in the *Euthyphro,* is the Good good because God chooses it, or does God choose the Good because it is good? Socrates answers that God chooses it because it is good.

Let us elaborate these theses. We first examine the first two theses together.

1. Care for the soul (or inner self) is all that matters.
2. Self-knowledge is a prerequisite for the good life.

Socrates asks us a similar question as Jesus did in the Gospel of Matthew: "What good would it do me to gain the whole world and lose my own soul?" What good is knowledge of the heavens if I am unhappy or spiritually diseased or in despair?

What good is it to live in a perfect society if I see no value in life itself or in my life? The one thing necessary is spiritual or psychological health. We need to discover the right sort of regimen to follow in order to promote excellence of soul. But this entails that we understand what the soul is. We need to scrutinize our values, measuring our lives by the highest possible standards. The unexamined life is not worth living.

How can we know the soul? Not necessarily through introspection but by understanding its function. Just as the function of a knife is to cut and the function of a ruler is to rule, the function of the soul is to attain virtue, to perfect itself in goodness and truth. In the *Phaedo,* Socrates describes this as the essence of philosophy: to prepare for death, that is, to purify one's soul through the attainment of wisdom that the soul will enter the next life worthy of blessedness:

> [As] a craftsman can only do good work if he is in command of his tools and can guide them as he wishes, an accomplishment which demands knowledge and practice, similarly life can only be lived well if the psyche is in command of the body. It meant purely and simply the intelligence, which in a properly ordered life is in complete control of the senses and emotions. Its proper virtue is wisdom and thought and truth. This identification of the psyche with the self and the self with the reason might be said to have roots both in Ionian scientific thought and in Pythagoreanism, yet there was certainly novelty in Socrates's development of it.[14]

3. Virtue is knowledge.

Self-knowledge, we saw, is a prerequisite for the good life. You cannot tend, care, or improve anything unless you know its nature. Virtue or moral goodness is simply that which is good for the soul, its health and salvation. Since the soul is spiritual, not material, it follows that neither physical harms or benefits nor material goods affect the soul's health, but only a spiritual regimen. Even as no one would voluntarily choose to be sick rather than healthy, so no one would voluntarily choose evil over good.

Why are there bad people, then? Because they do not know any better. Evil is a function of ignorance. Evil people simply do not know what is in their interest and so mistakenly believe that cheating or harming others will profit them, when just the reverse is the case. No wise person ever does evil voluntarily.

Similarly, goodness is a result of knowledge. To know the Good is tantamount to trying to do the Good, for everyone wants to succeed, to flourish, and to be happy; goodness is good for you and me. This is a thoroughly intellectualist ethic. It is not because we've been nurtured properly that we choose the Good. Nor is it because we love our neighbors as ourselves or feel sympathy for the less fortunate or love justice for its own sake. No, once we know the Good, we cannot help but do it. *Knowledge is virtue.* To know the Good is to do it.

There is no place for weakness of will. Evil is ignorance: "My own opinion is more or less this: no wise man believes that anyone sins willingly or willingly perpetuates any base or evil act; they know very well that every base or evil action is committed involuntarily."[15] Aristotle tells us that Socrates believed that the virtues are sciences, that doing well was analogous to knowing the truth of mathematics:

> Socrates believed that knowledge of virtue was the final aim, and he inquired what justice is, and what is courage and every other kind of virtue. This was reasonable in view of his conviction that all the virtues were sciences, so that to know justice was

at the same time to be just; for as soon as we have learned geometry and architecture we are architects and geometricians. For this reason he inquired what virtue is, but not how or from what it is acquired.[16]

Aristotle goes on to point out that although this relationship of knowing to being is true of the theoretical sciences, it is not so with the productive sciences where knowledge is only a means to the further end. For example, knowledge of medicine is necessary but not sufficient for health. Knowledge of the good state is necessary but not sufficient for producing the good state.

Again Aristotle points out:

> The effect of [Socrates's] making the virtues into branches of knowledge was to eliminate the irrational part of the soul, and with it emotion and moral character. So his treatment of virtue was in this respect mistaken. After him Plato, rightly enough, divided the soul into the rational and irrational parts and explained the appropriate virtues of each.[17]

We are more likely to agree with Euripides's Medea that sometimes people act against what they know to be good ("Evil be thou my good") and with St. Paul that sometimes people suffer weakness of will and do not do the good that they would but the evil that they would not.[18] Most of us are aware of yielding to temptation when we *know* better—going to the refrigerator for a high-caloric dessert when on a diet or saying something mean when it was wrong to do so.

Furthermore, Aristotle points out there is something deterministic about the Socratic theory of virtue:

> Socrates claimed that it is not in our power to be worthy or worthless men. If, he said, you were to ask anyone whether he would like to be just or unjust, no one would choose injustice, and it is the same with courage and cowardice and the other virtues. Evidently any who are vicious will not be vicious voluntarily. Neither, in consequence, will they be voluntarily virtuous.[19]

So what is the point of exhortation to seek the Truth and the Good if it is all determined? If we cannot help being virtuous or vicious?

It may well be that Socrates, the consummate rationalist, was harmed here by his own rationality. He apparently always chose according to the dictates of reason. He may have lacked a substantial degree of irrationality in the soul, and this may have blinded him to the fact that most people are less fortunate, that weakness of will and an evil will exist.

4. You cannot harm the good person, but in trying to harm the other, you harm yourself. The Good is good for you, and the Bad is bad for you.

The classic illustrations of this, which are found in Book 2 of the *Republic,* are the story of Gyges's ring and the thought experiment of the two men, the seemingly bad good man who suffers injustice and the seemingly good bad man who enjoys the fruits of the virtuous. Socrates argues that despite all appearances the tortured virtuous is really better off than the apparently happy evil man, for one has a healthy soul and the other a sick soul. Since it is the soul that truly defines our state of being, we can conclude that it always is better to suffer evil than to do evil!

This argument has been criticized by some who argue that unless there is an afterlife where justice rewards us according to our moral merit, it's hard to see why it isn't in our interest to act immorally when we can escape detection or punishment. Should Socrates have held to an afterlife, as his pupil, Plato, did? You will have to decide the answer to this question.

5.   The autonomy of ethics: To the dilemma set forth in the *Euthyphro,* is the Good good because God chooses it, or does God choose the Good because it is good? Socrates answers that God chooses it because it is good.

Socratic ethics lacks a transcendental dimension. If there is an afterlife, well and good; it's icing on the cake, but it is not necessary for the justification of morality. Goodness has to do with the proper functioning of the soul and can be discovered through reason alone. There is no need for revelation, and if there are gods, they too must obey the moral law and keep their souls pure through following virtuous living. Socrates doesn't even hint that religion helps motivate people to virtuous living. Goodness is its own reward, and it is obviously so to anyone who knows what virtue is and how the soul functions. Religion is a "fifth wheel," useless in the moral domain. The charge brought against him at his trial by Meletus that he didn't worship the gods of the city was not without some foundation. They certainly played no role in his moral theory.

We can sum up Socratic ethics by saying that it is based in an understanding of human nature and proper functioning; that the self has a *telos,* or purpose that involves living virtuously—that is, wisely and justly; that happiness is predicated on proper functioning, hence on living virtuously; that knowing the Good necessarily results in doing the good; and that we do not need religion to inform us of the Good or to motivate us to be virtuous.

In the hands of Plato—Socrates's disciple, successor, and promoter—Socrates's ideas become transformed from a simple theory of moral virtue into a global metaphysics and epistemology in which the pilgrimage from vice to virtue takes place on the road from ignorance to knowledge—something Socrates professed not to have! Just how far Socrates really believed he knew nothing except one thing—that he knew nothing—is an open question, but, as developed by Plato, Socratic wisdom takes on the aspect of a comprehensive worldview wherein philosophy is the way to salvation, a kind of soul cure. This is nowhere better illustrated than in Plato's "The Allegory of the Cave."

The Allegory of the Cave. Imagine a group of prisoners who from infancy have had their necks and legs chained to posts within a dark cave. Behind them is a raised walkway on which people and animals travel to and fro, bearing diverse objects. Behind the walkway is a large fire that projects the shadows of the people, animals, and objects onto the wall in front of the prisoners. The shadows on the wall grow and diminish, move up and down and around as the fire behind the objects wafts and wanes. But the prisoners do not know that the shadows are merely appearances of real objects. They take the shadows for reality, talk about them as though they were real, name them, reidentify them, and incorporate their knowledge of the various forms into their social life. Their lives are centered on the shadows.

Now imagine that someone tried to liberate one of the prisoners from the cave. At first, the prisoner kicked and screamed as he was forcibly moved from the only home and social milieu he had ever known. Being dragged through the cave against his will, he was, at last, taken outside, where the dazzling bright sunlight blinded him. Our prisoner cries to be allowed to be returned to his safe shelter in the cave,

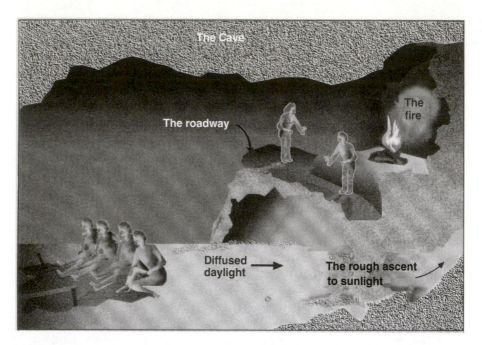

Plato's cave.

but the way is closed. Gradually, his eyes adjust to the sunlight, and he is able to see the beautifully colored flowers and wide-spreading branches of oak trees, hear the songs of birds, and watch the play of animals. Delighted, his powers of sight increase until, at last, he is able to look at the bright sun itself and not be harmed.

But now his liberator, who has become his friend and teacher, instructs him to return to the cave to teach the other prisoners of the real world and to get them to give up their chains and journey upward to the sunlight. But our hero quakes with fear at such an ordeal, for he wants no part of that dark, dismal existence, preferring to enjoy the light of day to the dark of the abyss.

He is told that it is his duty to go, and so he makes his way into the cave again, returns to his mates in chains, tells them that the shadows are merely illusions and that a real world of sunlight and beauty exists above outside the cave. As he is proclaiming this gospel, his former mates grab him, beat him for impugning their belief and value system, and put him to death. But every now and then, the liberator comes back, drags one or two prisoners out of the cave against their wills, teaches them to enjoy the light, and sends them back to instruct the slaves to appearances.

SUMMARY

In fifth-century B.C. Athens, the Sophists enabled the rising entrepreneurial class to succeed in litigation. They were cynics about truth and religion, relativists, pragmatists, and egoists, and they were very successful in making money. Socrates appeared on the scene, disillusioned with the speculations of the early

Cosmologists but possessed with their optimism and love of truth. He opposed the Sophists at every point, developed the first thorough–going moral philosophy —centered in the idea that virtue is knowledge—and suffered the death of a martyr for philosophy.

PLATO

The safest general characterization of the European philosophical tradition is that it consists of a series of footnotes to Plato (Alfred North Whitehead). Plato (427–347 B.C.) is generally recognized as the father of philosophy, the first systematic metaphysician and epistemologist, the first philosopher to set forth a comprehensive treatment of the entire domain of philosophy from **ontology** to ethics and aesthetics. He was born into an Athenian aristocratic family at the end of the Periclean Golden Age of Greek democracy. During most of his life, Athens was at war with Sparta, the Greek city-state to the south. He was Socrates's disciple, the systematizer and developer of his teacher's ideas, the founder of the first university and school of philosophy (the Academy in Athens), Aristotle's teacher, and an advisor to emperors, Dionysius and Dion. His goal was to found an ideal state where philosophers ruled with justice. Among his important works are the *Euthyphro, Apology, Crito, Phaedo, Meno,* and *Republic.* Most of his books are dialogues in which Socrates is the key spokesman and interlocutor, who seeks an understanding of difficult concepts.

In the early dialogues, Plato may be reporting Socrates's own thoughts, if not his own words, but as Plato developed his own philosophy, he continued to use Socrates as his mouthpiece. After the infamous trial and execution of Socrates in 399 B.C., Plato, then twenty-eight, abandoned thoughts for a political career, traveled, and then began his career as a philosopher.

What were Plato's distinctive ideas? The most famous idea is the *theory of Forms,* an instance of the idea of the *one and the many.* What do the *many* similar things have in common? The *one* Form. All beautiful things have in common participation in the Form of the Beautiful; all good things have in common participation in the Form of the Good.

What do all triangles or green objects have in common? Triangles come in different shapes and sizes. It is true that all triangles are closed plain figures with three sides and three angles adding up to 180 degrees, but the sides may be different sizes and the shape of the triangle may be isosceles or scalene. Even before we can articulate the definition of a triangle, we seem to know one when we see it. Regarding green objects, we cannot even define their common property— green. We cannot help a blind person understand what it is or even describe it to one who knows what green is. It is an unanalyzable simple property. All green things have this undefinable property in common. Now let us go from perceptual objects (triangles, colors, chairs, and tables) to abstract ideas: friendship, equality, justice, beauty, goodness. What do all exemplars of each of these properties have in common? Plato's theory of Forms (sometimes referred to as his theory of Ideas) seeks to give us a satisfactory answer to this question.

Whereas Socrates sought clear definitions of concepts in order to have a common basis for discussion (how can we even settle on an understanding of what a "just society" will be if we have different definitions of *justice?*), Plato went beyond verbal definitions and posited a comprehensive theory of reality. According to Plato, every significant word (noun, adjective, and verb) and thing partakes of and derives its identity from a Form or Forms. The Forms are single, common to all objects and abstract terms, perfect as the particulars or exemplars are not, independent of any particulars and yet their cause, having objective existence (they are the truly real, while particulars are only apparently so). While independent of the human mind, they are intelligible and can be known by the mind alone and not by sense experience. The Forms are a divine, eternal, simple, indissoluble, unchanging, self-subsisting reality, existing outside space and time. They are the cause of all that is.

We will encounter Plato's theory of the Forms as it relates to his doctrine of innate ideas and the theory of recollection in Chapter 10.

QUESTIONS FOR DISCUSSION

1. Explain the main ideas of the Sophists and show Socrates's response to each one. Is the debate between the Sophists and Socrates relevant for our own day? If so, in which ways?

2. Alcibiades, one of the Greek military heroes, who later was considered a traitor, said this of Socrates:

   When I listen to him, my heart leaps up much more than in a corybantic dance, his words move me to tears. I see this happening to many others too. When I listened to Pericles and other fine orators, I thought: they speak well. But nothing like this happened to me, my soul was not thrown into turmoil. I was not enraged at myself for living so like a slave. But this Marsyas has often put me into a state where I felt that the life I lived was not worth living. . . . He is the only man who ever made me feel ashamed.[20]

   Can you understand how people might feel this way about Socrates?

3. On the other hand, many people hated Socrates and thought of him as an elitist who unkindly and unnecessarily showed up their weaknesses. I. F. Stone, in his book *The Trial of Socrates,* accuses Socrates of being antidemocratic, arrogant, and ultimately responsible for his own downfall. Along these same lines, the late eminent Greek scholar Gregory Vlastos argues that for all his dialectical skill, Socrates lacked the virtue, so prominent in Christianity some four centuries later, of *agape,* which is altruistic love.

   How would you respond to the charges that Socrates was undemocratic and lacked sufficient love? Is it obvious that Socrates is less valuable for not believing in democracy and for not being as altruistic as Jesus or the Christian saints? Discuss your answer.

4. Is Socrates's ethics unreasonably intellectualist? Can it be amended?

5. When Socrates says that the Good is really good for you and that only ignorant people would do evil because it only harms them, is he implicitly appealing to a religious view of the world?

6. What meaning do you get out of "The Allegory of the Cave"? Explain.

NOTES

1. Diels-Kranz, *Fragments of the Pre-Socratics* 88b 25.

2. Aristotle, *Sophistic Elenchi* 171b.

3. Plato, *Gorgias,* in *The Dialogues of Plato,* ed. and trans. Benjamin Jowett (Scribner, 1889), 73. I have slightly edited this version.

4. Herodotus, *Histories* III.

5. This story may be apocryphal, but it illustrates sophistic reasoning. On the other hand, Protagoras is said to have remitted payment for anyone who did not benefit from his teaching.

6. Cicero, quoted in W. K. Guthrie, *Socrates* (Cambridge, Eng.: Cambridge University Press, 1971), 98. I have heard it argued that the Sophists were really the ones who first brought philosophy down from the heavens, but Plato, Aristotle, and Cicero would have rejected this thesis because the Sophists sought popularity and used philosophical methods for profit, not for wisdom or the pursuit of truth.

7. See Plato's *Apology* (Jowett, op. cit.) for the details of these matters as well as for the account narrated in the following paragraphs. See also Guthrie, op. cit.

8. Plato, *Apology,* in Jowett, op. cit.

9. Ibid.

10. Ibid.

11. Plato, *Phaedo,* in Jowett, op. cit.

12. Marsyas: A satyr (a man with horns and who was a goat from the waist down) who challenged Apollo to a flute-playing contest and lost and was punished by being flayed alive.—Ed.

13. Plato, *Symposium,* trans. W. Hamilton (New York: Penguin Books, 1951), 101.

14. *Phaedo,* in Jowett, op. cit., 147.

15. Plato *Protagoras* 345d; for similar expressions of this intellectual ethic, see *Meno* 78a; *Laws* 731c; *Republic* 589c.

16. Aristotle, *Eudemian Ethics* 1216b.

17. Aristotle, *Magna Moralia* 1182a.

18. Romans 7:19.

19. Aristotle, *Magna Moralia* 1187a and appendix.

20. Plato, *Symposium,* in Hamilton, op. cit.

FOR FURTHER READING

Allan, D. J., and H. E. Dale, eds. *The Dialogues of Plato.* Oxford: Oxford University Press, 1953. Jowett's translation is still among the best, literary and accurate.

Benson, Hugh, ed. *Essays on the Philosophy of Socrates.* Oxford: Oxford University Press, 1992.

Brumbaugh, Robert. *The Philosophers of Greece.* Albany, NY: SUNY Press, 1981. An easy-to-read, yet philosophically rich survey of classical Greek philosophy.

Grube, G. M. A. *Plato's Thought.* London: Methuen, 1935. An insightful discussion of Plato's thought, especially the Forms.

Grube, G. M. A. trans. Plato's *Republic.* Indianapolis: Hackett, 1980. This is an accessible, highly accurate translation.

Guthrie, W. K. C. *The History of Greek Philosophy,* vol. 3–5. Cambridge, Eng.: Cambridge University Press, 1969. A thorough study of Socrates and Plato.

Guthrie, W. K. C. *Socrates.* Cambridge, Eng.: Cambridge University Press, 1971. A clear, accessible, scholarly work of the first order, which has influenced me greatly.

Guthrie, W. K. C. *The Sophists.* Cambridge, Eng.: Cambridge University Press, 1971. A clear, comprehensive, and scholarly book.

Hamilton, Edith, and Huntington Cairns, eds. *Plato: The Collected Dialogues.* Princeton, NJ: Princeton University Press, 1982. This complete set of Plato's dialogues is the best single-volume collection of his works. The translations are typically excellent.

Irwin, Terrance. *Plato's Moral Theory: Early and Middle Dialogues.* Oxford: Clarendon Press, 1977. A complex, advanced but rich scholarly work.

Jones, W. T. *The Classical Mind.* New York: Harcourt, Brace, 1952. A helpful overview of the ancient Greeks and their culture.

Kerferd, G. B. *The Sophistic Movement.* Cambridge, Eng.: Cambridge University Press, 1981. A cogently argued contemporary study, challenging many of the standard views about the Sophists.

Kraut, Richard. *Socrates and the State.* Princeton, NJ: Princeton University Press, 1984.

Kraut, Richard, ed. *The Cambridge Companion to Plato.* New York: Cambridge University Press, 1992.

Plato. *Apology, Euthyphro, Crito, Protagoras, Gorgias, Republic,* and *Phaedo* are especially important for a firsthand account of Socrates.

Renault, Mary. *The Last of the Wine.* New York: Pantheon Books, 1956. A novel depicting Athens in the days of Socrates.

Stace, W. T. *A Critical History of Greek Philosophy.* New York: St. Martin's Press, 1967. Chapters 9 and 10 are especially relevant for this chapter.

Stone, I. F. *The Trial of Socrates.* Boston: Little, Brown, 1988. A provocative investigative probe into the causes of the downfall of Socrates.

Taylor, A. E. *Socrates.* New York: Methuen, 1933. A standard study, well written.

Vlastos, Gregory, ed. *The Philosophy of Socrates.* New York: Doubleday, 1971.

Vlastos, Gregory. *Socrates: Ironist and Moral Philosopher.* Ithaca, NY: Cornell University Press, 1991. A brilliant work by the best Plato scholar America has produced.

PART II

Philosophy of Religion

WILLIAM BLAKE
Europe, a Prophecy, Frontispiece: Ancient of Days

The Metropolitan Museum of Art, Rogers Fund, 1930

No other subject has exercised as profound a role in human history as religion. Offering a comprehensive explanation of the universe and of our place in it, religion offers us a cosmic map and shows us our place on the map; through its sacred books, religion provides lessons in cosmic map reading, enabling us to find our way through what would otherwise be a labyrinth of chaos and confusion. Religion tells where we came from, where we are, where we are going, and how we can get there. In this regard, religion legitimizes social mores, rituals, and morals. All have a coherent place on reality's map.

Moreover, religion is value-laden. It typically gives us a sense of dignity and self-worth. "We hold these truths to be self-evident," wrote Thomas Jefferson in the Declaration of Independence, "that all men are created equal, that they are endowed by their Creator with certain unalienable rights, that among these are life, liberty and the pursuit of happiness." The notions of equal worth and dignity are originally religious notions, derived from the idea of a benevolent Creator creating humans in his own image, and become problematic apart from a religious framework.

Religion offers comfort in sorrow, hope in death, courage in danger, inward peace in the midst of turmoil, and spiritual joy in the midst of despair. It tells us that this world is not a mere impersonal materialist conundrum but a friendly home, provided for us by our heavenly Father. As William James said, if religion is true, "The universe is no longer a mere *It* to us, but a *Thou,* and any relation that may be possible from person to person might be possible here."[1]

The sacred tomes of the religions of the world—the Vedas, the Bhagavad Gita, the Bible, the Koran, and the Dhammapada—are literary classics in their own right. In the Western tradition, who has not marveled at the elegance of the stories of the Creation, Joseph's brothers selling him into slavery, Moses leading the children of Israel out of bondage in Egypt, the birth of Jesus, the Sermon on the Mount, the reconciliation of the prodigal son, or the parable of the Good Samaritan?

Religion has inspired millions in every age. Its architecture—from the pyramids to the Parthenon, from the Hindu Juggernaut and the Sikh Golden Temple at Amritsar to the cathedrals of Chartres and Notre Dame—rises high above ordinary human commerce as a testimony to faith in the transcendent; its art from the Muslim mosaics in Grenada to Raphael's *Transfiguration* and Michelangelo's Sistine Chapel is without peer; its music from Hindu chants through Bach's cantatas and Handel's *Messiah* to thousands of hymns and spirituals have lit the hearts in weal and in woe of people in all times and almost all places. The Hindu Divali, the Muslim Ramadan, the Jewish Yom Kippur, the Christian Easter and Christmas, and a thousand other holidays—rituals marking the journey from birth through rites of passage and marriage to death—punctuate the lives of human beings in almost every time and place. Every time we date a letter, a check, or a contract, we pay homage to the founder of Christianity, dividing the calendar into B.C. ("before Christ") and A.D. (*anno Domini,* "the year of our Lord").

Religion holds a power over humanity like nothing else. Saints and martyrs have been created in its crucible, reformations and revolutions ignited by its flame, and outcasts and criminals have been catapulted to a higher level of existence by its propulsion. Auschwitz survivor Olga Lengyel writes that almost the only people to keep their dignity in the Nazi concentration camp were people animated by faith:

"priests and nuns in the camp [who] proved that they had real strength of charac-ter."[2] When I worked with the poor in Bedford-Stuyvesant, Brooklyn, the work of the Pentecostal Christian David Wilkerson astounded the civil authorities, for drug addicts who were considered incorrigible, upon being converted, suddenly would "kick the habit cold-turkey." Such is the power of religion.

Nonetheless, despite its enormous dynamics, religion's power and influence are no guarantees of truth. It could be that the impact of religion in human affairs only shows that humans are myth-making and myth-craving animals. We need a Big Myth to help us make it through the darkness of existence, whether it be a religion, Nazism, Marxism, or astrology. And it could be that humanity will someday "come of age," outgrow religion, and stand on its own as an autonomous adult. There is a dark side to religion, too—its bigotry, fanaticism, inquisitions, "holy" wars, and intolerance—which should give us pause in evaluating its merits.

All of this, however, is speculation. From a philosophical point of view, we want to know whether religion is true. We want to assess the evidence and argu-ments for and against its claims in an impartial, judicious, open-minded manner. And this is what we will endeavor to do in this part of our work.

The key notion of the great monotheistic religions of the West, Judaism, Christianity, and Islam, as well as part of Hinduism, is the idea of a God, an all-powerful, benevolent, and providential Being, who created the universe and all therein. Questions connected with the existence of God may be the most impor-tant that we can ask and try to answer. If God exists, then it is of the utmost importance that we come to know that fact and as much as possible about God and his plan. Implications follow that affect our understanding of the world and ourselves. If God exists, the world is not accidental, a product of mere chance and necessity, but a home that has been designed for rational and sentient beings, a place of personal purposefulness. We are not alone in our struggle for justice but are working together with One whose plan is to redeem the world from evil. Most importantly, there is Someone to whom we are responsible and to whom we owe absolute devotion and worship. Other implications follow for our self-understanding, the way we ought to live our lives and prospects for continued life after death. In short, if there is a God, we ought to do everything possible to dis-cover this fact, including using our reason in the discovery itself or as a means to test the validity of claims of such a discovery.

On the other hand, it may be that a supreme, benevolent being does not exist. If there is no God, we want to know this too. Whether we believe in God or not will make a difference in the way we view the universe and in the way we live.

Many people have lived well without believing in God. Pierre-Simon Laplace (1749–1827), when asked where God fit into his theory of the universe, is report-ed to have replied, "I have no need of that hypothesis." But the testimony of humanity is against him. Millions have needed and been inspired by this notion. So great is the inspiration issuing from the idea of God that we could say that if God doesn't exist, the idea is the greatest invention of the human mind. What are all the world's works of literature, art, music, drama, architecture, science, and phi-losophy compared to this simple concept? To quote Anthony Kenny,

> If there is no God, then God is incalculably the greatest single creation of the
> human imagination. No other creation of the imagination has been so fertile of

ideas, so great an inspiration to philosophy, to literature, to painting, sculpture, architecture, and drama. Set beside the idea of God, the most original inventions of
mathematicians and the most unforgettable characters in drama are minor products
of the imagination: Hamlet and the square root of minus one pale into insignifi-
cance by comparison.[3]

The field of philosophy of religion documents the history of humanity's quest
for a supreme being. Even if God does not exist, the arguments centering on this
quest are interesting in their own right, for their ingenuity and subtlety, even apart
from their possible soundness. It can be argued that the Judeo-Christian tradition
has informed our self-understanding to such a degree that it is imperative for
every person who would be well informed to come to grips with the arguments
and counterarguments surrounding its claims. Hence, even if one rejects the assertions of religion, understanding what is being rejected and why is important.

ARGUMENTS FOR THE EXISTENCE OF GOD

Can the existence of God be demonstrated or made probable by argument? The
debate between those who believe that reason can demonstrate that God exists
and those who do not has an ancient lineage, going back to Protagoras (ca. 450
B.C.) and Plato (ca. 427–347 B.C.) but made famous by the work of the greatest
Catholic philosopher of all time, St. Thomas Aquinas (1224–1274), who set forth
five different arguments for the existence of God. The Roman Catholic Church
has traditionally held that the existence of God is demonstrable by human reason.
The strong statement of the First Vatican Council (1870) indicates that human
reason is adequate to arrive at a state of knowledge:

> If anyone says that the one and true God, our creator and Lord, cannot be known
> with certainty with the natural light of human reason by means of the things that
> have been made: let him be anathema.

Many others, including theists of various denominations, including Catholics,
have denied that human reason is adequate to arrive at knowledge or demonstrate
the existence of God.

Arguments for the existence of God divide into two main groups: **a priori**
and **a posteriori.** An a posteriori argument is based on premises that can be
known only by means of experience of the world (e.g., there is a world, and
events have causes), whereas an a priori argument depends on no such premises.
It rests on premises that can be known to be true independently of experience of
the world. One need only clearly conceive of the proposition in order to see that
it is true.

In this part of our book, we will consider three types of a posteriori arguments for the existence of God and one a priori argument. The a posteriori
arguments are the cosmological argument, the teleological argument, and the
argument from religious experience. The a priori argument is the ontological
argument. We will then look at the main argument against the existence of
God, the argument from evil. Finally, we will examine the relationship of faith
to reason.

The question before us in this part of our work is, What do the arguments for the existence of God establish? Do any of them demonstrate beyond reasonable doubt the existence of a supreme being or deity? Do any of them make it probable (given the evidence at hand) that such a being exists? Can reason bring us to faith or is faith contrary to reason?

NOTES

1. William James, *The Will to Believe* (New York: Longmans, Green, 1897).

2. Olga Lengyel, *Five Chimneys* (New York: Grenada, 1972), 120.

3. Anthony Kenny, *Faith and Reason* (New York: Columbia University Press, 1983), 59.

4

The Cosmological Argument for the Existence of God: A First Cause

Asking people why they believe in God is likely to evoke something like this response: "Well, things just didn't pop up out of nothing. Someone, a pretty powerful Someone, had to cause the universe to come into existence. You just can't have causes going back forever. God must have made the world. Nothing else makes sense."

All versions of the cosmological argument begin with the a posteriori assumptions that the universe exists and that something outside the universe is required to explain its existence. That is, it is **contingent,** depending on something outside of itself for its existence. That "something else" is logically prior to the universe. It constitutes the reason for the existence of the universe. Such a being is God.

One version of the cosmological argument is called the *First Cause argument.* From the fact that some things are caused, we can reason to the existence of a First Cause. A version of this argument was given by the Catholic monk St. Thomas Aquinas (1224–1274); his "second way" is based on the idea of causation:

> We find that there is among material things a regular order of causes. But we do not find, nor indeed is it possible, that anything is the cause of itself, for in that case it would be prior to itself, which is impossible. Now it is not possible to proceed to infinity in causes. For if we arrange in order all causes, the first is the cause of the intermediate, and the intermediate the cause of the last, whether the intermediate be many or only one. But if we remove a cause the effect is removed; therefore, if there is no *first* among causes, neither will there be a last or an intermediate. But if we proceed to infinity in causes there will be no first cause, and thus there will be no ultimate effect, nor any intermediate causes, which is clearly false. Therefore it is necessary to suppose the existence of some first cause, and this men call God.[1]

The general outline, focusing on the second argument, goes something like this:

1. There exists things that are caused.
2. Nothing can be the cause of itself.
3. There cannot be an infinite regress of causes.
4. There exists an uncaused first cause.
5. The word *God* means uncaused first cause.
6. ∴ God exists.

What can we say of this argument? Certainly, premise 1 is true—some things have causes. We generally believe that every event has a cause that explains why the event happened. Premise 2 seems correct. Nothing can cause itself to come into existence (*causa sui*), for it would have to exist before it caused anything at all. To cause anything to happen implies that it has causal power, but nonexistent things have no power at all. Note that premises 2 and 4 do not contradict each other. There is nothing obviously incoherent about the idea that something or someone existed from eternity and so is uncaused, whereas there is something incoherent about the idea that something nonexistent caused itself to come into being.

One difficulty with the argument is premise 3: "There cannot be an infinite regress of causes." Why can't there be such a regress? You might object that there is an infinite regress of numbers, so why can't there be an infinite regress of causes?

One response to this objection is that there is a significant difference between numbers and events and persons. Numbers are just abstract entities, whereas events and persons are concrete, temporal entities, the sort of things that need to be brought into existence. Numbers exist in all possible worlds. They are eternal, but Napoleon, Mt. Everest, and you are not eternal but need a causal explanation. The child asks, "Mommy, who made me?" and the mother responds, "You came from my womb." The child persists, "Mommy, who made you and your womb?" The mother responds that she came from a fertilized egg in her mother's womb, but the child persists in the query until the mother is forced to admit that she doesn't know the answer or perhaps says, "God made the world and all that is in it."

God may be one explanatory hypothesis, answering the question why the world came to be, but the question is, Does the First Cause argument, even if it is valid, give us a full-blown proof of the existence of God?

Consider, does it rule out the possibility that this uncaused cause is matter itself? Does it prove that the First Cause is still around? There is a joke that God isn't dead, she's just moved to a better neighborhood. Could the Creator of this universe have moved off into a different, more satisfying neighborhood? Does the argument prove that just one Creator caused everything to come into being? Could there be many uncaused causes? Finally, does the First Cause argument give any indication that the First Cause is benevolent, let alone omnibenevolent? Furthermore, why couldn't the world simply be eternal, a *brute fact,* itself an uncaused entity? Before we comment further on these problems, let us examine a second form of the Cosmological Argument.

THE ARGUMENT FROM CONTINGENCY

Some philosophers believe that the English theologian and philosopher Samuel Clarke (1675–1729) has a superior version of the cosmological argument, called the *Argument from Contingency* (it may be helpful to read this passage out loud):

> There has existed from eternity some one unchangeable and independent being. For since something must needs have been from eternity; as hath been already proved, and is granted on all hands: either there has always existed one unchangeable and *independent* Being, from which all other beings that are or ever were in the universe, have received their origin; or else there has been an infinite succession of changeable and *dependent* beings, produced one from another in an endless progression, without any original cause at all: which latter supposition is so very absurd, that tho' all atheism must in its account of most things terminate in it, yet I think very few atheists ever were so weak as openly and directly to defend it. For it is plainly impossible and contradictory to itself. I shall not argue against it from the supposed impossibility of infinite succession, *barely and absolutely considered in itself;* for a reason which shall be mentioned hereafter: but if we consider such an infinite progression, as *one entire series of dependent* beings; it is plain that this whole series of beings can have no cause *from without,* of its existence: because in it are supposed to be included *all things* that are or ever were in the universe: and it is plain it can have no reason *within itself,* of its existence; because no one being in this infinite succession is supposed to be self-existent or *necessary* (which is the only ground or reason of existence of any thing, that can be imagined *within the thing itself*), but every one *dependent* on the foregoing: and where *no part* is necessary; it is manifest *the whole* cannot be necessary; absolute necessity of existence, not being an outward, relative, and accidental determination; but an inward and essential property of the nature of the thing which so exists. An infinite succession therefore of merely *dependent* beings, without any original independent cause; is a series of beings, that has neither necessity nor cause, nor any reason *at all* of its existence, neither *within itself* nor *from without:* that is, it is an express contradiction and impossibility; it is a supposing *something* to be *caused;* and yet that in the whole it is caused *absolutely by nothing:* Which everyone knows is a contradiction to be done *in time;* and because duration in this case makes no difference, it is equally a contradiction to suppose it done from eternity: And consequently there must *on the contrary,* of necessity have existed from eternity, *some one* immutable and *independent* Being.[2]

Clarke, like Aquinas before him, identifies this independent and necessary Being with God. We are dependent, or contingent, beings. Reduced to the bare bones, the argument from contingency goes like this:

1. Every being that exists is either contingent or necessary.
2. Not every being can be a contingent.
3. ∴ There exists a necessary being upon which the contingent beings depend.
4. A necessary being on which all contingent beings exist is what we mean by "God."
5. ∴ God exists.

A necessary being is self-existing and independent and has the explanation of its existence in itself, whereas contingent beings do not have the reason for their existence in themselves but depend on other beings and, ultimately, depend on a necessary being.

The argument from contingency has one advantage over the First Cause argument: the necessary being must still exist as that which supports all else that is. It cannot have ceased to be or have "moved to a better neighborhood." The world is like a set of chains that are supported in midair. You can trace the links of the chain backward, but somewhere there has to be a being sufficient to sustain the whole chain of dependent beings, and that is a necessary or independent Being, God.

But the argument is not without problems. The weak link occurs between premises 2 and 3. From the fact that not every being is contingent or dependent, it does not follow that there must be one necessarily existing, independent being. The mistake in this inference is called the *Fallacy of Composition,* whose form is the following:

1. Every member of the collection of dependent beings is accounted for by some explanation.
2. ∴ The collection of dependent beings is accounted for by one explanation.

Premise 2 does not follow from premise 1, because every member of the collection can be explained by some other member of the collection (just in case the collection is infinitely large) or by several different explanations rather than just one.

Consider these illustrations of the fallacy. First,

1. Every human being has a mother.
2. ∴ Every human being has the same mother.

That is, one woman and only one woman has had all the children who have ever been born. Second,

1. Every sailor loves a girl.
2. ∴ Some girl—say, Sally—is loved by every sailor.

It is absurd to believe that there is just one mother in the world or that every sailor loves the same girl, Sally. But just as it is absurd to infer from the fact that every sailor loves someone, that there is just one girl that is loved, so it is illicit to infer from the fact that every contingent fact needs to be grounded in a noncontingent fact that there is just *one noncontingent* or *necessary* being who explains all the contingent ones. Why couldn't there be many necessary beings? Or, referring to the chain metaphor mentioned earlier, why couldn't there be many individual chains held by various necessary beings?

But other problems are present. Some of the same ones that haunted the First Cause argument still trouble the argument from contingency. Is the necessary being good or omnibenevolent? Is it even personal? Could it be matter itself? Theists maintain that God, a necessary being, is a self-existent eternally brute fact (not needing further explanation). But why could not the universe itself be a self-existent eternally brute fact, needing no other explanation?

Although the cosmological arguments have problems, it may be precipitous to say that they are without any probative value at all. Perhaps they contribute in a modest but significant way to a total or cumulative case for the existence of God.

Imagine that you're hiking in the mountains above the tree line when spy a glowing, translucent sphere, twenty feet in diameter, sitting on the trail just ahead.

What would your reaction be? Wonder, no doubt. "How did this get here?" you ask yourself. Suppose that your hiking companion says, "No one lugged it way up here. It just happened by sheer chance." Would you be satisfied with that answer? I wouldn't, for I'd want to know the explanation for the translucent sphere. Merely being told that it happened by chance doesn't constitute a good explanation. If we venture beyond the city with its fog and lights, which block out the heavens, and gaze up into the spacious starry skies, contemplate the vast expanse of the heavens, and then consider the mystery of the subatomic world of neutrons, electrons, protons, positrons, mesons, and so forth, do we not have a mystery more wonderful than a twenty-foot glowing, translucent sphere? Shouldn't the universe, life, and especially, consciousness cause a sense of deep wonder within? Do we take this mystery for granted simply because we are used to it? Should we not sit like little children before the wonder of the universe and ask fundamental questions?

But even if the answer to these questions is affirmative, we may still ask whether God is the only answer to these perplexing mysteries. Does God constitute a good explanation for the universe? Couldn't we go on to ask, "Who caused God?" Does the answer that God is eternal and uncaused satisfy us any better than saying that the universe itself is eternal or that matter is uncaused and eternal?

The theist may claim, as an anonymous reviewer has, that this way of putting things misses the point. The whole point of the cosmological argument is that since the universe is contingent, it is the kind of entity that requires an explanation, but since God is necessary, he does not. But how do we know that the universe is contingent and not just a brute fact? Or even a necessary being, if there is such?

Consider some corroborating evidence from modern astronomy. In the early part of the twentieth century, many astronomers assumed that the universe was stationary, that is, in a steady state. But in 1929, an astronomer named Edwin Hubble noticed that light from distant galaxies was redder than it should be under the prevailing theory. Hubble and other astronomers hypothesized that the increasing red light was evidence for the fact that the universe was expanding, growing apart. Hubble likened the expansion to a balloon with buttons on its surface. As the balloon is inflated, the buttons move further apart as well as further from their original source. Astronomers soon inferred, working backward, that at some point in the distant past, the entire universe was contracted down to a single point, called *Singularity,* from which it exploded and quickly expanded, an event now referred to as the *Big Bang.* Astronomers calculate that the Big Bang occurred some 15 billion years ago. Here is how a group of astronomers describe the event:

> The universe began from a state of infinite density. Space and time were created in that event and so was all the matter in the universe. It is not meaningful to ask what happened before the *Big Bang,* any more than it is meaningful to ask what is north of the North Pole. Similarly it is not sensible to ask where the *Big Bang* took place. The point-universe was not an object isolated in space. It was the entire universe, and so the only answer can be that the *Big Bang* happened everywhere.[3]

It seems, then, that the primordial universe is reducible to an extensionless point, which somehow exploded from NOTHING. This feature is so analogous to the traditional Christian doctrine *Creatio ex nihilo* (creation from nothing, which seems to conflict with the ancient Greek dictum "Out of nothing comes nothing") that Christian theologians embrace the theory of the Big Bang as evidence for the Biblical story of creation. If the Big Bang is likened to an explosion, who or what caused it? The theist's answer is: God. God as the creator of the cosmos makes more sense and is more in line with contemporary cosmology than any other hypothesis.

The cosmological arguments seek to answer these questions: Why is there a universe at all? Why is there something and not just nothing? Why are we here? Some philosophers believe that these are inappropriate questions to ask because we have no basis for answering them. Others agree that they are valid questions, but the proper answer is, I don't know and I don't know anyone else who does. The religious person offers the existence of a personal, completely good creator as the answer to these questions. But unless he or she has more evidence than simply the cosmological argument, that answer will involve an extraordinary leap in logic. The cosmological argument may offer a hint of a divine creation, but more needs to be added before we can have the God of **theism.**

SUMMARY

The cosmological argument attempts to answer the question, Why is there a universe at all? It offers at least two types of arguments: (1) the First Cause argument, which rejects, as incoherent, the notions of an uncaused cause and an infinite regress; and (2) the argument from contingency, which argues from the idea that there are contingent beings to the necessity of an independent or necessary being. Two weaknesses of cosmological arguments are (1) that they don't provide us with a personal or benevolent God, and (2) that they do not rule out the possibility that the universe is itself eternal, a brute fact. Nevertheless, the argument raises an important question about the explanation of the universe, which religion seeks to answer satisfactorily.

QUESTIONS FOR DISCUSSION

1. The current view of physicists and astronomers is that the universe came into being about 15 or 16 billion years ago, when an extensionless point exploded in the Big Bang. From this explosion, the universe swiftly expanded and is still doing so. Does the Big Bang theory support Theism, or does it offer an alternative account of the origin of the universe to the religious account? Can the Big Bang itself be viewed as a contingent event? Can we ask what caused the Big Bang? What do you think is the explanation of the Big Bang?

2. Sometimes it is argued that the cosmological argument unwarrantedly assumes that an infinite regress is impossible and that we need a First Cause.

Does science accept the possibility of an infinite regress of causes? Or is the idea of a Big Bang itself an attempt to stop the regress?

3. Is the theist's answer that God is the explanation for the universe really a better explanation than the nontheist's claim that the universe itself is eternal or that matter is uncaused and eternal?

NOTES

1. Thomas Aquinas, *Summa Theologica,* trans. Laurence Shapcote (London: Benziager, 1911).

2. Samuel Clarke, "A Demonstration of the Being and Attributes of God" (1705), Part 2.

3. J. R. Gott et al. "Will the Universe Expand Forever?" in *Scientific American* (March 1976).

FOR FURTHER READING

Craig, William. *The Cosmological Argument from Plato to Leibniz.* New York: Barnes & Noble, 1980. A good survey of the history of the argument.

Gale, Richard. *On the Nature and Existence of God.* Cambridge, Eng.: Cambridge University Press, 1992. Chapter 7 is an excellent discussion of the argument.

Harrison, Jonathan. *God, Freedom and Immortality.* Aldershot, Eng.: Ashgate, 1999. Part II, especially, is now perhaps the most comprehensive and clearly written English-language attack on theism.

Hick, John. *Arguments for the Existence of God.* London: Macmillan, 1971. A clearly written, insightful examination of the central arguments.

Mackie, J. L. *The Miracle of Theism.* Oxford: Oxford University Press, 1982. A lively discussion of the proofs for the existence of God and other issues by one of the ablest atheist philosophers of our time.

Martin, Michael. *Atheism.* Philadelphia: Temple University Press, 1990. One of the most comprehensive and clearly written English-language attacks on theism.

Peterson, Michael, William Hasker, Bruce Reichenbach, and David Basinger. *Reason and Religious Belief.* New York: Oxford University Press, 1991. A clearly written, helpful book from a theist point of view.

Pojman, Louis, ed. *Philosophy of Religion: An Anthology,* 3d ed. Belmont, CA: Wadsworth, 1998. A comprehensive anthology, setting forth both sides of many issues. It contains the relevant selections from Aquinas, Edwards, Rowe, Craig, and Draper.

Rowe, William. *The Cosmological Argument.* Princeton, NJ: Princeton University Press. 1971. A thorough and penetrating study.

Rowe, William. *Philosophy of Religion: An Introduction.* Belmont, CA: Wadsworth, 1978. A readable, reliable introductory work by a first-rate scholar.

Swinburne, Richard. *The Existence of God.* Oxford: Oxford University Press, 1979. Perhaps the most sustained and cogent defense of theism in the literature.

Wainwright, William J. *Philosophy of Religion,* 2d ed. Belmont, CA: Wadsworth, 1998. A careful, well-argued text from a theistic perspective.

5

The Teleological Argument
for the Existence of God

A DESIGNER

The teleological argument for the existence of God begins with the premise that the world exhibits intelligent purpose or order and proceeds to the conclusion that there must be or probably is a divine intelligence, a supreme designer to account for the observed or perceived intelligent purpose or order. Although the argument was first cited in Plato and in Cicero, we find expressions of the argument in the Bible, both the Hebrew Bible (Old Testament) and the New Testament:

> The heavens declare the glory of God; and the firmament showeth his handywork. Day unto day uttereth speech, and night unto night showeth knowledge. There is no speech nor language where their voice is not heard. Their line is gone out through all the earth. (*Psalm 19*)
>
> The wrath of God is revealed from heaven against all ungodliness and unrighteousness of men who hold the truth in unrighteousness; because that which may be known of God is manifest in them; for God hath showed it unto them. For the invisible things of him from the creation of the world are clearly seen, being understood by the things that are made, even his eternal power and divinity. (*Romans 1*)

William Paley (1743–1805) gives the clearest sustained treatment of the argument in *Natural Theology* (1802), where he offers his famous "watch" argument. It begins as follows:

> In crossing a heath, suppose I pitched my foot against a stone, and were asked how the stone came to be there: I might possibly answer, that for any thing I knew to the contrary, it had lain there for ever: nor would it perhaps be very easy to shew the

absurdity of this answer. But suppose I had found a watch upon the ground, and it should be inquired how the watch happened to be in that place. I should hardly think of the answer which I had before given, that, for any thing I knew, the watch might have always been there. Yet why should not this answer serve for the watch as well as for the stone? Why is it not as admissible in the second case, as in the first?

For this reason, and for no other, namely, that when we come to inspect the watch, we perceive (what we could not discover in the stone) that its several parts are framed and put together for a purpose, e.g., that they are so formed and adjusted as to produce motion, and that motion so regulated as to point out the hour of the day; that, if the different parts had been differently shaped from what they are, of a different size from what they are, or placed after any other manner, or in any other order, than that in which they are placed, either no motion at all would have been carried on in the machine, or none that would have answered the use that is now served by it. This mechanism being observed, the inference is inevitable, that the watch must have had a maker. That there must have existed, at some time, and at some place or other, an artificer or artificers, who formed it for the purpose which we find it actually to answer; who comprehended its construction, and designed its use.

Every indication of contrivance, every manifestation of design, which existed in the watch, exists in the works of nature; with the difference, on the side of nature, of being greater and more, and that in a degree which exceeds all computation.[1]

Paley argues that just as we infer an intelligent designer to account for the purpose-revealing watch, we must analogously infer to an intelligent grand designer to account for the purpose-revealing world: "Every indication of contrivance, every manifestation of design, which existed in the watch, exists in the works of nature; with the difference, on the side of nature, of being greater and more, and that in a degree which exceeds all computation." The skeleton of the argument looks like this:

1. Human artifacts are products of intelligent design. (Purpose)
2. The universe resembles these human artifacts.
3. ∴ The universe is (probably) a product of intelligent design. (Purpose)
4. But the universe is vastly more complex and gigantic than a human artifact.
5. ∴ There probably is a powerful and vastly intelligent designer who designed the universe.

HUME'S CRITIQUE

Ironically, Paley's argument was attacked even before Paley had set it down, for David Hume (1711–1776) had long before written his famous *Dialogues Concerning Natural Religion* (published posthumously in 1779), which constitutes the classic critique of the teleological argument. Paley seems to have been unaware of it. In it, the natural theologian Cleanthes debates the orthodox believer Demea and the skeptic or critic Philo, who does most of the serious arguing.

Hume, through Philo, attacks the argument from several different angles. He first argues that the universe is not sufficiently like the productions of human design to support the argument. As Philo puts it,

But can you think, Cleanthes, that your usual phlegm and philosophy have been preserved in so wide a step as you have taken, when you compare to the universe, houses, ships, furniture, machines; and from their similarity in some circumstances infer a similarity in their causes? . . . But can a conclusion, with any propriety, be transferred from the parts to the whole? Does not the great disproportion bar all comparison and inferences? From observing the growth of a hair, can we learn anything concerning the generation of a man?[2]

Hume claims that we cannot argue from the parts to the whole, but is he correct? If I test the waters of the Atlantic Ocean off the coast of North Carolina and find them to be saltwater, then test the waters off the coast of New Jersey with the same result, and then off the coast of Wales, can't I make an inductive inference about the rest of the Atlantic Ocean, that it is probably filled with saltwater?

When is it and when is it not legitimate to reason from the parts to the whole? If all we have are a few instances that point to a common conclusion (like our ocean-water case), we have a *weak* inductive argument, though one that grows stronger each time new confirming evidence is forthcoming. But until it is well confirmed, as it is in the case of ocean water being salty, we should not base too much weight on our slight experience.

Hume's second objection is that the analogy fails because we have no other universe with which to compare this one, which would be necessary in order to decide if the universe was designed or simply developed on its own. As Charles Sanders Peirce (1839–1914) put it, "Universes are not as plentiful as blackberries." Because there is only one of them, we have no standard of comparison by which to judge it. Paley's answer to this would be that if we can find one clear instance of purposiveness in nature, we have a sufficient instance enabling us to conclude that there is probably an intelligent designer. Paley and Cleanthes thought that the eye provided such a clear example of purposiveness: "Consider, anatomize the eye, survey its structure and contrivance, and tell me from your own feeling, if the idea of a contriver does not immediately flow in upon you with a force like that of sensation."[3] Do you agree with Cleanthes here? Hume rejects this reasoning as sliding over strong objections, especially because no other universes are available for comparison.

The theist may object, however, that Hume misses the point of the argument from analogy. If the analogy comes close enough to what it is compared with, it makes its conclusion probable. Notice how the argument from analogy works:

1. We have an object O_1 and want to determine whether it has a property P_1. We note that it has other properties in common with objects O_2, O_3, and so on.
2. O_1, O_2, O_3 . . . all have P_2, P_3, and P_4.
3. Then we discover that O_2, O_3 . . . all have P_1, the property in question. So we infer that *probably* O_1 also has P_1.

Suppose I am interested in buying a certain kind of Ford. I reason that other Fords of this kind that I or my acquaintances have owned have served us very well; thus, I reason that this Ford will probably serve me well.

Or suppose I want to determine whether a mushroom (O_1), which I have just pulled up from the ground, is edible (P_1). I note that it is similar in shape, color, and constituency (P_2, P_3, P_4) with other mushrooms (O_2, O_3 . . .) that turned out to be edible (P_1). Thus, I infer that probably this mushroom (O_1) is edible (P_1).

Similarly, this world resembles man-made machines (O_2, O_3 . . .), so it probably has the property (P_1) of having an intelligent designer.

Hume, however, points out a problem with such reasoning from analogy. To the extent that the universe resembles a man-made artifact, to that extent God becomes finitized or limited (i.e., we are guilty of **anthropomorphism**—the tendency to humanize God), but if we go the other way and say that the universe is much vaster and different than anything (in order to save the infinity of God), the analogy breaks down, for then the necessary likeness becomes attenuated:

Anthropomorphism ◀———————————————▶ Infinity
(Analogy works but God is limited.)   *(Analogy breaks down.)*

Following up on this last point, Hume offers a third criticism of the analogy argument. The analogy leads us to infer the existence of a grand anthropomorphic designer, a human writ large, who has all the properties that we have: "Why not become a perfect anthropomorphite? Why not assert the Deity or Deities to be corporeal, and to have eyes, a nose, mouth, ears, etc.?"[4]

Hume's fourth objection is that the so-called design of the universe seems to be flawed with evil and inexactness, so that we should consistently infer that the designer is imperfect or not terribly intelligent or no longer interested in his work of bygone years. Perhaps there is a plurality of designers. (We will deal with the problem of evil in Chapter 8.)

Hume makes several other points against the design argument. The universe resembles in some ways an animal and in other ways a plant, in which case, claims Hume, the argument fails because it depends on our seeing the world as a grand machine rather than as an animal or plant. Do you agree with Hume here?

Hume also points out that the universe might well be the result of mere chance. However, Hume agrees that the hypothesis of a designer is not completely useless, just very weak and uninformative:

> In a word, Cleanthes, a man who follows your hypothesis is able, perhaps, to assert or conjecture that the universe sometime arose from something like design: But beyond that position he cannot ascertain one single circumstance, and is left afterwards to fix every point of his theology by the utmost license of fancy and hypothesis. This world, for aught he knows, is very faulty and imperfect, compared to a superior standard; and was only the first rude attempt of some infant deity who afterwards abandoned it, ashamed of his lame performance. [Or] it is the work only of some dependent, inferior deity, and is the object of derision to his superiors. [Or] it is the production of old age and dotage in some superannuated deity; and ever since his death has run on at adventures, from the first impulse and active force which it received from him.

THE DARWINIAN OBJECTION

A modern objection to the argument, one that was anticipated by Hume, is that based on Darwinian evolution, which has cast doubt upon the notion of the teleological explanation all together. Charles Darwin (1809–1882), in his *Origin of the Species* (1859), observed that the process from simpler organisms to more complex ones took place gradually over many centuries through an

apparently nonpurposive process of trial and error, of natural selection and survival of the fittest. As Julian Huxley (1887–1975) put it, the evolutionary
process

> results immediately and automatically from the basic property of living matter—that
> of self-copying, but with occasional errors. Self-copying leads to multiplication and
> competition; the errors in self-copying are what we call mutations, and mutations
> will inevitably confer different degrees of biological advantage or disadvantage on
> their possessors. The consequence will be differential reproduction down the genera-
> tions—in other words, natural selection.[5]

As important as Darwin's contribution is in offering us an alternative model
with respect to biological development, it doesn't altogether destroy the argument
from design, for the theist can still argue that the process of natural selection is the
way an ultimate designer is working out his purpose for the world. The argument
from design could still be used as an argument to the best explanation, as an
abductive argument.

The Oxford University philosopher Richard Swinburne, a modern Cleanthes,
rejects all deductive forms of arguments for the existence of God but in their place
sets a series of inductive arguments: versions of the cosmological argument, the
teleological argument, the argument from religious experience, and others.
Although none of these alone proves the existence of God or shows it to be more
probable than not, each adds to the probability of God's existence. Together they
constitute a cumulative case in favor of theism. There is something crying for an
explanation: Why does this grand universe exist? Together the arguments for God's
existence provide a plausible explanation of the existence of the universe, of why
we are here, of why there is anything at all and not just nothing.[6]

Swinburne's arguments are set in terms of confirmation theory. He distinguishes arguments that are *P*-inductive (where the premises make the conclusion
probable) from those that are *C*-inductive (where the premises confirm the probability of the conclusion or make it more probable than it otherwise would be—
although not showing the conclusion to be more probable than not). The cosmological and teleological arguments are, according to Swinburne, good
C-inductive arguments. Because there is no counterargument to theism and religious experience offers "considerable evidential force" in favor of theism, the
cumulative effect is "sufficient to make theism all over probable."[7]

Whether and how the cumulative case for theism can be made is a task I must
leave for you, but a common objection to it is the "ten leaky buckets" argument.
The objector claims that the theist is using several bad arguments to make a
cumulative case, much as one would try to carry water by putting it into ten leaky
buckets. Ten leaky buckets won't hold water any more than one leaky bucket will.

The counterobjection to this objection is that the ten leaky buckets will hold
water better than one leaky bucket if the buckets are put inside one another and
the leaks of each bucket are covered by the base of the one below it. Similarly,
although not a fool-proof set of arguments, the case for theism may be better than
rival explanatory theory.

The issue is complex and the leaky bucket metaphor may not do justice to the
problem. Perhaps we will be in a better place to evaluate the case for and against
theism after we have considered the other arguments in this part of the book.

SUMMARY

The teleological argument proceeds from the perceived orderly process in the world and argues to the conclusion that such orderly processes must have an orderer or designer. It is unreasonable to suppose that the incredible intricacy and lawlikeness of the world is just a product of chance. Nevertheless there are several problems with the argument, among these being the tendency toward anthropomorphism and our inability to make intercosmic comparisons.

QUESTIONS FOR DISCUSSION

1. Evaluate the teleological argument for yourself. What does it indicate about the origins of the universe? Is the hypothesis of a designer plausible? Or can the process of chance and necessity account for the orderliness we perceive?

2. Assess Swinburne's idea of a cumulative case for the existence of God. Is this a good use of abductive argument, discussed in Chapter 2? Is the case for the existence of God like a case in civil law where both sides try to assemble the evidence in a way that best supports their side of the issue?

3. It is sometimes objected that the ten leaky buckets argument begs the question for theism because the metaphor suggests that a composite arrangement of the buckets (and so the arguments) very likely can be made to hold water (demonstrate the existence of God). Evaluate this criticism.

4. Sometimes the objector to the teleological argument refutes that the orderliness of the universe must be taken as a given, not something to be accounted for, for if there were no orderliness, we could not even comment on the fact. Swinburne argues by analogy that this objection misses the point:

> Suppose that a madman kidnaps a victim and shuts him in a room with a card-shuffling machine. The machine shuffles ten packs of cards simultaneously and then draws a card from each pack and exhibits simultaneously ten cards. The kidnapper tells the victim that he will shortly set the machine to work and it will exhibit its first draw, but that unless the draw consists of an ace of hearts from each pack, the machine will simultaneously set off an explosion which will kill the victim, in consequence of which he will not see which cards the machine drew. The machine is then set to work, and to the amazement and relief of the victim the machine exhibits an ace of hearts drawn from each pack. The victim thinks that this extraordinary fact needs an explanation in terms of the machine having been rigged in some way. But the kidnapper, who now reappears, casts doubt on this suggestion. "It is hardly surprising," he says, "that the machine draws only aces of hearts. You could not possibly see anything else. For you would not be here to see anything at all, if any other cards had been drawn." But of course the victim was right and the kidnapper is wrong. There is indeed something extraordinary in need of explanation in ten aces of hearts being drawn. The fact that this peculiar order is a necessary condition of the draw being perceived at all makes what is perceived no less extraordinary and in need of explanation. The teleologist's starting-point is

not that we perceive order rather than disorder, but that order rather than disorder is there.[8]

Evaluate Swinburne's claim about the legitimacy of looking for an explanation for the orderliness in the universe. Does his way of stating the matter help the theist?

NOTES

1. William Paley, *Natural Theology* (1802).

2. David Hume, *Dialogues Concerning Natural Religion* (1779).

3. Ibid.

4. Ibid.

5. Julian Huxley, *Evolution as Process* (New York: Harper & Row, 1953), 4.

6. Richard Swinburne, *The Existence of God* (Oxford: Oxford University Press, 1979).

7. Ibid.

8. Ibid.

FOR FURTHER READING

Hume, David. *Dialogues Concerning Natural Religion,* 1779. A classic critique of the teleological argument.

Mackie, J. L. *The Miracle of Theism.* Oxford: Oxford University Press, 1982. A lively discussion of the proofs for the existence of God and other issues by one of the ablest atheist philosophers of our time.

Martin, Michael. *Atheism: A Philosophical Justification.* Philadelphia: Temple University Press, 1990. Chapters 5 and 13 contain a strong expression of the atheist's position.

McPherson, Thomas. *The Argument from Design.* London: Macmillan, 1972. A good introduction to several forms of the argument.

Pojman, Louis, ed. *Philosophy of Religion: An Anthology,* 2d ed. Belmont, CA: Wadsworth, 1994. A comprehensive anthology, setting forth both sides of many issues.

Swinburne, Richard. "The Argument from Design." *Philosophy* 43 (1968).

Swinburne, Richard. *The Existence of God.* Oxford: Oxford University Press, 1979. Perhaps the most sustained and cogent defense of theism in the literature.

6

The Ontological Argument for the Existence of God

The ontological argument for the existence of God is the most intriguing of all arguments for theism. It is one of the most remarkable arguments ever given. First set forth by Anselm (1033–1109), Archbishop of Canterbury in the eleventh century, the argument has continued to puzzle and fascinate philosophers ever since. Let the testimony of the agnostic philosopher Bertrand Russell (1872–1970) serve as a typical example here:

> I remember the precise moment, one day in 1894, as I was walking along Trinity Lane [at Cambridge University where Russell was a student], when I saw in a flash (or thought I saw) that the ontological argument is valid. I had gone out to buy a tin of tobacco; on my way back, I suddenly threw it up in the air, and exclaimed as I caught it: "Great Scott, the ontological argument is sound!"[1]

The argument is important for two reasons: (1) It claims to be an a priori proof for the existence of God, and (2) it is the primary locus of such philosophical problems as whether *existence* is a property and whether the notion of *necessary existence* is intelligible. Furthermore, it has special religious significance because it is the only one of the traditional arguments that clearly concludes to the necessary properties of God—that is, his omnipotence, omniscience, omnibenevolence, and other great-making properties.

ANSELM'S ARGUMENT

Although there are many versions of the ontological argument and many inter-pretations of some of these, most philosophers agree on the essential form of Anselm's version in the second chapter of his *Proslogium*. Anselm believes that God's existence is so absolutely certain that only a fool would doubt or deny it. Yet he desires understanding to fulfill his faith:

> And so, Lord, do thou, who dost give understanding to faith, give me, so far as thou knowest it to be profitable, to understand that thou art as we believe; and that thou art that which we believe. And indeed, we believe that thou art a being than which nothing greater can be conceived. Or is there no such nature, since the fool hath said in his heart, there is no God? (Psalms 14:1). But at any rate, this very fool, when he hears of this being of which I speak—a being than which nothing greater can be conceived—understands what he hears, and what he understands is in his under-standing; although he does not understand it to exist.
>
> For, it is one thing for an object to be in the understanding, and another to understand that the object exists. When a painter first conceives of what he will afterwards paint, he has it in his understanding, but he does not yet understand it to be, because he has not yet painted it. But after he has made the painting, he both has it in his understanding and he understands that it exists, because he has made it.
>
> Hence, even the fool is convinced that something exists in the understanding, at least, than which nothing greater can be conceived. For, when he hears of this, he understands it. And whatever is understood, exists in the understanding. And assured-ly that, than which nothing greater can be conceived, cannot exist in the under-standing alone. For, suppose it exists in the understanding alone: then it can be con-ceived to exist in reality; which is greater.
>
> Therefore, if that, than which nothing greater can be conceived, exists in the understanding alone, the very being, than which nothing greater can be conceived, is one, than which a greater can be conceived. But obviously this is impossible. Hence, there is no doubt that there exists a being, than which nothing greater can be con-ceived, and it exists both in the understanding and in reality.[2]

Anselm's reasoning may be treated as a reductio ad absurdum argument. That is, it begins with a supposition S (suppose that the greatest conceivable being exists in the mind alone) that is contradictory to what one desires to prove. One then goes about showing that S together with other certain or self-evident assump-tions, A_1 and A_2, yields a **contradiction,** which in turn demonstrates that the contradictory of S must be true.

Anselm's argument goes like this:

1. Suppose that the greatest conceivable being (GCB) exists in the mind alone (and not in reality). (S)
2. Existence in reality is greater than existence in the mind alone. (A_1)
3. We can conceive of a GCB that exists in reality as well as the mind. (A_2)
4. ∴ There is a being that is greater than the GCB. (From premises 1, 2, and 3)
5. But this is impossible, for it is a contradiction.
6. ∴ It is false that a GCB exists in the mind alone and not in reality (from premises 1 and 5). So a GCB must exist in reality as well as in the mind. This being is, *per defini-tion,* God.

CRITICISM OF ANSELM'S ARGUMENT

Questions immediately arise. Is existence a perfection, so that we can say that it is better to exist than not to exist? Or is such locution nonsense because you can't compare existing things with nonexisting ones? Does some possible entity become greater by becoming actual?

Gaunilo, Anselm's contemporary, sets forth the first objection to Anselm's argument. Accusing Anselm of "pulling rabbits out of hats," he tells the story of a delectable lost island, one that is more excellent than all lands. Because it is better that such a perfect island exists in reality than simply in the mind alone, this Isle of the Blest must necessarily exist. Anselm's reply is that the analogy fails, for unlike the greatest possible being, the greatest possible island can be conceived as not existing.

Is Gaunilo correct? Some philosophers say no because, simply, some properties do and some properties don't have intrinsic maximums. No matter how wonderful you make the Isle of the Blest, we can conceive of a more wonderful island. The greatness of islands is like the greatness of numbers in this respect. There is no greatest natural number, for no matter how large the number is that you choose, we can always conceive of one twice as large. On the other hand, the properties of God have intrinsic maximums. For example, we can define perfect knowledge this way. For any proposition, an omniscient being knows whether it is true or false.

A second criticism of the ontological argument was lodged by Immanuel Kant (1724–1804), who accused the proponent of the argument of defining God into existence. "Being" is not a real predicate like "red" or "six feet tall" or "rational." Here is the relevant passage:

> "*Being*" is obviously not a real predicate; that is, it is not a concept of something which could be added to the concept of a thing. It is merely the positing of a thing, or of certain determinations, as existing in themselves. Logically, it is merely the copula of a judgment. The proposition, "God is omnipotent," contains two concepts, each of which has its object—God and omnipotence. The small word "is" adds no new predicate, but only serves to posit the predicate *in its relation* to the subject. If, now, we take the subject (God) with all its predicates (among which is omnipotence), and say "God is," or "There is a God," we attach no new predicate to the concept of God, but only posit the subject in itself with all its predicates, and indeed posit it as being an object that stands in relation to my concept. The content of both must be one and the same; nothing can have been added to the concept, which expresses merely what is possible, by my thinking its object (through the expression "it is") as given absolutely. Otherwise stated, the real contains no more than the merely possible. A hundred real thalers do not contain the least coin more than a hundred possible thalers. For as the latter signify the concept, and the former the object and the positing of the object, should the former contain more than the latter, my concept would not, in that case, express the whole object, and would not therefore be an adequate concept of it. My financial position is, however, affected very differently by a hundred real thalers than it is by the mere concept of them (that is, of their possibility). For the object, as it actually exists, is not analytically contained in my concept, but is added to my concept (which is a determination of my state) synthetically; and yet the conceived hundred thalers are not themselves in the least increased through thus acquiring existence outside my concept.

By whatever and by however many predicates we may think a thing—even if we completely determine it—we do not make the least addition to the thing which we further declare that this thing is. Otherwise, it would not be exactly the same thing that exists, but something more than we had thought in the concept; and we could not, therefore, say that the exact object of my concept exists. If we think in a thing every feature of reality except one, the missing reality is not added by my saying that this defective thing exists.[3]

Kant claims that Anselm makes the mistake of treating "existence" or "being" as a first-order predicate, like "blue" or "great." When you say that the castle is blue, you are adding a property (viz., blueness) to the idea of a castle; but when you say that the castle *exists,* you are not adding anything to the concept of a castle, only saying that the concept is exemplified or instantiated. You are taking a possible property (B) and affirming that it is exemplified (A), claiming that it is actual.

(A) First-order property (actual)
(B) Nonexisting property (possible)

We might say that "real" predicates or properties are first-order properties, but the idea of existence is a second-order property, which asserts something about the status of possible properties. In Anselm's argument, "existence" is treated as a first-order predicate that adds something to the concept of an entity, making it *greater.* This, according to Kant and those who follow him, is the fatal flaw in the argument.

Here is another way to make this point. Consider the table on which you are writing and abstract from it all its properties except *existence.* That is, imagine that you could leave it existing without all the other properties: its color, shape, substance, function, and so forth. What would be left? Existence alone. But what is the difference between existence alone and nothing at all?

Existence is an odd kind of property that can't *exist* without first-order properties. This is why we label it a second-order property. It tells us whether the other properties are exemplified.

If existence is not a property, it is not a perfection either. Suppose Lisa and Jane each wrote down the qualities of a perfect husband. Here are their lists:

Lisa's List	Jane's List
Intelligence	Intelligence
Kindness	Kindness
Sense of humor	Sense of humor
Attractive	Attractive
Moral integrity	Moral integrity
	Existence

Lisa's and Jane's lists are identical except for the quality of existence on Jane's list. But is Jane's list really better? I don't think so. Jane has misunderstood the purpose of the list, which is to set forth the qualities a perfect husband would have. It's another matter whether these qualities are exemplified in an actual man.

If existence were a perfection, we could define things into existence simply by building the concept of existence into the definition. Suppose we define a "unicorn" as a horse with horns. No unicorns exist. But suppose we defined a "lunicorn" as a unicorn that exists. So unicorns must exist since lunicorns exist by definition. But, of course, this is just a verbal trick; we cannot define things into existence. This is the point of Kant's criticism.

THE SECOND VERSION
OF ANSELM'S ARGUMENT

Although Kant's criticism may work against the standard version of the ontological argument, some philosophers—namely, Charles Hartshorne, Norman Malcolm, and William Lawhead—argue that Anselm had a second version of the argument, based on *necessary* existence. They contend that while existence itself may not be a property or a perfection, necessary existence is. The second version of the ontological argument, as set forth by Lawhead, goes like this:

1. It is possible that God exists.
2. God must be conceived as being the greatest possible being.
3. The greatest possible being must be a necessary being.
4. The existence of a necessary being must be either (a) impossible, (b) merely possible (contingent), or (c) necessary.
5. We can exclude (a), for it cannot be impossible for a necessary being to exist. There is no contradiction in the concept of a necessary being.
6. Nor can it be (b), a mere possibility that God exists, for such existence would be (i) dependent and (ii) happenstance, and such a being could not be God.
7. ∴ A necessary being necessarily exists. That is, God exists.

Has this new improved version of the ontological argument proved that God exists? Consider the premises. Are they all true? Premise 1 seems right. Even most atheists acknowledge that it is logically possible that God exists. Premise 2 seems right. God must be thought to be unsurpassably great: omnipotent, omniscient, omnibenevolent, and so forth. Premise 3 also seems right. It cannot just be an accident that God exists, otherwise his existence needs an explanation. What caused it? A greatest possible being is not contingent or a mere outcome of luck but must necessarily exist, as premises 4 and 5 argue. So it would seem that a necessary being must necessarily exist. God exists! This, if it is true, is a momentous discovery.

Have we really proved that God exists? Well, there are two objections you might consider. The first is that the same argument can be used to prove the existence of an all-powerful devil, defined as the worst possible being. The argument goes like this:

1. It is possible that the devil exists.
2. The devil must be thought as the worst possible being.
3. The worst possible being must be a necessary being.
4. The existence of a necessary being must be either (a) impossible, (b) merely possible (contingent), or (c) necessary.

5. We can exclude (a), for it cannot be impossible for a necessary being to exist. There is no contradiction in the concept of a necessary being.

6. Nor can it be (b), a mere possibility that the devil exists, for such existence would be (i) dependent and (ii) happenstance, and such a being could not be the devil.

7. ∴ A worst possible being must necessarily exist. That is, the devil exists.

Since it seems contradictory to suppose a best possible being and a worst possible being both exist, for they could not both be all-powerful, something must be wrong with this form of the argument.

Some argue that we can only argue for the greatest possible being and not for a worst possible one, since all other qualities of the devil would be good ones (e.g., knowledge, power, and presence). But proponents of the devil argument would argue, following Kant, that the only intrinsically good quality is the good-will so that all other virtues turn out to be vice-enhancing. If this is correct, the devil argument seems valid.

There is a second objection to Anselm's second argument. The argument still defines things into existence, only this time it defines things into necessary existence. Suppose we list all the triangles ever drawn and someone argues that it is necessary that a greatest possible triangle exists:

1. It is possible that the perfect triangle exists.
2. The perfect triangle must be thought as the best possible triangle.
3. The best possible triangle must be a necessary being.
4. Something that necessarily exists must exist.
5. ∴ The greatest possible triangle must exist.

But something seems absurd about this argument. There is no reason to believe that such a thing really does exist. Furthermore, couldn't we use the concept of necessary existence to define other things into existence? Consider Lisa's and Jane's ideas of an ideal husband. When Jane argues that her ideal is better than Lisa's because hers (Jane's) contains the concept of existence, Lisa can shoot back, "But mine contains the property of necessary existence, so my notion of a husband is better." Of course, some would argue that the idea of necessary existence does not apply to such innately contingent beings as husbands, but the question for you to consider is, Why?

Suppose these two criticisms fail to dislodge Anselm's second version of the ontological argument; have we then proved that God exists? I don't think so. What we have done is something interesting but less than a proof. An opponent could still attack the first premise and say that, although it may not be obvious at first sight, it really is not possible that God exists. This is because the argument really gives us only two choices: Either God necessarily exists or necessarily does not exist. Since we do not know which to choose on the basis of the concept of necessary being alone, we may suppose that, given the lack of other evidence, God's existence is impossible.

So the ontological argument, at best, does not prove that God exists. At best it shows that it is reasonable to believe that he exists, but even that may be too generous. Perhaps it is simply that it is not altogether foolish to believe that a necessary being exists. It is a difficult question.

SUMMARY

The ontological argument is an a priori argument for the existence of God, which attempts to establish the necessity of the existence of God through an understanding of the concept of existence or necessary being. Its strength is that it gives one an idea of an adequate God, one who is maximally powerful and benevolent (a greatest possible being). Although it is difficult to assess in all its multivarious ramifications, no version has been completely successful in proving the existence of God. On the other hand, it may lend a measure of plausibility to the idea of the existence of a maximally powerful and benevolent being. The issue is controversial.

QUESTIONS FOR DISCUSSION

1. Go over the two versions of the ontological argument discussed in this chapter. How telling are Gaunilo's and Kant's criticisms? Does Anselm misunderstand the concept of being, as the critics claim?

2. Is it greater to exist than not to exist, as Anselm argues? Or is the term *greater* used ambiguously or wrongly here?

3. Could a similar argument as Anselm's be used to prove that a perfectly powerful devil exists as the supreme being and creator of the universe? In their article "An Ontological Argument for the Devil" (*Monist* 54, 1970) David and Marjorie Haight put forth such an argument:

   1. I have a concept of something than which nothing worse can be conceived.
   2. If that "something" did not actually, or in fact, exist, it would not be "that than which nothing worse could be conceived," because something could always be conceived to be much worse, viz. something that actually exists.
   3. The "greatest something" we shall call the Devil.
   4. ∴ The Devil exists.

   Evaluate this argument.

NOTES

1. Bertrand Russell, *Autobiography of Bertrand Russell* (New York: Little, Brown, 1967).

2. St. Anselm, *Proslogium,* trans. S. W. Deane, slightly edited (LaSalle, IL: Open Court, 1903).

3. Immanuel Kant, *Critique of Pure Reason,* trans. J. Meiklejohn (New York: Colonial Press, 1900), 335–336.

FOR FURTHER READING

Gale, Richard. *On the Nature and Existence of God*. Cambridge, Eng.: Cambridge University Press, 1991. Chapter 6 contains an excellent discussion of this argument.

Mackie, J. L. *The Miracle of Theism*. Oxford: Oxford University Press, 1982. A lively discussion of the proofs for the existence of God and other issues by one of the ablest atheist philosophers of our time.

Martin, Michael. *Atheism*. Philadelphia: Temple University Press, 1990. The most comprehensive, English-language attack on theism. Clearly set forth.

Plantinga, Alvin. *God, Freedom, and Evil*. New York: Harper & Row, 1974. Part 2 contains a brilliant contemporary defense of the argument.

Plantinga, Alvin, ed. *The Ontological Argument from St. Anselm to Contemporary Philosophers*. Garden City, NY: Doubleday, 1965. A good anthology on the subject.

Pojman, Louis, ed. *Philosophy of Religion: An Anthology*, 3d ed. Belmont, CA: Wadsworth, 1998. A comprehensive anthology, setting forth both sides of many issues.

7

The Argument
from Religious Experience

There was not a mere consciousness of something there, but fused in the central happiness of it, a startling awareness of some ineffable good. Not vague either, not like the emotional effect of some poem, or scene, or blossom, or music, but the sure knowledge of the close presence of a sort of mighty person, and after it went, the memory persisted as the one perception of reality. Everything else might be a dream, but not that.[1]

—WILLIAM JAMES

The Ego has disappeared. I have realized my identity with Brahman and so all my desires have melted away. I have arisen above my ignorance and my knowledge of this seeming universe. What is this joy I feel? Who shall measure it? I know nothing but joy, limitless, unbounded! The treasure I have found there cannot be described in words. The mind cannot conceive of it. My mind fell like a hailstone into that vast expanse of Brahman's ocean. Touching one drop of it, I melted away and became one with Brahman. Where is this universe? Who took it away? Has it merged into something else? A while ago, I beheld it— now it exists no longer. Is there anything apart or distinct from Brahman? Now, finally and clearly, I know that I am the Atman [*the soul identified with Brahman*], whose nature is eternal joy. I see nothing, I hear nothing, I know nothing that is separate from me.[2]

—SHANKARA

ENCOUNTERS WITH GOD

The heart of religion is and always has been experiential. Encounters with the supernatural, a transcendent dimension, the *Wholly Other* are at the base of every great religion. Abraham hears a Voice that calls him to leave his family in Haran and venture out into a broad unknown, thus becoming the father of Israel. Abraham's grandson, Jacob, wrestles all night with an angel and is transformed, gaining the name "Israel, prince of God." While Moses is tending his father-in-law's flock, Yahweh, or "I am that I am," appears in the burning bush and orders Moses to deliver Israel out of slavery into a land flowing with milk and honey. Isaiah has a vision of the Lord "high and exalted, and the train of his robe filled the temple" of heaven. In the New Testament, John, James, and Peter behold Jesus gloriously transformed on the Mount of Transfiguration and are themselves transformed by the experience. After the death of Jesus, Saul is traveling to Damascus to persecute Christians when he is met by a blazing light and hears a Voice asking him why he is persecuting the Lord.[3] Changing his name to Paul, he becomes the leader of the Christian missionary movement. The Hindu experiences the Atman (soul) as the Brahman (God), "That art Thou," or beholds the glories of Krishna. The Advaitian Hindu merges with the One, as a drop of water merges with the vast ocean. The Buddhist merges with Nirvana or beholds a vision of the Buddha.[4] Allah reveals his holy word, the Koran, to Mohammed. Joan of Arc hears voices calling on her to save her people, and Joseph Smith has a vision of the angel Moroni calling him to do a new work for God.

Saints, mystics, prophets, ascetics, and common believers of every creed, of every race, in every land, and throughout recorded history have undergone esoteric experiences that are hard to explain but impossible to dismiss as mere nonsense. Common features appear to link these otherwise disparate experiences to one another, resulting in a common testimony to this Otherness, a *consensus mysticum*. Rudolf Otto characterizes the religious (or "numinal" spiritual) dimension in all of these experiences as the "mysterium tremendum et fascinans."[5] Religion is an unfathomable mystery, *tremendum* ("to be trembled at"), awe-inspiring, *fascinans* ("fascinating"), and magnetic. To use a description from Søren Kierkegaard, religious experience is a "sympathetic antipathy and an antipathetic sympathy" before a deep unknown.[6] Like looking into an abyss, it both repulses and strangely attracts.

AN ANALYSIS OF RELIGIOUS EXPERIENCE

What, then, is the problem with religious experience? If I say that I hear a pleasant tune, and you listen and say, "Yes, I hear it now, too," we have no problem; but if you listen carefully and don't hear it, you might well wonder whether I am really hearing sounds or only imagining that I am. Perhaps we could bring in others to check out the matter. If they agree with me, well and good; but if they agree with you and don't hear the sounds, then we have a problem. Perhaps we could bring in an audiometer to measure the decibels in the room. If the meter confirms my report, then it is simply a case of my having better hearing than you and the rest of the witnesses; but if the meter doesn't register at all, assuming that it is in working order, we would then have good evidence that I am only imagining the sounds. Perhaps I need to change my claim and say, "Well, I seem to be hearing a pleasant tune."

One problem is that religious experience is typically private. You have the sense of God forgiving you or an angel speaking to you, but I, who am in the same room with you, neither hear, nor see, nor feel anything unusual. You are praying and suddenly feel transported by grace and sense the unity of all reality. I, who am sitting next to you, wonder at the strange expression on your face and ask you if something is wrong. Perhaps your brain is experiencing an altered chemical or electrical state?

Yet, religious experiences of various types have been reported by numerous people, from dairymaids like Joan of Arc to mystics like St. Theresa of Avila and St. John of the Cross. They cannot be simply dismissed without serious analysis.

There are two levels of problem here: (1) To what degree, if any, is the subject of a religious experience justified in inferring from the psychological experience (the subjective aspect) to the existential or ontological reality of that which is the object of the experience (the objective aspect)? (2) To what degree, if any, does the cumulative witness of those undergoing religious experience justify the claim that there is a God or transcendent reality?

Traditionally, the argument from religious experience has not been one of the "proofs" for God's existence. At best, it has confirmed and made existential what the proofs conveyed with icy logic. Some philosophers, such as C. D. Broad (1887–1971), as well as the contemporary philosophers Richard Swinburne and Gary Gutting, believe that the common experience of mystics is *strong justification* or evidence for all of us for the existence of God.[7] Others, such as William James (1842–1910), believe that religious experience is sufficient evidence for the experient to believe in the existence of a divine reality, but only constitutes a possibility for the nonexperient. That is, religious experience grants us only *weak justification*. Religious skeptics, like Walter Stace (1886–1967) and Bertrand Russell (1872–1970), doubt this and argue that a subjective experience by itself is never warranted for making an existential claim (of an object existing outside oneself). It is a fallacy to go from the psychological experience of X to the reality of X.

There are two main traditions regarding religious experience. One, which we can call *mystical,* posits the unity of all reality or the unity of the subject with its object (the mystic is absorbed in God, becomes one with God, etc.). The second type of religious experience can be called simply *religious experience* in order to distinguish it from the mystical. It does not conflate the subject with the object but is a numinal experience wherein the believer (or subject) experiences the presence of God or an angel or Christ or the Holy Spirit, either speaking to or appearing to the experient or forgiving him or her. While in prayer, believers often experience a sense of the presence of God or the Holy Spirit.

Many psychological explanations of religious experience cast doubt on its validity. One of the most famous is the Freudian interpretation. Sigmund Freud said that religious experience was the result of the projection of the father image within oneself. The progression goes like this. When you were a child, you looked upon your father as a powerful hero who could do everything, meet all your needs, and overcome the normal obstacles that hindered your way at every step. When you grew older, you sadly realized that your father was fallible and very finite, indeed, but you still had the need of the benevolent, all-powerful father. So, subconsciously, you projected your need for that long-lost parent onto the empty heavens and invented a god for yourself. Because this is a common phenomenon, all of us who have successfully "projected daddy onto the big sky" go to church or synagogue or mosque or whatever and worship the illusion on our favorite holy day. But it is a myth. The sky is empty, and the sooner we realize it, the better for everyone.

This is one explanation of religious experience and religion in general. It is not a disproof of God's existence, simply an hypothesis. Even if it is psychologically true that we tend to think of God as a powerful and loving parent, it could still be the case that the parental relationship is God's way of teaching us about himself—by analogy.

In his classic on the subject, *Varieties of Religious Experience* (1902), William James describes what he considers the deepest kind of religious experience, mystical experience, a type of experience that transcends our ordinary sensory experience and that cannot be described in terms of our normal concepts and language. It is "ineffable experience." The experient realizes that the experience "defies expression, that no adequate report of its content can be given in words. It follows from this that its quality must be directly experienced; it cannot be imparted or transferred to others."[8] And yet it contains a *noetic quality,* a content. It purports to convey truth about the nature of reality, namely, that there is a unity of all things and that unity is spiritual, not material. It is antinaturalistic, pantheistic, and optimistic. Two other characteristics are predicated to this state. Mystical states are *transient*—that is, they cannot be sustained for long—and they are *passive*—that is, the mystic is acted upon by divine deliverance, grace. We can prepare ourselves for the experience, but it is something that happens to us, not something that we do.

James is cautious about what can be deduced from mystic experience. Although mystic states are and ought to be absolutely authoritative over the individuals to whom they come, "no authority emanates from them which should make it a duty for those who stand outside of them to accept their revelations uncritically." But their value is that they provide us a valid alternative to the "nonmystical rationalistic consciousness, based on understanding and the senses alone. They open out the possibility of other orders of truth, in which, so far as anything in us vitally responds to them, we may freely continue to have faith."

Broad goes even further than James. In his book *Religion, Philosophy, and Psychical Research* (1930); he likens the religious sense to an ear for music. There are a few people on the negative end who are spiritually tone deaf and a few on the positive end who are the founders of religion, the Bachs and Beethovens. In between are the ordinary followers of religion who are like the average musical listener, and above them are the saints who are likened to those with a very fine ear for music.

The chief difference is that religion, unlike music, says something about the nature of reality. Is what it says true? Does religious experience lend any support to the truth claims of religion? Is religious experience "veridical," and are the claims about "the nature of reality which are an integral part of the experience, true or probable"? Broad considers the argument from mystical agreement:

1. There is an enormous unanimity among the mystics concerning the spiritual nature of reality.
2. When there is such unanimity among observers as to what they take themselves to be experiencing, it is reasonable to conclude that their experiences are veridical (unless we have good reason to believe that they are deluded).
3. There are no positive reasons for thinking that mystical experiences are delusive.
4. ∴ It is reasonable to believe that mystical experiences are veridical.

Premise 3 is weak, for there is evidence that mystics are neuropathic or sexually repressed. Broad considers these charges, admits some plausibility in them, but suggests that they are not conclusive. Regarding the charge of neuropathology, he urges that "one might need to be slightly '*cracked*' in order to have some peepholes into the super-sensible world"; with regard to sexual abnormality, it could simply be the case that no one who was "incapable of strong sexual desires and emotions could have anything worth calling religious experience."

His own guarded judgment is that, given what we know about the origins of religious belief and emotions, there is no reason to think that religious experience is "specially likely to be delusive or misdirected," so that religious experience can be said to offer us strong justification for a transcendent reality.

Gutting develops Broad's strong-justification thesis further, arguing that religious experience "establishes the existence of a good and powerful being concerned about us, and [this] justifies a central core of religious belief."[9] On this basis, he argues that the essential validity of religion is vindicated. However, like Broad, he finds that this sort of justified belief "falls far short of the claims of traditional religions and that detailed religious accounts are nearly as suspect as non-religious accounts. The heart of true religious belief is a realization that we have *access* to God but only minimal reliable *accounts* of his nature and relation to us." Gutting develops three criteria that veridical religious experiences must meet: They must be repeatable, be experienced by many in many diverse climes and cultures, and issue forth in morally better lives.

But in arguing for the strong-justification thesis, Gutting seems to me to have gone too far. A strong justification makes it rationally obligatory for everyone to believe in the conclusion of an argument, in this case, that God exists. A weak justification only provides rational support for those who have an "of-God" experience (or already accept the worldview that made such experiences likely). Gutting believes that he has given a strong justification for religious belief, sufficient to establish the existence of God, but there are reasons to suppose that the argument from religious experience offers, at best, only weak justification.

A CRITIQUE OF THE
STRONG-JUSTIFICATION THESIS

Three criticisms of the strong-justification thesis are the following:

1. Religious experience is too amorphous and disparate for us to generalize from in the way Gutting would have us do. That is, there are many varieties of religious experiences, which seem mutually contradictory or vague, so that it is not clear whether we can give the proper criteria necessary to select "of-God" experiences as veridical or having privileged status.

2. Justification of belief in the veridicality of religious experience is circular, so that the belief in it will rest on premises that are not self-evident to everyone. In effect, all assessment of the veridicality of such experience depends on nonuniversal background beliefs.

3. When taken seriously as a candidate for veridical experience, religious experience has the liability of not being confirmed in the same way that perceptual experience

is. That is, although religious experience may sometimes be veridical, it cannot be checked like ordinary perceptual experience, nor can we make predictions on account of it. This indicates that it cannot be used as an argument for the existence of God in the way that Gutting uses it.

Let us look closer at these counterarguments.

Religious Experience Is Amorphous and Varied Religious experience is amorphous and too varied to yield a conclusion with regard to the existence of God. Consider the various types of religious experiences, most of which can be documented in the literature:

1. S senses himself absorbed into the One, wherein the subject–object distinction ceases to hold.
2. One senses the unity of all things and that she is nothing at all.
3. The Buddhist monk who is an atheist senses the presence of the living Buddha.
4. One senses the presence of God, the Father of our Lord Jesus Christ.
5. The Virgin Mary appears to S (in a dream).
6. The Lord Jesus appears to Paul on the road one afternoon, though no one else realizes it but him.
7. One senses the presence of Satan, convincing him that Satan is the highest reality.
8. Achilles is appeared to by the goddess Athene, whom he believes to be descended from Zeus's head. She promises that he will win the battle on the morrow.
9. Allah appears to S and tells him to purify the land by executing all infidels (e.g., Jews and Christians), whose false worship corrupts the land.
10. A guilt-ridden woman senses the presence of her long-deceased father, assuring her that he has forgiven her for her neglect of him while he was aging and dying.
11. A mother senses the presence of the spirit of the river, telling her to throw back her deformed infant because it belongs to the river and not to her.
12. One senses the presence of the Trinity and understands how it could be that the three persons are one God, but he cannot tell others.
13. One senses the presence of the demiurge who has created the universe but makes no pretense to be omnipotent or omnibenevolent.
14. An atheist senses a deep infinite gratitude for the life of his son without in the least believing that a god exists (George Nakhnikian's personal example).
15. An atheist has a deep sense of nothingness in which she is absolutely convinced that the universe has manifested itself to her as a deep void.

The problem for those who would strongly justify the practice of religious experience (that is, show that we are rationally obligated to believe the content of the experience) is to differentiate the valid interpretations from the invalid. Which of these experiences are valid? That is, do any of these guarantee the truth of the propositions contained in the experience? For the believer or experient, each is valid for him or her, but why should the nonexperient accept any of these reports? And why should the experient continue to believe the content of the report after it is over and after he or she notes that there are other possible interpretations of it or that others have had mutually contradictory experiences? It would seem that they cancel each other out. Note the disparity of different types of "nonphysical" or religious experiences in the preceding list. There is not even any consensus that there is one supreme being, who is benevolent. Experiences 1 through 3 do not involve a divine being at all. Contrary to what Gutting says about the virtual universality of god experiences, the branches of Buddhism and Hinduism (in experiencing Nirvana) have religious experiences without experiencing a god. Furthermore, experience 7 supposes that the supreme being is evil, and experience 13 denies omnibenevolence. Experiences 14 and 15 have all the self-authenticating certainty of a religious experience but involve a conviction that no God exists. Do we understand how to distinguish genuine religious experiences from "spiritually" secular ones like experience 14? Why should we believe that the testimony of "of-God" experients is veridical, but not the other types (e.g., 1, 3, 7, 9, 11, 13, and 15) that are inconsistent with it? The very *private* nature of religious experience should preclude our being hasty in inferring from the psychological state to the reality of the object of the experience.

Gutting recognizes the diversity of religious experiences but fails to realize how troublesome this is for his thesis. He tries to find a core in these experiences to the effect that there is a "good and powerful non-human being who cares about us."[10] Gutting admits that we can't derive very much from "of-God" experiences, only that there is a being who is more powerful than us, very powerful and very good. But even if his argument were to show this, would it be sufficient as a definition of "God"? What would be the difference between this and experience 13, Plato's finite demiurge, or experience 10, the guilt-ridden woman's sense of her father, who presumably was both mentally and physically more powerful than she? (He was Arthur Conan Doyle, a genius and pugilist.) How would this show that there is a God, whom we should worship? How would this differ from ancestor worship or polytheism? Or a visitor from outer space? All of these could be "powerful, good, nonhuman, and caring for us." Why should we prefer the "of-God" experiences to the "of-a-supreme-devil" experiences? Gutting rejects the notion of self-authentication as the guarantee for the veridicality of these religious experiences,[11] but if this is so, how does the experient tell the difference between the nonhuman being who cares for her and one who only pretends to care? And how does one reidentify the being who has appeared to him in a nonsensory form?

Religious Experience Is Circular Justification of belief in religious experience is circular, so that the belief in it will rest on premises that are not self-evident to everyone. If I am right about the difficulties in singling out "of-God" experiences from other deeply felt experiences, it would seem that we can only justify belief in the content of religious experience through circular reasoning, by setting forth hypothetical assumptions that we then take as constraints on the experience itself. For example, we suppose that God's ways are mysterious and beyond finding out, and so we are ready to accept our fellow believer's testimony of a deep "of-God" experience. A polytheist in East Africa already believes that the hippopotamus-god appears to women with deformed children in dreams, asking for them back, and so credits his wife with a veridical experience when she reports that she has had such an encounter in a dream.

It would seem, then, that whether or not our interpretations of religious experience are justified depends on our background beliefs and expectations. Our beliefs appear to form a network, or web, in which all our beliefs are variously linked and supported by other beliefs. Some beliefs—call them "core beliefs" (e.g., my belief that $2 + 2 = 4$, or that I seem to see a computer monitor, or that there are other minds, or that I am not now dreaming)—are more centrally located and interconnected than other beliefs. If our core beliefs fall, our entire noetic structure is greatly affected, whereas some beliefs are only loosely connected to our noetic structure (e.g., my belief that the Yankees will win the pennant this year or that it is better to have an IBM PC computer than a TRS 80). Similarly, religious people and nonreligious people often differ by having fundamentally different propositions at or near the center of their noetic structure. The religious person already is predisposed to have theistic-type religious experiences, whereas the nonreligious person is not usually so disposed (in the literature, Christians have visions of Jesus; Hindus, of Krishna; Buddhists, of Buddha; ancient Greeks, of Athene and Apollo; etc.). If you had been brought up in a Hindu culture, wouldn't you be more likely to have Hindu religious experiences than Christian ones? Would there be enough in common for you to decide that both really converged to a common truth?

All experiencing takes place within the framework of a worldview. Certain features of the worldview may gradually or suddenly change in importance, thus producing a different total picture, but there is no such thing as neutral evaluation of the evidence. As we have noted, what we see depends to some degree on our background beliefs and expectations. The farmer, real estate dealer, and artist looking at the same field do not see the *same* field. Neither do the religious person and the atheist see the same thing when evaluating other people's religious experience.

It might be supposed that we could agree on criteria of assessment in order to arrive at the best explanatory theory regarding religious experience, and there are, of course, competing explanations. There are Freudian, Marxian, and naturalistic accounts that, suitably revised, seem to be as internally coherent as the sophisticated theist account. For one account to win our allegiance, it would be necessary for that account to win out over all others. To do this, we would have to agree on the criteria to be met by explanatory accounts. But it could turn out that there are competing criteria, so that theory A would fulfill criteria 1 and 2 better than theories B and C; but B would fulfill criteria 3 and 4 better than the others, whereas C might have the best overall record without fulfilling any of the criteria best of all. It could be a close second in all of them. At this point, it looks like the very formulation and preference of the criteria of assessment depend on the explanatory account that one already embraces. The theist may single out *self-authentication* of the "of-God" experience, but why should that convince the atheist who suspects that criterion in the first place? It seems that there is no unambiguous, noncircular consensus of a hierarchy of criteria.

Gutting is confident of a core content that would be experienced (1) repeatedly, (2) by many, and (3) in such a way that these will be led to live better moral lives.[12] But why should this convince a naturalist who already has a coherent explanation of this phenomenon? Plato's "noble lie" (a lie that is useful to achieve social harmony), recently advocated by the scientist Loyal D. Rue, presumably would have had the same effect, but it still was a lie. Even if we took a survey and discovered that the "of-God" experiences were common to all people, what would that in itself prove? We might still have grounds to doubt its veridicality. As Richard Gale notes, mere unanimity or agreement among observers is not a sufficient condition for the truth of what is experienced:

> Everybody who presses his finger on his eyeball will see double, everybody who stands at a certain spot in the desert will see a mirage, etc. The true criterion for objectivity is the Kantian one: An experience is objective if its contents can be placed in a spatiotemporal order with other experiences in accordance with scientific laws.[13]

Gale may go too far in limiting objectivity to that which is accessible to scientific laws, but his negative comments about unanimity are apposite.

Let me illustrate this point in another way. Suppose Timothy Leary had devised a psychogenic pill that had this result: Everyone taking it had a "deep religious experience" exactly similar to that described by the Western theistic mystics. Would this be good evidence for the existence of God? Perhaps some would be justified in believing it to be. We could predict the kinds of religious experience atheists would have upon taking the pill. But suppose, further, that upon taking *two* of the same pills, everyone had a deep religious experience common only to a remote primitive tribe: sensing the presence of a pantheon of gods, one being a three-headed hippopotamus who created the lakes and rivers of the world but didn't care a bit about people. The fact that there was complete agreement about what was experienced in these states hardly *by itself* can count as strong evidence for the truth of the existential claims of the experience. Theists would be likely to take the experience to be veridical until they had a double dosage, and the tribal people would be likely to believe the experience to be veridical until they took a single dosage. Doesn't this indicate that it is our accepted background beliefs that predispose us to accept or reject that which fits or doesn't fit into our worldview?

Religious Experience Cannot Be Confirmed When taken seriously as a candidate of veridical experience, religious experience fails in not being confirmable in the same way that perceptual experience is. There is, however, one criterion of assessment that stands out very impressively in the minds of all rational people (indeed, it is one of the criteria of rationality itself) but that is unduly ignored by proponents of the argument from religious experience, like Gutting. It is the Achilles' heel (if anything is) of those who would place too much weight on religious experience as *evidence* for the content of religion. This is the complex criterion of *checkability-predictability* (I link them purposefully). The chemist who says that Avogadro's law holds (i.e., equal volumes of different gases at the same temperature and pressure contain an equal number of molecules) predicts exactly to what degree the inclusion of certain gases will increase the overall weight of a gaseous compound. Similarly, if, under normal circumstances, we heat water to 100°C, we can predict that it will boil. If you doubt my observation, check it out yourself. After suitable experiment, we see these propositions confirmed in such a way as to leave little room for doubt in our minds about their truth. After studying some chemistry, we see that they play a role in a wider network of beliefs that are mutually supportive. Such perceptual beliefs force themselves on us.

This notion of predictability can be applied to social hypotheses as well. For instance, an orthodox Marxist states that if his theory is true, capitalism will begin to collapse in industrialized countries. If it doesn't, we begin to doubt Marxism. Of course, the Marxist may begin to revise her theory and bring in **ad hoc** hypotheses to explain why what was expected didn't occur, but the more ad hoc hypotheses she has to bring to bear in order to explain why the general thesis isn't happening, the weaker the hypothesis itself becomes. We come to believe many important propositions through experiment, either our own or those of others whom we take as authoritative (for the moment at least). With regard to authority, the presumption is that we could check out the propositions in question if we had time or need to do so.

How do we confirm the truth of religious experience? Does it make any predictions that we could test now in order to say, "Look and see, the fact that X occurs shows that the content of the religious experience is veridical"? How do we check on other people's religious experiences, especially if they purport to be nonsensory perceptions?

The checkability factor is weak in Gutting's account. He claims that we have a duty to believe simply on the report of others, not on the basis of our own experience or any special predictions that the experient would be able to make. But if the Bible is to be believed, this wasn't always the case, nor should it be today. We read in 1 Kings 18 that to convince the Israelites that Yahweh, and not Baal, was worthy of being worshiped, Elijah challenged the priests of Baal to a contest. He proposed that they prepare a bullock and call on Baal to set fire to it. Then he would do the same with Yahweh. The priests failed, but Elijah succeeded. Convincing evidence! Similarly, at the end of Mark, we read of Jesus telling his disciples that "signs shall follow them that believe; in my name shall they cast out devils; they shall speak with new tongues; they shall take up serpents; and if they drink any deadly thing, it shall not hurt them; they shall lay hands on the sick, and they shall recover" (Mark 16:17, 18). I once read of a sect in Appalachia who followed his principle and fondled poisonous snakes. Funerals outnumbered miracles. Some believers doubt whether this text is authentic, and others seek to explain it away (e.g., "Jesus only meant his apostles and was referring to the apostolic age"). But if a religion is true, we might well expect some outward confirmation of it, such as we find in Elijah's actions at Mt. Carmel or in Jesus' miracles. The fact that religious experience isn't testable and doesn't yield any nontrivial predictions surely makes it less reliable than perceptual experience.

Not only doesn't religious experience usually generate predictions that are confirmed but it sometimes yields false predictions. An example is an incident that happened to me as a student in an evangelical Christian college. A group of students believed that the Bible is the inerrant Word of God and cannot contain an untruth. Now the Gospel of Matthew 18:19 records Jesus as saying that "if two of you shall agree on earth as touching anything that they shall ask, it shall be done for them of my Father which is in heaven," and Matthew 17:20 tells of faith being able to move mountains: "Nothing shall be impossible for you." Verses in Mark confirm this, adding that God will answer our prayer if we pray in faith and do not doubt. So, one night, several believers prayed through the entire night for the healing of a student who was dying of cancer. We prayed for her in childlike faith, believing that God would heal her. As morning broke, we felt the presence of God among us, assuring us that our prayer had been answered. As we left rejoicing and were walking out of the room, we received the news that the woman had just died.

It is interesting to note that none of the participants lost faith in God over this incident, though I for one was traumatically shaken by it. Some dismissed it as one of the mysteries of God's ways, others concluded that the Bible wasn't to be taken literally, and still others concluded that they hadn't prayed hard enough or with enough faith. But as far as the argument for the veridicality of the content of religion is concerned, this failure has to be taken as part of the total data. How it weighs against empirically successful prayers or times when the content of the experience was confirmed, I have no idea, and I don't think Gutting has either. But unless we do, it is hard to see how the argument from religious experience could be used as strong evidence for the existence of God *to anyone else except those who had the experience.* As James concludes about mystical states (one form of religious experience), whereas those having the experience have a right to believe in their content, "no authority emanates from them which should make it a duty for those who stand outside of them to accept their revelations uncritically."

Let me close with an illustration of what might be a publicly verifiable experience of God, one that would be analogous to the kind of perceptual experience by which we check scientific hypotheses. What if tomorrow morning (8 AM CST) there were a loud trumpet call and all over North America people heard a voice speak out, saying, "I am the Lord, your God, speaking. I have a message for you all. I am deeply saddened by the violence and lack of concern you have for one another. I am calling upon all nations to put aside nuclear weapons and to stop burning dangerous fossil fuels. I will give a leading environmental scientist (Dr. J. Walker) the formula for producing an efficient, low-polluting fuel. At the same time, I will replenish the depleted ozone layer and help scientists with a cure for AIDS. This message is being delivered to over one hundred locales at different times today. I want you to know that I will take all means necessary to clean up the environment, prevent a nuclear war, and punish those nations and businesses who persist in following the mad course on which they are now embarked. I love each one of you. A few signs will confirm this message. Later today, while speaking to Israel and the Arab states, I will cause an island, which is intended as a homeland for the Palestinians, to appear west of Lebanon in the Mediterranean. I will also cause the Sahara desert to become fruitful in order to provide food for the starving people in the sub-Saharan region. But I will have you know that I will not intervene often in your affairs. I'm making this exception simply because it is an emergency situation."

Imagine that all over the world the same message is conveyed during the next twenty-four hours and the predictions are fulfilled. Would your religious faith be strengthened by such an event? The question is, Why don't religious experiences like this happen? If there is a God, why does he or she seem to hide from us? Why doesn't God give us more evidence? I leave this question for you to reflect on.

SUMMARY

Religious experience is at the core of the religious life. Throughout the ages, in virtually every culture, people have reported deeply religious, even mystical, experiences that have confirmed their beliefs and added meaning to their lives. Yet problems surround the phenomena: There are discrepancies between accounts, they tend to be amorphous and varied, and they seldom are verified.

QUESTIONS FOR DISCUSSION

1. To what degree, if any, is a person who has a religious experience (of God) justified in inferring the existence of God? Should he or she seriously consider that the experience might be delusionary? How can one tell the difference between veridical and delusionary experiences?

2. Supposing that we agree with William James that the subject of a deep religious experience is justified in believing it to be veridical: How much should this influence the rest of us who have not had such an experience to accept the content of his or her experience?

3. What do you make of the criticism that religious experiences are too amorphous and varied to yield conclusions with regard to the existence of God?

4. What do you make of the criticism that belief in religious experience tends to be circular so that the belief in it will rest on premises that are not self-evident to everyone?

5. What do you make of the criticism that religious experience is not a good candidate for veridical experience, because, unlike perceptual experience, it cannot be verified?

NOTES

1. William James, *The Varieties of Religious Experience* (New York: Modern Library, 1902), 63.

2. *Shankara's Crest Jewel of Discrimination,* trans. Swami Prabhavandanda (New York: Mentor Books, 1970), 103–104.

3. "Now as he journeyed, Saul approached Damascus, and suddenly a light from heaven flashed about him. And he fell to the ground and heard a voice saying to him, 'Saul, Saul, why do you persecute me?' And he said, 'Who are you, Lord?' And he said, 'I am Jesus whom you are persecuting; but rise and enter the city, and you will be told what you are to do.' The men traveling with him stood speechless, hearing the voice but seeing no one. Saul arose from the ground; and when his eyes were opened, he could see nothing; so they led him into Damascus" (Acts 9).

4. Here is an illustration of Buddhist meditation:

Of one who has entered the first trance the voice has ceased; of one who has entered the second trance reasoning and reflection have ceased; of one who has entered the third trance joy has ceased; of one who has entered the fourth trance the inspiration and expiration have ceased; of one who has entered the realm of the infinity of space the perception of form has ceased; of one who has entered the realm of the infinity of consciousness the perception of the realm of the infinity of space has ceased; of one who has entered the realm of nothingness the perception of the realm of the infinity of consciousness has ceased. [Samyutta-Nikaya 36:115, in Buddhism in Translation, ed. Henry C. Warren (New York: Atheneum, 1973), 384.]

5. Rudolf Otto, *The Idea of the Holy* (Oxford: Oxford University Press, 1958).

6. Søren Kierkegaard, *The Concept of Dread* (Princeton, NJ: Princeton University Press, 1939).

7. C. D. Broad, *Religion, Philosophy, and Psychical Research* (London: Routledge & Kegan Paul, 1930); Richard Swinburne, *The Existence of God* (Oxford: Clarendon Press, 1979); and Gary Gutting, *Religious Belief and Religious Skepticism* (Notre Dame, IN: University of Notre Dame Press, 1982).

8. James, op. cit., 371. Here is another testimony reported by James:

> I remember the night, and almost the very spot on the hilltop, where my soul opened out, as it were, into the Infinite, and there was a rushing together of the two worlds, the inner and the outer. I stood alone with Him who had made me, and all the beauty of the world, and love, and sorrow, and even temptation. I did not seek Him, but felt the perfect unison of my spirit with His. The darkness held a presence that was all the more felt because it was not seen. I could not any more have doubted that He was there than that I was. I felt myself to be, if possible, the less real of the two. (p. 67)

9. Gutting, op. cit.

10. Ibid., 113.

11. Ibid., 145.

12. Ibid., 152.

13. Richard Gale, "Mysticism and Philosophy," *Journal of Philosophy* (1960).

FOR FURTHER READING

Alston, William. *Perceiving God.* Ithaca, NY: Cornell University Press, 1991. An important recent work on the epistemology of religious experience.

Gale, Richard. *On the Nature and Existence of God.* Cambridge, Eng.: Cambridge University Press, 1991. Chapter 8 contains a penetrating critique.

Gutting, Gary. *Religious Belief and Religious Skepticism.* Notre Dame, IN: University of Notre Dame Press, 1982. A well-argued contemporary discussion.

Harrison, Jonathan. *God, Freedom and Immortality.* Aldershot, Eng.: Ashgate, 1999. See especially Chapter 10.

James, William. *Varieties of Religious Experience.* New York: Modern Library, 1902. This marvelous treatise is the definitive work on the subject.

Otto, Rudolf. *The Idea of the Holy,* trans. J. Harvey. Oxford: Oxford University Press, 1923. A classic study on religious experience.

Pojman, Louis, ed. *Philosophy of Religion: An Anthology,* 3d ed. Belmont, CA: Wadsworth, 1998. Part 2 contains several important articles.

Swinburne, Richard. *The Existence of God.* Oxford: Oxford University Press, 1979. Contains an important discussion of religious experience.

Wainwright, William. *Mysticism.* Madison: University of Wisconsin Press, 1981. A comprehensive and sympathetic study of mysticism.

8

The Problem of Evil

Is he willing to prevent evil, but not able? Then he is impotent. Is he able, but not willing? Then he is malevolent. Is he both able and willing? Whence then is evil?

—EPICURUS'S PARADOX

THE MYSTERY OF EVIL

Why is there evil in the world? Why do bad things happen to good people? "The whole earth is cursed and polluted," says Philo in David Hume's (1711–1776) famous dialogue on natural religion. He continues:

A perpetual war is kindled among all living creatures. Necessity, hunger, want, stimulate the strong and courageous; fear, anxiety, terror agitate the weak and infirm. The first entrance into life gives anguish to the new-born infant and to its wretched parent; weakness, impotence, distress attend each stage of that life, and it is, at last, finished in agony and horror. Man is the greatest enemy of man. Oppression, injustice, contempt, contumely, violence, sedition, war, calumny, treachery, fraud—by these they mutually torment each other, and they would soon dissolve that society which they had formed were it not for the dread of still greater ills which must attend their separation.[1]

In Fyodor Dostoyevsky's (1821–1881) *The Brothers Karamazov*, Ivan relates the following story to his religious brother Alyosha. There was an aristocratic Russian general who had two thousand serfs and hundreds of hunting dogs. One day an eight-year-old serf boy threw a stone in play and hurt the paw of the general's favorite hound. "Why is my favorite lame?" the general inquires. He is told that the boy threw a stone that hurt the dog's paw. "So you did it!" the general exclaimed and ordered the boy taken away from his mother and kept shut up all night. Early the next morning, the general came out on horseback with his hounds, servants, and huntsmen all mounted, ready for a hunt. The eight-year-old boy is summoned from his cell, undressed. He shivers in the cold, numb with terror. "Make him run," commands the general. The boy runs. "At him!" yells the general, and he sets the pack of a hundred hounds loose. The hounds catch him and tear the boy to pieces before his mother's eyes.

Ivan cannot accept a world where such incidents occur. No amount of utility can justify the torture of a child. He cannot accept God's entrance ticket:

> And so I hasten to give back my entrance ticket, and if I am an honest man I am bound to give it back as soon as possible. . . . Tell me yourself, I challenge you. Imagine that you are creating a fabric of human destiny with the object of making men happy in the end, giving them peace and rest at last, but that it was essential and inevitable to torture to death only one tiny creature—that baby beating its breast with its fist, for instance—and to found that edifice on its unavenged tears, would you consent to be the architect on those conditions? Tell me, and tell me the truth.[2]

We have been looking at arguments in favor of God's existence. The **agnostic** and **atheist** usually base their cases on the alleged unsoundness of the arguments for God's existence. But they have one arrow in their own quiver, an argument for disbelief: It is the problem of evil. From it the "atheologian" (one who argues against the existence of God) hopes either to neutralize any positive evidence for God's existence based on whatever in the traditional arguments survives their criticism or to demonstrate that it is unreasonable to believe in God. We will examine ways in which moral and natural evil are thought to provide evidence against the existence of a wholly good, omnipotent God, including the argument from evolution, which provides an alternative explanatory account of evil. We shall also consider the two main defenses against the argument from evil: the free-will defense and the theodicy defense. But first, let us examine the core argument from evil against the existence of God.

THE ARGUMENT FROM EVIL

The problem of evil arises because of the paradox presented by an omnibenevolent, omnipotent deity allowing the existence of evil (cited at the beginning of this chapter). The Judeo-Christian tradition has affirmed these three propositions:

1. God is all-powerful (including omniscient).
2. God is perfectly good.
3. Evil exists.

But if God is perfectly good, why does he allow evil to exist? Why didn't he create a better world, if not with no evil, at least with substantially less evil than in this world? Many have contended that this paradox, first schematized by Epicurus (341–270 B.C.), is worse than a paradox. It is an implicit contradiction, for it contains premises that are inconsistent with one another. They argue something like the following:

4. If God (an all-powerful, omniscient, omnibenevolent being) exists, there would be no (or no unnecessary) evil in the world.

5. There is evil (or unnecessary evil) in the world.

6. ∴ God does not exist.

To see whether they are right, let us review each of the basic propositions that generate the paradox.

Proposition 1: God is all-powerful. "God is all-powerful" has been a cornerstone of Christian theology since the early centuries of the church. Although it is debatable whether one can show that the biblical writers had such a strong concept (or whether the exact formulation is derived from a Platonic and Aristotelian metaphysics), most Judeo-Christian theologians have seen it as entailed by any adequate view of deity. Some philosophers and theologians, such as John Stuart Mill, William James, Alfred North Whitehead, Charles Hartshorne, and John Cobb, have relinquished this attribute of omnipotence to get God "off the hook" with regard to evil. They accept a *limited* God. God is perfectly good and the greatest possible being, but not omnipotent or omniscient. He cannot do many things, nor does he know the future. They argue that if God knew the future, we would not be free to act, for his knowledge would determine the future. I think this is fallacious, for the epistemic domain does not affect ontological domains. My knowing that you will decide not to cheat on a test, when you get a chance, does not determine your decision not to cheat. Similarly, God could simply know how we will use our free will. Since he exists in eternity beyond time, it seems reasonable to suppose that he knows what we regard as the future without causing it. But these philosophers, called *process philosophers,* suppose that God's knowledge is somehow determining, so that it is reasonable to relinquish the claim of omniscience. God, like other finite beings, is still learning. But because he is neither all-powerful or all-knowing, he cannot eliminate all evil from the world. God simply does the best he can. Does this argument work? Many think that this is too desperate a move. Other critics point out that even if God is not all-powerful, he certainly must be exceedingly powerful (and knowledgeable), and if so, he should have been able to prevent evil (or most evil) in the world. On the other hand, if he is not so powerful, why do we call him "God" rather than "demiurge," and worship, instead, the *ideal* of moral goodness? This is not to say that such *process* theologians and philosophers do not have a case, but it may not be any better than some of the alternative solutions. Many will find it too radical altogether.

Finally, when theists speak of God as being omnipotent, they usually mean that God can do anything that is *logically possible.* God cannot make a stone heavier than he can lift, or will that he never existed, or make 2 + 2 = 5. This will be important with regard to the defense of theism from the charge of the atheologian.

Proposition 2: God is perfectly good. The Judeo-Christian, Muslim, and Hindu traditions all subscribe to the doctrine of complete divine benevolence. Take the property of benevolence from God, and what is the difference between God and a supreme devil? If mere power constitutes God's essence, why should we love and worship him? We might fear him, but he would hardly deserve our adoration or love. No, it is not mere power or knowledge but his complete goodness, his omnibenevolence, that makes God worthy of our worship. God cannot do evil and still remain God. All the major religions—Hinduism, Islam, Judaism, and Christianity—agree on this point. As the psalmist exclaims, "Oh that men would praise the Lord for his goodness, and for his wonderful works to the children of men" (Psalms 107).

Proposition 3: There is evil. "There is evil" may be denied by some Eastern religions, which view it as an illusion, but the Judeo-Christian tradition has always taken it as a fundamental datum to be overcome, if not explained. Suffering and pain, disease and death, cruelty and violence, rape and murder, poverty and natural havoc have all been viewed as the enemy of the good. The millions of humans who have starved to death or died as victims of torture, bloody battle, and brutal wars and the myriads who have been abandoned, abused, and aborted all testify to the tragedy of the human condition: Evil exists in abundance.

Generally, Western thought has distinguished between two types of evil: moral and natural. *Moral evil* covers all those bad things for which humans are morally responsible. *Natural evil,* or *surd evil,* stands for all those terrible events that nature does of her own accord—for example, hurricanes, tornadoes, earthquakes, volcanic eruptions, and natural diseases—which bring suffering to humans and animals. However, some defenses of theism affirm that all evil is essentially moral evil. Here the devil is brought in as the cause of natural evil.

Sometimes students argue that evil is logically necessary for the good, so God could not remove all evil without removing all good. Evil is the necessary counterpart to goodness, as the tail of a coin is the necessary complement of the head of a coin. Without evil, there could not be good. This seems fallacious reasoning. A property need not have an actual opposite in order to exist, though we might not be able to appreciate the good without some contrasting experiences. First of all, Christian and Muslim doctrine has always taught that no evil exists in heaven, which is the paradigm of perfect goodness, so goodness apparently can exist without evil in these traditions. But even if we waive this point, and concede the contrast to the counterpart theorist, this doesn't get him very far. For God could equip us with enormous imaginative powers, so that we could (and do) imagine great evil without really experiencing it. Therefore, although some people may not be able to appreciate the good without some evil, evil is not necessary to the good. Let us turn to the two main defenses against the argument from evil. The first is the free-will defense.

THE FREE-WILL DEFENSE

The main defense of theism in the light of evil is the *free-will defense,* going back as far as St. Augustine (354–430) and receiving modern treatment in the work of John Hick, Alvin Plantinga, and Richard Swinburne. The free-will defense adds a fourth premise to Epicurus's paradox in order to show that propositions 1–3 are consistent and not contradictory. This premise is proposition 7:

7. It is logically impossible for God to create free creatures and guarantee that they will never do evil.

Because it is a good thing to create free creatures who are morally responsible agents, there is no assurance that they will not also do evil. Free agency is so important that it is worth the price of the evil it may cause or permit. As Plantinga puts it:

> God has actualized a possible world A containing significantly free creatures (angels, human beings, other kinds, what have you) with respect to whose actions there is a balance of good over evil (so that A on balance is a very good world); some of these creatures are responsible for moral and natural evil; and it was not within God's power to create significantly free creatures with respect to whose actions there would be a better balance of good over evil than that displayed in A.[3]

Imagine that God viewed an infinite set of possible worlds. In some of them, he saw humans as not sinning but also not free. In some, he saw humans as free and doing less evil than in this world, but he chose to create this world with its enormous amount of good and evil. Perhaps he could have created other worlds with more good or less evil, but he would not create a world with a lesser proportion of good over evil than this one has, and no world he could have created could have a better proportion of good over evil. This world, though not perfect, is the best an omnipotent, omnibenevolent God could do.

This defense assumes a libertarian view of freedom of the will. That is, humans are free to choose between good and evil acts. They are not caused (though they may be influenced) to do one deed rather than the other, but rather they are causally underdetermined. Given two identically similar situations, with identical causal antecedents, an agent could do act A at one time and act B at the other. This view is opposed to **determinism,** as well as **compatibilism** (a view that tries to reconcile freedom of action with determinism). If you are committed to compatibilism or determinism, the free-will defense will not be effective against the argument from evil. The theologian Marilyn McCord Adams thinks that the free-will defense overestimates the level of free agency in humans. She holds that humans have diminished agency before God, analogous to a small child's ability to act freely over against an adult, so that humans cannot be held responsible for the amount and quality of evil.[4]

Many philosophers go even further than Adams and argue that metaphysical libertarianism is unsupported by any sound arguments. Every event in the world, including every action, is the product of either cause or chance. If the event is the result of mere chance, it is not a deliberative act for which we can be held accountable. On the other hand, if it is the effect of prior causes, we are not fully or strongly responsible for it—though we could be said to be responsible in a weak sense (we did the deed voluntarily).

If this is sound, then the problem with the free-will defense discussion is that the same arguments against libertarian freedom can be used to undermine or diminish divine agency. The crucial argument against libertarian free will and responsibility consists of a dilemma:

1. To be really free and responsible for our actions, we must be the cause of what we are (our states of mind).
2. No one is the cause of one's self. Not even God is *causa sui.*
3. ∴ No one is really free and responsible.

As far as I can see, no one has explained what free will is (how it functions), let alone how it is possible. Roderick Chisholm calls it a mysterious *miracle*. Compatabilism, a form of *soft-determinism,* toward which Adams seems to lean, may well be successful in reconciling determinism and responsibility, but this is not the robust kind of freedom needed for the free-will defense. The fact that I voluntarily do *X,* makes me only the *proximate,* but not the *ultimate* cause of *X.* Even my attitude of voluntariness is determined. But if God does not create himself, he is not free to do otherwise than he does. His actions are as causally determined as ours. Either he acts out of his basic character for determining *reasons* or he acts in an arbitrary manner. Either way, he is not omnipotent in the robust way the orthodox tradition supposes. Is there a way between the horns of this dilemma?

To return to the main issue, the proponent of the free-will defense claims that all moral evil derives from creature freedom of the will. But what about natural evil? How does the theist account for it? There are two different ways. The first one, favored by Plantinga and Stephen Davis, is to attribute natural evil to the work of the devil and his angels. Disease and tornadoes are caused by the devil and his minions. The second way, favored by Swinburne and John Hick, argues that natural evil is part and parcel of the nature of things; a result of the combination of deterministic physical laws, which are necessary for consistent action, and the responsibility given to humans to exercise their freedom.

THE THEODICY DEFENSE

While the free-will defense is concerned to show that Epicurus's original argument from evil is not decisive, that the problem of evil does not prove that God does not exist, the theodicy defense, first set forth by Gottfried Leibniz (1646–1716) goes even further and argues that all evil will contribute to the greater good, so that this world, despite appearances, is the *best of all possible worlds.* The most prominent proponent of the theodicy defense is the British theologian John Hick.

Hick's thesis is particularly interesting because he endeavors to put forth a full-scale justification for God's permitting the evil in the world. Why does God allow natural evil and not normally intervene in either natural or moral evil? Hick answers: In order that human beings, as free responsible agents, may use this world as a place of "soul making," which involves the spiritual perfection of our character and persons. The skeptic errs in complaining about the recalcitrant structure of the world because he or she makes the assumption that God created humanity as a completed entity. The skeptic mistakenly thinks

> that God's purpose in making the world was to provide a suitable dwelling-place for this fully-formed creature. Since God is good and loving, the environment which he has created for human life to inhabit is naturally as pleasant and comfortable as possible. The problem is essentially similar to that of a man who builds a cage for some pet animal. Since our world, in fact, contains sources of hardship, inconvenience, and danger of innumerable kinds, the conclusion follows that this world cannot have been created by a perfectly benevolent and all-powerful deity.[5]

Hick, drawing on the work of the second-century theologian Irenaeus, argues that humanity was made in the *image,* but not the *likeness,* of God. As incomplete beings, we must aim at full and perfect likeness. Our world, with all its rough edges and obstacles, "is the sphere in which this second and harder stage of the creative process is taking place."

Suppose that the world were a paradise, without the possibility of suffering, pain, and death. In that case, we would not be seriously accountable for our deeds:

> No one could ever injure anyone else; the murderer's knife would turn to paper or his bullets to thin air; the bank safe, robbed of a million dollars, would miraculously become filled with another million dollars; fraud, deceit, conspiracy, and treason would somehow always leave the fabric of society undamaged. . . . The reckless driver would never meet with disaster. There would be no need to work, since no harm could result from avoiding work; there would be no call to be concerned for others in time of need or danger, for in such a world there could be no real needs or dangers.[6]

Our present ethical concepts would not apply in such a safe "playpen paradise"; concepts like courage, honesty, love, benevolence, and kindness would make no sense because no one could do any harm nor would there be need for heroism or saintliness. Such a world would certainly promote pleasure, but it would be wholly inadequate for character development. But our world is not such a hedonistic romper room. It is a place where we must take full responsibility for our actions, for they have serious consequences. It is a place where we can and should develop our characters into the full likeness of God.

PROBLEMS WITH THE THEODICY DEFENSE

I will leave it to you to analyze Hick's challenging argument fully, but a few questions are in order. First, if this world with all its "heartaches and the thousand natural shocks that flesh is heir to"[7] is useful for suffering, couldn't a world with less suffering and evil than this be adequate for the task? Were Auschwitz, My Lai, Buchenwald, and the torture chamber really necessary for soul building? While astronauts are in training, they are allowed to make mistakes, but built-in feedback mechanisms correct their mistakes before disaster sets in. This allows the trainees to learn from their mistakes. Couldn't God have given us free will, allowed us to learn from our mistakes, and still constructed a world in which feedback mechanisms prevented the kind of monstrous disasters that occur around the world every day? Hick's theodicy may overestimate the human capacity to use evil for good. It also seems inefficient. Why could God not aid us in our soul building without resorting to horrendous evils, perhaps in the way that astronauts are trained? A good teacher can educate and help build character without resorting to torture and brutality.

With or without the free-will defense, many philosophers maintain that the problem of evil persists. Some, like J. L. Mackie and William Rowe, contend that the burden of proof is on the theist to explain why God does not intervene in the suffering of the world. If, by the mere pressing of a button, I could have caused Hitler to have had a heart attack before he started World War II, I would have been obliged to do so. Why did God not intervene in 1939 and prevent the evil of World

War II, including the holocaust? Why didn't God intervene in the event, described by Dostoyevsky, where the mad general set his hounds on the eight-year-old boy? Why does God not intervene in the sufferings of millions all over the world? Perhaps some evil is impossible to prevent, but why is there so much of it? Couldn't an all-knowing God have foreseen the evil in this world and created one in which people would not commit the amount of evil that occurs in our world? Couldn't he have seen another possible world in which humans are free but do much better than we do? Couldn't he have created a world with less natural evil, with less gratuitous pain in humans and animals? Couldn't an all-powerful, all-knowing deity do better than this? We could formulate the argument this way:

1. A morally good being will eliminate evil as much as possible, unless he has good reason to allow it.
2. If there is evil in the world, God must have a good reason to allow it.
3. There is evil in the world.
4. ∴ God must have a good reason for allowing evil.

But the atheologian points out that even if God has such a reason, unless he communicates it to us, we are not in the epistemic position to appreciate that reason, and, hence, we are in no position to believe that he has a sufficient reason to allow seemingly gratuitous evil. If God does not intervene in human and animal suffering, don't we have grounds to suspect that he doesn't exist, doesn't care, or is severely limited? Or perhaps God is not omnibelevolent, but only partly good and partly bad? If this is sound, the problem of evil seems to be a strong argument against belief in the God of classical theism.

Of course, theists counter each of these objections. Some, we have noted, maintain that God is not all-powerful but limited in what he can do. Others argue that it is simply a mystery why God, although all-powerful, doesn't intervene to prevent more evil than he does. How do we know that he hasn't prevented much more evil than there is? Or perhaps in heaven there will be due recompense for the suffering here on earth. Perhaps the lesson of evil is to show us just how serious our moral responsibilities are. Why blame God for evil, when it is we humans who are producing it?

With regard to natural evil (e.g., genetic deformities, diseases, earthquakes, and volcanic eruptions that kill innocent people), the theist argues that this is simply part of an orderly process of nature. The laws of nature are necessarily such that the good is interconnected with the bad. The same rain that causes one farmer's field to germinate may cause another farmer's field to flood, ruining the crops. Although there are, no doubt, limits to the amount of evil God will allow, he cannot constantly intervene without eroding human responsibility or the laws of nature. Where those limits of evil are, not one of us can know. And yet, we wonder. Couldn't an all-powerful God have created a better world than this, a world with a significantly greater proportion of good over evil?

Finally, theists argue that in heaven, God will thank us for enduring the evil we have suffered and compensate us for it. The lame will walk with special ability, and the blind see with acuity. This thesis rests on the coherence and plausibility of the notion of survival in an afterlife. We will examine the topic of personal identity and immortality in Chapter 17. I must leave you to deliberate on how the debate should continue, but there is one more argument from evil that we should consider before leaving the topic—the argument from evolution.

EVOLUTION AND EVIL

As we saw in Chapter 5, when we discussed the argument from design, theists may have good reason to fear evolutionary theory and support creationist accounts of the origin of life and human beings, for evolution proposes a radical alternative paradigm to a theistic, purposive creation. This point can now be employed to undermine theism with regard to evil. Evolution holds that evil is not the result of Satan's sin, Adam's fall, or the human misuse of free will, but rather the consequence of the species developing adaptive strategies, which tend to be accompanied by pain, suffering, unhappiness, and conflicts of interest, the major categories of evil. It is our evolution first from nonsentient to sentient beings that enables us to experience pain. Pain can serve as a warming mechanism, but extreme contingencies may cause pain for no protective reason. The sensation of pain may cause me to withdraw my hand from a fire, but being immolated in a burning building or funeral pyre serves no warning purpose at all and seems entirely gratuitous. Much of our physical suffering is simply the failure of evolution's adaptive strategies. For example, bipedalism, the ability to walk upright on two limbs, enables "higher" primates, including humans, to use their forelimbs for other purposes, such as grasping and thrusting. Bipedalism incurs several liabilities, however, including slower locomotion than quadripedal creatures; an imbalanced vertebral column, which increases the likelihood of lower back pain; troublesome birth pangs; and even stomach problems and herniation, because the center of balance shifts and more pressure is placed on the abdominal region. A more specific problem involves sickle-shaped red blood cells. They are adaptive in areas where malaria is rampant, but where it is not, they are lethal: Children born with sickle-cell anemia have only one-fifth the chance of other children of surviving to maturity. Similarly, human aggressiveness may be adaptive in hunting and defending one's self against predators, but in social groups in which conflicts of interest may arise, it tends to be maladaptive, causing suffering, injury, and death. Use of reason is necessary for social cooperation and coexistence, but the instincts of our ancestor species are more reliable and efficient. Reason leads to concepts such as morality and lawfulness, which are necessary for civilization, but these concepts create liabilities in terms of guilt, shame, litigation, and frustration. A lion does not deliberate about killing an antelope or copulating with an available lioness, nor are his forays followed by guilt or remorse. He enjoys his conquests without worrying about whether he has violated antelope rights. He simply follows his instincts and usually gets away with it.

The point is not that we should to back to the state of the *noble savage*. We couldn't, even if we tried. The point I'm trying to make is that each evolutionary adaptive strategy tends to incur a loss of some other virtue or capability, and this is what accounts for evil. What we call *evil* is simply part of the natural evolutionary process, which, as Tennyson pointed out, "is red in tooth and claw."[8] Much, if not most, moral or man-made evil is the "unintended" result of nature having made us creatures with insatiable wants but limmited resources and sympathies.

This evolutionary account of the origins of evil fits within the broader framework of human biology and animal ethology. To that extent, it is confirmable by scientific research, whereas religious accounts of the origin of evil have less impressive credentials. How do we recreate or confirm the record of the fall of Adam and Eve? The naturalistic account holds that we don't need myths or dogmas about the fall or original sin. Simply investigating evolutionary processes of adaptation is sufficient as an explanation for our greatest problems. Evil has a biological basis, being simply the inextricable concomitant of characteristics that served an adaptive function.

The theist has responses to this account of evil. She may either reject evolution in favor of a creationist account or absorb the evolutionary account within a theistic framework. The first strategy seems a lost cause, since evolution is supported by all we know about animal biology and genetics. The second strategy is more promising but is haunted by problems of explaining why God wasn't more efficient and benevolent in developing the species. Couldn't he have avoided the waste (sacrificing the millions of less fit individuals and species) and done things more benevolently (e.g., made carnivorous animals herbivores and so avoided the predator-prey cycle of death and destruction)?

So the problem of evil persists in haunting theism, and theists continue to devise strategies to ward off the attacks. On which side do the best reasons lie?

SUMMARY

The problem of evil has to do with three propositions that, at first glance, seem incompatible: God's benevolence, God's omnipotence, and evil in the world. Why did an all-powerful and omnibenevolent God permit evil in the first place? Once evil was established, why did God not eliminate it? The theist generally replies that it is better that God creates free beings who sin but who can be redeemed than for God to create a paradise where automatons do good mechanically. John Hick provides a second argument in terms of evil being necessary for soul building, so that humans may perfect themselves by developing into full spiritual beings, in the likeness of God. The skeptic objects to both of these proposals, arguing that it is implausible to suppose that an all-powerful, omnibenevolent God couldn't do better than make a world with this much evil in it.

Finally, we noted how an evolutionary explanation of the origins of evil competes with a theological account. Not Adam's fall but the evolution of the species is the best explanation for evil in the world.

QUESTIONS FOR DISCUSSION

1. Go over the argument from evil against the existence of God. How cogent is it? Does the fact of evil or the amount of evil in the world count against the hypothesis that God exists? Explain your answer.

2. Does John Hick's account of soul making successfully answer the skeptic on why there is so much natural and moral evil? How would Hick meet the objection that God is "overdoing it" with Auschwitz and torture chambers?

3. What do you make of the suggestion that God is limited and is either not all-knowing or all-powerful, and thus is not ultimately responsible for the amount of evil in the world? Does this view solve the problem of evil? Or does it merely extinguish the notion of a sovereign deity?

4. Some Christians, like Marilyn McCord Adams, argue that part of the solution to the problem of evil is the incarnation (of God in Christ) and crucifixion, wherein God himself suffers horrendous evil, thus identifying with us in our suffering. How comforting is this thought?

5. Examine the evolutionary account of the origins and present reality of evil. Does it make more sense than theistic accounts? How should theists respond? By denial, accommodation, or surrender? Explain your answer.

NOTES

1. David Hume, *Dialogues Concerning Natural Religion* (1779). Section reprinted in *Philosophy of Religion: An Anthology,* 2d ed., ed. Louis Pojman (Belmont, CA: Wadsworth, 1993).

2. Fyodor Dostoyevsky, *The Brothers Karamazov,* trans. Constance Garnett (Portsmouth, NH: Heinemann, 1912).

3. Alvin Plantinga, *The Nature of Necessity* (Oxford: Clarendon Press, 1974), 164–193.

4. Marilyn McCord Adams, *Horrendous Evils and the Goodness of God* (Ithica, NY: Cornell University Press, 1999), chapter 1.

5. John Hick, *Philosophy of Religion* (Englewood Cliffs, NJ: Prentice-Hall, 1963), 45.

6. Ibid.

7. William Shakespeare, *Hamlet.* In *Shakespeare: The Complete Works,* ed. G. B. Harrison (New York: Harcourt Brace and World, 1952), 3.1.62–63.

8. Tennyson, Alfred, *In Memoriam,* 1850 (Prologue, 56, st. 4).

FOR FURTHER READING

Adams, Marilyn McCord. *Horrendous Evils and the Goodness of God.* Ithica, NY: Cornell University Press, 1999. A comprehensive and illuminating contemporary treatment of the problem of horrendous evil.

Anders, Timothy. *The Evolution of Evil.* LaSalle, IL: Open Court, 1994. A good account of the thesis set forth at the end of this chapter, defending an evolutionary explanation of evil.

Hick, John. *Evil and the God of Love.* New York: Harper & Row, 1977. Contains the account of a theodicy discussed in this chapter.

Lewis, C. S. *The Problem of Pain.* London: Geoffrey Bles, 1940. A clear and cogent defense of theism.

Mackie, J. L. *The Miracle of Theism.* Oxford: Oxford University Press, 1982. Chapter 9 is an insightful, well-argued essay from an atheist's perspective.

Martin, Michael. *Atheism.* Philadelphia: Temple University Press, 1990. A comprehensive critique of theist arguments regarding the problem of evil. See especially Chapters 14–17.

Plantinga, Alvin. *God, Freedom, and Evil.* New York: Harper & Row, 1974. A clear, cogent account of the free-will defense from a theist perspective.

Pojman, Louis, ed. *Philosophy of Religion: An Anthology,* 2d ed. Belmont, CA: Wadsworth, 1993. Contains important readings in this area.

Swinburne, Richard. *The Existence of God.* Oxford: Oxford University Press, 1978.

Chapter 11 contains a careful defense of theism against the charges of the skeptic.

Symons, Donald. *The Evolution of Human Sexuality.* New York: Oxford University Press, 1979.

Williams, George. *Adaptation and Natural Selection: A Critique of Some Current Evolutionary Thought.* Princeton, NJ: Princeton University Press, 1966.

9

Faith and Reason

THE CHALLENGE TO FAITH:
AN OUTLINE OF THE CENTRAL ISSUES

One of the most important areas of philosophy of religion is that of the relationship of faith to reason. Is religious belief rational? Or is faith essentially an irrational or, at least, an arational activity? If we cannot prove the claims of religious belief, is it nevertheless reasonable to believe these claims? For example, even if we do not have a deductive proof for the existence of God, is it nevertheless reasonable to believe that God exists? In the debate over faith and reason, two opposing positions have dominated the field. The first position asserts that faith and reason are compatible—that is, it is rational to believe in God. The second position denies this assertion. Those holding to the first position differ among themselves about the extent of the compatibility between faith and reason. Most adherents follow Thomas Aquinas (1224–1274) in relegating the compatibility to the "preambles of faith" (e.g., the existence of God and his nature) against the "articles of faith" (e.g., the doctrine of the incarnation). Few have gone as far as Immanuel Kant (1724–1804), who maintained complete harmony between reason and faith—that is, a religious belief within the realm of reason alone.

The second position divides into two subpositions: (1) Faith is opposed to reason and therefore exists in the area of irrationality (this position is held by such unlikely bedfellows as David Hume and Søren Kierkegaard). (2) Faith, being transrational, is higher than reason. John Calvin (1509–1564) and Karl Barth (1886–1968) assert that a **natural theology** is inappropriate because it seeks to meet unbelief on its own ground (ordinary, finite reason). Revelation, however, is "self-authenticating," "carrying with it its own evidence." We can call this position the "transrational" view of faith. Faith is not against reason as above and beyond it. Actually, Kierkegaard shows that the two subpositions are compatible, for he holds both that faith is above reason (superior to it) and against reason (because human reason has been corrupted by sin). The irrationalist and transrationalist positions are sometimes hard to separate in the incompatibilist's[1] argument. At least, it seems that faith gets such a high value that reason comes off looking not simply inadequate but culpable. To use reason where faith claims the field is not only inappropriate but irreverent and faithless.

Can faith be rationally justified? Is it rationally acceptable to believe in God? This is the challenge that rationalists put to religion. Can it be met? Should it be met?

PRAGMATIC JUSTIFICATION
OF RELIGIOUS BELIEF

Religious philosophers sometimes concede that religion cannot be justified through rational argument. They maintain, however, that it can be justified by its practical results. Religious belief has a *practical* reasonableness. That is, even if we cannot find good evidence for religious beliefs, would it perhaps be in our interest to get ourselves to believe in these propositions anyway? And would such believing be morally permissible? In his classic work *Thoughts,* Blaise Pascal (1623–1662), a renowned French physicist and mathematician, sets forth the "wager" argument, contending that if we do a cost-benefit analysis of the matter, it turns out that it is eminently reasonable to get ourselves to believe that God exists, regardless of whether we have good evidence for that belief. The heart of the argument is contained in the following passage:

> Either God exists or He does not. But to which side shall we incline? Reason can decide nothing here. A game is being played where heads or tails will turn up. What will you wager? According to reason, you can do neither the one thing nor the other; according to reason, you can defend neither proposition. But you must wager. It is not optional. You are embarked. Which will you choose then? Your reason is no more shocked in choosing one rather than the other, since you must of necessity choose. This is one point settled. But which course will affect your happiness? Let us weigh the gain and the loss in wagering that God is. Let us estimate these two chances. If you gain, you gain all; if you lose, you lose nothing. Wager, then, without hesitation that He is.
> —"That is very fine," you say. "Yes, I must wager; but I may perhaps wager too much."
> Let us see. Since there is an equal risk of gain and of loss, if you had only to gain two lives, instead of one, you might still wager. But if there were three lives to gain, you would have to play, and you would be imprudent, when you are forced to play, not to chance your life to gain three at a game where there is an equal risk of loss and gain. But there is an eternity of life and happiness.

You may object, "My hands are tied, my mouth is gagged. I am forced to wager, so I am not free. But, despite this, I am so made that I cannot believe. What then should I do?"

I would have you understand your incapacity to believe. Labor to convince yourself, not by more "proofs" of God's existence, but by disciplining your passions and wayward emotions. You would arrive at faith, but know not the way. You would heal yourself of unbelief, yet know not the remedies. I answer you: Learn of those who have been bound as you are. These are they who know the way you would follow, who have been cured of a disease you would be cured of. Follow the way by which they began, by acting as if you believe, taking holy water, having masses said, and so forth. Even this will naturally make you believe.[2]

The argument follows something like this. Regarding the proposition "God exists," reason is neutral. It can neither prove nor disprove it. But we must make a choice on this matter, for not to choose for God is in effect to choose against him and lose the possible benefits that belief would bring. Since these benefits promise to be infinite and the loss equally infinite, we might set forth the possibilities like this:

	God Exists	**God Does Not Exist**
I Believe in God	A. Infinite gain with minimal finite loss	B. Overall finite loss in terms of sacrifice of earthly goods
I Do Not Believe in God	C. Infinite loss with finite gain	D. Overall finite gain

There are only these four possible outcomes. If I believe in God, two outcomes are possible, depending on whether God exists. If God exists, I win eternal happiness, an infinite gain. If God does not exist, I suffer minor inconvenience. Perhaps I could have better enjoyed spending the money I gave to the church or synagogue, but the loss cannot be compared with the possibility of infinite gain. On the other hand, if I do not believe in God, two other outcomes are possible. If I do not believe and God does not exist, I may gain a little advantage in not having had to give my money to the church or sacrifice in other ways. But if I fail to believe and God exists, I lose eternal bliss. I suffer infinite loss.

Even if there is only a small chance that God exists (say, 1 percent), it still pays to bet on God, for no matter how enormous the *finite* gain in C and D, 1 percent probability multiplied by infinity equals infinity. So the only relevant considerations are A and C. Since A (believing in God) promises infinite happiness and C (not believing in God) infinite unhappiness, a rational cost-benefit analysis leaves no doubt about what we should do. We have a clear, self-interested reason for believing in God.

You should go over this argument closely. Are there any weaknesses in it? Does it demonstrate that we all should do whatever necessary to come to believe that God exists? Is such a belief necessary and sufficient for eternal happiness?

In a famous rejoinder to such gambling with God, the British philosopher W. K. Clifford (1845–1879) argued that believing has moral ramifications, so that believing without sufficient evidence is immoral. Pragmatic justifications are not justifications at all but counterfeits of genuine justifications, which must always be based on evidence.

Clifford illustrates his thesis with the example of a shipowner who sends an emigrant ship to sea. He knows that the ship is old and not well built, but he fails to have the ship inspected. Dismissing from his mind all doubts and suspicions of the unseaworthiness of the vessel, he trusts in Providence to care for his ship. He acquires a sincere and comfortable conviction in this way and collects his insurance money without a trace of guilt after the ship sinks, killing all the passengers.

Clifford comments that although the shipowner sincerely believed that all was well with the ship, his sincerity in no way exculpates him because "he had no right to believe on such evidence as was before him." One has an obligation to get one's self in a position where one will only believe propositions on sufficient evidence. Furthermore, it is not a valid objection to say that what the shipowner had an obligation to do was *act* in a certain way (viz., inspect the ship), not *believe* in a certain way. Although he does have an obligation to inspect the ship, the objection overlooks the function of believing as action guiding:

> No man holding a strong belief on one side of a question, or even wishing to hold a belief on one side, can investigate it with such fairness and completeness as if he were really in doubt and unbiased; so that the existence of a belief not founded on fair inquiry unfits a man for the performance of this necessary duty.

The general conclusion is that it is wrong always and for anyone to believe anything on insufficient evidence.

The classic response to Clifford's ethics of belief is William James's "The Will to Believe" (1896), in which James argues that life would be greatly impoverished if we confined our beliefs to such a Scrooge-like epistemology as Clifford proposes. In everyday life, where the evidence for important propositions is often unclear, we must live by faith or cease to act at all. Although we cannot make leaps of faith just anywhere, sometimes practical considerations force us to make a decision regarding propositions that do not have their truth value written on their faces.

In "The Sentiment of Rationality" (1879), William James defines faith as "a belief in something concerning which doubt is still theoretically possible; and as the test of belief is willingness to act, one may say that faith is the readiness to act in a cause the prosperous issue of which is not certified to us in advance." In "The Will to Believe," he speaks of belief as a live, momentous optional hypothesis on which we cannot avoid a decision, for not to choose is, in effect, to choose against the hypothesis. There is a good illustration of this notion of faith in James's "The Sentiment of Rationality." A mountain climber in the Alps finds himself in a position from which he can escape only by means of an enormous leap. If he tries to calculate the evidence of his success, believing only on sufficient evidence, he will be paralyzed by emotions of fear and doubt and hence be lost. Without evidence of being able to perform this feat successfully, the climber would be better off getting himself to believe that he can and will make the leap: "In this case . . . the part of wisdom clearly is to believe what one desires; for the belief is one of the indispensable preliminary conditions of the realization of its object. *There are then cases where faith creates its own verification.*"

James claims that religion may be such an optional hypothesis for many people, and where it is, the individual has the right to believe the better story rather than the worse. To do so, one must will to believe what the evidence alone is inadequate to support.

The reader should keep two questions in mind at this point; one is descriptive, and the other is normative. The first is whether it is possible to believe propositions at will. In what sense can we get ourselves to believe propositions that the evidence doesn't force on us? Surely, we can't believe that the world is flat or that $2 + 2 = 5$ simply by willing to do so, but which propositions (if any) are subject to volitional influences? Is it psychologically impossible to make the kinds of moves that Pascal and James advise? Does it involve self-deception? If we know that the only cause for our belief in a religious proposition is our desire to believe, can we, if rational, continue to believe that proposition? Is there something self-defeating about the whole enterprise of trying to get yourself to believe propositions just because they are comforting?

The second question deals with the ethics of belief, stressed by Clifford. If we suppose that we can get ourselves to believe or disbelieve propositions, is this morally permissible? What are the arguments for and against integrity of belief?

Note that Pascal's volitionalism is indirect, whereas James's might be interpreted as direct. In Pascal's case, one must will to believe the proposition p, discover the best means to get into that state (e.g., going to church, saying mass, taking holy water), and act in such a way as to make the acquisition of the belief likely. In direct volitionalism, one supposes that one can obtain some beliefs simply by fiat of will.

Finally, note that there is a difference between getting one's self to believe propositions where one has no control over the truth of the proposition and getting one's self to believe propositions where the truth has still not been decided, but where belief might help bring about the desired state of affairs (e.g., the mountain-climbing case). Should we have a different attitude about each of these types of cases?

FIDEISM: FAITH WITHOUT/AGAINST REASON

Fideism is the position that holds that objective reason is simply inappropriate for religious belief. Faith does not need reason for its justification, and the attempt to apply rational categories to religion is completely inappropriate. Faith creates its own justification, its own criteria of internal assessment. There are two versions of fideism. The first states that religion is bound to appear **absurd** when judged by the standards of theoretical reason, while the second merely says that religion is an activity where reason is properly inoperative. It is not so much against reason as above reason. The two positions are compatible. The third-century theologian Tertullian seemed to hold that religious faith was both against and beyond human reason (and perhaps St. Paul holds the same in I Corinthians 1), but many fideists (e.g., Calvin) would only subscribe to the latter position.

Søren Kierkegaard (1813–1855), the Danish philosopher and father of **existentialism,** seems to hold to both versions of fideism. For him faith, not reason, is the highest virtue a human can reach, a trait that is necessary for the deepest human fulfillment. If Kant, the rationalist, adhered to a "religion within the limits of reason alone," Kierkegaard adhered to "reason within the limits of religion alone." He unashamedly proclaimed faith as being higher than reason in the development of essential humanness, and that alone promised eternal happiness. In a more everyday sense, Kierkegaard thought that we all lived by simple faith in plans, purposes, and people. It is rarely the case in ordinary life that reason is our basic guide. Paraphrasing Hume, he might have said that "reason is and ought to be a slave to faith," for we all have an essential faith in something and reason comes in largely as an afterthought to rationalize our intuitions and commitments.

No philosopher writes more passionately about faith, nor values it more highly, than Kierkegaard. Whereas his predecessors had viewed faith largely as a necessary evil, a distant cousin to the princely knowledge, Kierkegaard reversed the order. Knowledge about metaphysical issues is really a liability, for it prevents the kind of human striving that is essential for our fullest development. Faith is the highest virtue precisely because it is objectively uncertain, for it involves risk and uncertainty that are crucial for personal growth into selfhood. Spiritual self-realization needs to venture forth, to swim over 700,000 fathoms of ocean water. Faith is the lover's loyalty to the beloved when all the evidence is against her. Faith is the soul's deepest yearnings and hopes, which the rational part of us cannot fathom. Even if direct proof for theism or Christianity were available, we would not want it, for such objective certainty would take the venture out of the religious pilgrimage, reducing it to a set of dull mathematical certainties.

Genuine theistic faith appears when reason reaches the end of its tether, when the individual sees that without God life ceases to have purpose:

> In this manner God becomes a postulate, but not in the otiose manner in which this word is commonly understood. It becomes clear rather that the only way in which an existing individual comes into relation with God, is when the dialectical contradiction brings his passion to the point of despair, and helps him to embrace God with the "category of despair" (faith). Then the postulate is so far from being arbitrary that it is precisely a life-necessity. It is then not so much that God is a postulate, as that the existing individual's postulation of God is necessary.[3]

Kierkegaard, often writing through pseudonyms like Johannes Climacus (John the Climber—presumably, to heaven), argues that there is something fundamentally misguided in trying to base one's religious faith on objective evidence or reason. It is both useless (it won't work) and a bad thing (it detracts one from the essential task of growing in faith). Then he goes on to develop a theory of subjectivity wherein faith finds an authentic home. One version of his argument is called the *approximation argument*, for it claims that reason and scholarship only give us approximate results, whereas faith demands infinite passion and subjective certainty. Here is a key passage:

> If a naked dialectical analysis reveals that no approximation to faith is possible, that an attempt to construct a quantitative approach to faith is a misunderstanding, and that any appearance of success in this endeavor is an illusion; if it is seen to be a temptation for the believer to concern himself with such considerations, a temptation to be resisted with all his strength, lest he succeed in transforming faith into something else, into a certainty of an entirely different order, replacing its passionate conviction by those probabilities and guarantees which he rejected in the beginning

when he made the leap of faith, the qualitative transition from non-belief to belief;—if this be true, then everyone who so understands the problem, insofar as he is not wholly unfamiliar with scientific scholarship or bereft of willingness to learn, must feel the difficulty of his position, when his admiration for the scholars teaches him to think humbly of his own significance in comparison with their distinguished learning and acumen and well merited fame, so that he returns to them repeatedly, seeking the fault in himself, until he is finally compelled to acknowledge dejectedly that he is in the right.[4]

Kierkegaard is here examining the need for biblical scholarship to establish the credibility of the Bible and Christian claims of revelation, but in other places he discusses attempts to prove the existence of God through rational demonstrations. All they give us is approximate objective results. For example, years ago most biblical scholars believed in the literal narrative of the Creation and Fall from Grace of Adam and Eve (in Genesis 2 and 3). Today, most biblical scholars do not believe in the literal interpretation of the Genesis account, so that the literal interpretation cannot serve as the basis for a believer's faith. But suppose that tomorrow new evidence turns up against the authenticity of the New Testament Gospels. Or suppose a noted biblical scholar sets forth a plausible theory that explains how the disciples were deluded into believing that Jesus of Nazareth rose from the dead. Kierkegaard contends that if the believer's faith is hostage to the fortunes of scholarship, one week the faith may be strong but the next week it may be very weak. Indeed, some weeks, there may be no faith at all because the evidence is insufficient.

But this is just silly, argues Kierkegaard. Because Christianity has made eternal happiness depend on faith, taking scholarship too seriously can cause us to lose eternity. Our eternal happiness can't rest on the luck of what scholars find or on intellectual hypotheses. Faith is not simply for scholars and intellectuals—perhaps it is least of all for them, for they are preoccupied with reason and miss the glory of faith; faith is something even peasants and uneducated people can possess. It is certain, something absolute, that demands one's whole heart and soul. The leap of faith transcends all scholarly pretensions. It's more like falling in love than figuring out a crossword puzzle, to which the scholars would have us liken it.

What do you make of this argument? Is faith wholly cut off from reason? Or is it simply a fact of life that most of us, at least, have no rational basis for religious certainty?

A question may be asked: Why do we value reason so highly? In most areas of life, it seems to give us good results. In science as well as in our daily lives, following reason is generally the best guarantee for success. Even the recognition of the limits of reason seems to be a function of reason at a higher reflective level—exactly what you might be doing right now—using reason to recognize the limits of reason.

This is a deep question, for which a lifetime of experience may be necessary. You must decide the answer for yourself. However, there is one advantage that the rationalist has over the fideist. The rationalist can bring his or her evidence into the discussion so that we may all evaluate it and decide how credible it is, but the fideist has no such justification. In most other important areas of life, we trust the person with good reasons over the person with no reasons. Why should religious belief be different?

ALVIN PLANTINGA'S THEORY
OF REFORMED EPISTEMOLOGY

One of the most innovative, brilliant, and controversial contributions to the debate on faith and reason is the theory set forth by Alvin Plantinga. It claims that the belief that God exists is rational even though it is not based on prior evidence. In a series of articles Plantinga has juxtaposed what he calls *Reformed Epistemology* (or Calvinist Epistemology) with classical foundationalism (which he finds in Aquinas, Descartes, Locke, Hume, and many others) and has concluded that the theist is rationally justified in believing in God without further evidence.[5] Plantinga finds classical foundationalism wanting, but he himself seems to prefer a revised version of foundationalism as the best available epistemological theory. In this section I shall exposit Plantinga's arguments, using his latest article, "Reason and Belief in God," as the focal point of my analysis. After this, I shall discuss two criticisms of his position.

Classical foundationaliam is the doctrine that all justified beliefs must either be properly basic by fulfilling certain criteria or be based on other beliefs that eventually result in a treelike construction with properly basic beliefs resting at the bottom, or at the foundations. According to a typical classical foundationalist:

> A proposition *p* is properly basic for a person S if and only if *p* is either self-evident to S or incorrigible for S or evident to the senses for S.

Foundationalists may differ about the exact makeup of the definition (Descartes accepting only the first two disjuncts, but Aquinas and Locke accepting all three), but they all agree that justified beliefs must be based on foundations having some of the above components. Self-evident propositions are those that a person just sees as true immediately, such as "that $1 + 2 = 3$" or "that nothing all green is all black" or that the law of noncontradiction is universally valid. Incorrigible propositions are those about one's states of consciousness in which one cannot mistakenly believe what is not true, such as "that I seem to see a red ball" or "I think, therefore I am" or "I am in pain." Aquinas and Locke add a third type of proposition, that which is evident to the senses, such as "that I see a tree" or "I see a red ball." The goal of the classical foundationalist is to protect our belief systems from error by allowing only solid or absolutely certain beliefs to make up the foundations of our belief systems.

Next, Plantinga develops the notion of a noetic structure. "A person's noetic structure is the set of propositions he believes together with certain epistemic relations that hold among him and these propositions." Plantinga analyzes the noetic structure from the point of view of foundationalism in general. There are three ways of classifying the contents of our noetic structure: (1) in terms of basicality; (2) in terms of degree of belief; and (3) in terms of the depth of ingress of a belief.

(1) *Basicality* refers to the dependency relationship of all other beliefs on basic beliefs. The relationship is irreflexive (it can't be justified by itself), one-many (nonbasic beliefs may depend on more than one belief), and asymmetrical (if belief A depends on belief B, belief B cannot legitimately depend on belief A).

(2) We believe propositions in various *degrees*. Classical foundationalists like Locke and Hume would define rationality in terms of believing propositions according to the strength of the evidence. Whereas Plantinga agrees that we do believe in varying degrees, he rejects any attempt to work out an exact correlation of degrees of evidence and degrees of belief. He does so because the only candidate is some sort of quantification test, which he rejects as unworkable.

(3) Regarding the matter of *depth of ingress,* Plantinga says that beliefs play different roles within our noetic structure. Some of our beliefs are more central and some more peripheral to our doxastic system, so that losing some beliefs will have a greater effect on us than losing others. We are less worried about being wrong about the trivial proposition that there are X number of steps in the city of Dallas than about the proposition that the snake we are about to handle is nonpoisonous.

Applying this theory of classical foundationalism to religious claims, we see that, according to it, belief in God has no legitimacy. The thesis excludes the belief from the foundations of one's noetic structure, for belief in God is neither self-evident, incorrigible, nor evident to the senses. Furthermore, because it does not seem possible to get from the types of propositions allowed in our noetic structure by these conditions to the conclusion that God exists, the present-day foundationalists tend to reject the belief that God exists as unjustified or irrational.

But classical foundationalism is not without problems. First of all, it seems that "relative to propositions that are self-evident and incorrigible, most of the beliefs that form the stock in trade of ordinary everyday life are not probable—at any rate there is no reason to think they are probable." Such propositions as that there are enduring physical objects, other minds, and that the world has existed for more than five minutes "are not more probable than not with respect to what is self-evident or incorrigible for me." Nor are the propositions that there are other minds or that the world existed five minutes ago evident to the senses. Furthermore, many propositions that do not meet the criteria of classical foundationalism seem properly basic for me." I believe, for example, that I had lunch this noon. I do not believe this proposition on the basis of other propositions; I take it as basic; it is in the foundations of my noetic structure. Furthermore, I am entirely rational in so taking it, even though this proposition is neither self-evident nor evident to the senses nor incorrigible for me."

The most devastating criticism of the formula of classical foundationalism, however, is that it is self-referentially incoherent. For the statement that we are rational only if either it is properly basic or derived from statements that are does not seem to be either properly basic or derived from other statements that are properly basic. To be properly basic, the statement must be either self-evident, incorrigible, or evident to the senses. But the statement that prescribes such rules does not seem to be any of these. Nor does it seem to be derived from statements that are. Hence, it seems irrational to accept it by its own standards.

Plantinga's alternative to classical foundationalism is rooted in the Reformed theological tradition, which contains the core of a nonevidentialist epistemology. The Reformed thinkers have eschewed the attempt to demonstrate the existence of God. From the outset such theologians as Calvin, Bavinck, Warfield, and, more recently, Barth have seen dangers in trying to prove theism, have recognized that arguments are not the source of the believer's confidence, and have insisted that they are not needed for rational justification. As Scripture "proceeds from God as the starting point," so should the believer. In this sense, belief that God exists is like belief in other minds or that I have had lunch this noon. It does not need argument before it can be properly basic. Starting from that premise, the theist could then go on and adhere to foundational rules:

> (1) In every rational noetic structure there is a set of beliefs taken as basic—that is, not accepted on the basis of other beliefs; and (2) In a rational noetic structure non-basic belief is proportional to support from the foundations.

Plantinga does not offer criteria for proper basicality, but he does want to protect Reformed epistemology from certain objections. Specifically, his position should not be confused with the view that any belief may be part of one's epistemic foundations, nor does he want to say that it is groundless. It is not a version of Wittgensteinian fideism. Some objectors have complained that Plantinga's views open the door to all sorts of irrationality in the foundations of our noetic structure. Why cannot belief in the Great Pumpkin be considered properly basic? Plantinga's answer is that the Reformed epistemologist agrees with Calvin that "God has implanted in us a natural tendency to see his hand in the world around us; the same cannot be said for the Great Pumpkin, there being no Great Pumpkin and no natural tendency to accept belief about the Great Pumpkin."

Plantinga does not give any criteria to help us distinguish unacceptable from acceptable candidates for proper basicality, but he suggests that the manner of arriving at such will be broadly inductive.

> We must assemble examples of beliefs and conditions such that the former are obviously properly basic in the latter, and examples of beliefs and conditions such that the former are obviously not properly basic in the latter. We must then frame hypotheses as to the necessary and sufficient conditions of proper basicality and test these hypotheses by reference to those examples.

But there is a certain relativity in the process of searching for criteria for proper basicality. Each community will assemble a different set of examples of beliefs and accompanying conditions, so that there is no reason to assume that everyone will agree on the examples.

> The Christian will of course suppose that belief in God is entirely proper and rational; if he does not accept this belief on the basis of other propositions, he will conclude that it is basic for him and properly so. Followers of Bertrand Russell and Madelyn Murray O'Hare may disagree; but how is that relevant? Must my criteria, or those of the Christian community, conform to their examples? Surely not. The Christian community is responsible to its set of examples, not theirs.

It may well be the case that we shall never arrive at universal agreement regarding the conditions for proper basicality. This does not mean that there is no truth in this area, but simply that at least one set of criteria is wrong. It is important to point out that Plantinga is not stating that no argument could ever cause the theist to give up his belief in God, but that the objector has yet to give any such argument. Argument for proper criteria is important, but until good reasons are given why the believer should not accept belief in God into the foundations of her noetic structure, there is no reason for the believer to be troubled. Plantinga distinguishes weak justification, where one is in one's epistemic rights in accepting a proposition, from strong justification, where one has what amounts to knowledge. He suggests that the believer may only have a weak justification for belief that God exists, but indicates that, in the absence of a successful defeater, it is rational to believe in God. One is prima facie, but not ultima facie, justified in so doing.

Regarding the objection that Reformed Epistemology makes belief in God groundless, Plantinga answers that the belief is properly grounded in other beliefs, such as "God is speaking to me" and "God forgives me," which are properly basic. They are analogous to perceptual beliefs (e.g., "I see a tree"), memory beliefs ("I had breakfast this morning"), and beliefs ascribing mental states to other persons (e.g., "that person is in pain"). In the proper circumstances (e.g., where there is no reason to believe that my noetic structure is defective), my having an experience of a certain sort confers on me the right to hold the belief in question. In like manner, having the experience that God is speaking to me or that God is forgiving me are properly basic in the right circumstances. In this sense, "it is not wholly accurate to say that it is belief in God that is properly basic." It is really these more experiential beliefs that are properly basic. They in turn entail that God exists. The proposition that God exists is a relatively high-level general proposition that is based on these other more basic propositions.

Finally, Plantinga's proposal is to be distinguished from fideism. Plantinga accepts the definition of fideism as "exclusive or basic reliance upon faith alone, accompanied by a consequent disparagement of reason and utilized especially in the pursuit of philosophical or religious truth." Extreme fideism disparages and denigrates reason, while moderate fideism simply prefers faith over reason in religious matters.

The Reformed epistemologist rightly rejects the extreme fideism of a Kierkegaard (who makes faith in the absurdity of the eternal entering time a necessary condition for being a Christian) and Lev Shestov (who holds that one can attain religious truth only by rejecting the proposition that $2 + 2 = 4$ and accepting instead $2 + 2 = 5$). If we understand the deliverances of reason to include basic perceptual truths, incorrigible propositions, certain memory propositions, certain propositions about other minds, and certain moral or ethical propositions, then the Reformed epistemologist would say that belief in God fits into this scheme as properly rational, rather than being an instance where faith overrides reason. There is a "tendency or nisus" to apprehend God's existence and to understand something of his nature and actions. "This natural knowledge can be and is suppressed by sin, but the fact remains that a capacity to apprehend God's existence is as much part of our natural noetic equipment as is the capacity to apprehend perceptual truths, truths about the past, and truths about other minds." Hence, belief that God exists is among the deliverances of reason as much as these other basic beliefs, and hence, the theist need not be a fideist of any sort.

Plantinga is one of the growing number of philosophers of religion who is sensitive to the matter of volitionalism (the idea that we can choose our beliefs directly) and the ethics of belief. He rejects direct volitionalism as a plausible account of belief formation. We cannot get ourselves to believe propositions just by fiat. Beliefs are not normally, at least, within our control. But if they are not under our control, how can we be said to have duties to believe rationally or according to the evidence?

Plantinga begins his answer by appealing to almost universal beliefs about moral responsibility. Nearly all of us have a deep belief that we can be held morally responsible for our actions even when they are based on what we presently believe. Sincere false belief does not excuse us from moral condemnation. The antisemite, who believes that she is following the evidence to this abhorrent conclusion and who acts on the conclusion that Jews are evil, is morally culpable. A person who believes that it is morally proper to arrive at beliefs carelessly or who is sincere in rejecting morality is still morally guilty. This is because we believe that there is an objective morality which each normal person could know if she cared to.

While we cannot get ourselves to believe anything at all by willing to believe it, we can affect our doxastic repertoires by paying attention to the evidence, in this case, to our inner moral prompting. The implication of this is that we may also be responsible for whether we believe in God. Perhaps the nonbeliever is one who has defiled his natural tendency to see God in nature.

Among the critiques of Plantinga's position, that of Gary Gutting merits special attention.[6] Gutting is troubled by the ease with which Plantinga dismisses the views of those who differ from him, his epistemic peers, who do not find the proposition "God exists" as properly basic. Let us take an instance of disagreement among epistemic peers.

> Suppose a mathematician has reflected long and hard on a given proposition (e.g., the axiom of choice) and, although he is not able to derive it as a theorem or even to put forward strong plausibility arguments for it, has come to an entirely firm conviction of its truth. He just "sees" that it is true. However, when he proposes his proposition to his equally competent colleagues, he meets mixed reactions. Some share his intuitive acceptance of the proposition, others do not. In such a case, is he entitled to continue believing the proposition or should he withhold judgment on it?

It would seem that the mathematician ought to take account of his opponents' views. He should see whether they have any good arguments against his views and, if he concludes that they do not, "he must see if there is any reason to trust his opponents' judgments (intuition) rather than his own on this point." But even if there is no reason to prefer their judgment to his own, he should be moved from his certainty by the fact of their difference. To cling tenaciously to his intuition rather than weakening his hold on the proposition is to be guilty of "epistemological egoism," which is just as "arbitrary and unjustifiable as ethical egoism is generally regarded to be." That is, there is something like peer review of important propositions within any given field. While such review may not always cause us to give up a belief that we cannot defend, it ought, at least, to cause us to loosen our grasp on the belief, to realize that we could be wrong.

A second criticism, which has been made by Robert Audi[7] and others, is that Plantinga has not shown us why almost anything cannot be allowed into the foundations of one's noetic structure. In letting belief in God in as properly basic, he seems to be permitting belief in the Great Pumpkin and much more—and this, in spite of his asseverations that there are limits on what is acceptable. His response that "God has implanted in us a natural tendency to see his hand in the world around us; the same cannot be said for the Great Pumpkin, there being no Great Pumpkin and no natural tendency to accept belief about the Great Pumpkin," seems circular, for the Pumpkin theologian could claim the same argument as the reason there are not more followers of the Pumpkin, viz., that unbelievers are disobeying their true nature or not being sufficiently reflective. Is Plantinga making "a natural tendency to believe something" a criterion for proper basicality? If so, belief that God exists does not seem to have that property. At least it does not have it to the extent that belief in other minds or in *modus ponens* has it. If there is a strong person-relative aspect to rationality, why can it not be the case that someone comes to believe some strange things about the Great Pumpkin? Plantinga's point seems to be that there is no reason to worry about fictions like the Great Pumpkin, which are not serious candidates for proper basicality, but he has not shown what is wrong with such a belief. Likewise, someone could well believe that God is evil or that Satan is the creator of heaven and earth and claim this belief as properly basic. I've met people who believe this and that God is a sadist who is out to harm them. As Plantinga himself points out, it may turn out that we will not find clear criteria to separate the theist's beliefs from the atheist's or Satanist's beliefs. It may be that the different set of criteria that characterize what is properly basic for different groups and persons will never be entirely harmonized, but it may also be true that rationality directs us to be deeply respectful of our epistemic peers and moderate our judgment in matters where we have great differences and cannot give good reasons for preferring our positions. Belief that God exists or that he is speaking to me is not, after all, subject to the almost universal confirmability of the statement "I see a tree."

SUMMARY

There are three main positions regarding the relationship of faith to reason:

(1) Faith and reason are compatible; they work in harmony.
(2) Faith transcends reason, so that there are limits to reason. But faith never contradicts reason rightly used.
(3) Faith is against reason. Human reason is fallible and should not be given much weight in religious affairs.

The weakness of positions 2 and 3 is that, if we give up reason, how do we distinguish nonsense, which claims to be transcendent, from the veridical message of God?

Pascal's wager offers a pragmatic justification for believing in God without sufficient evidence. We examined Clifford's critique and other problems with Pascal's position, as well as James's defense.

At this point, at the end of the twentieth century, the debate in Philosophy of Religion is largely between the evidentialists, both theists and nontheists, on the one side, and fideists or neofideists like Plantinga, on the other side. The foremost evidentialist, Swinburne, has made a cumulative case for the existence of God. Taking all the evidence into consideration, the cosmological and teleological arguments and the argument from religious experience, the case for theism has a slight edge. Swinburne's controversy with the agnostics and atheists looks like a family quarrel compared with Plantinga's work on religious foundationalism, which rejects the notion of needing arguments for one's belief in God. God is the beginning point for the religious person, not something that we arrive at by argument. The role of philosophy of religion becomes very limited, at best a negative enterprise of marshalling attacks that will be met by a polite rebuttal by the theist who will not let anything come in the way of his faith in God. Plantinga's work is, at present, the central focus of debate.

The verificationist and falsificationist attacks of the 1940s and 1950s are now mostly a matter of history (except, oddly enough, in certain theological apologetics where some theologians are still using them as the whipping post), and the extreme versions of fideism no longer hold prominence. Classical foundationalism (the view that a belief is properly basic if and only if it is either self-evident or incorrigible or evident to the senses) has been undermined by such counterexamples as memory beliefs and beliefs in other minds and by the embarrassing fact that no version of it has been devised that is not self-referentially incoherent, that is, the principle itself is neither self-evident, evident to the senses, nor incorrigible. Plantinga and others have put forward a version of weak foundationalism that has greater latitude in what is to be allowed as properly basic and that includes belief in God as properly basic. The question is whether this version is too broad and whether a narrower version may be constructed that is not open to some of the problems of Plantinga's version.

One such attempt, which seems compatible with the concerns of Gutting and Audi, is found in Anthony Kenny's recent lectures at Columbia University, now published as a book, *Faith and Reason*.[8] Kenny has been influenced by Plantinga and agrees that classical foundationalism is dead. However, he thinks that Plantinga's version of allowing belief in God into the foundations of one's noetic structure opens the door for letting in any proposition whatever, including the proposition that there is no God. Kenny's alternative version of foundationalism, which escapes both the self-referential incoherence of classical foundationalism and the latitudinarianism of Plantinga, states that a belief is properly basic if and only if it is "self-evident or fundamental,—evident to the senses or to memory,—defensible by argument, inquiry or performance."

By "fundamental" Kenny means such universal beliefs as that there are other minds, that cats do not grow on trees, that the earth has existed for many years, and the like. By being defensible by inquiry, Kenny merely means that sometimes we ourselves do not have the requisite evidence at our fingertips but are ready to take steps to get it. By being defensible by performance, he means such situations as where the person always gets the right answers even though he may not himself know how (e.g., the water diviner who knows but can't tell how he knows that there is water in certain places). Kenny believes that this reconstructed evidentialist version of foundationalism escapes the liabilities of classical foundationalism, as well as the attacks by the antievidentialists. Whether it does or not will doubtless be the subject of forthcoming work in the area of faith and reason.

QUESTIONS FOR DISCUSSION

1. Examine the three major positions regarding faith and reason. What are the strengths and weaknesses of each one? Which seems the most plausible to you and why?

2. Examine Pascal's wager. What are its strengths and weaknesses?

3. Do you think that you can get yourself to believe propositions (e.g., that God exists or that Hinduism is the true religion) just by willing to do so? Or do beliefs force themselves on people depending on how the evidence or testimony of others affects them? Discuss your answer.

4. Is it immoral to believe a proposition against the evidence? Why, or why not?

5. In arguing for the strongest fideism, where we claim that reason is contrary to faith, don't we use rational arguments to show it is reasonable to abandon reason? Does this prove that the fideist is still a rationalist?

6. Consider a woman who has faith in the faithfulness of her husband, who has been accused of committing adultery. Suppose the evidence is strong but not conclusive. Is she morally virtuous in persisting in believing in his fidelity, or is she simply foolish? What if the case against him is conclusive? Does reason ever tell us that it is rational to believe despite the evidence?

7. Review and evaluate Plantinga's Reformed Epistemology. Is it a sound theory? Are criticisms of it sound?

NOTES

The quotations in the first three sections of this chapter are in selections found in Part VII.B of my *Philosophy of Religion: An Anthology,* 2d ed. (Belmont, CA: Wadsworth, 1993); and Part III.C of my *Introduction to Philosophy: Classical and Contemporary Readings* (Belmont, CA: Wadsworth, 1991).

1. I use the term *incompatibilist* to stand for the position that reason is an inappropriate instrument for deciding religious matters. It includes both the irrationalist and transrationalist position.

2. Blaise Pascal, *Thoughts,* trans. W. F. Trotter (New York: Collier, 1910).

3. Søren Kierkegaard, *Concluding Unscientific Postscript* (1846), my translation.

4. Ibid.

5. Alvin Plantinga, "Is Belief in God Rational?" in *Rationality and Religious Belief,*

ed. C. F. Delaney, (Notre Dame, IN: University of Notre Dame Press, 1979) and "Reason and Belief in God" in *Faith and Rationality,* eds. A. Plantinga and N. Wolterstorff. (Notre Dame, IN: University of Notre Dame Press, 1983). All references to Plantinga are to these works.

6. Gary Gutting, *Religious Belief and Religious Skepticism.* (Notre Dame, IN: University of Notre Dame Press, 1982), chapter 3.

7. Robert Audi, "Direct Justification and Theistic Belief," in R. Audi and W. Wainwright, eds. *Religious Belief and Moral Commitment* (Ithaca, NY: Cornell University Press, 1986).

8. Anthony Kenny, *Faith and Reason.* (New York: Columbia University Press, 1983).

FOR FURTHER READING

Harrison, Jonathan. *God, Freedom and Immortality*. Aldershot, Eng.: Ashgate, 1999, chapters 27 and 28. Perhaps the most comprehensive study of Philosophy of Religion.

Kenny, Anthony. *Faith and Reason*. New York: Columbia University Press, 1983.

Mackie, J. L. *The Miracle of Theism*. Oxford: Oxford University Press, 1982. An atheist's defense of rationality and against religious belief.

Penelhum, Terrence, ed. *Faith*. New York: Macmillan, 1989. A good collection of classical and contemporary articles on the nature of faith.

Plantinga, Alvin, and Nicholas Wolterstorff, eds. *Faith and Rationality*. Notre Dame, IN: University of Notre Dame Press, 1983. Contains a set of articles defending the rationality of theism from the perspective of Reformed epistemology.

Pojman, Louis. *Religious Belief and the Will*. London: Routledge & Kegan Paul, 1986. An examination of the relationship between faith and reason, arguing for a compatibilist position.

Pojman, Louis, ed. *Philosophy of Religion, An Anthology*, 3d ed. 1998. Contains many of the readings discussed in this chapter.

Swinburne, Richard. *Faith and Reason*. Oxford: Clarendon Press, 1981. A strong defense of the rationality of religious belief.

PART III

The Theory of Knowledge

M.C. ESCHER
Belvedere

10

What Can We Know?

What can we really know? How can we be certain that we have the truth? How can we be certain that we know anything at all? What is knowledge, and how is it different from belief? If we know something, must we know that we know it? Can we have genuine knowledge of the external world, or must we be content with mere appearances?

KNOWLEDGE AND ITS TYPES

The theory of knowledge, or *epistemology* (from the Greek *episteme*, or "knowledge," and *logos*, or "science"—the science of knowing), inquires into the nature of knowledge and justification of belief. Many philosophers, I among them, believe that it is the central area of philosophy, for if philosophy is the quest for truth and wisdom, then we need to know how we are to obtain the truth and justify our beliefs. We need to know how to distinguish the true from the false and justified beliefs from unwarranted beliefs.

If we consult the *Oxford English Dictionary*, we will find the following definition of the verb *know*: "to recognize, to identify, to distinguish, to be acquainted with, to apprehend or comprehend as a fact or truth." This sort of definition puts us in the ballpark in terms of understanding the word, but it is too broad for philosophical purposes. So let us note some typical uses of the verb *know*.

1. I know my friend John very well.
2. I know how to speak English.

3. I know that Washington, D.C., is the capital of the United States.

These three sentences illustrate three different types of knowledge: knowledge by acquaintance, competence knowledge, and descriptive, or propositional, knowledge. We may characterize each type in this way:

1. *Knowledge by Acquaintance.* A person S knows something or someone X, where X is the direct object of the sentence. We have personal and direct experience with the objects in the world, our thoughts, and sensations. I know my friend Robert. I know Chicago (i.e., I am acquainted with it). I know the answer to that question. We know our headache pain, our personal strengths and weaknesses, our own bodies and sense experiences—for example, I am acquainted with a white computer screen appearing before me. We also have direct acquaintance knowledge of our introspective states: our loves and hates, desires, hopes, memory states, beliefs, and doubts. One version of acquaintance knowledge is sometimes called *objectionable knowledge,* where the object of knowledge is not a proposition but a particular object or thing. *Perceptual Knowledge* is often of this kind. We see a blue spot in front of us or hear a sound. Animals and small children, who do not think in propositions, have this kind of belief and knowledge.

2. *Competence Knowledge (sometimes called skill knowledge).* A person S knows how to D (where D stands for an infinitive). This is *know-how.* You know how to speak English and get around campus or at least your room, when it isn't too cluttered. You may know how to ride a bicycle, drive a car, use a computer, speak a foreign language as well as your native one, play the piano, or swim. Competence knowledge involves an ability to perform a skill and may be used consciously or unconsciously. You may not be able to explain how you accomplish your feat to others.

3. *Propositional Knowledge (or descriptive knowledge).* A person S knows *that p* (where p is some statement or proposition). Propositions have truth value; that is, they are true or false. They are the objects of propositional knowledge. When we claim to know *that p* is the case, we are claiming that p is true. Examples of the use of propositional knowledge are "I know that the sun will rise tomorrow"; "I know that Sacramento is the capital of California"; "I know that I have a mind"; and "I know that Columbus discovered America in 1492."

Many philosophers believe that only reflective beings, such as human beings and perhaps some adult primates and cetaceans (e.g., dolphins and porpoises), are able to have this kind of knowledge. An interesting question is whether all propositional knowledge is based on acquaintance knowledge. The model used by those who assert that this relation holds is *perceptual knowledge.* To know that the tree in front of me is green entails having experienced the properties "green" and "tree." Those who deny such dependence argue that the structures of our mind are such that we can have knowledge (or justified beliefs) of some universal propositions that are not dependent on experience. Examples of such propositions are "Every event has a cause"; "All events take place in time"; and "A contradiction cannot be true."

Although a lot more needs to be said about these three kinds of knowledge, I think that the central distinctions will be a good beginning point. Epistemology is primarily interested in this third kind of knowledge, propositional knowledge, and it is the kind of knowledge we shall mainly be examining in the following chapters. But this is only to scratch the surface of what we are concerned with in the theory of knowledge.

The field of epistemology seeks to throw light on the following kinds of questions:

1. What is knowledge? That is, what are its essential characteristics; what are its necessary and sufficient conditions?
2. What is truth? Since truth is the desideratum or goal of cognitive processes, how shall we define this vital concept?
3. Can we know anything at all? Or are we doomed to ignorance about the most important subjects in life?
4. How do we obtain knowledge? Is it through the use of our senses or our intellect, or both?

Let us briefly examine each of these questions.

What Is Knowledge? Can you know something that is really false? Consider these propositions: "The people in the Middle Ages knew that the earth was flat, but they were wrong"; "I know that the U.S. Declaration of Independence was signed in 1945, but it was not"; and "I used to know that Chicago was the capital of the United States, but now I know that Washington, D.C., is." Does it strike you that these are odd statements? Normally, when we use the word "know" or "knowledge," we are making a claim that we possess the truth. Statements like "I know the answer to that question" or "I know that Germany started World War II and not England" assert that we have access to the truth about "that question" or the cause of World War II. So first of all, knowledge entails truth.

THEORIES OF TRUTH

> "What is Truth?" Pontius Pilate to Jesus, just before he delivered him up to be crucified.—JOHN 18:38

What is the Truth? Religions like Christianity, Judaism, Hinduism, Buddhism, and Islam claim to have the Truth. Ideologies like Libertarianism, Marxism, Liberal Democracy, and Fascism all claim to *be* the Truth about how society should be governed. Freudians, Jungians, Skinnerian Behaviorists, and Existentialists debate about which theory of human nature is true. Does empirical science offer the Truth, or something close to it, about human nature and the world in general, or do art, literature, and religion approach more nearly to that ideal? What is Truth?

Throughout this part, we will make reference to the idea of truth. We have noted that it is one of the conditions of knowledge and a desideratum of our cognitive processes. Here I want briefly to consider the meaning of the concept of truth from a philosophical perspective. There have been three main theories of truth in the history of philosophy: the Correspondence Theory, the Coherence Theory, and the Pragmatic Theory. Each has present-day advocates. We want to examine each one of these theories.

The Correspondence Theory of Truth The Correspondence Theory of Truth is the theory that truth consists in the relationship between the proposition (or sentence) and the facts or states of affairs that verify or confirm the propositions. A belief is true if it asserts a proposition that corresponds to facts. This is probably the oldest general theory of truth, going back at least as far as Plato, who wrote:

> The true [sentence] states facts as they are . . . and the false one states things that are other than the facts. . . . In other words, it speaks of things that are not as if they were.[1]

Aristotle refined Plato's definition:

> To say that what is, is not, or that what is not is, is false; but to say that what is, is, and what is not is not, is true; and therefore also he who says that a thing is or is not will say either what is true or what is false.[2]

The Correspondence Theory captures our commonsense intuition that truth depends on something objective (or mind-independent) in the world that makes it true. Beliefs are not made true by mere wishful thinking or imagination but have an objective basis in reality. Ludwig Wittgenstein said that "A proposition is a picture of reality. A proposition is a model or reality as we imagine it."[3]

Consider the following:

1. The book is on the table.
2. The colors in the flag of the United States of America are red, white, and blue.
3. _____ is the true religion. (Fill in the blank any way you wish.)
4. One ought not cause unnecessary suffering.
5. The law of gravity is a true law.

According to this *commonsense* view, or picture theory, we judge sentence 1, ("The book is on the table") to be true if we perceive the book to be on the table and false if it is not on the table. The sentence and what it asserts can be tested for its truth value by observation. Likewise, we can look and see whether the U.S. flag has the three colors claimed in sentence 2. Regarding sentence 3 ("____ is the true religion"), if all the assertions of that religion turn out to be true, then the religion as a whole is true. In sentence 4 ("One ought not cause unnecessary suffering"), the picture theory doesn't seem to do justice to this universal normative statement. Similarly, 5 ("the law of gravity is a true law") fails to fit the picture theory. But they may still represent a wider version of the correspondence theory (see below).

Truth adheres to propositions (or statements), not facts. The locution "These are the true facts," sometimes heard in law courts, is a malapropism. For *facts* are not true or false; they just are. They are the subjects of propositions. We might now ask what is a *proposition*? It is a thought, the meaning of a sentence. For instance, the two sentences "Happy Dancer is a good horse" and "Happy Dancer is a good steed" express the same proposition, since the word *steed* means *horse.* Similarly, the sentences "Es ist heisst," "Il fait chaud," "Det er warm," and "It is warm" all express the same proposition, even though they are sentences in four different languages (German, French, Danish, and English). We speak of propositions as *bearers of truth,* since a proposition is *either* true or false. Propositions purport to assert the truth. In this way, propositions differ from questions and imperatives, which make no assertions (but question or command). Compare the following sentences:

1. The book is on the table.
2. Is the book on the table?
3. Put that book back on the table!

A second term in our formula, *facts* (or *states of affairs*), points to reality itself: the book on the table, the flag with three colors, the number of planets in the solar system. We need not have knowledge of reality for the facts to exist. For example, we may not know the facts about the origin of the universe, but if the universe did have an origin (and is not simply eternal), then it originated the way it did whether anyone knows what that way is or not. We may not know whether God exists, but there is a fact about the matter. Either God does or does not exist.

A third term of the formula, *correspondence,* seems most problematic. Is the correspondence between the proposition and the fact one of identity or close resemblance or simply rough correlation? The proposition "The turkey is in the oven" stands only for the fact that the turkey is in the oven. Unlike the turkey, the proposition cannot be weighed, seen, eaten, or savored. Do all the parts of the sentence have to correspond with items in the world? As mentioned above, Wittgenstein thought of true propositions as accurate pictures of facts in the world, but whereas my picture of the U.S. flag resembles a real flag, the sentence "The colors in the flag of the United States of America are red, white, and blue" neither resembles the flag nor is colored like the flag. No one has successfully shown how to get an exact one-to-one correspondence between the elements in propositions and the elements of the states of affairs to which they correspond. But this may be unnecessary, may require interpreting *correspondence* too literally.

Contemporary versions of the Correspondence Theory attempt to get around the vagueness involved in the idea of correspondence by confining its definition to a simple logical formula, such as the following:

(C)　The proposition *p* is true if and only if *p.*

Or, if you don't like the notion of a proposition, then:

(S)　The sentence *s* is true in language *L* if and only if *s.*

For example, the sentence "Snow is white" is true in English if and only if snow is white.[4]

Perhaps the best way to view beliefs (as the bearers of propositions) and propositions from the point of view of the Correspondence Theory is to see them as maps. They are conventions that locate relationships in reality. Our beliefs are maps by which we steer our way through life. True beliefs will direct us to our goals, whereas false beliefs will not get us to our goals but instead will get us lost.

Or we may resort to Aristotle's simple definition:

> To say that what is, is not, or that what is not, is, is false; but to say that what is, is, and what is not is not, is true; and therefore also he who says that a thing is or is not will say either what is true or what is false.

So sentence 4 ("One ought not cause unnecessary suffering") is true just in case it is morally wrong to cause unnecessary suffering, and sentence 5 ("The law of gravity is a true law") is true just in case it is always the case that objects fall at the required velocity. Otherwise, it is false.

The Coherence Theory of Truth   The Coherence Theory of Truth states that to say a proposition or belief is true is to say that it coheres with a system of other propositions or beliefs. A true proposition is true by virtue of its legitimate membership in the system whose individual parts are related to each other by logical necessity. Truth is the Whole whose parts are harmoniously conjoined.

Often a corollary thesis is connected to the Coherence Theory, resulting in the *Doctrine of Internal Relations.* This doctrine signifies that each member of the system necessarily implies every other member. Hence, the truth test will be a test as to whether the statement is consistent with every other (known) part of the system. At least, it must not contradict what is already known. This doctrine is illustrated by the sorts of internal relationships present in mathematical and logical systems. However, the adherent of the Coherence Theory claims that these sciences are models for all reality. In G. W. Hegel's words, "The real is the rational and the rational is the real."

A further feature of Coherence theories is the *Doctrine of the Degrees of Truth.* If the truth is essentially the whole, then, the individual parts will not be the complete truth, but only contextually true, or true to a certain degree. As finite beings, we can never know the truth, but only partial, fragmented truth. Some sets of beliefs will cohere better than other sets of beliefs, but no one will have a perfectly coherent set. In a sense, all our beliefs are false, since we only have the Truth when we know it as a whole, knowing all the individual parts and their interrelationships.

Hegel's dialectical method is one result of such a doctrine. According to Hegel, the individual parts must be viewed as segments of a dialectical process, The Way of Truth in the world, and must be interpreted teleologically, from the perspective of the End result. The truths of any one period of history are only relatively true, demanding an opposite truth and finding its meaning only in the Absolute Truth, which subsumes all relative truths within itself.

Søren Kierkegaard pointed out that a Coherence system like Hegel's was nicely suited to God, who could see the whole from a perspective beyond time (*sub specie aeternitates*), but it was useless for humans who had to live their lives with partial knowledge and limited information. There may be a Grand Scheme of Things, a Total Truth, but it is presumptive to claim that we are close to such a system.

The opponents of the Coherence Theory point out that there can be two incompatible coherent systems and that even fairy tales and Big Lies are coherent—that is, consistent and mutually supportive—and this fact would seem to undermine it as a definition of truth. They argue that coherence or consistency between propositions is a *necessary* condition for the truth of the propositions in question, but not a sufficient condition. The propositions must somehow correspond to the facts. When we ask the question, "Is the Coherence Theory of truth true?" it seems we want an answer in terms of broad correspondence, not coherence.

The Pragmatic Theory of Truth The Pragmatic Theory of Truth, as propounded by William James, states that a belief is true if it is useful or expedient: "The true is only the expedient in the way of our behaving, expedient in almost any fashion, and expedient in the long run and on the whole course."[5]

Truth seems synonymous with practical success. It is action oriented, aimed at reaching future goals. "Grant an idea or belief to be true, what concrete difference will its being true make in anyone's actual life? . . . What, in short, is the truth's cash-value in experential terms?"

James used this conception of truth to justify religious belief where the objective evidence was insufficient to prove the belief. Our passional nature has a right to choose whether we believe in God or in whatever will make us happy. One religion may be true for you, but a contradictory one true for me. As such, the Pragmatic Theory is a form of cognitive relativism, denying any objective, interest-independent reality, as the proponents of the Correspondence Theory and the Coherence Theory would maintain.

Bertrand Russell argued against the Pragmatic Theory that practical "success" is a dubious criterion for truth. By such a criterion, Nazism would have been true if it had succeeded in leading Germany to win World War II. James's proviso "in the long run and on the whole of the course," seems too vague to help his definition, since we can never know whether our beliefs are true (i.e., successful). For example, we would not be able to know whether our belief that love is better than hate were true until the whole course of history had finished. Likewise, we could not know whether analytic truths were true until we had made an exhaustive investigation into their utility. On the other hand, erroneous beliefs such as medieval beliefs in Aristotle's four elements (cold, hot, wet, and dry) could be said to be true as long as they gave successful results. Such a belief might be said to have been true for millions of people for over 2000 years until John Dalton showed decisively that it was false.

Even if we decided to use the term *true* in the pragmatic sense, we would still need to distinguish it from a more objective kind of truth. Suppose Jim believes against all evidence that he is the smartest person alive, a genius. Suppose his wife and friends all humor him by pretending that he is correct. For Jim, who doesn't know he is of only average intelligence, this belief in his genius is what gives meaning to his life. Because he is so self-confident, he usually performs to his optimum level. He is happy. Still, although he has a "true" belief from the point of view of Pragmatism, we still want to say that there is a misrelationship between his belief and the facts. He doesn't have a true belief as far as the *facts* are concerned, but he does have what constitutes a pragmatically successful belief.

Or suppose Christy believes in astrology. Because the astrological forecasts are so general, she always manages to find something helpful when she consults the daily astrology columns. Astrology is what gives her life meaning and she functions well. Without her astrological faith, her life would be miserable. Granting that she may very well live better because of her beliefs, those of us who believe that astrology is a false worldview (as I believe it is) can't allow that Christy has a *true* belief. Perhaps we need to distinguish *true-P* (P = pragmatic) from *true-C* (C = correspondence or coherence). When someone says, "This is true for me, though it may not be true for you," they may have a pragmatic view of truth.

Pragmatic notions of truth seem to interpret truth either as (1) what a subject *believes* to be true (judged by correspondence criteria) or (2) what a subject can be *justified* in believing. Interpretation 1 reduces truth to belief and interpretation 2 to justification, but we still need a concept that points to facts or the way things are independent of our beliefs or justifications. And so the Pragmatic Theory seems to miss the objective or mind-independent feature of the notion of truth.

At this point we must distinguish between what makes a proposition true and how we determine that it is true. The former is a semantic/metaphysical notion, having to do with how we define or characterize the concept of "truth," while the latter is an epistemic notion. The pragmatist Richard Rorty says that *true* means roughly "what you can defend against all comers, . . . what our peers will . . . let us get away with saying." He goes on to say that the line "between a belief's being justified and its being true is very thin" and that alternative definitions are "what it is better for us to believe" and "warranted assertibility."[6] Similarly, Hilary Putnam speaks of "internal realism," that which we are justified in believing, as a characterization of truth.

But it seems a mistake to conflate truth with justification. First of all, Rorty's definition seems self-refuting. I for one don't think that he has defended the definition against all comers, so if it's true, then it's false.

A.   Truth = df. "what one can defend against all comers."
B.   Rorty hasn't adequately defended A against many people, including me.

If you insist that Rorty has defended A against all comers, only we don't realize it, then aren't you appealing to an objective standard of truth, one which says that something is true whether anyone realizes it or not? If so, then Rorty's definition is mistaken.

To Rorty's claim that truth is "what our peers allow us to get away with saying," why can't we respond, "As one of Rorty's peers, I won't let him get away with saying that"?

Similarly, we may indicate a self-referential problem with Rorty's second definition of truth as "what it is better for us to believe."

C.   Truth = df. A proposition that "it is better for us to believe."
D.   But I don't think it is better to believe C than some other definition of *truth*.

Since we have a conflict over C, we need an objective standard to decide whether it really is better to believe C or not, but what could that be but an objective idea of *truth*. We want to know whether it is true (objectively) that it is better to believe C than not.

But, in case you are dissatisfied with these kinds of arguments, here is a concrete example of the distinction between truth and justification. Suppose that it is the final inning of the final game of the World Series between the Oakland A's and the New York Mets. Each team has won three games. Now, in the last of the ninth, there are two out and your team is winning 3 to 2, but the bases are loaded and the count is 3 and 2 on the batter. The pitch is a curve ball, which just crosses the inside lower corner of the strike zone. But just as you are about to throw your glove into the air to celebrate the championship, the umpire calls "Ball four!" The tying run comes in. You protest, but to no avail. Your team protests on principle, but no one but you really believes that the ball was within the strike zone. When the commotion dies down, the next batter comes to the plate and singles in the winning run. Protest as you do, it is to no avail. The umpire's word is final and is successfully defended to all but you, because no one really believes you.

Suppose that you are correct and the ball really was within the strike zone. The fact that you can't successfully defend your position is unfortunate, even deplorable, considering the stakes involved, but it has nothing to do with your lacking the fact of the matter. It is true that the ball was within the strike zone, regardless of what others believe. There can be true beliefs and propositions that can't be successfully defended (or justified) "against all comers," but so what? Justification is not the same thing as truth. Nor is it relevant to ask which proposition it is "better to believe," for it could turn out that going along with the umpire's decision in these kinds of cases has positive utilitarian consequences. But, again, this has nothing to do with the truth itself. Perhaps we can speak of *social truth* as that which a consensus of your peers believes at any time, but then we need to point out that from an objective perspective, social truth can be false. It would be better to reserve the term *truth* for that which communicates or corresponds to the facts. I've included a general survey of the main theories of truth in the appendix of this book.

Let us sum up our discussion of theories of truth. Three classical theories of truth are the Correspondence Theory of Truth, which views truth as an appropriate relationship between a statement and the facts it represents; the Coherence Theory of Truth, which views Truth holistically as a mutually supportive set of statements that together depict reality; and the Pragmatic Theory of Truth, which equates truth with usefulness, that which works "in the long run and on the whole course." We noted strengths and weaknesses in each theory.

In this part I follow J. L. Mackie in holding to the commonsense notion of truth first articulated by Aristotle. It is compatible with Alfred Tarski's *Disquotational,* or *Semantic Theory* and the *Classical Correspondence Theory* of Thomas Aquinas, Bertrand Russell, and others. Although I accept the idea of correspondence, I don't interpret correspondence as isomorphic between statements and facts. Rather, the sentence adequately represents the way things are.

Of course, we may be wrong about our knowledge claims. The drunk claims to know that there are pink elephants in the room with him; the child claims to know that Santa Claus exists; and one witness of an accident may claim to know how it happened but may contradict the report of another witness. I may have good evidence that I will inherit a fortune, so that I claim to know it, but, alas, be mistaken. We often falsely believe that we know. Sometimes the evidence on which our knowledge claim is based is inadequate or misleading or we misremember or misperceive. Sometimes our knowledge claims are contradicted by those of others, as when two people of different religious faiths each claims that his or hers is the only true religion or when one person claims with certainty that abortion is morally wrong and the other person claims with equal certainty that it is morally permissible.

KNOWLEDGE AND BELIEF

Knowledge involves possessing the truth, but *how* does it possess it? When you know something, must you be in a special psychological state? Or is knowing just a special kind of correct believing? Plato and Descartes held that knowledge was different from believing, involving an infallible state of mind, so that if you found yourself in that knowledge state of mind, you would be guaranteed to possess the truth. Belief, on the other hand, was a kind of uncertainty, "opinion." Whereas knowledge implied absolute certainty, belief implied only a high probability. No doubt there are self-evident truths, such as knowledge of your own existence, simple mathematical truths, and possibly some psychological states (e.g., "I know that I'm surprised"), but it seems doubtful that a sharp line of demarcation can be drawn. People often feel absolutely certain about all sorts of things. Mary is absolutely certain that the Catholic Church is the one and only true religion, whereas Hussein is just as certain that Islam alone deserves that distinction. A person in the Middle Ages might have been absolutely certain that the earth was flat and that the sun revolved around the earth, whereas we may be absolutely certain of just the opposite.

It seems wiser to see the state of knowledge as a type of believing—a type of believing what is true. Perhaps it is a type of true believing where *certainty* is required. How much certainty? Absolute certainty? This seems too strong. Some philosophers like John Pollock and A. Phillips Griffiths argue that knowledge does not require belief. You may know the truth of proposition (*p*) without believing it. Phillips Griffiths suggests that it is possible for a person to know that *p* even where he doubts *p*. He asks us to consider a child who is terrorized by a brutal teacher. "He may be so put off by fear that he makes mistakes or hesitates about things that he knows perfectly well. As a well-informed, conscientious, intelligent boy, he really does know the answers; yet on particularly tense occasions, he really does doubt that the correct answer that springs to his lips is correct."[7]

Is Phillips Griffiths correct about disbelieving what you know? I think that these borderline cases are difficult to be sure about and that before we can be confident of our answers, we need a full-blown epistemology. Nevertheless, let me make an important distinction that may throw light on this problem by suggesting that in a way, the terrorized boy does not know the answer—and in a way he does. We may divide beliefs into two varieties: *occurrent* and *dispositional*. An occurent belief is one that you are conscious of at the moment. If I ask you, "How are you feeling now?" you will probably find yourself believing something about your present state of mind. Right now, I believe that I have five fingers on each hand, and that it is raining outside. Those are occurrent beliefs.

But there is also a different type of belief, one that I would become conscious of under suitable conditions. I have not thought about my late younger brother, Everett, for days, but suddenly I realize that today is the tenth anniversary of his tragic death. Even though I had not thought about this fact for days, I believed it every day for the past ten years. You too have dispositional beliefs. You probably haven't thought about Venus or Jupiter lately, but you probably have had the dispositional belief that each of them is a planet and that they are a long distance away from Earth. You have dispositional beliefs about love being better than hate, happiness better than sadness, peace better than violence, and getting an A in a course being a lot more satisfying than failing it. While we are stocked full of dispositional beliefs, we can only handle a few occurrent beliefs at any one time.

Let us return to our terrorized, conscientious, intelligent boy. We may surmise that *dispositionally* he knew the answer to the question because he believed it in the right way, but we may also say that when it came to consciousness he did so under emotionally stressful conditions, so that he lacked the normal psychological certainty that usually accompanies such beliefs. The *occurrent* aspect of believing was not completely successful, but he possessed his data as surely as he possessed his gender, size, and name. The lesson of this example is that one need not always *know that one knows* in order to have knowledge.

Illustrations of knowing without knowing that you know abound. A child knows who its mother is and gradually comes to learn that the building block it has placed behind itself will still be there when it goes for it in a couple of minutes, without being self-conscious about its knowledge. I believe that many of my memory reports are knowledge, but I may not be able to give these second-order beliefs (about my memory claims) the kind of backing that knowledge would require. You probably knew that you were reading this paragraph before you realized that you knew that you knew that you were. But now that you think about it, you probably do know that you know this. Well, you could doubt it. We'll come to that possibility in a moment.

Knowledge and Justification So far we have concluded that knowledge is a sort of true belief. But it is more than just believing truly. Imagine that I am holding up four cards so that I can see their faces but you can see only their backs. I ask you to guess what types of cards I am holding. You feel a hunch or a weak belief that I am holding up four aces and correctly announce, "You are holding four aces in your hands." Although we both possess the truth, I have something you don't—an adequate justification for my belief that there are four aces in my hand. You have gotten the right answer accidentally, whereas I have gotten it by a more reliable process. Even a stopped clock is accidentally right twice a day. So knowledge differs from mere true belief in that the knower has nonaccidental grounds or, in normal philosophical parlance, an adequate "justification" for claiming to have true beliefs.

Now the question shifts to the nature of justification. What is *justification*? In general, *justification* is a normative term, indicating meeting an acceptable standard or doing the right thing. Examples of the use of justification language in ethics are "The end doesn't justify the means" and "President Truman's decision to bomb Hiroshima in 1945 was (or was not) justified, all things considered." There is also a pragmatic or prudential use of justification, as in "Linda's decision to get an MBA was justified since she would thereby increase her chances of getting a promotion."

Epistemic justification signifies meeting acceptable epistemic standards, having positive epistemic status. As reason-giving creatures, we seek to support our beliefs and knowledge claims in ways similar to the way we support moral and prudential claims. If someone asks you "Why do you believe _____ will win the election?" you cite the grounds or evidence for your belief: "Because the polls show _____ to have a significant lead over the other candidates." Likewise, we seek to support our moral, religious, political, and philosophical beliefs with good evidence. A general assumption is that, all things being equal, the more evidence you have or the better justified you are regarding a given belief, the more likely it is that your belief is true. But can we justify that assumption?

Guessing that I had four aces in my hands was not an example of knowledge. Hunches, guesses, conjectures, and wishful thinking do not yield cases of knowledge even if they are true, for they are not the kinds of things that justify beliefs. But what kinds of things do justify beliefs? Must the evidence be undeniable, such as when we believe that "2 + 2 = 4" or when we feel pain and cannot help but believe that we are in pain? Can we have sufficient evidence to justify belief in physical objects? Belief in other minds? Beliefs about metaphysical propositions, such as the existence of God or freedom of the will? How much evidence must one have before he or she can claim to know a belief is true? We will examine this problem as it pertains to skepticism and perception in Chapters 11 and 12.

Can We Know Anything at All? Let us turn to our third question: *Can we know anything at all?* Or are we doomed to ignorance about the most important subjects in life? Could it be that our most treasured beliefs are merely unjustified biases, that even our sense of being a self is an illusion? Could it be that we really know nothing at all? If knowledge entails being completely justified in our beliefs, do we ever possess complete justification for a belief? Could we be systematically deceived by Nature or an evil demon? *Skepticism* is the theory that we do not have any knowledge or at least that we do not know most of the things we claim to know. *Moderate Skepticism* claims that we cannot be completely justified regarding any of our beliefs. *Weak Skepticism* holds that we can know some obvious truths, such as mathematical and logical truths, but not metaphysical or empirical truths. *Radical Skepticism* goes even further and claims that we cannot even be certain of the belief that we cannot be completely certain that any of our beliefs are true. We cannot even know that we cannot have knowledge!

Can you defeat the skeptic? We will examine arguments for and against skepticism, as well as the historical significance of skepticism in Chapter 11.

How Do We Obtain Knowledge? We turn to our fourth question: *How do we obtain knowledge?* Is it through the use of our senses or our intellect, or both? There are two classic theories on the acquisition of knowledge: *Rationalism* and *Empiricism*. Rationalism may be a misleading name for the first theory since according to both theories we use reason in acquiring knowledge. Rationalists simply believe that reason is sufficient to discover truth, whereas Empiricists hold that all knowledge originates through sense perception (that is, through seeing, hearing, touching, tasting, and smelling).

The first comprehensive Rationalist theory was put forth by Plato (427–347 B.C.), who distinguishes between two approaches to knowledge: sense perception and reason.[8] Sense perception cannot be adequate for possessing the truth because its objects are subject to change and decay. All one gets in this way of apprehending things is beliefs about particular objects. Knowledge, on the other hand, goes beyond the particular and grasps universal *Ideas* or *Forms*. Plato argues that all knowing is the knowing of objects, so that these Ideas must exist in the really real world, the World of Being. The philosopher is a person who works his way through the World of Becoming, the empirical world, to this higher reality. Plato uses "The Allegory of the Cave" to illustrate his doctrine:

> Imagine a group of prisoners who from infancy have had their necks and legs chained to posts within a dark cave. Behind them is a raised walkway on which people and animals travel to and fro, bearing diverse objects. Behind the walkway is a large fire which projects the shadows of the people, animals, and objects onto the wall in front of the prisoners. The shadows on the wall grow and diminish, move up and down and around as the fire behind the objects wafts and wanes. But the prisoners do not know that the shadows are merely appearances of real objects. They take the shadows for reality, talk about them as though they were real, name them, reidentify them, and incorporate their knowledge of the various forms into their social life. Their lives are centered on the shadows.
>
> Now imagine that someone tries to liberate one of the prisoners from the cave. At first, the prisoner kicks and screams as he is forcibly moved from the only home and social milieu he has ever known. Being dragged through the cave against his will, he is, at last, taken outside, where the dazzling bright sun's light blinds him. Our prisoner cries to be allowed to be returned to his safe shelter in the cave, but the way is closed. Gradually, his eyes adjust to the sunlight, and he is able to see the beautifully colored flowers and wide spreading branches of oak trees and hear the songs of birds and watch the play of animals. Delighted, his powers of sight increase until, at last, he is able to look at the bright sun itself and not be harmed.
>
> But now his liberator, who has become his friend and teacher, instructs him to return to the cave to teach the other prisoners about the real world and to get them to give up their chains and journey upward to the sunlight. But our hero quakes with fear at such an ordeal, for he wants no part of that dark, dismal existence, preferring the light of day to the dark of the abyss.
>
> He is told that it is his duty to go, and so he makes his way into the cave again. Returning to his chained mates, he tells them that the shadows are merely illusions and that a real world of sunlight and beauty exists above outside the cave. While he is proclaiming this gospel, his former mates grab him, beat him for impugning their belief and value system, and put him to death.
>
> But every now and then the liberator comes back, drags one or two prisoners out of the cave against their will, and teaches them to enjoy the light. Such is the process of educating the soul to perceive the Truth, the form of the Good.

The bridge between the World of Being and the World of Becoming is *Innate Ideas.* Plato held that learning is really a recollecting of what we learned in a previous existence. He believed in reincarnation, that in a previous existence we saw all essential truths but have lost awareness of them through birth. The educator should be a spiritual midwife who stimulates the labors of the soul, so that a person recalls what he or she really possesses but has forgotten. In the *Meno*, Socrates (Plato's mouthpiece) claims to demonstrate this doctrine of recollection of Innate Ideas by teaching geometry to an uneducated slave. Drawing a square in the sand, Socrates asks the boy to try to double the area of the figure. Through a process of questions and answers, in which the boy consults his own unschooled understanding, he eventually performs this feat. He seems to have "brought up knowledge from within." Similarly, Socrates argues, we can teach virtue only by causing our auditors to recollect what they have forgotten about the Good.

Types of Propositional Knowledge Plato thought that all knowledge was *a priori knowledge* (that which is prior), which one has independently of sense experience, as opposed to *a posteriori knowledge* (that which is posterior), which is contingent, empirical knowledge that comes to us from experience through the five senses. Ordinary empirical beliefs, according to Plato, unless they are related to the Forms, are not knowledge but simply unstable appearances. Examples of candidates for a priori knowledge are the mathematical equation $2 + 2 = 4$, the statement "Nothing that is green all over is red," and the statement "Not both p and not-p." You don't have to appeal to experience in order to see that these propositions are true. As Immanuel Kant (1724–1804) said,

> Though all our knowledge begins with experience, it does not follow that it all arises out of experience. For it may well be that even our empirical knowledge is made up of what we receive through impressions and of what our own faculty of knowledge supplies from itself.[9]

Kant refined these notions, making a posteriori knowledge refer to judgments that depend on empirical experience, and a priori knowledge refer to those judgments that do not depend on empirical experience.[10] But he went further. He took the linguistic or semantic notions of analytic and synthetic statements and combined them with a priori and a posteriori knowledge. *Analytic statements* are those in which the predicate is already contained in the subject (e.g., "All mothers are women," in which the subject term "mother" already contains the idea of "woman," so that we learn nothing new in our statement). *Synthetic statements* are just the opposite; the predicate term adds something new about the subject. For example, "Mary is now a mother" is a sentence in which we learn something new about Mary.

The Empiricists John Locke (1632–1704) and David Hume (1711–1776) argued that at birth our minds are an empty slate, a *tabula rasa,* on which the world via our sense organs made impressions that, in turn, produce ideas.[11] All knowledge of the world is a posteriori knowledge and knowledge of logic and mathematics is purely analytic and a priori knowledge.

A classification of the relevant concepts is as follows:

1. Epistemologic Categories
   a. A priori knowledge does *not* depend on evidence from sense experience (Plato's Innate Ideas and Leibniz's "Truths of Reason"), for example, mathematics and logic.
   b. A posteriori knowledge depends on evidence from sense experience (Plato's Appearance and Leibniz's "Truths of Fact"), for example, empirical knowledge.
2. Semantic Categories
   a. Analytic: The predicate is contained in the subject and is explicative, not ampliative (e.g., "All mothers are women").
   b. Synthetic: The predicate is not contained in the subject but adds something to the subject and is ampliative, not explicative (e.g., "Mary is now a mother").

Kant rejected the theory that there were only two kinds of knowledge: a priori and a posteriori. Combining a priori knowledge with synthetic propositions, he argued that we have a third kind of knowledge, *synthetic a priori knowledge*—knowledge that may begin with experience but does not arise from experience, but that is nevertheless known directly.

The essential claim of those who hold to synthetic a priori knowledge is that the mind is able to grasp connections between ideas (concepts) that are not strictly analytically related. For example, we simply know upon reflection that all events have causes or that time and space are real without having an empirical proof or logical argument. Kant thought that our knowledge of mathematical truths was really synthetic a priori, rather than analytic. Likewise, the moral law, which dictates that we ought to act in such a way that we could will that the maxims of our actions would be universal laws, is known without appeal to experience. Other philosophers, such as Descartes and Søren Kierkegaard, believed that we have synthetic a priori knowledge of God's existence and the immortality of the soul.

Let us turn to Empiricism. *Empiricism,* the classic rival of Rationalism, is the doctrine that all knowledge originates in the senses. John Locke systematically attacked the notions of innate ideas and a priori knowledge, arguing that if our claims to knowledge are to make sense they must be derived from the world of sense experience.

> Let us then suppose the mind to be, as we say, white paper, void of all characters, without any ideas; how comes it by that vast store, which the busy and boundless fancy of man has painted on it with an almost endless variety? Whence has it all the materials of reason and knowledge? To this I answer, in one word, from experience: in that all our knowledge is founded.[12]

All knowledge comes through sensory experience. Our ideas are a product of sensory impressions. From simple ideas, like brown and hard and square, we construct complicated ideas like "a hard brown square." If an idea or belief cannot be analyzed in terms of these basic foundational ideas, it is unworthy of belief.

Locke goes on to set forth a Representational Theory of Knowledge, which claims that the core of what we know is caused by the world itself, though some qualities are the products of the way our perceptual mechanisms are affected by the world. The former qualities, called *primary qualities,* such as motion, size, shape, and number, are the true building blocks of knowledge, because these qualities are accurate representatives of the objective features of the world. On the other hand, *secondary qualities* are modes of apprehending the primary qualities. Examples of these qualities are taste, color, odor, and sound. Because the color or taste of an object can be different to different people or to the same person at different times, secondary qualities are subjective, even though they are caused by the objective primary qualities. We will examine these concepts further in Chapter 12 when we treat the problem of perception.

SUMMARY

In this chapter we have examined various types of knowledge and noticed that philosophy is most concerned with prepositional knowledge (having the formula *S knows that p*). We have examined the definition of knowledge, as true, justified belief. Then we examined various theories of truth, concluding that the Correspondence Theory makes the most sense. We also examined the relationship between belief and justification; and we looked at two types of propositional knowledge (*a priori* and *a posteriori*). In the next chapter we shall consider whether we can know anything at all and in Chapter 12, the problem of perceptual knowledge.

QUESTIONS FOR DISCUSSION

1. Distinguish three ways we use the verb *know*. Which way is most important from the view of the theory of knowledge?

2. Some people believe that we should concentrate on competence knowledge more than we do—and even make it the basic epistemic type (Michael Polanyi seems to do this sometimes; see "Further Reading"). Knowledge is a result of a holistic competence, an ability to perceive, reflect, *and* act correctly. Take riding a bicycle. One cannot easily separate the propositional knowledge, acquaintance knowledge, and competence knowledge in such a process. One acts holistically, integrating all of these types, and the process involves personal interest, concentration, and even emotions—thus going against the standard model of detached, impartial reasoning. Do you find this more existential type of knowledge appealing? Explain your answer.

3. Can there be false knowledge? Why or why not?

4. Can there be false beliefs? Can you name any of your false beliefs? Why or why not? Try to define the concept of "belief."

5. What is the best definition of truth? Critically examine the three theories of truth discussed in this chapter. What do people mean when they say, "This is true for me, though not necessarily for you?" Can (some) truth be mind-dependent? Consider ideas in the imagination. Explain.

6. Discuss the relation of justification to knowledge. What do we mean by the justification of a belief? Does this imply that we are irresponsible if we believe propositions without being able to give our evidence? Laurence BonJour writes:

> We cannot, in most cases at least, bring it about directly that our beliefs are true, but we can presumably bring it about directly . . . that they are epistemically justified.
>
> It follows that one's cognitive endeavors are epistemically justified only if and to the extent that they are aimed at this goal, which means very roughly that one accepts all and only those beliefs which one has good reason to think are true. To accept a belief in the absence of such a reason . . . is to neglect the pursuit of truth; such acceptance is, one might say, *epistemically irresponsible*. My contention here is that the idea of avoiding such irresponsibility, of being epistemically responsible in one's believings, is the core of the notion of epistemic justification. *The Structure of Empirical Knowledge*, 8.

Evaluate BonJour's claim as best you can at this point. The question is whether we have epistemic duties. In what sense can we be said to be responsible for the beliefs we have? Can we be held accountable for our beliefs? Take an example of a prejudicial belief. Is the prejudiced person responsible for his or her prejudicial beliefs?

7. The skeptic asks how it is possible to know anything at all. Does the skeptic's question make sense to you? What could he or she mean by "total skepticism"? We will get to this problem in the next chapter, so it would be helpful if you formulated your initial response before you read the text.

8. What is the difference between Rationalism and Empiricism?

9. Distinguish between a priori and a posteriori knowledge. Then go over Kant's notion of synthetic a priori knowledge. Do you agree with his view that we cannot think about the world apart from such concepts? Do you agree that time, space, causality, and arithmetic are examples of such knowledge?

10. Why do empiricists reject the notion of synthetic a priori knowledge?

NOTES

1. Plato, *Sophist,* 263.

2. Aristotle, *Metaphysics* IV:7, 1011b.

3. Ludwig Wittgenstein, *Tractatus Logico Philosophicus* (London: Routledge & Kegan Paul, 1921), 401.

4. This version was first put forth by the Polish-born logician Alfred Tarski (1901–1983).

5. William James, *Essays in Pragmatism* (New York: Hafner, 1948), 170.

6. Richard Rorty, *Philosophy and the Mirror of Nature* (Princeton, NJ: Princeton University Press, 1979), 176, 308. He opposes the metaphysical/semantical notion of truth as representation, saying:

> The aim of all such [representational] explanation is to make truth more than what Dewey calls "warranted assertibility": more than what our peers will, *ceteris paribus,* let us get away with saying. Such explanation, when ontological, usually takes the form of a redescription of the object of knowledge so as to bridge the gap between it and the knowing subject. To choose between the approaches is to choose between truth as "what is good for us to believe" and truth as "contact with reality."

Dewey's term "warranted assertibility" signifies what a speaker in a given social context is justified in asserting. The idea is that the social context, rather than some eternal perspective, defines justification and is the closest we can come to the truth. See also Hilary Putnam, *Meaning and the Moral Sciences* (London: Routledge & Kegan Paul, 1978), and *Reason, Truth and History* (Cambridge, Eng.: Cambridge University Press, 1981).

7. A. Phillips Griffiths, *Knowledge and Belief* (Oxford: Oxford University Press, 1967), 10.

8. Plato, "The Republic." In *Plato: The Collected Dialogues,* ed. Edith Hamilton and Huntington Cairns (Princeton, NJ: Princeton University Press, 1982). See especially Books VI and VII.

9. Kant, *Critique of Pure Reason,* trans. Normal Kemp Smith (New York: St. Martin's Press, 1969), 41.

10. Ibid., 41–44.

11. John Locke, *An Essay Concerning Human Understanding.* (Oxford: Oxford University Press, 1924), Book II, Chapter 1, 121.

12. Ibid.

FOR FURTHER READING

Audi, Robert. *Belief, Justification, and Knowledge.* Belmont, CA: Wadsworth, 1988. An excellent short introduction to the subject.

Audi, Robert. *Epistemology.* Routledge, 1998. A thorough, penetrating contemporary introduction to epistemology.

Blanshard, Brand. *The Nature of Thought,* vol. 2. London: Allen & Unwin, 1939.

BonJour, Laurence. *The Structure of Empirical Knowledge.* Cambridge, MA: Harvard University Press, 1985. A comprehensive treatment. Advanced but well written.

Capaldi, Nicholas. *Human Knowledge.* New York: Pegasus, 1969. A helpful, accessible introduction to the subject.

Chisholm, Roderick. *Theory of Knowledge,* 3d ed. Englewood Cliffs, NJ: Prentice-Hall, 1988. A rich exposition of the major problems.

Dancy, Jonathan. *Contemporary Epistemology.* New York: Basil Blackwell, 1985. This book defends a coherentist position against foundationalism.

Dancy, Jonathan, and Ernest Sosa, eds. *A Companion to Epistemology.* London: Basil Blackwell, 1992. An excellent comprehensive encyclopedia of epistemology.

Davidson, Donald. *Truth and Interpretation.* Oxford: Clarendon Press, 1984.

Horwich, Paul. *Truth.* London: Basil Blackwell, 1990.

James, William. *The Meaning of Truth.* London: Longmans Green, 1909.

Lehrer, Keith. *Theory of Knowledge.* Boulder, CO: Westview, 1990. A thorough and thoughtful survey of the subject.

Moser, Paul, Dwayne H. Mulder, and J. D. Trout. *The Theory of Knowledge.* New York: Oxford University Press, 1998.

O'Connor, D. J., and Brian Carr. *Introduction to the Theory of Knowledge.* Minneapolis: University of Minnesota Press, 1982. A good survey of the basic issues.

Plantinga, Alvin. *Warrant and Proper Function.* Oxford: Oxford University Press, 1993. A penetrating and comprehensive work in contemporary epistemology.

Plantinga, Alvin. *Warrant: The Current Debate.* Oxford: Oxford University Press, 1993. A thorough critique of contemporary epistemology. An advanced but clearly written text, so that a beginning philosopher can understand most of it without too much trouble.

Pojman, Louis. *The Theory of Knowledge: Classical and Contemporary Readings.* 2d ed. Belmont, CA: Wadsworth, 1999. A comprehensive anthology containing many authors referred to and works used in this part of our book.

Polanyi, Michael. *Personal Knowledge.* Chicago: University of Chicago Press, 1958. An important work on nonstandard accounts of knowledge, especially competence knowledge.

Pollock, John. *Contemporary Theories of Knowledge.* Totowa, NJ: Rowman & Littlefield, 1986. A lively challenging study that focuses primarily on epistemic justification.

Rorty, Richard. *Mind and the Mirror of Nature.* Princeton, NJ: Princeton University Press, 1979.

Rorty, Richard. *Philosophy and the Mirror of Nature.* Princeton, NJ: Princeton University Press, 1979. A critique of the whole enterprise of epistemology, aiming to replace it with "social knowledge" and intellectual conversation.

Russell, Bertrand. *The Problems of Philosophy.* Oxford: Oxford University Press, 1912. A classic—pithy, succinct, and engaging. Contains a classic treatment of the correspondence theory of truth.

Steup, Matthias. *Contemporary Epistemology.* Englewood Cliffs, NJ: Prentice-Hall, 1996.

Wittgenstein, Ludwig. *Tractatus Logico-Philosophicus.* London: Routledge and Kegan Paul, 1922.

11

Skepticism

C an we know anything at all? Can we ever be certain that we have the truth?
If we know something, must we know that we know it? If so, can we know
that we have knowledge? Are any truths so certain as to exclude all reasonable doubt? Is some knowledge infallible or is everything subject to some legitimate doubt? Can we know that there is an external world, that we are truly perceiving the objects that we seem to be perceiving? Or could we be systematically
deceived, so that none of the things we seem to be seeing, hearing, feeling, and so
forth are what they appear to be? Could we be wrong about all our empirical
beliefs? How do we know that the future will be like the past or, even, that the
past existed at all, let alone as we seem to have remembered it? Can we have
knowledge of other minds, or could it be that other people are simply robots or
figments of our imagination? What can we know and how can we be sure that
we have knowledge?

THE CHALLENGE OF SKEPTICISM

Skepticism is the theory that we do not have any knowledge (or almost no knowledge). We cannot be completely certain that practically any of our beliefs are true.
More precisely, two types of skeptics exist. The *global skeptic* asserts and generally
argues that we can know nothing or next to nothing. The *local,* or *mitigated, skeptic,* argues that while we can have knowledge of some general and specific truths,
we have no knowledge about the external world, induction, other minds, the self,
immortality, free will, and other metaphysical truths. Traditionally, one who rejects

skepticism and claims that we do have knowledge is a "dogmatist," from the Greek word *dogma* for opinion or belief. I will use the term *dogmatist* in its original epistemological sense.

I am in my study (at least I strongly believe I am) in a house in Berkeley, California. I see a white wall with a brown shelf before me. On the left-hand side of the shelf are six Russian dolls (which successively fit into the next largest). How do I know that I am really in my study or that the house I'm in is in Berkeley? Can I be sure that the wall in front of me is white or that there really are six Russian dolls on the shelf projecting from the wall? I, like most people, sometimes dream. Like many people my dreams are so vivid that while I am dreaming, I believe the events in my dream to be occurring. I have even had dreams within my dreams. Could I be dreaming now? How would I prove that I was not dreaming?

Or could I be hallucinating? My mother claims that after my twenty-year-old brother died in an automobile accident he appeared to her two or three times while she was sitting alone in her bedroom. I think she was hallucinating. Could I be hallucinating now? How do you know that you are not hallucinating now?

Or suppose that a malevolent demon exists who is causing you to have all the appearances that you're now having. Do you know for sure that such a demon is not affecting you, causing you to have the kinds of sense experiences that you're having?

Or you are a brain suspended in a large vat full of chemical solution in a neuroscientist's laboratory and wired to a computer that is causing you to have the simulated experiences of what you now seem to be experiencing. The neuroscientist has programmed your brain to "feel" and "touch" and "see" and "hear" the very appearances you are now having. Could you tell the difference between these appearances and reality? Can you demonstrate that you are not a brain in a vat, being manipulated by a neuroscientist (or a whole team of them)? Even your attempt to prove that you are not a brain in a vat has been programmed into you by the neuroscientist. Even your comparison of your beliefs with your perceptions has been caused by this superprogram. Your vat is your destiny.

How do you know that you are not the only person who exists and that everyone else is not a robot programmed to "listen" to a robot teacher; to speak, ask questions, and smile; to sit in class and take notes and write exams; to stand up after class and walk out the door? Can you prove that other people have consciousness? Have you ever felt their consciousness, their pain, or their sense of the color blue? How do you know that other persons really exist?

Do you have any answers to these questions? Do you have an argument establishing that you have some knowledge? Can you refute the skeptic?

DESCARTES

The classic work on global skepticism is *Meditations* by René Descartes (1596–1650). In this work, Descartes places all his previous knowledge in doubt in order to build a secure house of knowledge.

> It is now some years since I detected how many were the false beliefs that I had from my earliest youth admitted as true, and how doubtful was everything I had

since constructed on this basis; and from that time I was convinced that I must once for all seriously undertake to rid myself of all the opinions which I had formerly accepted, and commence to build anew from the foundation, if I wanted to establish any firm and permanent structure in the sciences.

He begins by showing that sensory experience is unstable:

All that up to the present time I have accepted as most true and certain I have learned either from the senses or through the senses; but it is sometimes proved to me that these senses are deceptive, and it is wiser not to trust entirely to any thing by which we have once been deceived. . . . Reason persuades me that I ought to withhold my assent from matters which are not entirely certain and indubitable.[1]

Certainty demands reliable sources, but the senses are fickle and fallible, unreliable witnesses, and wisdom teaches that unreliable witnesses are not to be completely trusted, so that I should withhold assent from them.[2] The unreliable witness argument can be formulated like this:

1. Whatever has been found to be an unreliable witness should (prudentially) never again be trusted, since I can never be sure that it is not presently deceiving me.
2. The senses have sometimes been found to be unreliable witnesses.
3. ∴ The senses should not be trusted.

Is this a sound argument? No. From the fact that someone or something sometimes deceives me, I cannot infer that it may always deceive me—at least not without supplementary reasons. I may have evidence that the senses or witnesses sometimes do not deceive me. Descartes recognizes that there are some experiences that only a lunatic would doubt, such as, that this body is mine, and that I have two hands and feet. All the unreliable witness argument does is make us aware of our fallibility, that we are sometimes mistaken about what we take ourselves to be perceiving or remembering. Fallibility doesn't entail universal skepticism. But, it may cause us to become aware of the possibility of skeptical situations. It checks the dogmatist, the person who is certain of his or her beliefs, and forces him or her to consider the possibility of the skeptical hypothesis.

I said that Descartes recognizes that there are some experiences that only a lunatic would doubt, such as, that this body is mind and that I have two hands and feet. But on deeper reflection these believes too should be called into question. For I sometimes sleep and therein dream:

How often it has happened to me that in the night I dreamt that I found myself in this particular place, that I was dressed and seated near the fire, whilst in reality I was lying undressed in bed! At this moment it does indeed seem to me that it is with eyes awake that I am looking at this paper; that this head which I move is not asleep, that it is deliberately and of set purpose that I extend my hand and perceive it; what happens in sleep does not appear so clear not so distinct as does all this. But in thinking over this I remind myself that on many occasions I have in sleep been deceived by similar illusions, and in dwelling carefully on this reflection I see so manifestly that there are no certain indications by which we may clearly distinguish wakefulness from sleep that I am lost in astonishment. And my astonishment is such that it is almost capable of persuading me that I now dream.[3]

Barry Stroud comments on this passage:

With this thought, if he is right, Descartes has lost the whole world. He knows what he is experiencing, he knows how things appear to him, but he does not know whether he is in fact sitting by the fire with a piece of paper in his hand. It is, for him, exactly as if he were sitting by the fire with a piece of paper in his hand, but he does not know whether there really is a fire or a piece of paper there or not; he does not know what is really happening in the world around him. He realizes that if everything he can ever learn about what is happening in the world around him comes to him through the senses, but he cannot tell by means of the senses whether or not he is dreaming, then all the sensory experiences he is having are compatible with his merely dreaming of a world around him while in fact that world is very different from the way he takes it to be. That is why he thinks he must find some way to tell that he is not dreaming. . . . He thinks it is eminently reasonable to insist that if he is to know that he is sitting by the fire he must know that he is not dreaming that he is sitting by the fire.[4]

I could be dreaming or hallucinating or a demon could be deceiving me about my experiences. The essential point is that we do not have a criterion to distinguish illusory experience from veridical perception. The argument may be formulated in this way:

1. In order to have knowledge we need to be able to tell the difference between a hallucination (deception) and a perception. (Where there is no relevant difference, no epistemological distinction can be made.)
2. It is impossible to distinguish between a hallucination (or deception) and a normal perception.
3. ∴ We do not know whether any of our perceptual beliefs are true.

If this is so, then we do not have knowledge of the external world. All our experiences could be illusory. Not only Descartes, but all of us have "lost the whole world."

But Descartes goes on to doubt even our mathematical judgments. He imagines that an ingenious demon is deceiving him about everything, even about the most secure mathematical sums, so that it is possible that he is mistaken about adding $2 + 2$.

This seems preposterous. Surely, we know that "$2 + 2 = 4$" and many other logical and mathematical truths as well. Surely, we know that a contradiction cannot be true, that the laws of logic are valid, and that nothing that is black is at the same time white. Perhaps, but the skeptic's challenge is for you to give a cogent reason defeating his or her challenge. If you can't demonstrate or give a cogent reason to show that you are not dreaming or are not a brain in a vat, how can you be sure you know anything that you seem to know?

Descartes, himself, thought he could defeat the skeptic. First, he reasoned that if he was doubting everything, he could be sure of one thing: that he existed. For if I am doubting, I must exist in order to doubt. Doubting is a form of thinking, so I must exist in order to think. *Cogito ergo sum*: I think therefore I exist.

[Suppose] that there is some deceiver or other, very powerful and very cunning, who ever employs his ingenuity in deceiving me. Then without doubt I exist also if he deceives me, and let him deceive me as much as he will, he can never cause me to be nothing so long as I think that I am something. So that after having reflected well and carefully examined all things, we must come to the definite conclusion that this proposition: I am, I exist, is necessarily true each time that I pronounce it, or that I mentally conceive it.[5]

While I think that I am thinking, I cannot doubt that I exist. I have certain, indubitable knowledge of my own existence.

From this one item of certain knowledge, Descartes derives a criterion of certainty. Self-knowledge is self-authenticating. It is clear and distinct, self-evident. Generalizing from this, he concludes that whatever is clear and distinct is true and cannot be doubted. It is knowledge. He thinks that the existence of God is such a clear and distinct idea or is deduced from ideas that are clear and distinct. When the question arises, "How do you know that a demon isn't deceiving you into thinking that whatever is clear and distinct is always true?" Descartes answers that God, being good and all powerful, would not allow us to be so deceived. It has been noticed that Descartes is reasoning in a circle here. From the premise that clear and distinct ideas are true he infers the existence of God, but to infer the truth of the premise that clear and distinct ideas are always true, he appeals to the premise that God exists and is not a deceiver. So Descartes's argument doesn't establish that whatever is clear and distinct is true. Something could appear clear and distinct and yet be false. It could also appear clear and distinct and not be clear and distinct. Besides, as many critiques have pointed out, the notions "clear" and "distinct" themselves are not clear or distinct, but somewhat vague and indistinct. Descartes never defines these characteristics, but they seem to signify self-evidence, obviousness, and distinguishability from other things. But, again, these qualities seem contextually conditioned. What is self-evident to a computer engineer about my computer may be incomprehensible to me.

Descartes's justification of the thesis that we have knowledge of the external world rests ultimately on the idea that God exists and is not a deceiver. If the world didn't exist as our critical perceptions (our best science) says it does, God would be a deceiver. Since this is not so, the best explanation of our belief in the reality of the external world is that the world really does exist. Unless you think that Descartes has established the existence of God, which almost all inquirers agree he hasn't, his argument for the reality of the external world fails. He has not defeated skepticism about the external world.

But I think that Descartes's ingenious argument has established at least one bit of knowledge: If I am thinking, then I must exist—and the same goes for you. If you are thinking, then you must exist. A good reason to exercise your thought—it gives you a bit of knowledge—about your existence. Strictly speaking, it doesn't prove that "I" exist, for the "I" is still undefined. But it shows that *something* exists that is conscious and thinking and we may identify with this something, whatever it is. But apart from this, Descartes hasn't really defeated the skeptic.

HUME

David Hume (1711–1776), the next great skeptic, was both narrower and deeper than Descartes. He was deeper or more authentic (in the sense of putting forth the skeptical hypothesis as a plausible option) in that while Descartes was only a *methodological* skeptic, Hume was a *substantive* skeptic. Descartes sought to use skepticism to filter out error and so arrive at indubitable knowledge of metaphysical truth. Hume believed metaphysics was doomed by the skeptical hypothesis. On the other hand, Hume was narrower in scope than his French counterpart, for he conceded that we can know the truths of mathematics and logic as well as commonsense truths (e.g., memory reports and reports about our impressions). There is no equivalent to the Cartesian demon operating systematically to deceive us. Simplifying a bit, we may call Descartes a global, but methodological, skeptic and Hume a local or mitigated, but substantive, skeptic.

Hume's epistemology is grounded in the experience of having sense impressions—having appearance of sights, sounds, smells, and so forth. He supposes that all our beliefs (or ideas) are caused by impressions (both internal and external, the passions and the perceptions). But we cannot get behind the impressions to check whether the world is really like what we are experiencing, so we can never know to what extent our impressions and ideas resemble the world (supposing there is a world behind the impressions). Hume goes on to argue that since all our beliefs are founded on these insecure impressions, we can have no metaphysical knowledge. We cannot even trace our belief in cause and effect, induction, matter, the self, the existence of God, or free will to impressions. Hence, they lack justification and we lack knowledge of them. Here is a brief summary of Hume's skeptical musings on these subjects.

Cause and Effect Hume points out that the inferences we make about causality are not logical ones but arise out of experience. Going against the standard view of his day that the connection between cause and effect is necessary, like the connection between triangularity and three-sidedness, Hume attributed our belief in causality to the observation of regular conjunctions of events.

> When many uniform instances appear, and the same object is always followed by the same event; we then begin to entertain the notion of cause and connexion. We then *feel* a new sentiment or impression, to wit, a customary connexion in the thought or imagination between one object and its usual attendant.[6]

We cannot prove that every event has a cause, nor that the same cause will always have a like effect, but we see two events in constant conjunction and *unjustifiably* infer a necessary connection. But there is no *necessity* about this connection. We do not have a priori knowledge of such a connection, nor can we infer it from other truths. Our belief that every event has a cause is simply a psychologically habitual inference derived from our experience. We know nothing about how things are in themselves.[7]

Modern quantum physics comes to a conclusion similar to Hume's about our notion of *omnicausality* (that every event has a cause). It posits that at a subatomic level, noncausal events occur. Chance is at the heart of reality. But if chance is at the heart of physics, why should we hold on to the idea of omnicausality on the macroscopic level of the world?

Induction Hume argues that our belief that the future will be like the past is founded on the idea of the uniformity of nature, which in turn depends on the idea that the future will be like the past. There is no contradiction in denying induction or the uniformity of nature. We cannot reason that the sun will rise tomorrow because it has always done so in the past, for that assumes that the future will be like the past, which in turn assumes the uniformity of nature. In fact the future is not always like the past. As Bertrand Russell once pointed out, the chicken who comes to the farmer each day to be fed one day finds herself the object of feeding.

Matter (Material Substance) Hume asks,

> Whether the idea of *substance* be derived from the impression of a sensation or reflection? If it be conveyed to us by our senses, I ask, which of them; and after what manner? If it be perceived by the eyes, it must be a color; if by the ears, a sound; if by the palate, a taste; and so of the other senses. But I believe none will assert, that substance is either a color, or a sound, or a taste. The idea of substance must therefore be derived from an impression or reflection, if it really exist.[8]

If we cannot locate the impression on which substance is based, we have no idea of substance "distinct from that of a collection of particular qualities, nor have we any other meeting when we either talk or reason concerning it." Matter, according to Hume, is simply a confused idea, a collection of ideas that are conjoined by the imagination.

The Self Even the reality of the *self* and personal identity are called into question. If all knowledge about reality comes through impressions, where is the impression that produces the notion of a self that exists over time?

> From what impression could [the idea of the self] be derived? . . . It must be some one impression, that gives rise to every real idea. But self or person is not any one impression, but that to which our several impressions and ideas are supposed to have a reference. If any impression gives rise to the idea of self, that impression must continue invariably the same, through the whole course of our lives; since self is supposed to exist after that manner. But there is no impression constant and invariable. . . . For my part, when I enter most intimately into what I call *myself*, I always stumble on some particular perception or other, of heat or cold, light or shade, love or hatred, pain or pleasure. I never can catch *myself* at any time without a perception, and never can observe any thing but the perception. . . . If any one upon serious and unprejudiced reflection, thinks he has a different notion of *himself*, I must confess I can reason no longer with him. All I can allow him is, that he may be in the right as well as I, and that we are essentially different in this particular. . . . But setting aside some metaphysicians of this kind, I may venture to affirm of the rest of mankind, that they are nothing but a bundle or collection of different perceptions, which succeed each other with an inconceivable rapidity, and are in a perceptual flux and movement.[9]

The self is a fiction, what our imagination projects on the basis of various perceptions and a need for coherence and constancy. The mind is simply a "kind of theater, where several perceptions successively make their appearances; pass, re-pass, glide away, and mingle in an infinite variety of postures and situations."[10] Of course, we may ask who is the "our" whose imagination manufactures a self out of particular perceptions?

Existence of God Hume claims that the classic proofs, the cosmological and teleological arguments, fail to establish the existence of omnipotent, omnibenevolent designer of the universe. Since all our ideas derive from initial impressions, the idea of God must be an imaginative construction from simple ideas (power, knowledge, goodness, and so forth) based originally on impressions.

Free Will Perhaps all our actions are determined by antecedent states of affairs so that we are not free. To suppose that an action, such as deciding to raise my hand in order to vote for a candidate, is deliberate is to suppose that I could have done otherwise and that I am fully responsible for my act. But if something caused me to raise my hand, libertarian free will is a fiction and responsibility boils down to nothing more than being the locus of causal processes.

So, it seems that Nature systemically deceives us. We cannot help believing that we are free when acting, but, on reflection, the notion of free will does not even seem to make sense. It doesn't make sense, not only because it contrasts with a notion of causal determination (which Hume doubts anyway), but because the notion of chance doesn't give us a notion of freedom and responsibility either. If my behavior is produced, not by determinate causes, but by random events, then that behavior is arbitrary and capricious, not rationally grounded. So either my actions are caused in a lawlike manner and I am not free or my actions are the product of chance and they are not really *my* acts, but the irrational product of a randomizing nature. Either way I am not free. Nevertheless, when I act I feel that I am in control, that I could have done otherwise if I had willed to do otherwise (and I could have willed to do otherwise).

According to Humean reason, this feeling is unsupported by reflection. Nonetheless, Hume is not a hard determinist, but a compatibilist (trying to reconcile determinism and freedom of the will). He believes that we must be held accountable for our voluntary actions, because we *chose* to do them—even though we were caused to choose to do them.

But if we cannot help believing in causation, induction, matter, the identity of the self, freedom of the will (at least while acting), and (possibly) the existence of a higher being, in spite of their absence of rational justification, the skeptic has a firm basis for his or her contention that we know very little and that we may be systematically misled by Nature (perhaps for our own good).

> As long as our attention is bent upon the subject, the philosophical and studied principle may prevail; but the moment we relax our thoughts, nature will display herself, and draw us back to our former opinion. . . . The skeptical doubt, both with respect to reason and the senses, is a malady, which can never be radically cured, but must return upon us every moment, however we may chance it away. . . . As the skepitcal doubt arises naturally from a profound and intense reflection on those subjects, it always increases, the farther we carry our reflections, when in opposition or conformity to it. *Carelessness and inattention alone can afford us any remedy.*[11]

Fortunately, Hume concludes,

> It happens that since reason is incapable of dispelling these clouds, nature herself suffices to that purpose, and cures me of this philosophical melancholy and delirium, either by relaxing this bent of mind, or by some avocation, and lively impression of my senses, which obliterate all these chimeras. I dine, I play a game of backgammon, I converse, and am merry with my friends; and when after three or four hours' amusement, I would return to these speculations, they appear so cold, and strained, and ridiculous, that I cannot find in my heart to enter into them any farther.[12]

A natural propensity prohibits perseverance in skepticism and forces us to act as though the deliberations of reason were chimeras. But when we come back to philosophical reflection, we must suspect, if not profoundly conclude, that we know very little indeed.

DO WE HAVE KNOWLEDGE
OF THE EXTERNAL WORLD?

Suppose that we follow Hume and allow that we do know mathematical and logical truths. The question now is whether we can know anything else. For example, do we have knowledge of the external world? Are the particular things we seem to perceive really what they seem to be? Suppose we are looking at a lush red McIntosh apple. We take it in our hands, feel its firmness, bring it to our mouths, bite into it, and experience its luscious taste. Our senses work in harmony, it seems, conveying powerful experiences about the McIntosh apple. But could we not be deceived about all of this? Could not the taste be due to our taste buds—lusciousness not being a property of the apple but of our taste mechanisms; redness not being a property in the world but an effect manufactured in our minds; firmness being likewise a property in us, not the apple (which physics tells us is made up of mostly space and microphysical particles)? Or could we not be hallucinating or be brains in a vat?

We might set forth the argument this way.

1. If I know that I have a McIntosh apple in my hand then I know that I am not hallucinating or dreaming this.
2. But I do not *know* that I am not hallucinating or dreaming this, since knowledge entails having a complete justification for what is known and I have no complete justification that I am not hallucinating.
3. ∴ I do not know that I have a McIntosh apple in my hand.

What can we make of this argument? It seems valid. Premise 1 seems true. If I really do have a McIntosh apple in my hand, then I am not simply hallucinating that I do (of course, I could be hallucinating and still have a McIntosh apple in my hand, but let us ignore that complication for the moment).

Premise 2 seems true also. I can't prove that I am not hallucinating or dreaming, for even if I am not hallucinating or dreaming, I wouldn't know the difference if I were. My experiences would be relevantly similar to what they are now.

So the argument seems sound. If I don't know that I'm not hallucinating or dreaming all this, how can I know that I really do have a McIntosh apple in my hand? If I can't prove or don't know that I am not hallucinating at any particular moment of my life, how can I know anything about the external world—even if I'm not hallucinating?

The force of the argument is not that we don't have *justified* beliefs or even true, justified beliefs. We're doing the best we can and perhaps that's enough to give us truth. But it's not enough, claims the skeptic, to give us knowledge or justified certainty about the truth of our experiences. We could be wrong about any of our appearances. So we don't have knowledge.

Of course the antiskeptic will try to counter the skeptic's argument. He or she will claim that it is unsound. I can know that I have a McIntosh apple in front of me even if I cannot know that I am not hallucinating. This is based on the premise H: If I know that a McIntosh apple is in front of me and I know that if a McIntosh apple is in front of me then I am not hallucinating, then I know that I am not hallucinating. Let K stand for "I know," p for the proposition "a McIntosh apple is in front of me," q for the proposition "that I am not hallucinating," and $\rightarrow$ for "entails." We get the following modus ponens formal argument:

1. Kp & $K(p \rightarrow q) \rightarrow Kq$ (formulation of proposition H).
2. Kp (statement of knowledge based on my commonsense perception).
3. $K(p \rightarrow q)$ (analytic statement about the knowing relationship: I know that if p then q; and I know this because, given the p and q in question, the conditional p q is analytic).
4. $\therefore$ Kq (I know that I'm not hallucinating).

Of course, the skeptic uses modus tollens to argue just the reverse:

1. Kp & $K(p \rightarrow q) \rightarrow Kq$ (formulation of H).
2. Not-Kq (I don't know that I'm not hallucinating, for I can't refute the skeptic).
3. $K(p \rightarrow q)$ (analytic truth as above: I know that if a McIntosh apple is in front of me, then I am not hallucinating).
4. $\therefore$ Not-Kq (I do not know that a McIntosh apple is in front of me).

So we seem to come to a standoff. It's all a matter of quickness—who can draw his logical pistol first? Can the believer draw his modus ponens before the skeptic draws his modus tollens? Obviously something is wrong here. Either the antiskeptic must find a way around this standoff or the skeptic wins by default because the skeptic is claiming not that we don't have true beliefs but that we don't have complete justification or certainty—knowledge.

THE RELEVANT ALTERNATIVES MODEL

A similar attempt to solve the problem of skepticism is the relevant alternatives model set forth by Fred Dretske.[13] Dretske asks you to imagine taking your son to a zoo where you see several zebras. When questioned by your son, you tell him that the animals in the pen before you are zebras. Do you know that they are zebras? Most of us would say without hesitation that we do, for we have a pretty good idea what zebras look like, the pen is marked "Zebras," and the like. "Yet," says Dretske, "something's being a zebra implies that it is not a mule and, in particular, not a mule cleverly disguised by the zoo authorities to look like a zebra. Do you know that these animals are not mules cleverly disguised by the zoo authorities to look like zebras?" No, you don't. If they were cleverly disguised mules, you wouldn't know the difference.

> Have you checked with the authorities? Did you examine the animals closely enough to detect such a fraud? You might do this, of course, but in most cases you do nothing of the kind. You have some general uniformities on which you rely, regularities to which you give expression by such remarks as "That isn't very likely." . . . Granted, the hypothesis [that the "zebras" are disguised mules] is not very plausible,

given what we know about people and zoos. But the question here is not whether this alternative is plausible, not whether it is more or less plausible than that there are real zebras in the pen, but whether *you know* that this alternative hypothesis is false. I don't think you do.[14]

But does this mean that you and your son don't know that zebras are in front of you? No, you do know that (we're assuming that they're zebras). The point is simply that you need not rule out the possibility of implausible alternatives in order to be said to have knowledge. "To know that *x* is *A* is to know that *x* is *A* within a framework of relevant alternatives, *B, C,* and *D.*" As long as you can pick out a zebra from a horse or an elephant or an elm tree and correctly identify it, you may be said to know that you're seeing a zebra—even if you can't rule out the possibility that it is a painted mule or a weird hologram or a robot from a Steven Spielberg epic.

Dretske's argument emphasizes that knowledge has a contextual aspect. What you know about the external world depends to some extent on your discriminating ability in various contexts—your ability to distinguish between genuine objects and relevant alternatives—but our knowledge does not depend on being able to discriminate between real objects and all logically possible appearances. Knowledge is a practical affair and must only be able to meet real objections and actual possibilities.

There are problems with the relevant alternative theory:

1. First, it is unclear what a relevant alternative is. The notion of relevance is vague. How do we know whether the possibility of a mule being painted to look like a zebra is relevant to picking out zebras? If I believe in demons who intervene in human affairs, does the possbility of a demon causing these animals to look like zebras become a relevant alternative? This leads to a second problem.

2. The theory relativizes knowledge in a way that may be unduly subjective. What you know may depend on whether or not you have certain background beliefs. I may be said to know that the zebra in front of us is truly a zebra because I can just barely distinguish it from painted mules and because I don't believe in demons. You, however, may not be said to know that the same zebra in front of us is a zebra even though you can distinguish it from painted mules even better than I can. You, we may suppose, believe in demons who could disguise mules as zebras, hence your added belief robs you of knowledge—even though your perceptual mechanisms are more discriminating than mine.

Or while I am out in the garage building a table or repairing a chair I may be said to know that there is an external world, but in my study or in an epistemology class where the possibility arises that I may be systematically mistaken about my experiences, that knowledge is suddenly withdrawn—since the possibility of systematic error is now a relevant alternative. Usually, we think that the more we reflect and find evidence for our beliefs, the closer to certainty and knowledge we come. But paradoxically the idea of relevant alternatives seems to take knowledge away from us. The more I seem to know about or reflect on a subject, the less I can be said to know it. As Bernard Williams puts it "reflection destroys knowledge."[15]

At first glance, tying our attributions of knowledge to such vague and relativized notions with such paradoxical results seems to make knowledge an extremely unstable entity. But if it is this unstable, doesn't the skeptic win the day?

3. A third criticism of the theory of relevant alternatives concerns whether knowledge is externalist or internalist, and works if knowledge is externalist. There are two radically different theories of justification and/or knowledge: *internalism* and *externalism*. The internalist says that one must have or be able to give the reasons for one's belief in order to have knowledge of the proposition in question, but the externalist says that one need not have reasons for a belief in order to have knowledge of that proposition. All that is necessary is that the true belief has been brought about by a reliable (nonaccidental) process.

If internalism is correct and we accept the closure argument (i.e., if Kp & $K(p \rightarrow q) \rightarrow Kq$; not-$Kq$; therefore, not-$Kp$), that statement "If you don't know that the animal before you is not a painted mule, then you don't know that it is not a zebra" tends toward a skeptical conclusion. You don't know that the animal before you is a zebra.

But if externalism is correct, as long as your belief that a zebra is before you has been caused in the right way, you don't have to be able to rule out all the alternatives. You know that the animal in front of you is a zebra because that knowledge has been caused in the right way. Since you know that if it is a zebra it is not a painted mule, a hologram of a zebra, an illusion caused by a malicious demon, and so forth, you can be said to know that it is not a painted mule, a hologram of a zebra, an illusion, and so forth. Of course, this antiskeptical argument works only if a form of externalism is true.

For all its problems, the idea of relevant alternatives may play a role in defeating the skeptic. Not all doubts are rational ones or justified. And the burden of proof does seem to be on the shoulders of the skeptic to at least give us positive reasons for doubting self-evident, commonsense beliefs about the external world.

MOORE'S DEFENSE OF COMMON SENSE

Can you defeat the skeptic? Two other related refutations of skepticism have been attempted.

G. E. Moore (1873–1958) claims that we can know that there is an external world, because we can know we have bodies. I can know that my body was born at a certain time in the past, and has existed continuously ever since.

> It was much smaller when it was born, and for some time afterwards, than it is now. Ever since it was born, it has been either in contact with or not far from the surface of the earth; and, at every moment since it was born, there have also existed many other things, having shape and size in three dimensions, from which it has been at various distances.[16]

In a famous lecture Moore claimed that he would then and there prove two things, that he had two hands. How? Here is Moore's proof.

> I can prove now . . . that two human hands exist. How? By holding up my two hands, and saying, as I make a certain gesture with the right hand, "Here is one hand," and adding, as I make a certain gesture with the left, "and here is another." But now I am perfectly well aware that, in spite of all that I have said, many philosophers will still feel that I have not given any satisfactory proof of the point in question. . . . If I had

proved the proposition which I used as *premises* in my two proofs, then they would perhaps admit that I had proved the existence of external things. . . . They want a proof of what I assert *now* when I hold up my hands and say "Here's one hand and here's another." . . . They think that, if I cannot give such extra proofs, then the proofs that I have given are not conclusive proofs at all. . . . Such a view, though it has been very common among philosophers, can, I think, be shown to be wrong. . . . I can know things which I cannot prove; and among things which I certainly did know were the premises of my two proofs. I should say, therefore, that those, if any, who are dissatisfied with these proofs merely on the grounds that I did not know their premises, have no good reasons for their dissatisfaction.[17]

Moore claimed that we do not need to be able to prove all the premises of our argument in order to end up with a sound argument. If our premises are self-evident, we may consider them innocent until proven guilty. Accordingly, Moore claimed to have thereby given a rigorous proof that there was an external world, because the premises are known to be true (even though we can't prove them), and the conclusion follows by valid inference from these premises.

The general form of Moore's strategy is

1. If skepticism is true, we do not have knowledge of the external world.
2. But we do have knowledge of the external world (the examples given).
3. ∴ Skepticism is false.

Accordingly, we do not have to provide a complete explanation of the difference between dream states (or hallucination states) and veridical experiences in order to know that some of my self-evident perceptions are veridical. Common sense is innocent until proven guilty.

Skeptics have not taken kindly to Moore's refutation, claiming that it has all the virtues of "theft over honest toil" (in Bertrand Russell's phrase). Moore, they claim, is begging the question against the skeptic, for the question of whether Moore—or those "watching" him—are dreaming or hallucinating cannot be so easily ruled out.

WEAK VERSUS STRONG KNOWLEDGE

In the second type of attempt, related to the first and set forth by the American philosopher Norman Malcolm (1911–1990), two types of knowledge are distinguished: *weak* and *strong*.[18] There are some knowledge claims about which, on being challenged, I would be wise to admit I could be wrong; these are "weak" knowledge. For example, I believe that the sun is about 90 million miles from the earth, but if someone were to challenge me on this, I might well admit that I'm not certain about it. Likewise, I claim to know that I was born in Chicago, Illinois, to Louis and Helen Pojman, but if someone challenged me, claiming that there was evidence that I was adopted at six months of age or not born in Chicago but in Madison, Wisconsin, I might well retract my knowledge claim.

But there are other kinds of knowledge claims that are so certain that no conceivable challenges could cause me to give them up; "strong knowledge" is the kind about which Moore was so adamant. For example: I have a body; I have two hands; my dog is called Caesar; I am now reading a philosophy book; I am now sitting on a chair; I am not sleeping or dreaming.

So while we are willing to let further investigation determine whether we really have knowledge in the instances of weak knowledge, we do not concede that anything whatsoever could prove us mistaken in the cases of strong knowledge.

Malcolm's argument is really an elaboration of Moore's, but the distinction is important. There are experiences about which we cannot imagine being wrong. We want to say that the burden of proof is on the skeptic to tell us why we should doubt these things.

If this is so, then while the skeptic cannot be refuted, he or she can be *rebutted*. We can accept our claims to knowledge as working hypotheses, challenging the skeptic to show us what is wrong with any specific knowledge claim. If we are at least prima facie justified in making claims to knowledge, if we cannot in good faith discover defeaters to these claims, then we may have knowledge after all.

Of course, the skeptic is not going to be convinced about this sort of claim to knowledge. The skeptic's point is that we are not completely justified in our knowledge claims. Since we could be wrong, we should hold back claims to knowledge.

Whatever the truth of the matter is on making knowledge claims, at least one value of skepticism is to make us modest about our pretensions to knowledge. It is harder than most of us imagine to justify our claims to knowledge, and much of what we claim to know turns out to be mistaken. Such lessons in humility are steps toward wisdom. Mark Twain once said, "The real trouble isn't in what we believe, but in what we know that ain't so."

SUMMARY

Skepticism is the theory that we do not have any knowledge at all. One of the goals of epistemology is to come to terms with skepticism—either defeating it or conceding its force. Global skepticism denies that we can know anything at all—except *perhaps* mathematical and simple logical truths. Local skepticism admits that we can have empirical knowledge but denies that we can have metaphysical knowledge. René Descartes represents the global skeptic, arguing that a demon could be deceiving us about even simple mathematical statements. David Hume, while denying that we can have empirical *knowledge,* admits that we are justified in our empirical *beliefs,* but denies metaphysical knowledge. We are systematically deceived by nature about causation, induction, the identity of the self, the reality of matter, free will, and the existence of God. Philosophical reflection informs us that we have no metaphysical knowledge, but we must act as though we do. We cannot live as skeptics.

Fred Dretske seeks to break the hold of skepticism by denying that knowledge is closed under known entailment and that only relevant alternatives should be taken into consideration when evaluating knowledge claims. Both of these attempts are fraught with difficulties, among them the question of whether it makes sense to say that knowledge is not closed under known entailment.

G. E. Moore and Norman Malcolm have each tried to undermine the skeptic's arguments by shifting the burden or proof back to the skeptic, demanding that he or she tell us why we should not trust our commonsense judgments where no specific defeater is forthcoming. They claim that while the skeptic cannot be refuted, he or she can be rebutted.

Perhaps it is helpful to see the three main positions discussed in this chapter as responses to the following proposition: If you know that *p* and know that *p* entails *q,* then you know that *q* (e.g., if I know that I have a body and know that if I have a body then I am not a brain in a vat, then I know that I am not a brain in a vat).

$$Kp \mathrel{\&} K(p \to q) \to Kq$$

The standard dogmatists, Moore and Malcolm, directly assert that we have knowledge. So they simply assert the antecedent:

$$Kp \mathrel{\&} K(p \to q)$$

I do know that I have a body and know that if I have a body, I am not a brain in a vat.

Therefore, by modus ponens, *Kq:* I know that I am not a brain in a vat.

The nonclosurist, Dretske, denies the entailment between the antecedent and consequent: $Kp \mathrel{\&} K(p \to q) \to Kq$.

They accept *Kp* and $K(p \to q)$ but deny that I know that I am not a brain in a vat. They hold not-*Kq*.

Skeptics respond to the proposition $Kp \mathrel{\&} K(p \to q) \to Kq$ by denying the consequent and so, by modus tollens, denying the antecedent, $Kp \mathrel{\&} K(p \to q)$. They accept the second conjunct but deny the first *Kp.* I do not know that I have a body.

It seems then that the question of skepticism hangs on whether or not one accepts closure under known entailment and if one does, whether one is inclined to draw a modus ponens or a modus tollens argument. Perhaps we need to understand the various characterizations of knowledge, perception, and justification before we can fully appreciate this issue. So you will want to come back to the question of skepticism after you have worked through the rest of this book.

QUESTIONS FOR DISCUSSION

1. Go over the various types of skepticism. Distinguish Descartes's methodological skepticism from Humean substantive skepticism. Which are the strongest types?

2. Can you refute the skeptic? Which arguments against skepticism seem most plausible?

3. Descartes says that Wisdom teaches us that we should never entirely trust a witness who has deceived us. He uses this idea to cast doubt on the deliverances of the senses. But doesn't this assertion presuppose that we (or Descartes) know that our senses have sometimes deceived us?

4. Hume noted that skeptical arguments "admit of no answer and produce no conviction." What do you think Hume meant by this?

5. What is the difference between global and local skepticism? Which do you find more plausible or cogent?

6. Can you think of a belief or theory held by many people with certainty, that should be subject to the skeptic's doubt?

7. Consider Dretske's relevant alternative scheme for knowledge. Explain its strengths and weaknesses.

8. Do you think that Moore's strategy is convincing? Why can't the skeptic accuse Moore of begging the question against skepticism? Can the skeptic simply argue that Moore has not provided a justification for why he believes he has two hands?

9. Evaluate Malcolm's notion of weak and strong knowledge.

10. Can the skeptic live by his or her skepticism? Examine this passage from Hume's *Treatise:*

> A Stoic or Epicurean displays principles, which may not only be durable, but which have an effect on conduct and behavior. But a Pyrrhonian [skeptic] cannot expect, that his philosophy will have any constant influence on the mind: or if it had, that its influence would be beneficial to society. On the contrary, he must acknowledge, if he will acknowledge anything, that all human life must perish, were his principles universally and steadily to prevail. All discourse, all action would immediately cease; and men remain in a total lethargy, till the necessities of nature, unsatisfied, put an end to their miserable existence. It is true; so fatal an event is very little to be dreaded. Nature is always too strong for principle. And though a Pyrrhonian may throw himself or others into a momentary amazement and confusion by his profound reasonings; the first and most trivial event in life will put to flight all his doubts and scruples, and leave him the same, in every point of action and speculation, with the philosophers of every other sect, or with those who never concerned themselves in any philosophical researches. When he awakes from his dream, he will be the first to join in the laugh against himself, and to confess, that all his objections are mere amusement, and can have no other tendency than to show the whimsical condition of mankind, who must act and reason and believe; though they are not able, by their most diligent enquiry, to satisfy themselves concerning the foundation of these operations, or to remove the objections, which may be raised against them. (David Hume, *An Enquiry Concerning Human Understanding,* Sec. XII).

Do you agree with Hume that we cannot live as skeptics? What then is the lesson, if any, of skepticism?

NOTES

1. René Descartes, *Meditations on First Philosophy,* trans. Elizabeth Haldane and G. Ross (Cambridge: Cambridge University Press, 1931), 145.

2. Note that Descartes's argument seems to assume that we *know* that our senses have sometimes deceived us.

3. Descartes, 148.

4. Barry Stroud, *The Significance of Philosophical Scepticism* (Oxford: Oxford University Press, 1984), 12.

5. Descartes, 150.

6. David Hume, *Enquiry Concerning Human Understanding* (Oxford: Clarendon Press, 1748), 78.

7. Michael Levin has pointed out (in correspondence) that when Hume speaks of beliefs about the future being derived from experience, he seems to be assuming causation himself.

8. Hume, 15.

9. Hume, *Treatise of Human Nature* (Oxford: Clarendon Press, 1739), 252.

10. Ibid.

11. Ibid., 218. Hume's conclusions regarding metaphysics is worth quoting:

> When we run over libraries, persuaded of these principles [of empiricism], what havoc must we make? If we take in our hands any volume of divinity or school metaphysics, for instance, let us ask, Does it contain any abstract reasoning concerning quantity or number? No. Does it contain any experimental reasoning concerning matter of fact and existence? No. Commit it to the flames, for it can contain nothing but sophistry and illusion. (*Enquiry*) 165.

12. Ibid., 269.

13. Fred Dretske, "Epistemic Operators," *Journal of Philosophy* (December 24, 1970); Gail Stine, "Dretske on Knowing the Logical Consequences," *Journal of Philosophy* (May 6, 1971). For a critique of the relevant alternatives approach, see Palle Yourgrau, "Knowledge and Relevant Alternatives," *Synthese* 55 (1983).

14. Dretske, 1016.

15. Bernard Williams, *Ethics and the Limits of Philosophy* (Cambridge, MA: Harvard University Press, 1985), 167.

16. G. E. Moore, "A Defense of Common Sense," *Philosophical Papers* (London: Allen & Unwin, 1959).

17. G. E. Moore, "Proof of the External World," *Philosophical Papers* (London: Allen & Unwin, 1959), 144f.

18. Norman Malcolm, *Knowledge and Certainty* (Englewood Cliffs, NJ: Prentice-Hall, 1963).

FOR FURTHER READING

Burnyeat, Myles, ed. *The Skeptical Tradition.* Berkeley: University of California Press, 1983. A set of scholarly essays on the skeptical tradition from the Greeks to Kant.

Descartes, René. *The Philosophical Works of Descartes,* trans. by Elizabeth Haldane and G. Ross. Cambridge: Cambridge University Press, 1931. Especially Descartes's classic *Meditations on First Philosophy.*

Hookway, Christopher. *Scepticism.* London: Routledge & Kegan Paul, 1990. Contains both an important historical survey, especially of Pyrrhonism, Descartes, and Hume, and a philosophical analysis of the problem of skepticism.

Hume, David. *Enquiries Concerning the Human Understanding and Concerning the Principles of Morals,* edited by L. A. Selby-Bigge. Oxford: Clarendon Press, 1902.

Hume, David. *A Treatise of Human Nature,* edited by L. A. Selby-Bigge. Oxford: Clarendon Press, 1896.

Klein, Peter. *Certainty: A Refutation of Scepticism.* Minneapolis: University of Minnesota Press, 1981. A clear and cogent argument against skepticism.

Pojman, Louis, ed. *The Theory of Knowledge,* 2d ed. Belmont, CA: Wadsworth, 1999. Part II contains several relevant essays.

Sextus Empiricus. *Selections from the Major Writings on Scepticism, Man & God,* trans. by Sanford G. Etheridge; edited by Philip Hallie. Indianapolis: Hackett, 1985.

Stroud, Barry. *The Significance of Philosophical Skepticism.* Oxford: Oxford University Press, 1984. A sympathetic exposition of the major skeptical arguments.

Unger, Peter. *Ignorance: A Case for Skepticism.*
Oxford: Clarendon Press, 1975. A radical, superglobal skeptical view.

Williams, Michael. *Unnatural Doubts.*
Oxford: Blackwell, 1991. An advanced
discussion, arguing that skeptical doubts
are not natural or intuitive, but founded
on a false theory of "epistemological
realism."

12

Perception: Our Knowledge of the External World

In daily life, we assume as certain many things which, on a closer scrutiny, are found to be so full of apparent contradictions that only a great amount of thought enables us to know what it is that we really may believe. In the search for certainty, it is natural to begin with our present experiences, and in some sense, no doubt, knowledge is to be derived from them. But any statement as to what it is that our immediate experience makes us know is very likely to be wrong. It seems to me that I am now sitting in a chair, at a table of a certain shape, on which I see sheets of paper with writing or print. . . . I believe that, if any other normal person comes into my room, he will see the same chairs and tables and books as I see, and that the table which I see is the same as the table which I feel pressing against my arm. All this seems to be so evident as to be hardly worth stating, except in answer to a man who doubts whether I know anything. Yet all this may be reasonably doubted, and all of it requires much careful discussion before we can be sure that we have stated it in a form that is wholly true.[1]

APPEARANCE AND REALITY

Appearance is different from reality. An object may look, sound, feel, taste, or smell differently from the way it actually is. We see two parallel railroad tracks as if they converge in the distance. We hear the sound of an ambulance gradually increase in loudness as it approaches us and gradually diminish as it recedes into the distance, though the sound remains constant to those in the ambulance. Place one hand on a warm stove and the other in a bowl of ice cubes and then place both hands in a bowl of lukewarm water. What happens? The hand that was in the warm place feels as though the water is cold, while the other hand feels as though the water is hot, yet the temperature of the water remains constant. Mirages of oases appear in the desert or on a road during a sunny summer day. A coin looks elliptical when viewed from a certain angle and stars that are several times larger than our sun appear as tiny sparks in the heavens. We never see these gigantic objects as they really are. (What size would that be? How close would we have to be to see a star in its actual size?) A straight stick placed halfway in water looks bent. White shirts, walls, and paper appear red in red lighting and blue in blue lighting. When we put sunglasses on, the colors around us appear different from what they are. Pineapples and yogurt taste different before and after we have brushed our teeth with a pungent toothpaste or when we have a fever.

In more serious cases, in hallucinations, we see ghosts and people who are not present. Remember Shakespeare's *Macbeth:*

> Is this a dagger which I see before me,
> The handle toward my hand? Come, let me clutch thee:
> I have thee not, and yet I see thee still.
> Art thou not, fatal vision, sensible
> To feeling as to sight? or art thou but
> A dagger of the mind, a false creation,
> Proceeding from the heat-oppressed brain?
>
> (Act II, i, 33)

We want to distinguish these appearances from veridical perceptions. It is clear that these illusory appearances are not the way the world really is. They are images in our mind, caused by the world but not in the world. Philosophers call these images or appearances "sense data" or "sense impressions."

So far, so good, but now the real problem arises. How do we know that we ever do have veridical appearances of the world? How do we know that what we take for nonillusory appearances really are such? For there doesn't seem to be any intrinsic difference between illusions and veridical appearances. We see a "white table" as blue in blue lighting and red in red lighting, but the only reason we see it as white is because of the way light waves reflect off the surfaces of the table onto our retina, which sends information to the visual center at the back of our brain. The table is not really colored at all. And sounds are simply wave frequencies in the atmosphere picked up by our eardrums and translated in the auditory centers of our brains.

So the question is forced upon us. What exactly do we know of the external world?

THEORIES OF PERCEPTION

What is the direct object of awareness when we perceive? Traditionally, three answers have been given to this question: (1) Direct Realism (sometimes referred to as "Naive Realism" or "Commonsense Realism"), (2) Representationalism, and (3) Phenomenalism. Direct Realism claims that the immediate object of perception is a physical object that exists independently of our awareness of it. Representationalism and Phenomenalism answer that the immediate object of perception is a *sense datum* (or *sense impression*), an object that cannot exist apart from

our awareness of it. Sense data, according to these two theories, are internal pre-
sentations, for example the colors, shapes, and sizes of appearances in our minds.

But Representationalism and Phenomenalism divide over the relationship of
sense data to the physical world. For the Representationalist the physical world
exists independently of and is the cause of our perceptions. Physical objects give
rise to the sense data we perceive, so we only have mediate knowledge of the
external world. For Phenomenalism, on the other hand, physical objects are simply constructions of sense data. They do not exist independently of sense
impressions. Both theories agree that all our experience is confined to sense
data, only Representationalism says that there really is something outside us,
which they represent, whereas Phenomenalism says that there is nothing besides
sense data in the world.

Common sense rejects both Representationalism and Phenomenalism and
tells us that we, through our five senses—sight, hearing, touch, taste, and smell—
do directly perceive the *real* world. It tells us that the physical world exists independently of our awareness of it and that the things we perceive are pretty much
the way we perceive them. They exist here and now. Common sense supports
Naive or Direct Realism.

Unfortunately for common sense, science casts doubt on this simple picture of
our relationship to the world. As Bertrand Russell succinctly says, "Naive realism
leads to physics, and physics, if true, shows that naive realism is false. Therefore, naive
realism, if true, is false; therefore it is false."[2] Science tells us that the physical objects
we perceive are not what they seem to be nor do we ever see things in the present.
Colors are not in the objects but are the way objects appear as they reflect light. Since
light travels at 186,000 miles per second, it takes time to reach our eyes. All that we
see really existed in the past. It takes 8 minutes for the light from the sun to reach us,
over 8 years for it to reach us from the distant and brightest star, Sirius, and 650 years
for the light from the distant star, Rigel, to reach us. So when we look up into the
heavens at the stars, we do not see any of them as they now are, but as they existed in
the near or distant past. Indeed, some of these stars may no longer exist. In fact, since
it takes light time to reach us, we never see anything as it is in the present. Even near
objects are not seen as they presently exist. All sight is of the past.

Likewise, science tells us that the sounds we hear, the flavors we taste, the sensations we feel, and the odors we smell are not what they seem to be. They are
mediated through our ways of perceiving, so that we seldom or never experience
them as they really are in themselves.

So Representationalism seems to succeed in giving an explanation of perception that is more faithful to science than Direct Realism. Representationalism
holds that the real world causes our appearances or perceptions by representing
the physical world through sense data, mental entities that are private to individual perceivers.

Locke's Representationalism John Locke (1632–1704) set forth the classic
expression of this view. Attacking the notion that we have innate knowledge of
metaphysical truths, Locke argued that all our knowledge derives ultimately from
sense experience. "Let us then suppose the mind to be, as we say, white paper,
void of all characters, without any ideas; how comes it by that vast store, which
the busy and boundless fancy of man has painted on it with an almost endless

variety? Whence has it all the materials of reason and knowledge? To this I answer, in one word, from experience: in that all our knowledge is founded."[3]

Locke held a causal theory of perception in which processes in the external world impinge on the perceiver's sense organs, which in turn send messages to the brain, where they are transformed into mental events. We may diagram Locke's Causal Theory of Perception this way:

Although the process is physical and mechanistic, it yields a nonphysical result, a mental event, the perceptual experience, which subsequent philosophers described as a *percept* (sense datum or sense impression).

We are aware of, not the thing in itself, the object which is perceived and which causes the idea to arise in our Mind, but only the idea or *representation* of the object. We are directly aware of the idea but in as much as the object is the *cause* of the idea, we may be said to be indirectly aware of the object.

Now a problem arises. Do these ideas that occur in the Mind faithfully, accurately represent the external world taken to be their cause?

Locke said, Yes and No. His answer has to do with two types of qualities of physical objects. Let me explain.

Locke divides the qualities of physical objects into two basic classes: *primary qualities* and *secondary qualities*. Here is Locke's classic passage.

> Qualities thus considered in bodies are, First, such as are utterly inseparable from bodies, in what estate soever it be; such as, in all the alterations and changes it suffers, all the force can be used upon it, it constantly keeps; and such as sense constantly finds in every particle of matter which has bulk enough to be perceived, and the mind finds inseparable from every particle of matter, though less than to make itself singly be perceived by our senses; e.g., take a grain of wheat, divide it into two parts, each part has still *solidity, extension, figure,* and *mobility;* divide it again, and it retains still the same qualities: and so divide it on till the parts become insensible. They must retain still each of them all those qualities. For, division . . . can never take away either solidity, extension, figure, or mobility from any body, but only makes two or more distinct separate masses of matter of that which was but one before; all which distinct masses, reckoned as so many distinct bodies, after division, make a certain number. These I call *original* or *primary* qualities of body, . . . solidity, extension, figure, motion, or rest, and number.[4]

Primary qualities are really in their objects and inseparable from their objects, and so our ideas of them truly represent the objects. Such qualities are solidity (or bulk), extension, figure, movement (and rest), and number. These are the true building blocks of knowledge because they accurately represent features in the world. Ultimately, the world is made up of indivisible, minute atoms, which underlie physical objects. Secondary qualities are not in the things themselves but are powers to cause various sensations in us. The powers themselves are in the object. What is not in the object is the quality that our secondary-quality idea represents as being in the object.

For example, an object's color is its power to cause color ideas in us. It does this by reflecting certain kinds of light and not others. And it reflects certain kinds of light because its surface has a certain structure. That surface structure is a primary quality. When, under normal circumstances, we look at an object it looks a certain color, say, red. The redness that we are acquainted with is not in the object itself but in the way the light reflects off the object into our eye and is communicated to our brain. The primary quality (the surface structure) is what gives the object the power to reflect some kinds of light and so cause some kinds of sensation (idea), but it doesn't really cause the secondary quality. All there really is to objects are their primary qualities. Because of their primary qualities those same objects have the power to cause certain kinds of sensations (ideas). They really have that power. The power is in the object. However, some of those ideas represent the object as having qualities—color, smell, sound, taste, and the like— that aren't really in the object. These secondary qualities are types of powers, or potentialities or *dispositions,* that reside in a physical object.

Locke adds a third quality, dispositional, which has the power to cause changes in the external world. For example, fire has the power to change liquids into gases, sugar is soluble in warm water, and glass is fragile. Solubility, flammability, and fragility are dispositional qualities in bodies.

Locke's Dualism   There is a problem with Locke's theory of Representationalism; it is difficult to see how we could justify any knowledge claim regarding the external world if we are never directly aware of anything except the ideas in our mind. Locke, aware of this problem, said, We have as much certainty as our condition needs but, in reality, we can't know very much. Our senses only represent large objects and not their smaller particles, so that the mysteries of the natural world are forever hidden from our view.

But the critic can press the point, making a criticism that has been labeled the "permanent picture gallery" objection. Ordinarily, we check a picture of a landscape against the scene pictured, but in perception, if Locke is right, we never get a look at the scene itself. So how can we know if the picture faithfully represents it? No comparison seems possible, so we pause to wonder whether Locke's theory doesn't really lead to skepticism? or, if not skepticism, immaterialism?

Locke thought that it was incoherent to speak of qualities existing in their own right, so he relied on the Aristotelian notion of substance as that which underlies all other properties, the foundation of matter itself. Substance is an unknown "something I know not what."

Being a devout Christian, Locke inferred that this mechanistic materialism could not be the last word on the subject of substance, so he posited a second, spiritual substance with nonmaterial properties, including the soul, consciousness, and sensations. Locke was aware that he had no philosophical grounds for this distinction. Faith dictated dualism.

Berkeley's Idealist Attack on Representationalism   Locke thought that he had done justice to both science and faith with this dualism, but his theory soon came under attack as being dangerous, repugnant, and absurd. The philosopher who led the attack was an Irish bishop, George Berkeley (1685–1753), who was unsparing in his zeal to demolish the damned doctrine of mechanistic materialism. In its place, Berkeley erected an ingenious Idealism called *Immaterialism*. First, let us note Berkeley's criticisms of Locke's Representationalism.

1. Locke's ideas are *dangerous,* because they made religion (and God) unnecessary, reducing all to a Newtonian mechanistic model of the universe, under physical causation. All is matter in motion, with bodies interacting in accordance with rigorously formulated mechanical laws. If this is true, where does God fit in?

Locke's God is reduced to a prime mover (or the Big Push), largely superfluous for daily purposes.

Furthermore, Locke's notion of atomism and his vague concept of substance really was a thinly disguised materialism (not that he thought Locke realized this), for Locke made it possible that the world was exclusively material, and that there were no souls or spirits, but that consciousness was merely a property of matter. So, the Mind would cease to exist at death.

Berkeley, being a devout Christian and a bishop, felt it his duty to combat this incipient materialism, secularism, and atheism. Locke, though a Christian himself, had played right into the enemy's hands, yielding either Skepticism or Materialism.

2. Locke's ideas are *loathsome* because they took away the beauty of the physical world. Common sense was outraged in supposing, as Locke's theory did, that the visible beauty of creation was no more than "a false imaginary glare" (e.g., the flowers in our garden are not really colored and have no fragrant aroma).

3. Locke's ideas yield *absurd consequences*. First, Berkeley noted that Locke's primary/secondary qualities distinction was very weak. The primary qualities are no more "in" the objects of perception than the secondary ones. Both types or qualities are relative to the perceiving mind.

> It is said that heat and cold are affections only in the mind, and not at all patterns of real beings existing in the corporeal substances which excite them, for that the same body which appears cold to one hand seems warm to another. Now, why may we not as well argue that figure and extension are not patterns or resemblances of qualities existing in matter, because to the same eye at different stations, or eyes of a different texture at the same station, they appear various and cannot, therefore, be the images of anything settled and determined without the mind.[5]

Secondly, he argued that there were logical problems in the theory that our perceptions resembled physical objects ("an idea can be like nothing but an idea"). Locke's theory led to skepticism because it offered no basis for comparing representations with their objects. Recall our permanent picture gallery objection. Thirdly, Berkeley undermined the whole notion of substance, which Locke needed to maintain his theory. What is the difference, Berkeley rhetorically asked, between a "something I know not what" (Locke's notion of substance) and nothing at all? Ultimately, Locke's causal theory really supports materialism.

4. Finally, Berkeley charged that Locke's system was an *explanatory failure*. Locke asserted that ideas in the Mind were caused by mechanical actions upon our sense organs and brains. But Berkeley pointed out that this fails to explain mental events both in detail and in principle: in *detail* because it was impossible to explain why a certain physical event should produce certain but quite different (in character) mental states (e.g., light waves producing the color red); in *principle* because the whole notion of dualistic interactionism was incoherent, misusing the notion of "cause." A cause makes something happen, but for this you need a notion of a will, or agency—all causation is agent causation. But events in Nature do not make other events happen; one only sees two events in temporal succession—with regularity. But this only signals the reality of a cause; it is not the cause because it is not an agent and exerts no will. If Locke's model for the world was a clock, Berkeley's was an agent with radical free will.

What was Berkeley's own solution to the problem of how we know the external world? It was incredibly simple: to deny matter. In one fell swoop the intractable problems of substance, dualist interactionism, causation, and knowledge of the external world are swept away in the supposition that material substance doesn't exist.[6]

Berkeley held that there were only two realities: minds and mental events. Ideas exist in the mind alone. All qualities are essentially secondary and attain their reality by being perceived (*esse est percipi*—"To be is to be perceived"). There is no material world. Physical objects are simply mental events. "The table I write on exists, that is, I see and feel it; and if I were out of my study I should say it existed—meaning thereby that if I was in my study I might perceive it, or that some other spirit actually perceives it."[7] All physical objects are mental phenomena that would cease to exist if they were not perceived. Why do physical objects continue to exist when no one is perceiving them? What happens to them when we are not looking at trees or mountains? Do they cease to be? No, someone is always perceiving them. God's eye keeps the world from dissolving.

> There was a young man who said, "God
> Must think it exceedingly odd
> If he finds that this tree
> Continues to be
> When there's no one about in the quad."

> Dear Sir, your astonishment's odd
> I'm always about in the quad,
> And that's why the tree
> Will continue to be
> Since observed by,
> Yours faithfully, God.

Hence, we bring God back into philosophy and science as the necessary being that keeps our world intact. This thought frees us from mechanism, skepticism, and atheism all at once and offers us dignity—for we are not mere machines but infinitely valuable souls, finite and infinite spirits.

God communicates directly with our finite minds by the mediation of ideas, the orderly, regular, and admirable connection of which forms the rational discourse of the infinite Creator with finite spirits.

Berkeley sought to stave off the charge that his theory eliminated the need for scientific investigation. He argued that his theory reduces science to general rules (instrumentalism). The atomistic theory is a useful myth (serviceable fiction).

Phenomenalism Contemporary Phenomenalism differs with Berkeley only in his theological moorings. It doesn't posit God as necessary to hold the physical world in existence. Instead, it views the physical world as a construct of ideas. In Mill's words, objects are "permanent possibilities of sensation," meaning that if one were to get into the appropriate condition, one would experience the sense data. Philosophers like W. T. Stace (1886–1967) argue that the realist's view of the world as containing material objects behind the perceived world is an unjustified faith. The world of scientific discourse (e.g., "atoms," "gravity," and "conservation of energy") is not to be taken literally, but instrumentally, as providing useful fictions that help us to predict experiences. Consider his argument.

> So far as I know scientists still talk about electrons, protons, neutrons, and so on. We never directly perceive these, hence, if we ask how we know of their existence the only possible answer seems to be that they are an inference from what we do directly perceive. What sort of an inference? Apparently a causal inference. The atomic entities in some way impinge upon the sense of the animal organism and cause [it] to perceive the familiar world of tables, chairs, and the rest.
>
> But is it not clear that such a concept of causation, however interpreted, is invalid? The only reason we have for believing in the law of causation is that we *observe* certain regularities or sequences. We observe that, in certain conditions, *A* is always followed by *B*. We call *A* the cause, *B* the effect. And the sequence *A-B* becomes a causal law. It follows that all *observed* causal sequences are between sensed objects in the familiar world of perception, and that all known causal laws apply solely to the world of sense and not to anything beyond or behind it. And this in turn means that we have not got, and never could have, one jot of evidence for believing that the law of causation can be applied *outside* the realm of perception, or that the realm can have any causes (such as the supposed physical objects) which are not themselves perceived.[8]

Strictly speaking, Stace continues, "*Nothing exists except sensations* (and the minds which perceive them). The rest is mental construction or fiction." All that the so-called laws of science do is enable us to organize our experiences and predict future sensations.

Bertrand Russell (1872–1970) has defended Representational Realism, developing Locke's causal theory of perception in the light of contemporary science. According to Russell, our knowledge of physical objects is inferred from percepts (sense data) in our brain. One may ask why Russell does not simply accept Phenomenalism since he makes percepts primary to our knowledge. Russell concedes that Phenomenalism is not impossible. But there are deeper reasons for rejecting it. Let me mention three of them, together with the Phenomenalist response.[9]

1. *Appearance and Reality* The stick in water appears bent, and we all agree that this is an illusion, but the Phenomenalist can find no essential difference between this and our visual perception of the stick out of water (or our tactile perception of the straightness of the stick even while in water) as the way it really is shaped, for the Phenomenalist can admit no difference between appearance and reality. The real–unreal and genuine–counterfeit distinctions vanish. Material things consist of sense data and nothing else.

But the Phenomenalist responds that the everyday distinctions between reality and appearance are not metaphysical ones but practical, enabling us to deal with the experiences we encounter.

> What causes us to condemn an experience as an "illusion" is that it leads us astray. A mirage is an illusion because it causes us to make a mistake. But what kind of mistake? Surely, not the mistake of thinking that we now see trees and water, but the mistake of expecting that we shall soon be able to have a drink and sit down in the shade. The mistake consists in the false expectation of certain other sense data. Thus, the illusoriness is not in the sense data itself, but in the expectation which we form when we sense it.[10]

The bent stick in the water is an illusion too because sticks that "look bent" usually "feel bent" as well, and so we are surprised to find that it feels straight.

2. *The Permanency of Material Things* Sensations are flighty, intermittent, depending on our sense organs, but material objects, we intuitively suppose, are permanent things, enduring uninterruptedly for long periods of time (and are not mind dependent).

I don't annihilate this room and all of you every time I close my eyes. On a Phenomenalist account it would seem that we could not say this stone has existed ten years or one million years without it having a rotation shift of nurse–watchers to keep it in existence.

The Phenomenalist replies with John Stuart Mill that sense data are "permanent possibilities of sensation," so we may distinguish between an actual or possible sense datum. To say that there is a table in my office now is to say that if there were anyone in the room he would be having the kind of experience that we call seeing a table. "There is a table" means "Go and look and you will see a table."

Still, we might ask, What sense can be given to the directive "Go and look and you will see a table"? Does it mean that you will have experiences as if you were going to look and you will have experiences as if you were seeing a table? The problem is that you could have such experiences in a dream or hallucination.

3. *Causal Activity* Causal interaction in Nature seems undermined by Phenomenalism. As Whiteley says, "Surely, the room cannot be warmed by my visual sense datum of a fire! Still less can it be warmed by the possibility of a visual sense datum of a fire during my absence, when I am not looking at the fire, but the room gets warmed all the same." Ideas are inert and can do nothing.

The Phenomenalist responds, as Stace does in the earlier quotation, We should reinterpret the concept of causality. We never see "causes," but only regular succession of events.

I think that this response is inadequate, for we generally believe that a cause is something that actually exists and that something that does not actually exist or occur can have no effects. Phenomenalism implausibly makes causality a relation between something and nothing, since most of the causes are unperceived.

Representationalism, we saw, led to Phenomenalism, and Phenomenalism seems to take the world away from us, landing us, if not completely back into skepticism, then into solipsism, the view that no one else exists besides me. If I can only have sense experiences of my own, then how can I take other people's experiences into account?

A Return to Direct Realism So where does that leave us? Perhaps you will choose between Phenomenalism and Representationalism, but some philosophers, like D. M. Armstrong, John Searle, and William Alston have returned to Direct Realism, though not a "naive" variety, but one chastened by the long history of the problem. Armstrong defines perception as the acquiring of beliefs (true or false) about the current state of our bodies or environment. In perceiving, we do encounter the world directly, though always through the interpretive powers of our mind.

One reason Armstrong rejects Representationalism and Phenomenalism is the problematic notion of sense data. These intermediary things seem unnecessary and even paradoxical. They are unnecessary because we can give an account of our perceptions as taking in objects in the world directly. They are paradoxical in two ways.

The first is the nontransitivity of perception. Take three pieces of red colored paper. Suppose that we cannot distinguish between samples *A* and *B*. They seem exactly the same color. Likewise, samples *B* and *C* are indistinguishable. But we can distinguish between *A* and *C*! Given the notion of sense data this is puzzling, since we should be able to distinguish our sense data from one another. The second puzzle is indeterminateness. Suppose we see a speckled hen. How many speckles does our sense datum hold? If we say that it is indeterminate, we seem to have a paradox between the indeterminate sense datum and the determinate objects that are supposed to be represented.[11]

Adverbial Perception   Many philosophers have sought to avoid taking a strong stand on the philosophy of perception by simply using adverbial language. For example, when seeing a red book, I state my perception in appearance language, "I am appeared to redly and bookishly," or when seeing a red ball, "I am appeared to redly and ballishly." This is known as the "adverbial theory of perception," and it receives its fullest expression in the work of Roderick Chisholm (1916–).[12] The theory has the advantage of doing without the troublesome notion of sense data and being compatible with Direct Realism, Representationalism, and Phenomenalism. It points to the fact that we experience things in particular ways. The question of whether they are appearing the way they really are or are not is a separate question. One questions whether this adverbial locution isn't just a grammatically awkward manuever to cover our perplexity. It may be wiser to admit how little we know about the nature of perception, choose the least objectionable theory, and interpret ordinary language accordingly.

SUMMARY

The problem of perception concerns our knowledge of the external world. Three theories have been advanced to solve that problem: (1) Direct Realism, which holds that we know the world directly and pretty much as it is; (2) Representationalism, which holds that we know the world indirectly pretty much as it is—at least regarding the primary qualities; and (3) Idealism or Phenomenalism, which holds that all we really know are sense data. John Locke set forth the classical rendition of Representationalism, distinguishing between primary and secondary qualities. George Berkeley, criticizing Locke's theory as dangerous, loathsome, and absurd, put forth the classic version of Idealism, whose motto was "to be is to be perceived." The fact that God is always perceiving us and the world insures our continued existence. Modern Phenomenalists follow Berkeley, but subtract the notion of God from the epistemic domain. There has been a move by contemporary epistemologists like D. M. Armstrong and John Searle back to Direct Realism, but the issue is one of lively debate.

QUESTIONS FOR DISCUSSION

1. Why is the subject of perception a philosophical problem? Do you think that science has decided on the answer? Explain.

2. Explain the theory of Direct Realism. What are the objections to it? Can you defend a version of Direct Realism against criticisms?

3. Examine Locke's theory of indirect realism (Representationalism). What are its strengths and weaknesses? Do you agree with Berkeley's criticisms?

4. What are sense data? What are the objections to their existence?

5. Examine Phenomenalism. What are its strengths and weaknesses?

6. Having worked through the problem of perception, which theory makes the most sense?

NOTES

1. Bertrand Russell, *Problems of Philosophy* (Oxford: Oxford University Press, 1912), 7, 8.

2. Bertrand Russell, *Inquiry into Meaning and Truth* (London: Allen & Unwin, 1940), 15.

3. John Locke, *An Essay Concerning Human Understanding,* vol. II (London: Awsham & John Churchill, 1689), 104.

4. Ibid., II. viii. 9.

5. George Berkeley, *A Treatise Concerning the Principles of Human Knowledge* (Oxford: Oxford University Press, n.d.), par. 14.

6. Berkeley wrote in his notebook, "I wonder not at my sagacity in discovering the obvious though amazing truth, I rather wonder at my stupid inadvertency in not finding it out before." He was astonished at the strong reaction against his position.

7. Berkeley, op. cit.

8. W. T. Stace, "Science and the Physical World," *Man Against Darkness and Other Essays* (Pittsburgh: University of Pittsburgh Press, 1967).

9. I am indebted to C. H. Whiteley, *An Introduction to Metaphysics* (London: Methuen & Co, 1950), who points out three advantages of Phenomenalism. It removes doubt and skepticism. We can't really doubt that there is a table before us,

but the Representationalist program would lead us to doubt it. The sense data are all there is, so there is no cause to doubt—unless we suspect that there are pseudosense data.

It answers the problem of deception but does it solve the problem of Descartes's demon or dream hypothesis?

It saves us from worrying about involvement with unobservable matter. We can preserve our empiricism. Science becomes "the recording, ordering, and forecasting of human experience."

10. Ibid. See also A. J. Ayer, *Central Questions of Philosophy* (New York: Holt, Rinehart and Winston, 1973), 106.

11. D. M. Armstrong, *Perception and the Physical World* (London: Routledge & Kegan Paul, 1961). See also John Searle, *Intentionality* (Oxford: Oxford University Press, 1983) and William Alston, *Epistemic Justification* (Ithaca, NY: Cornell University Press, 1989).

12. See Roderick Chisholm, *Perceiving: A Philosophical Study* (Ithaca, NY: Cornell University Press, 1957) and *Theory of Knowledge* (Englewood Cliffs, NJ: Prentice-Hall, 1989). Robert Audi has a good discussion of this theory in *Belief, Justification, and Knowledge* (Belmont, CA: Wadsworth, 1988), 21–24.

FOR FURTHER READING

Alston, William. *The Reliability of Sense Perception*. Ithaca, NY: Cornell University Press, 1993. Alston argues that we must rely on circular arguments to defend the view that sense perception is a reliable source of beliefs.

Armstrong, D. M. *Perception and the Physical World*. London: Routledge & Kegan Paul, 1961. A thorough defense of Direct Realism. Advanced.

Berkeley, George. *Three Dialogues Between Hylas and Philonous*. Oxford: Oxford University Press, 1713. The classic defense of Idealism.

Heil, John. *Perception and Cognition*. Berkeley: University of California Press, 1983. A clear, thoughtful presentation.

Landesman, Charles. *Color and Consciousness*. Philadelphia: Temple University Press, 1989. A provocative defense of Representationalism.

Locke, John. *An Essay Concerning Human Understanding*. London: Awsham & John Churchill, 1689. The classic defense of Representationalism.

Pojman, Louis, ed. *The Theory of Knowledge*, 2d ed. Belmont, CA: Wadsworth, 1999. Contains several relevant essays on the topics discussed in this chapter.

PART IV

Philosophy of Mind

13

The Mind-Body Problem

The curiosity of Man and the cunning of his Reason have revealed much of what Nature held hidden. The structure of spacetime, the constitution of matter, the many forms of energy, the nature of life itself; all of these mysteries have become open books to us. To be sure, deep questions remain unanswered and revolutions await us still, but it is difficult to exaggerate the explosion in scientific understanding we humans have fashioned over the past 500 years.

Despite this general advance, a central mystery remains largely a mystery: the nature of conscious intelligence.[1]

—PAUL CHURCHLAND

DUALISTIC INTERACTIONISM

Intuitively, there seem to be two different types of reality: *material* and *mental.* There are bodies and minds. Bodies are solid, material entities, extended in three-dimensional space, publicly observable, measurable, and capable of causing things to happen in accordance with invariant laws of mechanics. Minds, on the other hand, have none of these properties. Consciousness is not solid or material, is not extended in three-dimensional space, does not occupy space at all, is directly observable only by the person who owns it, cannot be measured, and seems incapable of causing things to happen in accordance with invariant laws of mechanics. Only the person himself can think his thoughts, feel his emotions, and suffer his pain. Although a neurosurgeon can open the skull and observe the brain, she cannot observe a person's mind or its beliefs, sensations, emotions, or desires. Unlike physical bodies, mental entities have no shape, weight, length, width, height, color, mass, velocity, or temperature. It would sound odd indeed to speak of a belief weighing 10 pounds like a sack of potatoes, a feeling of love measuring 8 feet by 10 feet like a piece of carpet, a pain being as heavy as a bag of cement, or a desire being green and having a temperature of 103 degrees.

Yet common sense tells us that these two entities somehow interact. We step on a nail, and it pierces our skin, sending a message through our nervous system that results in something altogether different from the shape or size of the nail or skin, something that does not possess size or shape and that cannot be seen, smelled, tasted, or heard—a feeling of distress or pain. Whereas the nail is public, the pain is private.

Our mind informs us that it would be a good thing to get a bandage to put over the cut that has resulted from stepping on the nail (maybe a tetanus shot, too); in this way, the mind causes us to move our body. Our legs carry us to the medicine cabinet, where we stop, raise our arms, and with our hands take hold of the cabinet, open it, and take the bandage out, and then apply it dexterously to the wound. Here we have an instance where the body affects the mind and the mind in turn affects the body. So *common sense* shows that a close interactive relationship exists between these two radically different entities. This position is called **Dualistic Interactionism,** the theory, classically set forth by the French philosopher, René Descartes (1596–1650), that the body and the mind are different substances that causally interact on each other. We can represent it pictorially in the following manner: Let *BS* represent "brain state," *MS* represent "mental state," and → represent "causation." The dualistic interactive picture of reality looks like this:

For example, stepping on the nail causes the first brain state (BS_1) that in turn causes the first mental state (MS_1—the feeling of pain in one's foot) that in turn causes us (via a brain state) to decide to move our foot (BS_2) that in turn brings relief from the pain (MS_2) as well as the intention to get a bandage for our wound (MS_3) that leads to the third brain state (BS_3) that causes us to move toward the first-aid kit in the bathroom. But the questions arise: Exactly *how* does this transaction between the mind and brain occur? How can something completely physical (the body and brain) affect something nonphysical (the mind)? Is there a semiphysical hook that connects the two different realities? And *where* does the interaction take place? Descartes thought it was the pineal gland, which we now know to be implausible. The problem of interactive causation haunted Duelist Interactionism. Materialists seek to solve the problem by denying the existence of the spiritual or mental, or arguing that the mind is just a function of the body, not a separate substance at all? Or could the **Idealist Monists** be correct in asserting that the body is really an illusion and that there is only one substance, the mind alone? The following schema (Table 13.1) represents the three main positions discussed in this chapter. Note that both idealism and materialism are **monisms,** reducing all reality to one underlying substance. Dualism opposes both types of monism.

Table 13.1

Theory	Nature of Substance	Philosophers	Religion
Dualist interactionism	Mental and physical	Plato René Descartes John Locke John Eccles J. P. Moreland David Chalmers	
Ideal monism	Mental	George Berkeley	Hinduism Christian Science
Material monism	Physical	Thomas Hobbes Julien La Mettrie Bertrand Russell Paul Churchland Daniel Dennett	
Behaviorism	Physical	B. F. Skinner Gilbert Ryle W. V. Quine	

There are several types of dualism besides interactionism. The most notable is **Epiphenomenalism,** which posits a one-way causal relationship: The body affects the mind, causing mental events, but the mind does not affect the body. Mental events are like the babbling of brooks, the exhaust from a car's engine, or the smoke from a train's chimney. They are effects of physical processes but do not themselves cause motion in the water, the car, or the train. Epiphenomenalism is represented in the following schema:

$$MS_1 \quad MS_2 \quad MS_3 \quad MS_4$$
$$\uparrow \qquad \uparrow \qquad \uparrow \qquad \uparrow$$
$$BS_1 \rightarrow BS_2 \rightarrow BS_3 \rightarrow BS_4$$

There is also a view known as **Parallelism,** which holds that there are two parallel realities: one mental and one physical connected with human action. Gottfried Wilhelm Leibniz (1646–1716) held that God established two separate causal series that were set to run side-by-side, like two clocks, in a preestablished harmony, so that it appears that they are related to each other:

$$MS_1 \rightarrow MS_2 \rightarrow MS_3 \rightarrow MS_4$$

$$BS_1 \rightarrow BS_2 \rightarrow BS_3 \rightarrow BS_4$$

A similar theory is **Occasionalism,** held by Nicholas Malebranche (1638–1715), which explains the problem of how the body and mind interact by asserting that when humans have a mental desire (e.g., to raise one's arm), God causes the event to occur (the arm is raised by God.

There is also a view called **Panpsychism,** which holds that everything in nature has a mind or a soul. Panpsychism is a correlate to pantheism, which holds that everything is God or contains God. According to panpsychism, soul or mind is in the ultimate particles of physics, and only because of this can we experience consciousness.

Finally, one other theory should be noted: **Neutral Monism,** the view that one common but unknown substance underlies all reality, matter, and mind. Baruch Spinoza (1632–1677) first put forth this position, though it was developed by William James (1842–1910) at the end of the nineteenth century. Although this may seem a suitable compromise between those who are attracted to monism and those who are inclined to dualism, neutral monism actually compounds the problem: Now not only do we not understand matter and mind, but we also have a third mystery to worry about. If it is true, there seems little evidence for it. Yet, given the difficulties with the other positions, you may finally select it as the least objectionable of the lot. Mind and body are just two aspects of one reality. That is, matter has a double aspect.

MATERIALISM

Materialism, the theory that matter and the law of physics constitute ultimate reality, has several versions. The simplest version is **Behaviorism,** which either denies mental events or denies their importance in understanding behavior. **Methodological Behaviorism** holds that since we cannot study the soul (we cannot measure soul states), we are simply forced to confine our scientific research to the body's behavior, using *input* stimulation together with behavioral *outputs.* **Logical or Metaphysical Behaviorism,** on the other hand, goes further and denies that mental events exist. They can be reduced to behavioral dispositions and events. Proponents of this theory include W. V. Quine, Karl Hempel, and Gilbert Ryle. They characterized behavior in terms of hypothetical dispositions. For example, the claim that Tom believes it is raining can be translated into the condition, *If Tom believes it is raining, he will close the windows where rain may come in and will take an umbrella when he goes outside.* The input of information about rain will yield an output of his closing windows and taking an umbrella outside. However, on analysis, it soon became apparent that one needed mental categories to define these dispositions. Tom will not take an umbrella with him if he wants to get wet (say after a dry summer).

A more basic objection is simply the fact that we know we have mental states that are not reducible to behavior. Mental states are self-evident phenomena. I know I am in pain even when I don't admit it to you or neglect to take an aspirin. Patients undergoing operations who are given a paralyzing drug, such as curare, manifest no outward behavior, yet feel pain. These facts led the linguists Ogden and Richards to accuse the behaviorists of "feigning anesthesia." Metaphysical behaviorism was prominent in the first half of this century, but two strong objections have caused it to be virtually abandoned in philosophy of mind. The successor of behaviorism is **Functionalism,** which we will study in Chapter 15. Functionalism denies that there is any one type of brain state or event that can always be correlated with a type of mental event. For example, I may feel pain in my hand on two different occasions, but may have two *different* areas of the brain activated. Actually, functionalism need not be materialist at all. It could be agnostic on the mind-body problem, confining itself to outputs of human activity.

The third version of materialism is **Reductive Materialism,** which attempts to find a one-to-one correlation between mental states and brain states and identifies the former with the latter. Beliefs, pains, and desires will turn out, on this account, to be simply brain states.

The final version is **Eliminative Materialism,** which contends that our ordinary talk about mental events is mistaken. Our commonsense conceptual scheme is labeled **Folk Psychology** and includes the concepts of belief, desire, emotion, perception, and sensation. When we learn more about our brains and the way they work, we will be able to replace this subjectivist speech with a more scientific discourse. For example, instead of talking about a headache in my forehead, we might talk about certain C-fibers firing in my brain. (We will examine reductive and eliminative materialism in Chapter 14.)

First, we turn to René Descartes's classic rendition of interactive dualism (sometimes called *substance dualism*). After doubting everything that it is possible to doubt, including that he has a body, Descartes asks, "What am I?" and comes to the conclusion that he is not essentially a body but a mind:

> I am not a collection of members which we call the human body: I am not a subtle air distributed through these members, I am not a wind, a fire, a vapor, a breath, nor anything at all which I can imagine or conceive; because I have assumed [through doubt] that all these were nothing.[2]

But he cannot doubt that he himself, as a thinking thing, exists:

> But what then am I? A thing which thinks. What is a thing which thinks? It is a thing which doubts, understands, conceives, affirms, denies, wills, refuses, which also imagines and feels.

According to Descartes, three kinds of objects or substances exist in the universe: (1) the eternal substance, God; (2) his creation in terms of mind; (3) his creation in terms of matter. Humans are made up of the latter two types of substance.

> We may thus easily have two clear and distinct notions or ideas, the one of created substance which thinks, and the other of corporeal substances, provided we carefully separate all the attributes of thought from those of extension.

That is, mind and matter have different properties, so they must be different substances.

We are thinking substances, or embodied minds,

> for I am not only lodged in my body as a pilot in a ship, but I am very closely united to it, and so to speak so intermingle with it that I seem to compose with it one whole. For if that were not the case, when my body is hurt, I, who am merely a thinking thing, should perceive this wound by the understanding only, just as the sailor perceives by sight when something is damaged in his vessel.[3]

The two kinds of substances that make us each a person intermingle in such a way that they causally act on each other. Although it might be that a mind interacts with each part of its body separately, Descartes's view is that the mind interacts only with the brain. The material event that causally stimulates one of our five senses (e.g., light hitting the retina of the eye) results in a chain of physical causation that leads to a certain brain process from which a certain sensation results. Then, in turn, being affected by the brain, the mind through mental events acts on the brain that in turn affects the body. Descartes thought he could pinpoint the place in the brain where the interaction between mind and brain took place:

> The part of the body in which the soul exercises its function immediately is in nowise the heart, nor the whole of the brain, but merely the most inward of all its parts, to wit, a certain very small gland which is situated in the middle of its substance."[4]

This gland, the pineal gland, is the seat of the mind. It functions as the intermediary that transmits the effects of the mind to the brain and the effects of the brain to the mind. There is no reason to believe that the pineal gland is the seat of the mind, and neuroscience has given a better explanation of its function. We will disregard Descartes's mistake about the pineal gland and accept the essential structure of his theory as the classic expression of dualistic interactionism.

Descartes's view seems close to what we arrive at through common sense. We seem to be aware of two different kinds of events: physical and mental, as described earlier in this chapter. Mental events cause physical events, and physical events cause mental events. At this point, the interactionist argues that epiphenomenalism is mistaken in making the causal direction only one way. What evolutionary use is the mind if it does no work? Epiphenomenalism seems to violate Newton's dictum that "nature does nothing in vain." It is a useless fifth wheel. On the contrary, the dualist avers, our intuitions inform us that the reasons (grasped by the mind) initiate causal chains resulting in physical actions and other mental events. For example, I may decide (a mental event) to imagine all the friends I have ever had and call them up to consciousness. The epiphenomenalist account glosses over the introspective process and states that all of these decisions and imaginings are simply the by-products of mysterious physical processes. With friends like that, the interactionist concludes, who needs materialist enemies?

Most of our mental states seem private and incorrigible. Only I can know whether I am really in pain, whether I really believe that God exists, whether I really intend to keep a promise or to be a moral person. True, perhaps I can misremember or be mistaken about a borderline feeling (is it a slight pain or a sharp tickle? lemon-flavored ice cream or a variety of orange-flavored ice cream?), but for a whole host of experiences, introspection is reliable. Folk Psychology works.[5]

A CRITIQUE
OF DUALISTIC INTERACTIONISM

Nonetheless, there are severe problems with dualistic interactionism. Here are the five most prominent ones:

1. Where does the interaction of the soul and body take place?
2. How does the interaction occur?
3. How can the idea of the mental causing the physical be reconciled with the principle of the conservation of energy?
4. How can the idea of two realities, body and mind, be reconciled with Occam's Razor, the principle of simplicity?
5. How can one, who knows himself as a mental being, account for other minds, which he never directly experiences?

Let's take up each problem in turn. We have already discussed the first two problems, so we can be brief there. Where does the interaction take place? Descartes thought it was in the pineal gland, but no evidence supports this or that the pineal gland has anything to do with consciousness. The problem is that whereas physical states have spatial location, mental states do not. Mental substance is not subject to the laws of physics (otherwise, we would conclude it was material). But if we cannot speak of mental states having location, it seems odd to speak of a *where* in which they "touch" or "meet" or "interact" with physical objects.

This certainly raises an interesting puzzle. The dualist responds that we do not have to understand where the mind is located (that may be a nonsensical question) to be able to say that it affects the brain *in* the brain. That is, we posit that there are metaphysical laws in addition to physical laws. God, mind, and the realm of the spirit operate within the realm of the former kind of laws.

The second problem—how does the interaction occur?—is very similar to the first. How can physical states result in something wholly other, something mental? To move a stalled car, several people must push it. Force must be exerted in every physical change, and force is a product of mass and acceleration, so that whatever exerts force must be capable of physical movement. But nothing mental has mass or acceleration (mental objects do not travel through space from your hometown to the university). So nothing mental can exert physical force or be affected by force. Thus, nothing physical can be causally affected by anything mental, nor can anything mental be causally influenced by anything physical.

How might dualists reply to this difficult problem? One way might be to respond like Hamlet, that "there are more things in heaven and earth, Horatio, than is written in your philosophy." Why should we suppose that substances must be qualitatively similar before they can influence each other? Doesn't the very thought that someone is out to harm you cause a state of psychological and physical depression or fear? Isn't my decision to raise my hand obviously an example of the mind causing the body to move? Isn't agency itself testimony to the truth of interactionism? Perhaps free agency, the source of the second example, is a myth or an illusion, but it cannot be dismissed out of hand. An argument is needed to exclude introspective reports for free will as evidence for dualistic interaction. We will turn to the problem of freedom of the will in Part V.

The third problem involves the principle of the conservation of energy. This principle states that the amount of energy in a closed physical system remains constant; so if there is causal interaction between mental events and physical events, the principle of conservation of energy is violated. Energy is a function of matter, not mind. But the dualist believes that my decision to pick up the book in front of me somehow creates the necessary energy to cause the book to rise. So it would seem, on dualist premises, that the principle of the conservation of energy is violated.

Once again dualists are faced with a formidable challenge. At least three options are open for them:

1. The principle of the conservation of energy applies only to closed systems, but the universe may be an open system. Energy may come and go at different points. The trouble with this answer is that contemporary physics operates on the assumption that the universe is a closed system. This has ramifications for the notion of divine

intervention. The theist, believing that God sometimes intervenes in the universe, thus altering energy states from without, seems committed to an open universe.

2. There may be a replacement of energy within the closed system, so that when ten ergons appear via my decision to lift the book, ten ergons disappear in another place. This is possible, but, of course, it is just an ad hoc hypothesis necessary to save the theory.

3. It may not be necessary that mental causation involves a transfer of energy but only a harnessing or redirection of energies. The problem with the redirection hypothesis is that one would like to know how the mind can affect the direction of energy flow without itself being a form of energy. This brings us back to problem 2 discussed previously.

We turn to the fourth objection to dualism, which gets us into the arguments for materialist monism. The idea of two realities, body and mind, seems to violate Occam's Razor, the principle of simplicity. The principle of simplicity is an abductive principle (i.e., one having to do with arriving at the best explanation) that claims we should prefer explanations that minimize the number of entities postulated. All things being equal, isn't it better to have one all-embracing explanation of several different events rather than two? Instead of the puzzle of substance interaction, wouldn't the posit of a single substance with a single set of laws have the advantage of giving us a unified picture of reality?

Imagine that two murders have been committed in a large nearby city, one in the southern part of town on Monday afternoon during rush hour, and one in the northern part a half hour later. In both cases, a woman has been killed by an assailant who sucks blood from her neck and leaves a picture of Dracula on the corpse. On the one hand, the evidence points to two murderers, committing the crimes independently, for it would be difficult for someone to get from the southern part of town to the northern part of town in a half hour, especially during rush hour. However, it would greatly simplify the police's investigation if they could assume some way of traveling between the two places in 30 minutes and so be on the lookout for one murderer instead of two. It would be too great a coincidence if two vampires acting independently should both strike in the same city within a half hour of each other. The quest for economy and reduction to simpler basic units seems to be of great importance in explaining phenomena.

This is the commonsense motivation that informs the tendency toward monism. Unless there is a compelling reason not to do so, simplicity and economy of explanation, reducing differences to an underlying unity, are desirable for problem solving. The question is whether there is a compelling reason for not making a move to simplicity. Since the duelist's response at this point is global, having to do with the entire product of materialist monism, we might well postpone it until we see the case for materialism.

Finally, the dualist has difficulty explaining other minds. I am aware of my mental events, that I feel pain and pleasure and have fears, hopes, and beliefs, but I never directly experience anyone else's mental states. When I hit my finger with a hammer, I feel pain, but when I hit someone else's finger with the hammer, I don't feel a thing. The dualist tries to answer this by arguing that we can infer from the same input of physical happening, the same state of mental experience would result, but this is unsound logic. Normally, we reason from many experiences to the next one or to an inductive generalization, but in this case we're doing just the reverse, arguing from one experience to the many. The dualist seems driven to *solipsism,* the view that only I exist as a mental being, everyone else being a mere physical robot. Of course, no one really believes this, but the logic of dualism tends in that implausible direction.

DUALISM REVIVED

Recently David Chalmers has sought to defend dualist interactionism. His main argument, **The Zombie Argument,** is contined in the following passage from his book *The Conscious Mind:*

> . . . consider the logical possibility of a *zombie:* someone or something physically identical to me (or to any other conscious being), but lacking conscious experiences altogether. At the global level, we can consider the logical possibility of a *zombie world:* a world physically identical to ours, but in which there are no conscious experiences at all. In such a world, everybody is a zombie.
>
> So let us consider my zombie twin. This creature is molecule for molecule identical to me, and identical in all the low-level properties postulated by a completed physics, but he lacks conscious experience entirely. (Some might prefer to call a zombie "it," but I use the personal pronoun; I have grown quite fond of my zombie twin.) To fix ideas, we can imagine that right now I am gazing out the window, experiencing some nice green sensations from seeing the trees outside, having pleasant taste experiences through munching on a chocolate bar, and feeling a dull aching sensation in my right shoulder.
>
> What is going on in my zombie twin? He is physically identical to me, and we may as well suppose that he is embedded in an identical environment. He will certainly be identical to me *functionally:* he will be processing internal configurations being modified appropriately and with indistinguishable behavior resulting. He will be *psychologically* identical to me . . . He will be perceiving the trees outside, in the functional sense, and tasting the chocolate, in the psychological sense. All of this follows logically from the fact that he is physically identical to me, by virtue of the functional analyses of psychological notions . . . It is just that none of this functioning will be accompanied by any real conscious experience. There will be no phenomenal feel. There is nothing it is like to be a zombie.[6]

According to the Zombie argument, then, it is logically possible that there be a world in which people are exactly like us in every physical detail, but do not have experiences, or have experiences that are not like anything to have. These people would be indistinguishable from us in terms of behavior and physical structure down to the last detail. Chalmers thinks that since we can conceive of zombies who are physically identical to us but lacking consciousness, and following Hume, whatever can be conceptually distinguished is different, we must have consciousness as a separate substance. We must be minds as well as physical bodies.

What do you make of Chalmers' theory? It has stirred up a lot of debate, but the essential problem is that it doesn't disprove that consciousness is a biological process, ontologically part of the brain's make-up and processes. The main objection is that it could well be that zombies are impossible. A being could not be exactly like us but lack conciousness. Interactive Dualism is certainly a logical possibility. But so is Epiphenomenalism. Or some kind of Materialism or Functionalism could be the true explanation. One has to make a case that one theory is explanatorily richer than the others. In the next two chapters we will examine rivals to Substance Dualism.

SUMMARY

The mind-body problem arises because we have at least two separate types of strong beliefs: On the one hand, it seems obvious that consciousness and mental states like pains and feelings are not physical entities. They are mental, not material. On the other hand, neuroscience seems to indicate that our mental states are reducible to brain states, where there is no place for a separate mental faculty. Interactive dualism seems intuitively obvious until we notice the philosophical objections to it.

Epiphenomenalism, the one-way causal traffic from matter to mind, though logically possible, seems to make mind a useless fifth wheel. Thus, we are led to examine forms of materialism.

THE MIND-BODY PROBLEM

Here is a table of the main positions in this chapter, followed by a summary.

Theory	Substance	Theory	Substance
Idealism (monistic idealism)	Mental	Materialism	
Dualism		Metaphysical behaviorism	All is physical
Dualistic interactionism	Focuses on mental and physical relations	Material monism (reductive and eliminative)	All is physical
Epiphenomenalism	Mental and physical but primarily physical	Functionalism	Focuses on input-output relations and mental events
Parallelism	Mental and physical	Neutral monism	A third reality underlies the other two substances
Panpsychism	Everything has mind		
Pantheism	Everything is God		

Idealism (Monistic Idealism)
Only the mental exists: minds and ideas. Matter is an illusion. This position is held by Hindus and Christian Scientists and received its fullest defense in the work of Bishop George Berkeley (1685–1753).

Dualism
Dualistic Interactionism
Mind and matter both exist. This is the position of René Descartes (1596–1650), which most people in Western culture have held. We can represent it pictorially in the following manner: Let BS represent "brain state," MS represent "mental state," and let $\rightarrow$ represent "causation." The dualistic interactive process looks like this:

$$MS_1 \qquad MS_2 \rightarrow MS_3 \qquad MS_4$$
$$BS_1 \quad BS_2 \qquad\qquad BS_3 \quad BS_4 \rightarrow BS_5$$

Epiphenomenalism
Epiphenomenalism posits a one-way causal relationship: The body (including the brain) affects the mind, causing mental events, but the mind does not affect the body. Mental events are like the babbling of brooks, the exhaust from a car's engine, or the smoke from a train's chimney. They are effects of physical processes but do not themselves cause motion in the water, the car, or the train. The process looks like this:

$$MS_1 \qquad MS_2 \qquad MS_3 \qquad MS_4$$
$$BS_1 \rightarrow BS_2 \rightarrow BS_3 \rightarrow BS_4$$

Parallelism
Parallelism holds that two parallel realities are connected with human action, one mental and one physical. This view was put forth by the German philosopher Gottfried Wilhelm Leibniz (1646–1716), who said that God established two separate causal series, like two clocks, each set to run in preestablished harmony. The process looks like this:

$$MS_1 \rightarrow MS_2 \rightarrow MS_3 \rightarrow MS_4$$

$$BS_1 \rightarrow BS_2 \rightarrow BS_3 \rightarrow BS_4$$

Panpsychism
Panpsychism holds that everything in nature has mind or soul.

Pantheism
Pantheism holds that everything is God. There is no distinction between God and the world. They are the same reality. In the East this view is found in the Hindu scriptures and in the West in the writings of Paracelsus and Spinoza.

Materialism (Physicalism)
Metaphysical Behaviorism
Metaphysical behaviorism either denies mental events or their importance in understanding behavior.

Reductive Materialism
Reductive materialism (identity theory) finds a one-to-one correlation between mental states and events and brain states and events. Beliefs, pains, and desires are mental events that occur in the brain—that is, they are happening in the brain.

Eliminative Materialism
Eliminative materialism, like reductive materialism, denies mental states but goes further and denies our way of characterizing mental events as beliefs, desires,

pains, and the like. Our commonsense views of mental events constitute a faulty Folk Psychology that cannot stand up to inspection. A science of brain events should replace Folk Psychology. Eventually, we will not talk of pain but of a C-fiber firing in a certain place.

Functionalism
Functionalism emphasizes the input-output relations of behavior. But unlike behaviorism, it admits the importance of mental events (and of introspection). Against reductive materialism, it denies that just one type of brain state can always be correlated with a type of mental event. Just as a watch can be operated by a battery or springs, different material constructions could yield the same kind of mental event.

Neutral Monism
Neutral monism is a fourth type of position (neither idealism, dualism, nor materialism). It posits a third underlying reality, of which matter and mind are manifestations. The view was first put forward by Baruch Spinoza (1632–1677) and developed by William James (1842–1910).

QUESTIONS FOR DISCUSSION

1. What are the primary issues involved in the mind–body problem? How do the various theories discussed in this chapter answer those concerns?

2. Examine the arguments for and against dualistic interactionism. How strong are the criticisms against this position? Can these criticisms be answered?

3. What is epiphenomenalism? What are its strengths and weaknesses?

4. What is the principle of simplicity, and how does it affect the discussion of dualism?

5. What is behaviorism? What are some problems with it?

6. Examine David Chalmers' Zombie Argument. What do you think of it? Why?

NOTES

1. Paul Churchland, *Matter and Consciousness* (Cambridge, MA: MIT Press, 1990), 1.

2. *The Philosophical Works of Descartes,* vol. 1, trans. E. Haldane and G. R. T. Ross (Cambridge, Eng.: Cambridge University Press, 1911), 152. Reprinted in Louis Pojman, ed., *Philosophy: The Quest for Truth,* 4th ed. (Belmont, CA: Wadsworth, 1999), 221.

3. Ibid., 192. In Pojman, ibid., 222.

4. Ibid., 345. In Pojman, ibid., 222.

5. Interactive dualism has come under much attack recently by eliminative materialists, as an outmoded Folk Psychology, but so far nothing is even near to taking its place. See both Stich and Churchland, listed in "For Further Reading."

6. Chalmers, David. *The Conscious Mind: In Search of a Fundamental Theory.* (Oxford: Oxford University Press, 1996), 94–95.

FOR FURTHER READING

Beakley, Brian, and Peter Ludlow, eds. *The Philosophy of Mind: Classical Problems and Contemporary Issues.* Cambridge, MA: MIT Press, 1992. An excellent anthology.

Chalmers, David. *The Conscious Mind: In Search of a Fundamental Theory.* Oxford: Oxford University Press, 1996.

Churchland, Paul. *Matter and Consciousness.* Cambridge, MA: MIT Press, 1990. A superb introductory text from a materialist perspective.

Dennett, Daniel. *The Intentional Stance.* Cambridge, MA: MIT Press, 1989. A brilliant discussion of the mental states.

Levin, Michael E. *Metaphysics and the Mind-Body Problem.* Oxford: Clarendon Press, 1979. An excellent defense of materialism. My illustration of the principle of simplicity was taken from this work.

Lycan, William, ed. *Mind and Cognition.* Oxford: Blackwell, 1991. An excellent anthology.

McGinn, Colin. *The Character of Mind.* Oxford: Oxford University Press, 1982. A rich, compact exposition of the major issues.

Moreland, J. P. *Scaling the Secular City.* Grand Rapids, MI: Baker Books, 1987. Contains a defense of dualistic interactionism from a Christian perspective.

Rosenthal, David M., ed. *The Nature of Mind.* Oxford: Oxford University Press, 1992. The best anthology of contemporary work available.

Searle, John. *Mind, Brains and Science.* Cambridge, MA: Harvard University Press, 1984. A perceptive work, setting forth puzzles and providing a brilliant analysis of the issues.

Stich, Stephen. *From Folk Psychology to Cognitive Science: The Case Against Belief.* Cambridge, MA: MIT Press, 1983. A provocative work, well worth reading.

14

Materialist Monism

In the afternoon of September 13, 1848, in the Vermont countryside, an affable twenty-five-year-old foreman, Phineas P. Gage, was leading a group of men in laying a new line of the Rutland and Burlington Railroad. They needed to blast a huge rock blocking their way, and so Phineas poured gunpowder into the narrow hole that had been drilled in the rock. Powder in place, the next step was to tamp down the charge, which Phineas proceeded to do. But the iron tamping rod rubbed against the side of the shaft, and a spark ignited the powder, causing an explosion. The iron rod—three and a half feet in length and an inch and a quarter in diameter—burst from the hole, struck Phineas just beneath his left eye, tore through his skull, and landed fifty feet away.

Phineas was thrown to the ground, his limbs twitching convulsively, but soon was able to speak. He was taken to a hotel where doctors were able to stop the bleeding. Amazingly, Phineas lived, but he was transformed from a friendly intelligent leader into an intemperate, unreliable, childish ox with the evil temper to match it.

Materialism says that what we call mind is really a function of the brain; that when the brain is injured, as was the case with Phineas P. Gage, or diseased, the effect is seen in behavior and impaired mental functioning. In Alzheimer's disease, for example, the cerebral cortex and the hippocampus contain abnormal twisted tangles and filaments as well as abnormal neurites. The loss of neurons in the nucleus basalis results in a reduction of choline acetyltransferase, an enzyme needed for normal brain life. The result is the slow death of the brain. Without the brain (or some physical equivalent), no mental states are possible.

Cutting the corpus callosum, the thick band of nerves linking the two hemispheres of the cerebral cortex, can result in two separate centers of consciousness.

Different parts of the brain are responsible for different mental operations. Over thirty years ago, the Canadian neurosurgeon Wilder Penfield conducted a set of experiments in which he used electrodes to stimulate the cerebral cortex of patients. They began to recall memories from the past and even sang lullabies learned in early childhood, which they had forgotten, lending support for the thesis that memories are stored in the neurons of the cerebral cortex.

Furthermore, a systematic correspondence seems to exist between the structure of different animals' brains and the sort of behavior they exhibit. Why do we need such a complex brain with billions of cells and trillions of connections if the mind is located in its own separate substance? If dualism is correct, this intricately constructed, complex brain is unnecessary baggage, superfluous machinery. All that the mind should require is some channel for linking the mental with the physical worlds.

Metaphysical Materialism, the doctrine that matter and the laws of physics make up and govern the entire universe, has a long history. It was held by the first Greek Cosmologists, expounded in greater detail by the Greek philosopher Democritus (ca. 460–370 B.C.) and the Roman Atomist Lucretius (ca. 99–55 B.C.), and given still deeper expression in the work of Thomas Hobbes (1588–1679). Hobbes was a *theist* materialist, who believed that all reality except God is material. God alone is spirit. We are entirely material beings:

> The world (the universe, that is the whole mass of all things that are) is corporeal, that is to say, body; and hath the dimensions of magnitude, namely, length, breadth, and depth; also every part of body, is likewise body, and hath the like dimensions; and consequently every part of the universe is body; and that which is not body, is no part of the universe. And because the universe is all, that which is no part of it, is nothing; and consequently no where. Nor does it follow from this that spirits are nothing; for they have dimensions, and are therefore really bodies; though that name in common speech is only given to visible bodies. Spirit, that which is incorporeal, is a term that rightly belongs to God himself, in whom we consider not what attribute expresses best his nature, which is incomprehensible, but that which best expresses our desire to honor him.[1]

Bringing the discussion into the present, the British philosopher Colin McGinn puts it this way:

> What we call mind is in fact made up of a great number of subcapacities, and each of these depends upon the functioning of the brain. [Neurology] compellingly demonstrates . . . that everything about the mind, from the sensory-motor periphery to the inner sense, is minutely controlled by the brain: if your brain lacks certain chemicals or gets locally damaged, your mind is apt to fall apart at the seams. . . . If parts of the mind depend for their existence upon parts of the brain, then the whole of the mind must so depend too. Hence the soul dies with the brain, which is to say it is mortal.[2]

By materialism neither Hobbes nor contemporary materialists, like McGinn, mean *value materialism,* the thesis that only money and the things money can buy have any value, nor do they necessarily mean that religion or the spiritual aspects of life are ruled out. Indeed, some scholars interpret the biblical view of humanity as materialist rather than dualist (see Chapter 17). The materialists mean simply that the physical system of the brain and the physical events that take place within it are the entirety of our conscious lives. There is no separate mental substance, and mental events are really physical events.

There are two central varieties of materialist monism: reductive and eliminative. Both distinguish themselves from **Metaphysical Behaviorism,** the view that denies or ignores mental events and describes the human condition in terms of dispositions to act. In this chapter, we will examine both forms of materialism.

Reductive Materialism, sometimes known as the **Identity Theory,** admits mental events (though not a separate mental substance) but claims that each mental event is really a brain state or event. Our center of consciousness resides in the brain, probably about two inches behind the forehead. We are conscious of happenings in our cerebral cortex even though they appear to be different from measurable brain states. Thus, a pain in my foot can be identified with a brain event—say, a C-fiber firing—and a belief can be identified with certain sentences symbolically stored in some area of the cerebral cortex.

Eliminative Materialism goes even further in rejecting dualism, calling on us to reject as false the whole Folk Psychology language that makes reference to pains, beliefs, and desires. Such language supposes that our introspective states are incorrigible or infallible reporters of our inner life. Psychological experiments seem to show that we can be mistaken about our introspective reports. So we should reject Folk Psychology for a richer scientific theory. Here is how Richard Rorty, one of the earliest proponents, puts it:

> A certain primitive tribe holds the view that illnesses are caused by demons—a different demon for each sort of illness. When asked what more is known about these demons than that they cause illness, they reply that certain members of the tribe—the witch-doctors—can see, after a meal of sacred mushrooms, various (intangible) humanoid forms on or near the bodies of patients. The witch-doctors have noted, for example, that a blue demon with a long nose accompanies epileptics, a fat red one accompanies sufferers from pneumonia, etc. They know such further facts as that the fat red demon dislikes a certain sort of mold which the witch-doctors give people who have pneumonia. If we encountered such a tribe, we would be inclined to tell them that there are no demons. We would tell them that diseases were caused by germs, viruses, and the like. We would add that the witch-doctors were not seeing demons, but merely having hallucinations.[3]

Rorty goes on to argue that this belief in demons is analogous to our belief that we have pains:

> The absurdity of saying, "Nobody has ever felt a pain" is no greater than that of saying "Nobody has ever seen a demon," if we have a suitable answer to the question, "What was I reporting when I said I felt a pain?" To this question, the science of the future may reply, "You were reporting the occurrence of a certain brain-process, and it would make life simpler for us if you would in the future, say 'My C-fibers are firing' instead of saying 'I'm in pain.'" In so saying, he has as good a prima facie case as the scientist who answers the witch-doctors' question, "What was I reporting when I reported a demon?" by saying, "You were reporting the content of your hallucination, and it would make life simpler if, in the future, you would describe your experience in those terms."[4]

If philosophers like Rorty are right, our Folk Psychology language is as superstitious and misleading as the witch doctors' belief that demons cause illness.

Mental events like pains should not merely be identified with brain states (like C-fibers firing) but should be *replaced* by neurological language, Neurospeak. Instead of saying, "I've a pain in my foot," Neurospeak will say something like "A C-fiber is firing in quadrant A2 of brain LP" (it's unclear whether "persons" will survive Neurospeak). Instead of saying "I believe that so and so will win the presidential election," Neurospeak will tell us to say, "The sentence S17 is manifesting itself in quadrant C56 of cerebral cortex LP."

Whatever the future prospects of eliminative materialism, at present it seems like science fiction or, at best, a research project to excite neuroscientists and their philosopher kin. But we need not choose between reductive and eliminative materialism for our purposes. They both suppose a materialist monism, and the question is whether materialist monism is true.

The main criticism of such monism is that it is obvious on introspection that we have mental events and that any theory that would deny them has a strong presumption of self-evidence to overcome. Reductivism, under the guise of reinterpreting mental events, claims it is not doing away with the events, only showing their true identity as physical events lodged in the brain.

The dualist's criticism of this identification rests on an appeal to *Leibniz's Law* (identity of indiscernibles): Two things are numerically identical if and only if they have all the same properties in common. It can be expressed in this formula (don't be afraid of the symbols):

$$\text{If } (x)(y)[(x = y), \text{ then } (P)\ (Px, \text{ if and only if } Py)]$$

That is, for any two entities x and y, if they really are the same, then if x has property P, y must also have it (and vice versa—if y has the property, x must also). For example, if Superman is really Clark Kent, then it could not be the case that if Superman is six feet tall, Clark Kent is five feet nine inches tall. You certainly couldn't have Superman not being located in space!

The dualist points out that the mind has different properties from the body. The body occupies space and is subject to the laws of physics, whereas the mind doesn't occupy space and doesn't appear to be subject to the same laws. We might set forth the argument like this. Let M stand for "mind," B for "body," and P for "property." Then,

1. B has property P (e.g., extension in space, so can be measured).
2. M lacks property P (so it can't be measured).
3. If B has P and M lacks P, then M is not identical with B.
4. ∴ The mind is not identical with the brain.

As we noted in Chapter 13, bodies are solid, material entities, extended in three-dimensional space, publicly observable, and measurable, whereas minds have none of these properties. Consciousness is not solid or material, is not extended in three-dimensional space, does not occupy space at all, is directly observable only by the person who owns it, cannot be measured, and seems incapable of causing things to happen in accordance with invariant laws of physics. Only the person himself or herself can think his (her) thoughts, feel his (her) emotions, and suffer his (her) pain.

How might the materialist respond to this? Materialists point out that what seems to be different is not always so. In times past, lightning was deemed a mysterious and spiritual force. The ancient Greeks thought that lightning was a thunderbolt of Zeus. Now we know that it is a luminous electrical discharge in the atmosphere, produced by the separation of electrical charges in thunderstorm clouds. Although it may not *appear* to us as electrical charges, physics assures us of that identity.

For eons the nature of life was held to be a mysterious *élan vital:* a spiritual substance that animated whatever was living. But in this century, such vitalism was undermined by discoveries in molecular biology. Life is made up of the same basic elements as other material, nonliving things. The difference between living and nonliving things, biology tells us, is not in the kind of substance that underlies the two types of things but in the arrangement of those substances.

Similarly, water has different properties than hydrogen and oxygen (such as wetness) but is nevertheless nothing but H_2O. So, it could turn out that mental events are really physical events and states and nothing more. Materialists believe we are especially likely to be misled by thinking that consciousness has certain "phenomenological" properties it really does not have. For instance, when we imagine a green apple, we are inclined to say that our memory image is green. But nothing in our brain is green, so the critic of materialism triumphantly concludes that the mental image is not in our brain. But the materialist replies that the image is not literally green and that, indeed, we do not literally have an image before our mind's eye, as we might literally have a picture of an apple before our physical eye in an art gallery. What is happening when you imagine an apple, according to the materialist, is that the same thing is going on in your brain as what goes on when you see a real green apple. You are imagining seeing something green, and in that sense your imagination may be said to be green, but there is nothing literally green in your mind. So nothing impedes the identification of mental with physical processes.[5]

The materialist points out that our increased understanding of brain behavior makes it a plausible hypothesis that conscious thought and feeling are simply phenomenological descriptions of that which neuroscience describes from an externalist point of view.

The goal is to have a unified, explanatory mind-brain theory in which both science and common sense can take satisfaction.

Where does this leave us? The materialist has a certain amount of empirical success to his or her credit, which should give the dualist pause. The more that neuroscience can explain, the more impressive the credentials of materialism become. But can it really explain the self? Consciousness? Free will? Or is there an element of hubris at the very core of the materialist project?

The dualist agrees with the materialist monist that a unified explanation would be a good thing if we could obtain it. The questions, however, arise: Does something get left out in the shuffle? What is the price of such unity? Free will? How is free will possible in a world governed by deterministic law? It seems that materialism cannot support freedom of the will. Further, how can humans be said to have infinite or intrinsic value and dignity, if they are no more than simply relatively competent, material computers? Not only does the materialist take away our intentional states, beliefs, desires, and feelings, but there seems no room for God or a spiritual order in the materialist world. If there is independent evidence for these things, then unity of explanation may not be worth the price.

Tom Nagel expresses nagging doubts about the attempt to capture the essence of humanness via a detached, scientific approach to the subject:

> There are things about the world and life and ourselves that cannot be adequately understood from a maximally objective standpoint, however much it may extend our understanding beyond the point from which we started. A great deal is essentially connected to a particular point of view . . . , and the attempt to give a complete account of the world in objective terms detached from these perspectives inevitably leads to false reductions or to outright denials that certain patently real phenomena exist at all. . . . To the extent that such no-nonsense theories have an effect, they merely threaten to impoverish the intellectual landscape for a while by inhibiting the serious expression of certain questions. In the name of liberation, these movements have offered us intellectual repression.[6]

Is Nagel right? The dualist fears that he is, whereas the materialist is "exhilarated by the prospect . . . by the [prospect of developing] an evolutionary explanation of the human intellect."[7] Why should we fear honest inquiry? Isn't the search for truth at the heart of scientific inquiry?

Perhaps the mind-body problem cannot be viewed in isolation from the rest of philosophy. What you decide regarding the theory of knowledge generally, philosophy of religion, and the problem of free will and determinism will influence your conclusion on the mind-body problem. However, we should look at one more theory before we move on—that is, functionalism, a theory that claims to get around the problems inherent in reductivism. We will turn to that theory in the next chapter.

SUMMARY

Reductive and eliminative materialism seem to satisfy the principle of simplicity and conform to a scientific view of the world. Eliminative materialism seems a promissory note that science will eventually reinterpret our experience in a new framework and language. As such, we probably should admit it is a possibility, but not one for which there is presently much evidence. Reductive materialism is less radical, but it still faces problems, especially that of seeming to leave out of its account the phenomenology of conscious experience, of consciousness itself.

QUESTIONS FOR DISCUSSION

1. What do you make of the story of Phineas Gage? Do such examples provide evidence that we are mistaken in supposing that the mind or consciousness is a separate reality?

2. If someone accepts materialism, is he or she thereby committed to determinism? Determinism will be discussed in Part V, but you should be thinking about the relationship between the mind-body and free will–determinism.

3. If someone opts for materialism, which version (reductive or eliminative) is more plausible? What are the main criticisms of materialism?

4. Jeffrey Olen offers the following analogy on the relation of interactive dualism, epiphenomenalism, and the identity theory:

> Some people who have never seen a watch find one alongside a road. They pick it up and examine it, noticing that the second hand makes a regular sweep around the watch's face. After some discussion, they conclude that the watch is run by a gremlin inside. They remove the back of the watch but cannot find the gremlin. After further discussion, they decide that it must be invisible. They also decide that it makes the hands go by running along the gears inside the watch. They replace the watch's back and take it home.
>
> The next day the watch stops. Someone suggests that the gremlin is dead. Someone else suggests that it's probably sleeping. They shake the watch to awaken the gremlin, but the watch remains stopped. Someone finally turns the stem. The second hand begins to move. The person who said that the gremlin was asleep smiles triumphantly. The winding has awakened it.
>
> For a long time the people hold the gremlin hypothesis, but finally an innovative citizen puts forth the hypothesis that the watch can work without a gremlin. He dismantles the watch and explains the movements of the inner parts. His fellows complain that he has left out the really important aspect, the gremlin. "Of course," they agree, "the winding contributes to the turning of the gears. But only because it wakes up the gremlin, which then resumes its running." But gradually the suggestion of the innovative citizen converts a number of others to his position. The gremlin is not vital to run the watch. Nevertheless, they are reluctant to reject the gremlin altogether. So they compromise and conclude that there is a gremlin inside, but he is not needed to run the watch.
>
> But the man who figured out that the watch worked without the intervention of a gremlin is dissatisfied. If we do not need the gremlin to explain how the watch works, why continue to believe that it exists? Isn't it simpler to say that it does not?[8]

Apply this story to the mind–body problem and think of the watch as the human body and the gremlin as the mind. Olen suggests that the people who believed that the gremlin operated the watch are equivalent to dualistic interactionists, and the people who believed that the gremlin was inside the watch but inactive were like epiphenomenalists, and the man who held that the watch was self-operating was like the materialist: "A nonphysical mind is just as suspect as the gremlin. The only difference between the two cases is this: whereas there is no gremlin at all, there is a mind. The mistake is in thinking that it is anything over and above the brain."[9] Do you agree with Olen? Evaluate the various hypotheses.

NOTES

1. Thomas Hobbes, *Leviathan* (New York: Dutton, 1950), Chapter 46.

2. Colin McGinn, *The London Review of Books* (January 23, 1986): 24–25.

3. Richard Rorty, "Mind-Body Identity, Privacy, and Categories," *Review of Metaphysics* (1965): 28–29.

4. Ibid., 30–31.

5. Here is J. J. C. Smart's description of the phenomenological fallacy:

> The phenomenological fallacy: to say that an image or sense datum is green is not to say that the conscious experience of having the image or sense datum is green. It is to say that it is the sort of experience we have when in normal

conditions we look at a green apple, for example. Apples and unripe bananas can be green, but not the experiences of seeing them. An image or a sense datum can be green in a derivative sense, but this need not cause any worry, because, on the view I am defending, images and sense data are not constituents of the world, though the processes of having an image or a sense datum are actual processes in the world. The experience of having a green sense datum is not itself green; it is a process occurring in grey matter. The world contains plumbers, but does not contain the average plumber; it also contains the having of a sense datum, but does not contain the sense datum.[10]

6. Tom Nagel, *A View from Nowhere* (Oxford: Oxford University Press, 1986), 7, 11.

7. Daniel Dennett, *The Intentional Stance* (Cambridge, MA: MIT Press, 1987), 5.

8. Jeffrey Olen, *Persons and Their Worlds* (New York: Random House, 1983), 223.

9. Ibid.

10. J. J. C. Smart, "Materialism," *Journal of Philosophy* 22 (1963).

FOR FURTHER READING

See "For Further Reading" at the end of Chapter 13.

15

Functionalism and Biological Naturalism

Consciousness: The having of perceptions, thoughts, and feelings; awareness. The term is impossible to define except in terms that are unintelligible without a grasp of what consciousness means. Many fall into the trap of confusing consciousness with self-consciousness—to be conscious it is only necessary to be aware of the external world. Consciousness is a fascinating but elusive phenomenon: it is impossible to specify what it is, what it does, or why it evolved. Nothing worth reading has been written about it.

—THE INTERNATIONAL DICTIONARY OF PSYCHOLOGY, 1989

At this point, you may be frustrated by the problems surrounding each theory that we have examined so far. The debates over whether we are made of one or two different substances, whether mental events can be reduced to brain events, and whether mental events exist at all seem fraught with insurmountable problems. "A plague on all your houses," we are tempted to shout, after working through these theories. There is a group of philosophers who feel exactly the same way. In the 1960s and early 1970s, philosophers like Jerry Fodor of MIT and Hilary Putnam of Harvard criticized the current versions of materialist monism, the identity theory (roughly, what we have examined in Chapter 14 as reductive materialism), and in its place they offered a new theory, **Functionalism.**[1] In this chapter, we will examine both the functionalist's critique of the identity theory and functionalism itself as a replacement of other theories. Then we will look at criticisms of functionalism.

Functionalists take issue with aspects of the identity theory, the form of reductivism that identifies types of mental events with types of brain events, and with metaphysical behaviorism, which denies the reality of mental events. First, they argue against the behaviorists and those holding the identity theory, that mental states and events must be accounted for. The behaviorist, we noted in Chapter 13, is interested in input and output states. Functionalism, which is the heir to behaviorism, argues that this formula leaves out the uniqueness of mental states. Not only must environmental input and behavioral output be accounted for, but a third factor, types of mental states, must be recognized (see Figure 15.1).

A similar first criticism is leveled by the functionalists against the reductivists (or identity theory). Functionalists argue that, although it may or may not be the case that physical matter is the only substance of which we partake, mental events exist and must be accounted for. Second, they accuse reductivists of "chauvinism," in thinking that material brains like those found in humans and mammals are the *only* things that can account for mental events. Just as racism is chauvinism about race, sexism a prejudice about gender, and speciesism an unjustified view about one's own species, so reductivism is a chauvinism that unwarrantedly excludes all other forms of realization of mental events. "Just because Martians don't have brains like ours doesn't mean that they don't suffer or use reason!" the functionalist is apt to insist. Here functionalism sets forth the doctrine of *multiple realizability,* the view that mental events could be realized in many different forms and structures.

Note that the identity theorists hold that mental events are reducible to types of brain events, that consciousness is really nothing but a brain state or event. It is this doctrine of type identity at which the functionalist aims his or her attack.

Functionalists draw their inspiration from Aristotle, who distinguished between form and matter, arguing that a form could be realized in many different ways, in different substances. For example, a statue of Abraham Lincoln could be made of marble, wood, clay, steel, aluminum, or papier mâchè. That is, for Aristotle there is no single *type* of matter that defines an entity. The form of the substance, not the substance itself, is the defining feature.

The doctrine of multiple realizability applies this insight to mental events, interpreting them as functions. Let's illustrate the doctrine itself by applying it to an artifact. Consider the mousetrap. Here are five different examples of mousetraps:

- A standard spring trap. Cheese is placed on a trigger; the mouse is attracted to the cheese and trips the trigger that in turn releases a spring, causing a metal bar to come crashing down on the head or neck of the mouse.

- Like the standard trap, only instead of a bar coming down, a rope is released by the trigger. It surrounds the neck of the mouse, tightens and at the same time pulls the mouse off the ground, hanging him.

- A trapdoor mousetrap. When the mouse touches the cheese, a trapdoor opens, and the mouse falls into a shoot, leading directly to an incinerator.

- A scented model of a mouse of the opposite sex is poisoned with a lethal perfume and left for the mouse to embrace. When he or she does so, the mouse imbibes the poison and soon expires.

- An awesome model of a ferocious cat, which when seen by mice causes them to die of fright.

All these instruments qualify as mousetraps. They all have the same purpose or function. We could invent other ways of trapping mice. Enumerating the different types of mousetraps is not the way of accounting for the idea of a mousetrap,

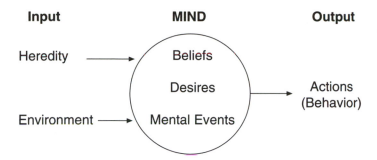

FIGURE 15.1

however. There is no single material feature that all and only mousetraps have in common. All that they have in common is the *abstract* idea that their purpose or function is to catch mice. They can realize that function in multiple ways—hence the name, the doctrine of multiple realizability.

Similarly, the functionalist hypothesizes that there is no reason to rule out the possibility that mental events are realized in different ways in different structures. They could be realized in brain tissue like ours or a different kind of tissue in other animals, in the silicon chips of computers, in some other structure of Galacticans, or in an unknown substance that makes up angels. From artificial intelligence to angels, all that counts is that mental events be the result and that these mental events be part of the causal process mediating environmental input and behavioral outputs.

Similarly, in different humans, there may be different ways in which the same function is realized. The cerebral cortex may have more than one type of structural mechanism that produces mental events. And two different people may function identically though they have different types of inward processes taking place.

At the core of the functionalist position is the idea that what makes a mental state like pain what it is is its functional role: Pain simply is whatever causes the rapid withdrawal of hands from the fire and whatever results from putting one's hand in the fire. So if a creature with entirely different wiring than ourselves were behaviorally isomorphic to ourselves, the inner states that mediated its behavior would be our inner states because the essence of an inner state is the causes and effects it has.

Yet, this is just where functionalism runs into problems. If the processes that produce the same function are too different, couldn't functionalism be missing an important feature of mental events? The *inverted-spectrum argument* is offered to illustrate this point.

You have a particular type of sensation when you look at a red object and a different kind of sensation when you look at a green object. But isn't it possible for someone else to have the reverse sensations? When he looks at the green apple, he has a red sensation, and when he looks at the red apple, he has a green sensation. His behavior, his use of the words *red* and *green* would be *functionally* identical with yours, and his sensations of seeing a "red" and "green" apple would be functionally identical with yours, but the inner states are really different despite the functional equivalence. Would this show that functionalism has missed an essential feature in accounting for mental events? That it is not just the function that counts but the reality of what is going on inside of one's mind or brain?

Functionalism concentrates on the input-output relationships. I step on a nail (the input), and that action sends a message to my brain that in turn *causes* me to cry "Ouch" (the output). Other people simply withdraw their feet. Some grimace, others cry out, and still others cry. Concentrating on the functional analysis of cause and effect, however, seems to have the defects of behaviorism (which is what functionalism was in part meant to answer). The functionalist account leaves out precisely what is important, the *quality* of the inner state. That is, it is not enough to say that there are functionally equivalent types of mental events in conscious beings, we must also pay attention to the conscious experience itself that could be of a different type despite functional identity. The functionalist generally meets this objection by denying the possibility or likelihood of the inverted-spectrum case or radically different qualitative states given the same biological state, but they seem conceivable.

In the 1930s and 1940s, the British mathematician Alan Turing (1912–1954) devised an idealized finite calculating program to determine whether computers could think. Two rooms are equipped with input/output devices, both going to an experimenter in a third room. A human is placed in one room and a computer in the other, each communicating with the experimenter. By issuing instructions, asking questions, and receiving replies, the experimenter tries to determine which room has the human and which the machine. If he cannot tell the difference, this constitutes strong evidence that computers can think. It turns out that under standard conditions the experimenter cannot tell the difference. Hence, many scientists and philosophers concluded that computers can think. The Turing machine supported the functionalist account of the philosophy of mind, which, for a time, became the dominant theory of the mind.

One philosopher demurred. John Searle of the University of California argued that the Turing Test failed to prove that computers can think. He offered the following thought-experiment. Suppose I am in a room with boxes filled with Chinese symbols, which I can identify by their shapes, but have no understanding of their meaning. People in another room send questions written in Chinese to me with instructions in English on how to match the questions with the symbols in the box. Suppose that I get so good at following the instructions and matching the Chinese symbols that a third party, a native Chinese speaker, cannot tell the difference between my responses and those of a native Chinese speaker. "Nobody just looking at my answers can tell that I don't speak a word of Chinese." I neither speak nor understand Chinese. All I have proved is that I can manipulate symbols.

Now imagine that these people also give you stories in English, which you understand, and they then ask you questions in English about these stories, and you give them back answers in English. Suppose also that after a while you get so good at following the instructions for manipulating the Chinese symbols and the programmers get so good at writing the programs that from the external point of view (i.e., someone outside the room), your answers to the questions are absolutely indistinguishable from those of native Chinese speakers. Nobody just looking at your answers can tell that you don't read a word of Chinese. Let us also suppose that your answers to the English questions are, as they no doubt would be,

indistinguishable from those of other native English speakers, for the simple reason that you are a native English speaker. From the point of view of an observer,
the answers to the Chinese questions and the English questions are equally good.
But in the Chinese case, unlike the English case, you produce the answers by
manipulating uninterpreted formal symbols; you simply behave like a computer
performing computational operations on formally specified elements. You are
"simply an instantiation of the computer program." You have inputs and outputs
that are indistinguishable from a Chinese speaker, but you understand nothing.[2]
Similarly, a computer can be programmed to manipulate symbols but it, nevertheless, still lacks understanding of the meaning of what it is doing. So, Searle concludes, contrary to Turing and his followers, the adherents of Strong Artificial
Intelligence (AI), computers, unlike humans, cannot think. They lack consciousness, intentionality, and understanding. There are no grounds to suppose that
robots or other types of artificial intelligence can understand, have feelings, have
intentions, or perform mental acts. Do you agree? Can you think of a response
that the functionalist might make to Searle's Chinese Room Objection?

Whether functionalism is a significant advance over behaviorism, which it
sought to replace, and whether it is superior to reductive materialism is a highly
controversial question in contemporary philosophy of mind. What seems correct
is the idea of multiple realizability. No reason has been given against the possibility that some types of behavioral or mental events have different types of structural accounts. The question is, Can some form of eliminative materialism or
other theory account for this feature while giving a better account of how the
various structures actually work? This is one of the exciting challenges of contemporary philosophy of mind, which I must leave you to ponder.

Meanwhile Searle has set forth a positive outline for a solution to the problem of consciousness. Consciousness is a biological property, one which emerges
from lower-level neuronal functions in the cerebral cortex. Intentional properties,
as well as consciousness itself, are simply aspects of biological events. Just as the
molecular structure on the surface of a table gives rise to the property of smooth-
ness (when in contact with our finger) and as a sufficient number of H_2O molecules give rise to the phenomenon of liquidity, so consciousness emerges on a
higher level from the neuronal activity at lower levels of the cerebral cortex. The
value of Searle's solution is that it takes consciousness seriously, rather than denying it, as the behaviorists and materialists do. It is a fundamental reality and not a
mere epiphenomenon. But, in a sense, isn't it a type of materialism or physical-
ism? Emergent biological materialism? For consciousness still is a property of the
physical brain. Perhaps it is a version of the double aspect theory discussed in
Chapter 13. In any case, it represents one of the most fascinating theories in the
literature. Still, no one understands how consciousness arise, what causes the phenomenal feel or awareness that accompanies our every waking moment, and how
consciousness unifies all our various experiences. While it may be an exaggeration
to say, as does *The International Dictionary of Psychology,* that "Nothing worth reading has been written about it," we have neither solved the mind-body problem
nor learned how consciousness works.

SUMMARY

We have noted the strengths and weaknesses of functionalism, the theory that different structures could give rise to mental events and that we need not understand these processes to have a workable understanding of the workings of our mind. The strength of functionalism is that it improves on behaviorism by recognizing the reality of psychological states and events and it keeps open the possibility of mental events in other types of structures (physical or nonphysical) different from ours. Its weakness is that it omits that ideas of consciousness and intentionality. Functionalism, like its parent behaviorism, is essentially a black box theory, failing to recognize the reality of consciousness and intentionality. We have noted Searle's charge that computers cannot think, so that Strong Artificial Intelligence is a mistaken project, and we have noted his proposal of consciousness as a biological process.

You must ask yourself whether functionalism or any of its rivals discussed in Chapters 13 to 15, gives a satisfactory account of the central mystery of humanity, the conundrum of intelligent consciousness.

INTENTIONALITY

Intentionality (from the Latin *intendo,* "to aim at" or "point at") refers to the directness (or *aboutness*) of mental states. Consciousness is often directed at an object, its content—objects of desires, fear, belief, and appearances. Intentions are bi-directional; (1) from Mind to World; and (2) from World to Mind. An example of (1) from Mind to World is our desire to change the world or an aspect in it, such as when I kick the soccer ball, aiming at scoring a goal, or when one invests money in stocks, hoping to improve one's financial situation. Examples of (2) from World to Mind is an accurate belief that is formed about the makeup of this room when I open my eyes to perceive its content. When intentional acts are successful, they accomplish their task—fulfill a desire to obtain a true belief.

The term was used in the Middle Ages but revived by the nineteenth century German philosopher Franz Brentano, who claimed that *intentionality* defined the distinction between the mental and the physical: all mental events but no merely physical events have intentionality. This thesis *Brentano Irreducibility* is sometimes used to argue that the mind cannot be a feature of the brain. John Searle argues that *intentionality* is an emergent property caused by neurophysiological processes. Functionalists, such as Daniel Dennett, argue that so long as a system manifests the right kind of behavior, as a conscious being would, it can be said to be *intentional.*

QUESTIONS FOR DISCUSSION

1. What are the advantages of functionalism? How plausible a theory is it? What does it do that the other theories don't? What does it leave out that is important? Can eliminative materialism answer the problems raised by functionalism?

2. Review the major theories discussed in Chapters 13 to 15. Assess their strengths and weaknesses. What is your conclusion?

3. The functionalist claims that what defines a mental state like pain is its functional role. Is this a plausible claim? Is what makes pain pain its causes and effects or, rather, what it is in itself?

4. Consider Searle's Chinese Room Objection. Is Searle's concept of *understanding* (see note 2) clear? Could you argue that we really understand in degrees, so that robots and computers simply have low-level understanding whereas we have high-level understanding?

5. Examine the quotation at the beginning of this chapter:

> The having of perceptions, thoughts, and feelings; awareness. The term is impossible to define except in terms that are unintelligible without a grasp of what consciousness means. Many fall into the trap of confusing consciousness with self-consciousness—to be conscious it is only necessary to be *aware* of the external world. Consciousness is a fascinating but elusive phenomenon: it is impossible to specify what it is, what it does, or why it evolved. Nothing worth reading has been written about it. (*International Dictionary of Psychology,* 1989)

Do you agree with its conclusion? Why or why not? Has Searle provided a beginning to a better answer?

NOTES

1. See Jerry Fodor, *Psychological Explanations* (New York: Random House, 1968); and Hilary Putnam, "The Nature of Mental States" in *Mind, Language and Reality* (London: Cambridge University Press, 1975). Both articles are found in Beakley and Ludlow's anthology and Rosenthal's anthology, both listed in "For Further Reading."

2. John Searle, "Minds, Brains and Programs," *The Behavioral and Brain Sciences* 3 (1980). Searle describes *understanding* as "implying both the possession of mental (intentional) states and the truth (validity, success) of these states." *Intentionality* is that "feature of certain mental states by which they are directed at or about objects and states of affairs in the world. Thus, beliefs, desires, and intentions are intentional states; undirected forms of anxiety and depression are not."

FOR FURTHER READING

Beakley, Brian, and Peter Ludlow, eds. *The Philosophy of Mind: Classical Problems and Contemporary Issues.* Cambridge, MA: MIT Press, 1992. An excellent anthology.

Chalmers, David. *The Conscious Mind.* Oxford: Oxford University Press, 1996. The most thorough discussion of consciousness in the literature, from a dualist position.

Churchland, Paul. *Matter and Consciousness.* Cambridge, MA: MIT Press, 1990. A superb introductory text from a materialist perspective.

Dennett, Daniel. *The Intentional Stance.* Cambridge, MA: MIT Press, 1989. A brilliant discussion of the mental states.

Levin, Michael E. *Metaphysics and the Mind-Body Problem.* Oxford: Clarendon Press,

1979. An excellent defense of materialism. My illustration of the principle of simplicity was taken from this work.

Lycan, William, ed. *Mind and Cognition.* Oxford: Blackwell, 1991. An excellent anthology.

McGinn, Colin. "Can We Solve the Mind-Body Problem?" *Mind* 98 (1989).

McGinn, Colin. *The Character of Mind.* Oxford: Oxford University Press, 1982. A rich, compact exposition of the major issues.

Moreland, J. P. *Scaling the Secular City.* Grand Rapids, MI: Baker Books, 1987. Contains a defense of dualistic interactionism from a Christian perspective.

Rosenthal, David M., ed. *The Nature of Mind.* Oxford: Oxford University Press,

1992. The best anthology of contemporary work available. Contains an excellent bibliography.

Searle, John. *Mind, Brains and Science.* Cambridge, MA: Harvard University Press, 1984. A perceptive work, setting forth puzzles and providing a brilliant analysis of the issues.

Searle, John. *The Rediscovery of Mind.* Cambridge, MA: MIT Press, 1992. A further development of Searle's ideas.

Stich, Stephen. *From Folk Psychology to Cognitive Science: The Case Against Belief.* Cambridge, MA: MIT Press, 1983.

Turing, A. "Computing Machinery and Intelligence." *Mind* 59 (1950).

16

The Problem
of Personal Identity

Suppose you wake up tomorrow in a strange room. There are pictures of unfamiliar people on the light blue walls, and you don't recognize the furniture. You wonder how you got here. You remember being in the hospital where you were dying of cancer. Your body was wasting away, and your death was expected soon. Your physician, Dr. Matthews, had kindly given you an extra dose of morphine to kill the pain. That's all you can remember. You notice a calendar on the wall in front of you. The date is April 1. "This can't be," you think, "for yesterday was January 2." Not quite your normal, alert self, you try to take this all in. "Where have I been all this time?" Suddenly, you see a mirror. You reel back in horror, for it's not your body that you spy in the glass, but a large woman's body. Your color has altered, and, if you're male, so has your sex. You have more than doubled your previous normal weight and look twenty-five years older. You feel tired, confused, and frightened and can scarcely hold back tears of dismay. Soon a strange man, about forty-five years of age, comes into your room. "I was wondering when you would waken, Maria. The doctor said that I should let you sleep as long as possible, but I didn't think that you would be asleep two whole days. Anyway, the operation was a success. We had feared that the accident had ended your life. The children and I are so grateful. Jean and John will be home in an hour and will be so happy to see you awake. How do you feel?"

"Can this be a bad joke, an April Fool's prank?" you wonder, noting the date on the calendar. "Who is this strange man, and who am I?" Unbeknown to you, Dr. Matthews needed a living brain to implant in the head of Mrs. Maria Martin, mother of four children, who had been in a car accident. After arriving at the hospital, her body was kept alive by technology, but her brain was dead. Your brain, in excellent shape, lacked a healthy body. Maria Martin's body was intact but needed a brain. Being an enterprising brain surgeon, Dr. Matthews saw his chance of performing the first successful brain transplant. Later that day, Matthews breaks the news of your transformation to you. He congratulates you on being the first human to survive a brain transplant and reminds you, just in case you are not completely satisfied with the transformation, that you would have been dead had he not performed the operation. Still dazed by the news, you try to grasp the significance of what has happened to you. You wonder whether you'd be better off dead. The fact that the operation was a success is of little comfort to you, for you're not sure whether you are you!

The problem of personal identity is one of the most fascinating in the history of philosophy. It is especially complicated since it involves not one but at least three, and possibly four, philosophical questions. What is it to be a person? What is identity? What is personal identity? How is survival possible given the problems of personal identity? Let's look briefly at the first three questions. (Chapter 17 discusses the fourth question.)

WHAT IS IT TO BE A PERSON?

What is it that sets us human beings off as having special value, as being entities with serious moral rights? What characteristics must one have to have high moral value? The Judeo-Christian tradition generally defines personhood in terms of our ability to reason and make moral choices. Writing within the Judeo-Christian tradition, the English philosopher John Locke (1632–1704) said that a person is defined as

> a thinking intelligent being, that has reason and reflection, and can consider itself as itself, the same thinking thing, in different times and places; which it does only by that consciousness which is inseparable from thinking, and as it seems to me, essential to it.

That is, our ability to reason, introspect, and survey our memories and intentions sets us apart from the animals as being of greater value. The view may be challenged by the materialist who says that it is really our brain (or our brain and our body) that defines our personhood. It is the fact that we have a more developed brain that sets us apart from other animals. We are, of course, conscious beings. Although we do not understand how consciousness works, the physicalist believes that consciousness is a function of the brain. David Hume (1711–1776) argued that the notion of a self or soul is very likely a fiction. "I" am merely a bundle of perceptions. There is consciousness of a continuing succession of experiences but not of a continuing experiencer. This view is compatible with the physicalist view of personhood.

How do we decide what it is that makes us valuable? Perhaps self-consciousness is a necessary or minimal condition, but is it a sufficient one? Are primates and other mammals persons? The subject is a difficult philosophical problem whose solution will likely depend on wider metaphysical and theoretical considerations. But if the question of personhood is a difficult problem, the question of identity is no less so.

WHAT IS IDENTITY?

At first glance, this sounds like an absurdly simple question. Identity is the fact that everything is itself and not another. In logic, the law of identity (the formula $A = A$) formally states the definition. We are not interested, however, in a formal definition of mere identity but identity *over time* or reidentification (sometimes this is referred to as *numerical identity*). What is it to be the *same* thing over time? Suppose you go to an automobile dealership in order to buy a new car. You see several blue Fords parked side-by-side. They resemble one another so much that you cannot tell them apart. They are the same type of car and are *exactly similar* to one another. Suppose you pick one out at random and buy it. Your car is different from the other blue Fords even though you couldn't tell the difference between them. A year passes, and your blue Ford now has 20,000 miles on it and a few scratches. Is it the same car that you originally bought? Most of us would probably agree that it is. The changes have altered but not destroyed its identity as the blue car that you bought and have driven 20,000 miles.

What does your blue Ford have that causes it to be the same car over the period of one year? A common history, continuity over time. The car is linked by a succession of spatiotemporal events from its origins in Detroit to its present place in your driveway. This distinguishes it from all other Fords that were ever built, no matter how similar they appear. So we might conclude that *continuity over time* is the criterion of identity.

But immediately we find problems with this criterion. The Rio Grande dries up in places in New Mexico every summer, only to reappear as a running river in the early spring. Is the Rio Grande the same river this year as it was the last? There isn't any continuity over time of water flowing over the riverbed. Perhaps we can escape the problem by saying that by "river" we really mean the riverbed that must hold running water sometimes but need not always convey it. Does this solve the problem?

Consider another counterexample: The Chicago White Sox are playing the New York Yankees in Yankee Stadium in late April. The game is called in the fifth inning with the Yankees leading 3 to 2. Shortly afterward, there is a baseball strike, and all players take to the picket lines while a new set of players comes up from the minor leagues to fill their positions. The "game" is continued in Chicago in August with a whole new set of players on both sides. The White Sox win, and the game decides who wins the division pennant. Suppose the Yankee shortstop, who had been a philosophy major in college, protests that this hybrid game must not count and that a new game must be played in its stead. He argues that since there was no continuity between the two segments of the "game," that not even the same players played in both halves, the two segments cannot count as constituting one and the same baseball game. Does the shortstop have a point? Should the Yankee manager accept his argument and appeal the game to the commissioner of baseball? Should the commissioner call for a new game? Why, or why not?

The most perplexing problem with regard to the notion of "sameness" or identity over time is illustrated by the ancient tale of Theseus's ship. Suppose you have a small ship that is in need of some repairs. You begin (at time t_1) to replace the old planks and material one-by-one with new planks and material. After one year (time t_2), the ship is completely made up of different material. Do you have

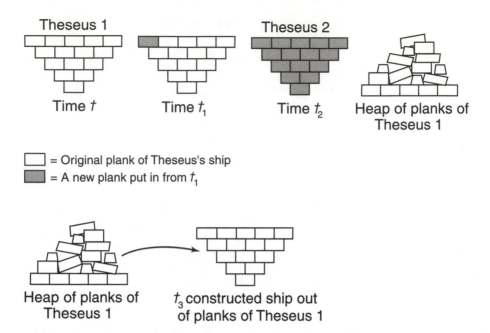

FIGURE 16.1

the same ship at t_2 as you had at t_1? If not, at what point did it (call it *Theseus 2*) become a different ship? (See Figure 16.1.)

People disagree about whether Theseus's ship has changed its identity. Suppose you argue that it is the same ship that you started with, for it had a continuous history over time and therefore is the same ship. But now suppose your friend takes the material discarded from *Theseus 1* and reconstructs *that* ship (call it *Theseus 3*). Which ship is now Theseus's ship? There is the *continuity of the ship* between *Theseus 1* and 2 but *continuity of material* between *Theseus 1* and *3*. Which type of continuity should be decisive here? If it worries you that there was a time when the material of *Theseus 1* was not functioning as a ship, we could alter the example and suppose that as the planks were taken from *Theseus 1* they were transferred to another ship *Argos,* where they replaced the *Argos's* planks, ending up with a ship that contained every board and nail from the original *Theseus* (call this transformed *Argos Theseus 4*). Which is now the original *Theseus*? (See Figure 16.2.)

Does there not seem something puzzling about the notion of identity?

Now we must take the two puzzling concepts, personhood and identity, and combine them.

WHAT IS PERSONAL IDENTITY?

What is it to be the same person over time? Are you the same person that you were when you were one year old or even sixteen years old? We recall Locke's idea of *personhood,* that mental characteristics (ability to reflect or introspect) constitute personhood. *Personal identity* is indicated by the successive memories

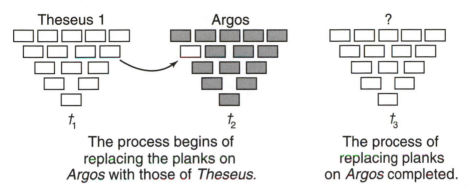

The process begins of replacing the planks on *Argos* with those of *Theseus*.

The process of replacing planks on *Argos* completed.

FIGURE 16.2

that the person has had, the continuity over time of a set of experiences that were remembered. We can call this the psychological states criterion of personal identity. The main competitor of this view is the brain criterion of personal identity, although some philosophers hold to a body criterion. Let's examine each of these briefly.

The **psychological states criterion** holds that our memories constitute our identity over time. You are the same person you were at ten years of age because you have a continuous set of memories that contains all those that you had at age ten plus others that continued after that year. Can you detect any problems with this view? Consider the following. In the first place, our memories are not continuous in our consciousness. When we sleep, we cease to have memories at all. In partial amnesia, do we cease to be who we are? Thomas Reid (1710–1796), questioning Locke's theory of personhood, argued that there is a problem of transitivity with regard to memories. Suppose there is a gallant officer who at age twenty-five years is a hero in a battle and who remembers getting a flogging in his childhood. Later at age sixty-five years, he recalls the heroic deed done at age twenty-five but cannot recall the flogging. Since he cannot remember the flogging, is he the same person he was when he did remember it? Can Locke answer Reid?

What about the phenomenon of split personalities and multiple personalities, the most famous of which is Sybil, who allegedly expressed sixteen different personalities with sixteen different sets of memories? On a psychological states account, would we have to say that one body contains (or is associated with) sixteen persons? Are there different persons inside each of us, expressed by different "sides" of our personality?

Sometimes a person expresses apparent memories of events that occurred in distant times and to different "persons." Is the body of the contemporary being possessed by another person? If your friend suddenly starts reminiscing about the Battle of Waterloo and the beautiful Empress Josephine, has Napoleon suddenly come alive in your friend's body? This would truly be a case of reincarnation! But what if two of your friends came to you with the same "foreign" memories? Your friend Bill recites in great detail the events of the Battle of Waterloo and describes in minute detail the wardrobe of the Empress Josephine. Then, shortly after, your friend Joyce describes similar events and details that she could not possibly have read in books. If memory constitutes the criterion for personal identity, then Bill is Napoleon and Joyce is Napoleon. But if they both are Napoleon, then Bill is Joyce. Since Bill is Joyce's husband, he is married to himself!

Furthermore, on this account, what is to prohibit complete soul flow, a different person inside you each day? How do you know that the soul that is remembering today is the same soul that remembered yesterday? You might object that this couldn't be the case because you have the same body, but that objection won't work since the body has nothing to do with the psychological states criterion. If you think that the body is important, this might be an indication that the memory criterion is inadequate on its own and depends on a physical body for continuity.

The *body criterion* has difficulties, one of which is the fact that the body can undergo radical changes and we would still want to call the person the same person. Almost all cells in our body change every seven years. Do we become a new person every seven years? Or think of the story at the beginning of the chapter in which Dr. Matthews transplants your brain into Maria Martin's body. Despite these physical changes, wouldn't you still be you?

This suggests a third criterion, the *brain criterion of personal identity.* Our memories are contained within our brains, so we might want to say that having the same brain constitutes the same person. But this has difficulties, which are brought out by the Oxford University philosopher Derik Parfit. If the corpus callosum (the thick band of fibers that unites the two hemispheres of the brain) is cut, two different centers of consciousness can be created. When either side of the cerebral cortex of the brain is destroyed, the person can live on as a conscious being. It is also possible, in principle, to transplant brains. Suppose your body is destroyed and neurologists transplant each half of your brain into a different body. Dr. Matthews transplants one-half of your brain into Maria Martin and the other half into the head of a seven-foot-tall basketball player. "You" wake up with two personalities. Do you survive the operation? There seem to be just three possible answers: (1) You do not survive; (2) you survive as one of the two; or (3) you survive as two people.

All these options seem unsatisfactory. It seems absurd to say that you don't survive (option 1), for there is continuity of consciousness (in the Lockean sense), as though you had gone to sleep and awakened. If you had experienced the destruction of one-half of your brain, we would still say you survived with half a brain, so why not say so now when each half is autonomous? The logic of option 1 would seem to say that double life equals death.

But option 2 seems arbitrary. Why say that you only survive as one of the two? And which one is it? Option 3—that you survive as both—is not satisfactory either, since it gives up the notion of identity. You cannot be numerically one with two centers of consciousness and two spatiotemporal bodies. Otherwise, we might say when we wreck our new Ford that the other Ford left in the automobile dealer's parking lot (the blue Ford that was exactly like yours) was indeed yours.

If this is an accurate analysis of the personal identity problem, what sense can we make of the concept? Not much, according to Parfit. We should speak of the survival of the person, not the identity of the person. Persons, as psychological states, survive and gradually merge (like Theseus's rebuilt ship) into descendent persons. Your memories and personality gradually emerged from the fifteen-year-old who gradually developed from the six-year-old and, before that, the one-year-old who bore your name. These were your ancestor selves. But you too will merge with future or descendent selves as you have different experiences, take on new memories, and forget old ones. Suppose every year neurologists could transplant half of your brain into another body, in which a new half would duplicate the present state of the transferred half. In this way, a treelike operation would continue to spread successors of yourself as though by psychological parthenogenesis. You would survive in a sense, but it would make no sense to speak of personal identity, a concept that Parfit wants to eliminate. We could also imagine a neurological game of "musical hemispheres" as half of your brain was merged with half of someone else's brain in a third person's head. Suppose something like "The Branching Brain Game" catches on (see Figure 16.3). The brains of John, Mary, Bill, Pat, and others are split every year or so and the hemispheres joined inside different heads. In year 1, half of Mary's brain is joined with half of John's, half of Bill's brain is joined with Mary's, and half of Pat's brain is joined with Bill's. The next year, they split again, and different halves are joined by the corpus callosum in a different head (Ross, R; and Arthur, A), and so on. Suppose you were one of these brain-branching people. You could continue the hemisphere-moving game every year so that you might even get remerged with your own other half at some future time—much like meeting your high school companion again after years of separation and interesting adventures. You'd have much to talk about through the medium of the corpus callosum!

Parfit's point is that we are going through significant changes all the time, so that as we have new experiences, we take on new selfhood. Something in us survives but with a difference. If Parfit is right about the relativity of identity in survival, then we might be less interested in our distant future than our immediate future. After all, that person ten years down the line is less like us than the person we'll be tomorrow. This might encourage a sort of general **utilitarianism,** for since our distant interests really are not as closely related to us as the needs of our contemporaries, we could be free to work for the total greater good. On the other hand, it could have a deleterious effect of making us indifferent to the future of society. This notion of proximate identity also raises the question of whether we should be concerned about our distant death fifty years down the line, which one of our successor selves will have to face. Why should we fear death, when it won't touch us but only one of our successor selves in the distant future? Of course, one of our successor selves might be angry with us for not taking out an insurance policy or pension plan necessary for his or her well-being.

This notion of relative and proximate identity might also cause us to prohibit long-term prison sentences for criminal actions, for why punish a descendent for what one of his or her ancestors did? It could be used to argue against exorbitant awards in malpractice litigation. Often a jury is asked to award a sum of money (as high as $12 million) to a severely retarded child whose brain damage had been incurred through medical malpractice. The justification for the large sum is the expectation that the child could have become a highly talented professional (physician or lawyer) and made an enormous sum of money in his or her lifetime. But if we were to take the notion of proximate identity seriously, we

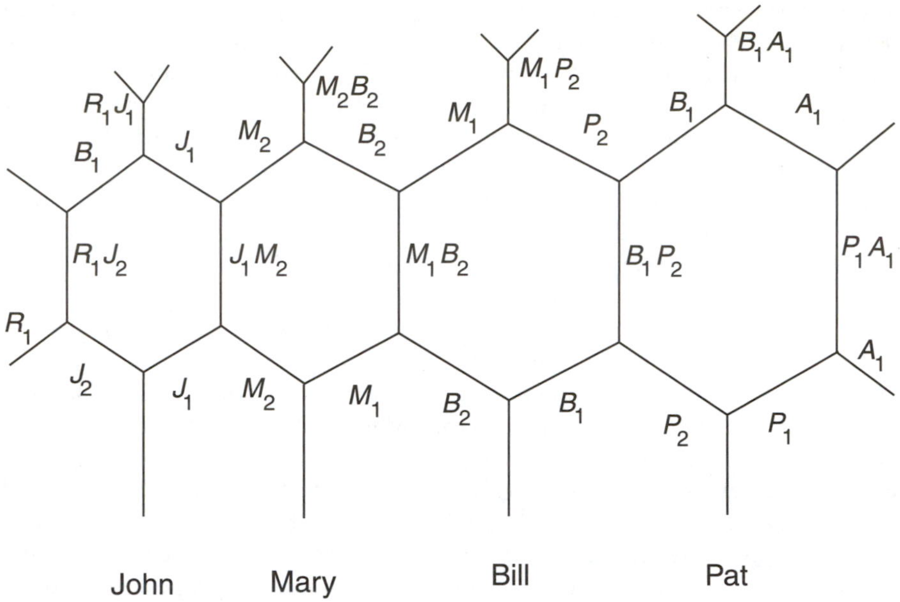

FIGURE 16.3

could only sue the physician for the damages done to the immediate person, not to his descendent selves.

What is the truth about personal identity? What constitutes the essential you? The issue is as perplexing as it is important. The challenge of solving this problem is before you. Who are you?

SUMMARY

The problem of personal identity is a compound set of paradoxes and puzzles that involves three difficult questions: What is a person? What is identity over time? What is it to be the same person through change and time? The first question relates to the body-mind problem in general and cannot be satisfactorily answered without a solution to that problem. The second question seems to be context-dependent; that is, the answer will depend on subtleties of meaning that depend on various contexts. The third question, which depends in part on the first two, has had two main answers: the psychological state criterion and the brain criterion. Far-reaching implications flow from how we decide this issue.

QUESTIONS FOR DISCUSSION

1. How would you respond to the question raised by the brain operation? Do you survive the operation? Consider the three possible answers: (a) You do not survive; (b) you survive as one of the two; or (c) you survive as two people. Discuss the reasons for and against each answer.

2. How would you solve the puzzle about the identity of Theseus's ship? What happens to it at t_2? One of my students said, "It just disappears." Do you agree? Why, or why not?

3. Explain the difference between the psychological states criterion for personal identity and the brain criterion. Which has the best case in its favor? Why?

4. What do you make of the phenomenon of split personalities and multiple personalities, such as the case of Sybil, who allegedly expressed sixteen different personalities with sixteen different sets of memories? On a psychological states account, would we have to say that one body contained sixteen persons? Are there different persons inside each of us, expressed by different "sides" of our personalities?

5. In the last section of this chapter, we discussed the implications flowing from relative and proximate identity. Discuss these consequences. Can you think of other implications?

FOR FURTHER READING

Parfit, Derek. *Reasons and Persons.* Oxford: Clarendon Press, 1984. Part 3 contains an excellent discussion.

Perry, John. *A Dialogue on Personal Identity and Immortality.* Indianapolis: Hackett, 1978. A philosophically rich, entertaining discussion of the problem of personal identity.

Perry, John, ed. *Personal Identity.* Berkeley: University of California Press, 1975. Contains the essential classical readings.

Pojman, Louis, ed. *Philosophy: The Quest for Truth,* 4th ed. Belmont, CA: Wadsworth, 1999. Contains Parfit's discussion.

Rorty, Amelie, ed. *The Identities of Persons.* Berkeley: University of California Press, 1976. A good selection of essays on the nature of personhood.

Unger, Peter. *Identity, Consciousness, and Value.* New York: Oxford University Press, 1990. A highly imaginative, penetrating discussion of the issues discussed in this chapter.

17

Is There Life after Death? Personal Identity and Immortality

Is there life after death? Few questions have troubled humans as deeply as this one. Is this finite, short existence of seventy or so years all that we have, or is there reason to hope for a blessed postmortem existence where love, justice, and peace, which we now experience in fragmented forms, will unfold in all their fullness and enable human existence to find fulfillment? Are we merely mortal or blessedly immortal?

Anthropological studies reveal a widespread and ancient sense of immortality. Prehistoric societies buried food, clothes, and tools with their dead so that the deceased would not be lacking in the next life. Most cultures and religions have some version of a belief in another life, whether it be in the form of a resurrected body, a transmigrated soul, reincarnation, or an ancestral spirit present with the tribe.

Let's begin by understanding what we mean by *immortality*. For our purposes, we will not mean living on through our works in the memories of our loved ones but rather a conscious existence where the individual continues to exist. The definition given in *A Catholic Dictionary* is

> that attribute in virtue of which a being is free from death. A being is incorruptible if it does not contain within itself a principle of dissolution; it is indestructible if it can resist every external power tending to destroy or annihilate it. If the indestructible and incorruptible being is endowed with life it is called immortal. Annihilation is always possible to God by the mere withdrawal of his conserving act.[1]

For most humans **Death** is the ultimate tragedy. It is the paramount evil, for it deprives us of all that we know and love on Earth. Although there may be fates worse than death for some of us (living a completely evil life, being a heavy burden on others), our fear of death is profound. We want to live as long as possible (given a certain quality of life). We have a general craving for continued existence. The more life, the better. Unfortunately, there is precious little direct evidence for life after death. After the brain ceases to function, a person cannot be resuscitated. We don't know of anyone personally who has come back from the dead to tell us about the next life.

So on the one hand, we have a passionate longing to live again and be with our loved ones; on the other hand, there is little or no direct evidence that we will live again. The grave seems the last environment for humankind. And yet we search for indirect evidence for immortality. We welcome any news from this possible distant clime as good news indeed and cannot but regard the promise of eternal life as an incentive to meet whatever a credible guide states as the necessary conditions for entry.

In the Western tradition, three views have dominated the scene; one denies life after death, and two affirm it. The negative view, going back to the ancient Greek Atomist philosophers Democritus (ca. 460–370 B.C.) and Leucippus (ca. 450 B.C.), holds that we are identical with our bodies (including our brains) so that when the body dies, so does our self. There is nothing more. We can call this view *materialist monism* because it does not allow for the possibility of a soul or spiritual self that can live without the body.

The positive views divide into dualist and monist theories of life after death. The dualist views separate the body from the soul or self of the agent and affirm that it is the soul or self that lives forever. This view was held by the pre-Socratic philosopher Pythagoras (ca. 580–496 B.C.) and developed by Plato (ca. 427–347 B.C.). In modern philosophy, it is represented by René Descartes (1596–1650). It is sometimes referred to as the Platonic–Cartesian view of immortality. These philosophers argue that we are essentially spiritual or mental beings and that our bodies are either unreal or not part of our essential selves, so that death is merely the separation of our souls from our bodies, a sort of spiritual liberation. Although Plato has many arguments for this thesis, one of the most famous is found in the *Phaedo,* where Plato writes,

> When the soul employs the body in any inquiry, and makes use of sight, or hearing, or any other sense—for inquiry with the body must signify inquiry with the senses —she is dragged away by the body to the things which are impermanent, changing, and the soul wanders about blindly, and becomes confused and dizzy, like a drunken man, from dealing with things that are changing. . . . [But] When the soul investigates any question by herself, she goes away to the pure and eternal, and immortal and unchangeable, to which she is intrinsically related, and so she comes to be ever with it, as soon as she is by herself, and can be so; and then she rests from her wandering and dwells with it unchangingly, for she is related to what is unchanging. And is not this state of the soul called wisdom?[2]

The argument can be analyzed as follows:

1. If a person's soul while in the body is capable of any activity independent of the body, then it can perform that activity in separation from the body (i.e., after death, surviving death).

2. In pure or metaphysical thinking (i.e., in contemplating the forms and their interrelationships), a person's soul performs an activity independently of the body. No observation is necessary for this investigation.

3.   ∴ A person's soul can engage in pure or metaphysical thinking in separation from the body. That is, it can and must survive death.

This is a positive argument for the existence of the soul. It does seem that we can think about logic, mathematics, metaphysics, and other subjects without reference to bodies. Unfortunately, the second premise is dubious, for it could be the case that the mind's activity is epiphenomenal, that is, dependent on the brain. So although Plato is right in saying that we need not make an empirical examination of the world in order to think analytically or metaphysically, he has not shown that analytic and metaphysical thinking can go on without a brain.

As far as I know, no one has offered a sound argument to *prove* that we have a soul that outlives our physical existence. However, this is not to say that there is no evidence for this point of view. We will note some below.

The second positive view on immortality is associated with the Christian tradition, namely, St. Paul's statement in 1 Corinthians 15. It is interesting to note that very little mention is made in the Old Testament of life after death. It is at best a shadowy existence in Sheol, the place under Jerusalem where the dead lie dormant or vaguely aware, a place comparable to Hades in Greek mythology. The one exception, celebrated in Handel's *Messiah,* is the famous passage in the Book of Job (19:25–26):

> I know that my Redeemer liveth,
> And that He shall stand at the latter day upon the earth,
> And though worms destroy this body,
> Yet in my flesh shall I see God.

Note that it is *in the flesh,* not as a disembodied spirit, that Job expects to live again.

In the New Testament, although there are references to a spiritual existence, the soul (*psyche*) is not separated from the body (*soma*) after death, but remains a holistic, unified being with the soul or self being the form of the material body (in an almost Aristotelian sense). In death the soul is not liberated from the body as from a corpse, but rather a new, glorified *body* comes into being, which is somehow related to our present earthly body. The classic passage is from Paul's first letter to the Corinthians, which reads as follows:

> Now if Christ be preached that he rose from the dead, how say some among you that there is no resurrection of the dead? But if there be no resurrection of the dead, then is Christ not risen: And if Christ be not risen, then is our preaching in vain, and your faith is also in vain. . . . Ye are still in your sins. Then they which are fallen asleep in Christ are perished. If in this life only we have hope in Christ, we are of all men most miserable.
>
> But now is Christ risen from the dead, and become the first fruits of them that slept. For since by man came death by man came also the resurrection of the dead. . . . For Christ must reign until he hath put all enemies under his feet. The last enemy that shall be destroyed is death.
>
> But some man will say, How are the dead raised up? and with what body do they come? Thou fool, that which thou sowest is not quickened, except it die: and that which thou sowest, thou sowest not that body that shall be, but bare grain, it may chance of wheat, or of some other grain. But God giveth it a body as it hath pleased him, and to every seed his own body. All flesh is not the same flesh; but there is one

kind of flesh of men, another flesh of beasts, another of fishes and another of birds. There are also celestial bodies, and bodies terrestrial: but the glory of the celestial is one, and the glory of the terrestrial is another. There is one glory of the sun, and another glory of the moon, and another glory of the stars: for one star differeth from another star in glory. So also is the resurrection of the dead. It is sown in corruption; it is raised in incorruption; . . . it is sown in weakness; it is raised in power: It is sown a natural body; it is raised a spiritual body. . . . And so it is written, The first man Adam was made a living soul; the last Adam was made a quickening spirit. Howbeit that was not first which is spiritual, but that which is natural; and afterward that which is spiritual. The first man is of the earth, earthly: the second man is the Lord from heaven. As is the earthly, such are they also that are earthly: and as is the heavenly, such are they also that are heavenly. And as we have borne the image of the earthly, we shall also bear the image of the heavenly. Now this I say, brethren, that flesh and blood cannot inherit the kingdom of God; neither doth corruption inherit incorruption. Behold, I show you a mystery; We shall not all sleep, but we shall all be changed. In a moment, in a twinkling of an eye, at the last trump: for the trumpet shall sound, and the dead shall be raised incorruptible, and we shall be changed. For this corruptible must put on incorruption, and this mortal must put on immortality.[3]

When I approach the subject of immortality in an undergraduate philosophy class, I poll the students to ask them which is the Christian view of life after death: the view that in death the soul leaves the body and goes to heaven or the view that our bodies will be raised. Almost every student chooses the first view, which I then point out is basically Platonic, not Christian. This view is reflected in popular religion, not the least being the bedtime prayer taught to children: "Now I lay me down to sleep, I pray the Lord my soul to keep. If I should die before I wake, I pray the Lord my soul to take." Of course, one could have a view that although there is eventually a new body, there is an intermediate state where the soul dwells disembodied, waiting for the resurrection day, at which time it will receive its new form.

Are there good arguments for either of these versions of survival after death? Each raises the question of personal identity, discussed in Chapter 16. Given the fact that we all undergo physical and mental change, under what conditions can we be said to be the *same* person over time (i.e., what gives us the right to say that some person P is the same person at t_2 as P was at some time earlier, t_1)?

You will recall (from Chapter 16) the two standard views on this matter: the psychological states criterion and the body (including the brain) criterion. The psychological states (or memory) criterion goes back to John Locke (1632–1704) and states that a person is the same person if and only if he or she is psychologically continuous in character, desires, and memories. There are, at least, three problems with this view:

1. There is no way to distinguish *apparent* memories from *genuine* remembering, so that it could be the case that someone came among us, detailing the events of Napoleon's life in such a way as to cause us to believe that he had somehow captured those memories. But we would probably be reluctant to say that this person was Napoleon, especially if we already knew him to be our uncle.
2. There is a problem with multiple rememberers. That is, it could be the case that our memories (and characters and desires for that matter) could be duplicated in other people, so that multiple subjects have the same "memories." We would not be able to

tell which of the persons was the rememberer. As we noted in Chapter 16, if Bill and Joyce both possess the same memories, they would be each other!

3.   There is the problem of whether memory itself makes any sense apart from a body. What would a purely mental existence be like? Would it be in time and space? If it were in space, how does it, a nonsensory entity, perceive anything at all? It seems that memory and character predicates are tied to a physical existence. This leads us to consider the body criterion as the proper criterion for personal identity.

The body criterion states that a person is the same person over time if he or she is continuous with his or her body. The notion of resurrection (or reconstitution) states that I will continue to survive my death in a new glorified body. God will reconstitute me. This is eloquently stated on Benjamin Franklin's tombstone:

This body of B. Franklin in Christ Church cemetery,
Printer, Like the Cover of an old Book,
Its Contents torn out,
And stript of its Lettering and Gilding,
Lies here, Food for Worms.
But the work shall not be lost;
For it will, as he believed,
Appear once more in a new and more elegant Edition,
Corrected and Improved by its Author.

But the resurrection view supposes that God will create a new being like yourself. The problem with this view is that it does not seem all that comforting to learn that someday there will be someone just like you who will enjoy a blessed existence, for if there is no continuity between you and your future self, it is really not you but your successor (someone very similar, even exactly similar to you, a sort of twin) who will enjoy eternal life.

Taking this criterion literally, we would have to conclude that when a zygote divides into identical twins during the first weeks of its existence, the two resulting entities are identical to each other (rather than being exactly similar). Furthermore, we can imagine situations where the personality of one person is transferred to another, such as in Locke's story of the prince and the cobbler, where the body of the prince wakes up one day with all the memories, desires, and character of the cobbler. We might be inclined to say that although the prince's body was before us, we were really speaking with the cobbler. We could also imagine futurist split body-brain operations where our bodies and/or brains are divided and merged with prosthetic bodies or brains. The notions of continuity and uniqueness would conflict.

Suppose the ingenious neurologist Dr. Matthews designed, in his laboratory, a brain and a body like yours, which was virtually indestructible (well, a nuclear bomb could destroy it, but failing that it would be impervious to alteration). The brain is now dormant, but at your death Dr. Matthews will activate it and bring it to life within the prosthetic body. Now Matthews tells you that he needs to kill you in order to allow your alter ego to exist. You complain, but he assures you that one exactly similar to you will live again with all your memories (or copies of them, but alter ego won't know the difference). Would you be comforted by that news? Would you take comfort in the fact that "you" will live again?

Where does all of this leave us with regard to survival after death? If there is no continuity of consciousness, is it the same person who would be resurrected or reconstituted by God at some future time? Or is the reconstituted person like Matthews's replica? A different token of the same generic type? Could God make several tokens of your type—say, five of you—that could be reconstituted and go on to live a new and eternal life? Quintuple resurrection!

Is the survival of the disembodied memories of a person sufficient to satisfy you with regard to your survival after death? The question is perplexing. On the one hand, it seems that our identity is somehow tied to our psychological states (e.g., memories and personality traits), which don't seem to depend on a body. But then if this is so, would our survival occur if a computer stored much of the information about our personalities and memory states?

We seem to need both a body and a brain to instantiate our consciousness and personalities. It is hard to imagine any learning or experiencing or communication with others without a recognizable body. And the brain seems to be the locus of conscious experience. But our bodies and brains die and are disintegrated. What happens to our consciousness and our personal identity? Is the gap between the present conscious life and the next simply like a long sleep during which God prepares a new and glorified body for our personality? Or does the fact that there will have to be a new creation rule out the possibility of personal survival altogether? Or can it be that there is an intrinsically spiritual character to ourselves that both survives the death of the body and perdures in a life beyond this one?

Of course, many Christians believe that although there must be a body for one's full existence, it could be the case that the personality is preserved in an interim state of disembodiment between the first corruptible bodily existence and the second incorruptible bodily existence. But this still has the problem of whether it makes sense to speak of a disembodied self.

However, there is indirect evidence for a soul or the disembodied survival of the self, that recorded by individuals who have been pronounced clinically dead

REINCARNATION

Reincarnation is the view that after death, souls live again in other forms. The doctrine was held by Plato and is a tenet in Hinduism and Buddhism. In the Hindu Scripture *Bhagavad Gita* (ca. 500 B.C.), Lord Krishna comforts the unenlightened Arjuna by telling him that there is no reason to grieve over the death of someone we love, for the "eternal in man cannot die." "We have all been for all time: I, and thou, and those kings of men. And we shall be for all time, we all for ever and ever."

A person's body is different in every incarnation, but the same mind inhabits each body. As the *Bhagavad Gita* states, "As a man leaves an old garment and puts on the one that is new, the Spirit leaves his mortal body and then puts on one that is new." The goal is to end the cycle of rebirths and be absorbed into God (or Nirvana).

Reincarnation is typically linked with *karma*, the doctrine that whatsoever a person sows, whether in action or thought, the fruits will eventually be reaped by him or her—if not in this life, then in the next. Thus, a person who led an evil existence might be reborn as a lower animal (e.g., a reptile or an insect).

> Evidence cited for reincarnation includes déjà vu experiences, the sense that you've been in this place before, seen this person some other time—in another existence—as well as reports of children, of experiences that they couldn't have had in this life.
>
> Objections to reincarnation include the problem of uniform age. When a ninety-year-old man dies, one would expect him to be reborn as an old man or at least with the maturity and the memories of an old man, but he is always born as a baby without wisdom, maturity, or apparent memories. Why is that? If memories are a criterion of personal identity, can the baby be said to be the same person as the ninety-year-old man? Or is it simply a successor self—or does this problem indicate that reincarnation is a myth? Furthermore, what happens to the soul in the interregnum between incarnations? Where do these souls rest while they are awaiting rebirth?
>
> Finally, if one holds the view that consciousness is dependent on the brain, then the very idea of a disembodied soul will seem implausible. The burden of proof will rest with the proponent of reincarnation to give us evidence as to why we should believe this doctrine.

and reported having had out-of-body experiences. James Moody documents several cases of "clinically dead" persons who were revived and reported remarkably similar experiences. Moody sets down a composite of the reports in the following passage:

> A man is dying and, as he reaches the point of greatest physical distress, he hears himself pronounced dead by his doctor. He begins to hear an uncomfortable noise, a loud ringing or buzzing, and at the same time feels himself moving very rapidly through a long dark tunnel. After this, he suddenly finds himself outside of his own physical body, but still in the immediate physical environment, and he sees his own body from a distance, as though he is a spectator. He watches the resuscitation attempt from this unusual vantage point and is in a state of emotional upheaval.
>
> After a while, he collects himself and becomes more accustomed to his odd condition. He notices that he still has a "body," but one of a very different nature and with very different powers from the physical body he has left behind. Soon other things begin to happen. Others come to meet and to help him. He glimpses the spirits of relatives and friends who have already died, and a loving, warm spirit of a kind he has never encountered before—a being of light—appears before him. This being asks him a question, nonverbally, to make him evaluate his life and helps him along by showing him a panoramic, instantaneous playback of the major events of his life. At some point he finds himself approaching some sort of barrier or border, apparently representing the limit between earthly life and the next life. Yet, he finds that he must go back to the earth, that the time for his death has not yet come. At this point he resists, for by now he is taken up with his experiences in the afterlife and does not want to return. He is overwhelmed by intense feelings of joy, love, and peace. Despite his attitude, though, he somehow reunites with his physical body and lives.[4]

This passage is not meant to represent any one person's report but is the model, or composite, of common elements found in many stories. Moody himself makes no claims for the interpretation that the patients really experienced what they claim to have experienced. There could be neurological causes for the experiences, or they could be attributed to wish fulfillment. The point is, simply, that these experiences should be considered as part of the evidence to be examined carefully—perhaps being followed up with further research.

But even if these reports survive close scrutiny, in themselves they do not constitute a strong case for immortality. It could be the case that we do survive our death for one or two more existences but then perish. But for those who can find other arguments for life after death, the Moody reports may serve as a corroboration of this doctrine.

SUMMARY

The question whether there is life after death has haunted human beings from time immemorial. Virtually every religion addresses it and attempts to answer it. Plato and many through the ages have held that our essential self is spiritual, so that it does not die with the body but endures, either in heaven or as reincarnated in another body. The Hebrew view, which is reflected in Paul's writings in the New Testament, holds that our personhood is a function of our bodies, so that you cannot separate body from soul in any absolute manner. Paul taught that after death the redeemed will inherit a new and glorified body. We noted problems with both views. Moody has recorded evidence of out-of-body experiences, although these testimonies have been challenged.

QUESTIONS FOR DISCUSSION

1. The noted anthropologist Sir James Frazier has written the following statement about immortality. Evaluate it.

   Of all the many forms which natural religion has assumed none probably has exerted so deep and far-reaching an influence on human life as the belief in immortality and the worship of the dead; hence [a discussion] of this momentous creed and of the practical consequences which have been deduced from it can hardly fail to be at once instructive and impressive, whether we regard the record with complacency as a noble testimony to the aspiring genius of man, who claims to outlive the sun and the stars, or whether we view it with pity as a melancholy monument of fruitless labour and barren ingenuity expended in prying into that great mystery of which fools profess their knowledge and wise men confess their ignorance.[5]

2. Analyze the Platonic and Judeo-Christian views on life after death. Which view is more plausible? Explain your answer.

3. What do you make of the evidence for out-of-body experiences described by Moody? What are the arguments for and against using this evidence for the thesis that we survive our deaths?

NOTES

1. *A Catholic Dictionary,* ed. D. Attwater (New York: Macmillan, 1941), 261.

2. Plato, *Phaedo,* 79c, d; my translation.

3. 1 Corinthians 15:12–53, King James Version, edited.

4. Raymond Moody, *Life After Life* (New York: Bantam Books, 1976), 21.

5. Sir James Frazier, *The Belief in Immortality,* vol. 1 (London: Macmillan, 1913), vii–viii.

FOR FURTHER READING

Ducasse, C. J. *Nature, Mind and Death.* La Salle, IL: Open Court, 1951. A defense of immortality.

Edwards, Paul, ed. *Immortality.* New York: Macmillan, 1992. The best collection of articles available. Edwards's own introductory article is valuable.

Flew, Anthony. "Immortality." In *Encyclopedia of Philosophy,* vol. 4. New York: Macmillan, 1967, 139–150.

Geach, Peter. *God and Soul.* London: Routledge & Kegan Paul, 1969. A defense of the Judeo-Christian view of survival after death.

Johnson, Raynor. *The Imprisoned Splendor.* London: Hodder & Stoughton, 1953. A defense of reincarnation.

Moody, Raymond. *Life After Life.* New York: Bantam Books, 1976. A fascinating but controversial account of near-death experiences.

Plato, *Phaedo* (any standard translation).

Scriptures of the various religious traditions.

PART V

Freedom of the Will
and Determinism

MICHELANGELO
Adam and Eve Choosing the Forbidden Fruit

Sistine Chapel, The Vatican Museum

There is the unmistakable intuition of virtually every human being that he is free to
make the choices he does and that the deliberations leading to those choices are also
free flowing. The normal man feels too, after he has made a decision, that he could have
decided differently. That is why regret or remorse for a past choice can be so disturbing.[1]

—CORLISS LAMONT

The actions of man are never free; they are always the necessary consequence of his
temperament, of the received ideas, and of the notions, either true or false, which he has
formed to himself of happiness.[2]

—BARON HENRI D'HOLBACH

The problem of freedom of the will and determinism is one of the most
intriguing and difficult in the whole area of philosophy. It constitutes a paradox. If we look at ourselves, at our ability to deliberate and make choices,
it seems obvious that we are free. On the other hand, if we look at what we
believe about causality—namely, that every event and thing must have a cause—
then it appears that we do not have free wills but are determined. So we seem to
have inconsistent beliefs.

Let's look closer at the two theses involved, to see how they work and what
support there is for each of them:

1. Determinism: The theory that everything in the universe (or at least the macroscopic
   universe) is entirely determined by causal laws, so that whatever happens at any
   given moment, including human actions, is the effect of some antecedent cause.
2. Libertarianism: The theory that claims some actions are exempt from the causal laws,
   in which the individual is the sole (or decisive) cause of the act, the act originating
   ex nihilo (out of nothing), cut off from all other causes but the self's doing it.

A third position tries to combine the best of the two positions. Called compatibilism, it says that although everything is determined, we can still act voluntarily.

Chapter 18 presents the classical picture of determinism. Chapter 19 sets forth
arguments for and against libertarianism, and Chapter 20 set forth the case for and
against compatibilism, concluding with some thoughts on the implications of the
debate for moral responsibility.

NOTES

1. Corliss Lamont, *Freedom of Choice
Affirmed* (New York: Horizon, 1967), 3.

2. Baron Henri d'Holbach, *System of Nature*
(1770).

18

Determinism

Baron Henri d'Holbach (1723–1789) stated the determinist thesis in its classic form when he wrote,

In whatever manner man is considered, he is connected to universal nature, and submitted to the necessary and immutable laws that she imposes on all the beings she contains, according to their peculiar essences or to the respective properties with which, without consulting them, she endows particular species. Man's life is a line that nature commands him to outline upon the surface of the earth, without his ever being able to swerve from it, even for an instant. He is born without his own consent; his organization does in nowise depend upon himself; his ideas come to him involuntarily; his habits are in the power of those who cause him to contract them; he is unceasingly modified by causes, whether visible or concealed, over which he has no control, which necessarily regulate his mode of existence, give the hue to his way of thinking, and determine his manner of acting. He is good or bad, happy or miserable, wise or foolish, reasonable or irrational, without his will counting for anything in these various states. . . .[1]

H. T. Buckle (1821–1862), who published Holbach's work, sums up his position in this way:

If I were capable of correct reasoning, and if, at the same time, I had a complete knowledge both of his disposition and of all the events by which he was surrounded, I should be able to foresee the line of conduct which, in consequence of those events, he would adopt.[2]

Extending this further, we can say that if we knew all the possible states of matter and motion in the universe, we could know all the events of the universe past, present, and future. We could predict every future event and postdict every past event.

Determinism is the theory that everything in the universe is governed by causal laws. That is, everything in the universe is entirely determined so that whatever happens at any given moment is the effect of some antecedent cause. If we were omniscient, we could predict exactly everything that would happen for the rest of this hour, for the rest of our lifetime, for the rest of time itself, simply because we know how everything hitherto is causally related. This theory—which, it is claimed, is the basic presupposition of science—implies that there is no such thing as an uncaused event (sometimes this is modified to include only the macrocosmic world, leaving the microcosmic world in doubt). Hence, since all human actions are events, human actions are not undetermined, are not *free* in a radical sense but are also the product of a causal process. Hence, although we may self-importantly imagine that we are autonomous and possess free will, in reality we are totally conditioned by heredity and environment.

The outline of the argument for determinism goes something like this:

1. Every event (or state of affairs) must have a cause.
2. Human actions (as well as the agent who gives rise to those actions) are events (or states of affairs).
3. ∴ Every human action (including the agent himself) is caused.
4. Hence, determinism is true.

UNIVERSAL CAUSALITY

Although the hypothesis of universal causality cannot be proved, it is something we are assumed—either because of considerable inductive evidence or as an a priori truth that seems to make sense of the world. We cannot easily imagine an uncaused event taking place in ordinary life. For example, imagine how you would feel if, on visiting your dentist for relief of a toothache, she were to conclude her oral examination with the remark, "I certainly can see that you are in great pain because of your toothache, but I'm afraid that I can't help you, for there is no cause of this toothache." Perhaps she calls her partner over to confirm her judgment. "Sure enough," he says, "this is one of those interesting noncausal cases. Sorry, there's nothing we can do for you. Even medicine and pain relievers won't help these noncausal types."

Let's consider another example. In Melbourne, Australia, weather forecasts for a twenty-four-hour period are exceedingly reliable. The predictions based on the available atmospheric data and the known meteorological laws are almost always correct. On the other hand, on Star Island off the New Hampshire coast, the official forecasts for a twenty-four-hour period are more often wrong than right. Suppose someone came along and said, "There is an easy explanation for the success of the Australian forecasts and the lack of success of the Star Island forecasts. In Melbourne, the weather is caused by preceding conditions, but on Star Island, more often than not, the weather has no cause. It's cut off from what happened before." Most of us would explain the failure of the meteorologists differently, believing that the weather on Star Island is just as much the outcome of preceding conditions as the weather in Melbourne. The forecasts are less reliable on Star Island because of the greater complexities of the factors that have to be taken into account and the greater difficulty of observing them, but not because sufficient causal factors do not exist.

It's an interesting question, whether the belief in causality is universal in humans or simply a product of experience. When does it arise in children? When our children were about ages four and six years, respectively, I discovered one day a mess made in the pantry. A package of cookies had been opened, and the cookies and cookie crumbs were strewn about on the floor, some having been eaten. We asked our children which one of them had pilfered cookies. Both denied having anything to do with the matter. We pressed them, for there were no other people but ourselves who had access to the cookies. Finally, my exasperated four-year-old son volunteered, "Why does someone have to have done it? Why couldn't it just have happened?" "Impossible," I remonstrated, "every event must have a sufficient cause!" My son looked at me with bewilderment. Two weeks later I went to the pantry again and saw a similar sight. Bags of cookies had been broken into, and cookies were scattered all over the floor. But in the midst of the cookies was a dead mouse caught in a mousetrap with a piece of cheese in his mouth but cookie crumbs lining his whiskers. Greed summoned his downfall. Exhilarated by the discovery and confirmation of my theory, I summoned my children to the scene of the crime and triumphantly exclaimed, "Behold, every event must have a cause!" And so the not-so-subtle indoctrination commences.

Why do we believe that everything has a cause? Most philosophers have echoed John Stuart Mill's (1806–1873) answer that the doctrine of universal causality is a conclusion of inductive reasoning. We have had an enormous range of experience wherein we have found causal explanations to individual events, which in turn seem to participate in a further causal chain. The problem with this answer, however, is that we have only experienced a very small part of the universe, not enough of it to warrant the conclusion that every event must have a cause.

It was David Hume (1711–1776) who pointed out that the idea of causality is not a logical truth (like the notion that all triangles have three sides). The hypothesis that every event has a cause arises from the observation of regular conjunctions: "When many uniform instances appear, and the same object is always followed by the same event; we then begin to entertain the notion of cause and connexion."[3] So after a number of successful tries at putting a pot of water to heat over a fire and seeing the water disappear, we can conclude that heat (or fire) causes water to disappear (or vaporize, turn into gas). But we cannot prove causality. We never see it. All we see are two events in constant spatiotemporal order and infer from this constant conjunction a binding relation between them. For example, we see billiard ball A hit ball B, we see B move away from A, and we conclude that A's hitting B at a certain velocity is the cause of B's moving away as it did. However, we cannot prove that it is the sufficient cause of the movement.

It was Immanuel Kant (1724–1804) who first suggested that the principle of universal causality is a synthetic a priori—that is, an assumption that we cannot prove by experience but simply cannot conceive not to be the case. Our mental construction demands that we read all experience in the light of universal causation. We have no knowledge of what the world is in itself or whether there really is universal causation, but we cannot understand experience except by means of causal explanation. The necessary idea of causality is part and parcel of the framework of our noetic structure. We are programmed to read our experience in the causal script.

Kant saw that there was a powerful incentive to believe in determinism, but he also thought that the notion of morality provided a powerful incentive to believe in freedom of the will. Kant was faced with a dilemma: "How can I reconcile the free will necessary for morality and the causal determinism necessary for science?" (We will say more about his problem in Chapters 19 and 20.)

The man who used the idea of determinism more effectively for practical purposes than anyone before him was the great American criminal lawyer Clarence Darrow. In the 1920s, in a sensational crime, two teenage geniuses, named Leopold and Loeb, students at the University of Chicago, committed what they regarded as the perfect murder. They grotesquely dismembered a child and buried the parts of his body in a prairie. Caught, they faced an outraged public who demanded the death penalty. The defense attorney was Clarence Darrow, champion of lost causes. He conceded that the boys committed the deed but argued that they were, nevertheless, "innocent." His argument was based on the theory of determinism. It is worth reading part of the plea:

> We are all helpless. . . . This weary world goes on, begetting, with birth and with living and with death; and all of it is blind from the beginning to the end. I do not know what it was that made these boys do this mad act, but I do know there is a reason for it. I know they did not beget themselves. I know that any one of an infinite number of causes reaching back to the beginning might be working out in these boys' minds, whom you are asked to hang in malice and in hatred and injustice. . . .
>
> Nature is strong and she is pitiless. She works in her own mysterious way, and we are her victims. We have not much to do with it ourselves. Nature takes this job in hand, and we play our part. In the words of old Omar Khayam, we are:
>
> But helpless pieces in the game He plays
> Upon the chess board of nights and days;
> Hither and thither moves, and checks and slays,
> And one by one back in the closet lays.
>
> What had this boy to do with it? He was not his own father, he was not his own mother; he was not his own grandparents. All of this was handed to him. He did not surround himself with governesses and wealth. He did not make himself. And yet he is to be compelled to pay.[4]

This was sufficient to convince the jury to go against public opinion and recommend a life sentence in lieu of the death penalty. If Leopold and Loeb were determined by antecedent causes to do the deed they did, we cannot blame them for what they did, any more than we can blame a cow for not being able to fly.

But Darrow may have gotten away with an illicit move here. For if determinism is true, as he argues, the same argument he uses to exculpate the two boys can be used to show that *no one* is responsible for his or her deeds, whether they be good or bad. There are no grounds for punishment according to desert, nor rewarding people for their good deeds—at least not on the basis of desert, for if determinism is true, it will be argued, no one deserves anything. We will return to the problem of moral responsibility in the next two chapters. Here we note that it is a problem.

Determinism has received new attention and respect due to modern neurological studies. These studies suggest this hypothesis: There is a one-to-one correlation between mental states and brain states so that every conscious action can be traced back to a causally sufficient brain state. In other words, the laws of physics deterministically produce mental states.[5]

TELEOLOGICAL DETERMINISM

Let me immediately point out that determinism need not be crudely mechanistic but can take into account rational intentions and purposes. Although it generally holds that mental events are dependent on neural events or brain states, sophisticated teleological determinism (as opposed to simple phhsical determinism) can recognize the conceptual connection between intention and action. That is, in analyzing why you raised your hand, I need to know whether you were intending to wave to a friend, to vote, or to swat a fly. A purely physical description of your bodily motions is inadequate as a full account of what you are doing.

However, despite what some libertarians have argued, intentions are no great problem for determinism. Guided missiles, thermostats, and chess-playing computers are also purposive and self-regulating, having feedback mechanisms that enable them to reach their goals despite changing factors in the environment. Chess-playing computers, for example, can learn, devise new strategies, and decide between alternate moves. Although computers are not conscious, they have purposes. The determinist notes that the only advantages that human chess players have over the artifact is that the humans are conscious while playing chess. But the question is, What exactly is so important about consciousness? How does consciousness—mere awareness—add to our ability to act freely? We could well imagine a chess-playing computer suddenly conscious of its strategies and moves. Would that awareness by itself make it free?

SUMMARY

The determinist argues that all human action can be subsumed under scientific causal laws that govern the rest of physical behavior. Since every action is completely caused by heredity and environmental factors, there are no free actions. Since there are no free actions, we are not responsible for any of our actions.

QUESTIONS FOR DISCUSSION

1. Go over the arguments for determinism. How strong are they? What are the chief problems?

2. Assess Darrow's defense of Leopold and Loeb. Do you think his argument is sound? How would an opponent challenge it? Do you agree that if determinism is true, no one is really responsible for his or her actions?

3. What kind of punishment system should we have if determinism is true?

NOTES

1. Baron Henri d'Holbach, *System of Nature* (1770).

2. H. T. Buckle in his *History of Civilization in England* (1857), cited in *An Introduction to Modern Philosophy,* eds. Albury Castell and Donald Borchert (New York: Macmillan, 1976), 76.

3. David Hume, *Enquiry* (1748), 78.

4. Clarence Darrow, *Attorney for the Damned* (New York: Simon & Schuster, 1957).

5. See Donald M. MacKay, *Freedom of Action in a Mechanistic Universe* (Cambridge, Eng.: Cambridge University Press, 1967).

FOR FURTHER READING

Dennett, Daniel. *Elbow Room: The Varieties of Free Will Worth Wanting.* Cambridge, MA: MIT Press, 1984. A well-argued defense of compatibilism.

Double, Richard. *The Non-reality of Free Will.* New York: Oxford University Press, 1991. A penetrating, readable work.

Honderich, Ted. *How Free Are You?* Oxford: Oxford University Press, 1993. A good introduction to the subject by a leading proponent of determinism.

Lehrer, Keith, and James Cornman. *Philosophical Problems and Argument,* 3rd ed. New York: Macmillan, 1982. Lehrer's essay in Chapter 3 is excellent.

Pojman, Louis, ed. *Introduction to Philosophy: Classical and Contemporary Readings,* 2d ed. Belmont, CA: Wadsworth, 1999. Part 5 contains several important readings on free will, responsibility, and the implications for a theory of punishment.

Stace, Walter T. *Religion and the Modern Mind.* Philadelphia: Lippencott, 1952. Contains a lucid account of compatibilism.

Trustead, Jennifer. *Free Will and Responsibility.* Oxford: Oxford University Press, 1984. A clear, accessible introduction to the subject.

van Inwagen, Peter. *An Essay on Free Will.* Oxford: Clarendon Press, 1983. A highly original study, criticizing compatibilism.

Watson, Gary, ed. *Free Will.* Oxford: Clarendon Press, 1982. Contains important articles, especially those by Frankfurt, van Inwagen, and Watson himself.

19

Libertarianism

Libertarianism is the theory stating that we do have free wills. It contends that given the same antecedent (prior) conditions at time t_1, an agent S could do either act A_1 or A_2. That is, it is up to S what the world will look like after t_1, and that his act is causally *underdetermined,* the self making the unexplained difference. Libertarians do not contend that all our actions are free, only some of them. Neither do they offer an explanatory theory of free will. Their arguments are indirect. They offer two main arguments for their position. The first is the argument from deliberation, and the second is the argument from moral responsibility.

THE ARGUMENT FROM DELIBERATION

The position is nicely summed up in the words of Corliss Lamont:

> There is the unmistakable intuition of virtually every human being that he is free to make the choices he does and that the deliberations leading to those choices are also free flowing. The normal man feels too, after he has made a decision, that he could have decided differently. That is why regret or remorse for a past choice can be so disturbing.[1]

As an example, there is a difference between a knee jerk and purposefully kicking a football. In the first case, the behavior is involuntary, a reflex action. In the second case, we deliberate, notice that we have an alternative (viz., not kicking the ball), consciously choose to kick the ball, and if successful, we find our body moving in the requisite manner so that the ball is kicked.

Deliberation may take a short or long time, be foolish or wise, but the process is a conscious one wherein we believe that we really can do either of the actions (or any of many possible actions). That is, in deliberating, we assume that we are free to choose between alternatives and that we are not determined to do simply one action. Otherwise, why deliberate? This should seem obvious to everyone who introspects on what it is to deliberate.

Furthermore, there seems to be something psychologically lethal about accepting determinism in human relations; it tends to curtail deliberation and paralyze actions. If people really believe themselves totally determined, the tendency is for them to excuse their behavior. Human effort seems pointless. As Arthur Eddington put it, "What significance is there to my mental struggle tonight whether I shall or shall not give up smoking, if the laws which govern the matter of the physical universe already preordain for the morrow a configuration of matter consisting of pipe, tobacco, and smoke connected to my lips?"[2]

The Determinist's Objection to the Argument from Deliberation   The determinist responds to this by admitting that we often feel "free" and feel that we could do otherwise, but that these feelings are illusory. The determinist may admit that at any given time t_1, while deliberating, she feels that she is free—at least on one level. But on a higher level or after the deliberation process is over, she acknowledges that even the deliberation is the product of antecedent causes. Ledger Wood suggests that the libertarian argument from deliberation can be reduced to this formula: "I feel myself free, *therefore,* I am free." He analyzes the deliberative decision into three constituents: (1) the recognition of two or more incompatible courses of action, (2) the weighing of considerations favorable and unfavorable to each of the conflicting possibilities of action, and (3) the choice among the alternative possibilities. "At the moment of making the actual decision, the mind experiences a *feeling* of self-assertion and of independence both external and internal." However, Wood insists that the determinist can give a satisfactory account of this feeling, regarding it as "nothing but a sense of relief following upon earlier tension and indecision."

> After conflict and uncertainty, the pent-up energies of the mind—or rather of the underlying neural processes—are released and this process is accompanied by an inner sense of power. Thus the feeling of freedom or voluntary control over one's actions is a mere subjective illusion which cannot be considered evidence for psychological indeterminacy.[3]

Sometimes, the determinist will offer an account of action in terms of action being the result of the strongest motive. Adolf Grunbaum puts it this way:

> Let us carefully examine the content of the feeling that on a certain occasion we could have acted other than the way we did in fact act. What do we find? Does the feeling we have inform us that we could have acted otherwise under exactly the same external and internal motivational conditions? No, says the determinist, this feeling simply discloses that we were able to act in accord with our strongest desire at the time, and that we could indeed have acted otherwise if a different motive had prevailed at that time.[4]

We could break up the concept of motivation into two parts, that of belief and desire (or wants), resulting in the combination of a desire based on certain beliefs. If Mary strongly desires to fly to New York from Los Angeles at a certain time and believes that taking a certain American Air Lines flight is the best way to do this, she will, unless there are other intervening factors, take such a flight. There is no mystery about the decision. She may deliberate on whether she really wants to pay the $50 more on American than she would have to pay on a later economy flight, but once she realizes that she values getting to New York at a certain time more than saving $50, she will act accordingly. If Mary is rational, her wants and desires will function in a reliable pattern. Because wants and beliefs are not under our direct control, are not products of free choice, and the act is a product of desires and beliefs, the act is not a product of free choice either. The argument goes something like this:

1. Actions are the results of (are caused by) beliefs and desires.
2. We do not freely choose our beliefs and desires.
3. Beliefs and desires are thrust on us by our environment in conjunction with innate dispositions.
4. ∴ We do not freely choose our actions, but our actions are caused by the causal processes that form our beliefs and desires.

If this is so, it is hard to see where free will comes into the picture. The controversial premise is probably premise 2, whether we choose our beliefs and desires. The determinist would maintain that we do not choose our beliefs but that they, as truth-directed, are events in our lives, the way the world represents itself to us. That is, beliefs function as truth detectors; that as it is not up to us what the truth is, so it is not up to us to form beliefs about the world. You can check this in a small way by asking why it is you believe that the world is spherical and not flat. Because of evidence, or because you choose to believe it? If the latter, could you give up the belief by simply deciding to do so? Neither do we choose our desires, but our desires simply formulate choices. We do not choose to be hungry or to love knowledge, although when we find ourselves in conflict between two conflicting desires (e.g., the desire to eat ice cream and the desire to lose weight), we have to adjudicate the difference. But this decision is simply a process of allowing the strongest desire (or deepest desire—a deep dispositional desire could win out over a sharply felt occurrent desire) to win out. But all this can be explained in a purely deterministic way, without resorting to a mysterious free act of the will.

The Libertarian Counterresponse: Agent Causation Now the libertarian objects that this is too simplistic a notion of action. We cannot isolate the desires and beliefs in such a rigid manner. There are intangibles that are at work here and that may be decisive in bringing all factors of desire and belief together and formulating the final decision.

Some libertarians, such as Roderick Chisholm and Richard Taylor, respond to this view of motivation by putting forward an alternative picture of causation to account for actions. According to Chisholm and Taylor, it is sometimes the case that *agents themselves* are the cause of their own acts. That is, the agent causes actions without himself changing in any essential way. No account need be given on how this is possible:

> The only conception of action that accords with our data is one according to which men . . . are sometimes, but of course not always, self-determining beings; that is, beings which are sometimes the causes of their own behavior. In the case of an action that is free, it must be such that it is caused by the agent who performs it, but such that no antecedent conditions were sufficient for his performing just that action. In the case of an action that is both free and rational, it must be that the agent who performed it did so for some reason, but this reason cannot have been the cause of it.[5]

This notion of the self as agent differs from the Humean notion that the self is simply a bundle of perceptions; instead, the self is a substance and self-moving being. Human beings are not simply assemblages of material processes but complex wholes, with a different metaphysical status than physical objects. Furthermore, the self is a substance and not an event. It is a being that initiates action without being moved to act by antecedent causes. If I raise my hand, it is not the events leading up to the raising of my hand that cause this act, but I myself am the cause.

In a sense the self becomes a "god," creating *ex nihilo,* in that reasons may influence but do not determine the acts. In the words of Chisholm,

> If we are responsible, and if what I have been trying to say [about agent causality] is true, then we have a prerogative which some would attribute only to God: each of us, when we act, is a prime mover unmoved. In doing what we do, we cause certain events to happen and nothing—or no one—causes us to cause those events to happen.[6]

Perhaps the libertarian draws some support for this thesis from Genesis 1:26, where God says, "Let us make man in our image." The image of God may be our ability to make free, causally underdetermined decisions. In a sense, every libertarian believes in at least one "god" and in creative miracles.

This theory, although attractive in that it preserves the notion of free agency, suffers from the fact that it leaves agent causation unexplained. The self is a mystery that is unaccounted for. Actions are seen as miracles that are unrelated to antecedent causal chains, detached from the laws of nature. Nevertheless, something like the argument from agency seems to be intuitively satisfying upon introspection. We do feel that we are free agents.

Along these lines, the libertarian dismisses the determinist's hypothesis of a complete causal explanation based on a correlation of brain events with mental events. Memories are stored in the brain, but the self is not. Whether as an emergent property, a transcendent entity, or simply an unexplained mystery, the self must be regarded as primitive. In a Cartesian manner, it is to be accepted as more certain than anything else and the source of all other certainties.

Objection to Arguments from Introspection   The problem with the argument from introspection, which underlies the agency theory, is that our introspections and intuitions about our behavior are often misguided. Freudian psychology and common sense tell us that sometimes when we believe that we are acting from one motive, another hidden subconscious motive is really at play. The hypnotized person believes that she is free when she is uttering her preordained speech, while the audience looks on knowingly. Dr. Chris Frederickson, a neuro-physiologist at the University of Texas at Dallas, has told of experiments with electrodes that illustrate this point nicely. Patients with electrodes attached to their neocortex are set before a button, which sets off a bell. The patients are told that they may press the button whenever they like. The patients proceed to press the buttons and ring the bells. They report that they are entirely free in doing this. However, the monitoring of the brain shows that an impulse is started in the cere-bral cortex before they become aware of their desire and decision to press the but-ton, and when this impulse reaches a certain level, the patients feel the volition and press the button. Is it fair to suppose that all our behavior may follow this model? Do we only become conscious of the workings of our subconscious at discrete moments? Notice in this regard that often we seem to have unconsciously formulated our speech before we are conscious of what we are saying. The words flow naturally, as though some inner speech writer were working them out beforehand.

It seems, then, that our introspective reports must be regarded as providing very little evidence in favor of free will in the libertarian sense. As Baruch Spinoza (1632–1677) said, if a stone hurled through the air were to become conscious, it would probably deem itself free.

The Argument from Quantum Physics (A Peephole of Free Will) At this point, libertarians sometimes refer to an argument from quantum mechanics in order to defend themselves against the insistence of determinists that science is on their side in their espousal of universal causality. The argument from quantum mechanics is negative and indirectly in support of the libertarian thesis. According to quantum mechanics as developed by Neils Bohr (1885–1962) and Max Born (1882–1970), the behavior of subatomic particles does not follow causal process-es but instead yields only statistically predictable behavior. That is, we cannot pre-dict the motions of individual particles, but we can successfully predict the per-centage that will act in certain ways. A certain randomness seems to operate on this subatomic level. Hence, there is a case for indeterminacy.

This thesis of quantum mechanics is controversial. Albert Einstein (1879–1955) never accepted it. "God doesn't play dice!" he said. Quantum physics may only indi-cate the fact that we do not know the operative causes at subatomic levels. After all, we are only in the kindergarten of subatomic physics. So the indeterminist may be committing the fallacy of ignorance in reading too much into the inability of quan-tum physicists to give causal explanations of subatomic behavior.

On the other hand, perhaps quantum physics should make impartial persons reconsider what they mean by "causality" and whether it could be the case that it is an unclear concept in the first place. The fact that our notion of "causality" is vague and unanalyzed was pointed out long ago by David Hume (1711–1776) and reiterated in this century by William James (1842–1910):

> The principle of causality . . .—what is it but a postulate, an empty name covering simply a demand that the sequence of events shall some day manifest a deeper kind of belonging of one thing with another than the mere arbitrary juxtaposition which now phenomenally appears? It is as much an altar to an unknown god as the one

that Saint Paul found at Athens. All our scientific and philosophic ideas are altars to unknown gods.[7]

Recent work by philosophers on the subject of causality hasn't substantially improved this state of affairs. The notion, although enjoying an intuitively privileged position in our noetic structure, is still an enigma.

Nevertheless, although the quantum theory and doubts about causality may cause us to loosen our grip on the notion of universal causality, it doesn't help the libertarians in any positive way, for it only shows at best that there is randomness in the world, not that there is purposeful free agency. Uncaused behavior suggests erratic, impulsive, reflex motion without any rhyme or reason, the behavior of the maniac, lacking all predictability and explanation, behavior out of our rational control. But free action must be under my control if it is to be counted as my behavior. That is, the thesis of libertarianism is that the agent is underdetermined when he makes a purposeful, rational decision. All that quantum mechanics entails is that there are random events in the brain (or wherever) that yield unpredictable behavior for which the agent is not responsible.

THE ARGUMENT
FROM MORAL RESPONSIBILITY

Determinism seems to conflict with the thesis that we have moral responsibilities, for responsibility implies that we could have done otherwise than we did. We do not hold a dog responsible for chewing up our philosophy book or a one-month-old baby responsible for crying because they could not help it, but we do hold a twenty-year-old student responsible for her cheating because (we believe) she could have done otherwise. Black-backed seagulls will tear apart a stray herring seagull baby without the slightest suspicion that their act may be immoral, but if humans lack this sense, we judge the behavior as pathological, as substandard.

Moral responsibility is something that we take very seriously. We believe that we do have duties, oughts, over which we feel rational guilt at our failure to perform. But there can be no such things as duties, oughts, praise, blame, or rational guilt if we are not essentially free. The argument form is the following:

1. If determinism is true and our actions are merely the product of the laws of nature and antecedent states of affairs, then it is not up to us to choose what we do.
2. But if it is not up to us to choose what we do, we cannot be said to be responsible for what we do.
3. So if determinism is true, we are not responsible for what we do.
4. But our belief in moral responsibility is self-evident, at least as strong as our belief in universal causality.
5. So if we believe that we have moral responsibilities, determinism cannot be accepted.

We must reject the notion of determinism even if we cannot give a full explanatory account of how agents choose.

Here the determinist bites the bullet and admits that we do not have moral responsibilities and that it is just an illusion that we do. However, we are determined to have such an illusion, so there is nothing we can do about it. Perhaps we cannot consciously live as determinists, in the sense that when I act I cannot help feel that I am free to do otherwise, but why should we think that we can? We are finite and fallible creatures, driven by causal laws, but with self-consciousness that makes us aware of part (but only a part) of the process that governs our behavior. We can accept determinism, realize that we are not really free, and take account of this in our institutional arrangements—perhaps by basing punishment on the principles of deterrence, prevention, and rehabilitation, rather than on desert and responsibility.

The libertarian will not accept this reply as an adequate answer because determinism seems to make us into robots who are responding to forces beyond our control—the antecendent determining factors.

However, there is another response to the problem of free will and determinism, which claims to save both the notion of determinism and the notion of moral responsibility. To this reconciling project, called compatibilism, we will turn in Chapter 20.

SUMMARY

Libertarianism is the theory that we have free will and that we are not totally determined by heredity or environment. It appeals to the arguments from deliberation, introspection, quantum physics, and moral responsibility to make its case. Libertarians argue that without a commitment to free will, we have no basis for holding people accountable for their actions. The determinist challenges each of these arguments.

QUESTIONS FOR DISCUSSION

1. Go over the two major theories (determinism and libertarianism). What are the strengths and weaknesses of each theory? Which do you think is the best answer, and why?

2. It is often claimed that our moral intuitions—that we are responsible for our actions and have duties, that people should be praised or blamed and punished or rewarded for their actions—turn out to be illusory if the libertarian answer is not true. The argument, which we noted above, goes as follows:

    1. If determinism is true and our actions are merely the product of the laws of nature and antecedent states of affairs, then it is not up to us to choose what we do.

    2. But if it is not up to us to choose what we do, we cannot be said to be responsible for what we do.

    3. So if determinism is true, we are not responsible for what we do.

    4. But our belief in moral responsibility is self-evident, at least as strong as our belief in universal causality.

    5. So if we believe that we have moral responsibilities, determinism cannot be accepted.

We must reject the notion of determinism even if we cannot give a full explanatory account of how agents choose.

Of course, even if this is a sound argument, the determinist can bite the bullet and admit that we do not have moral responsibilities and that it is just an illusion that we do. We are determined to have such an illusion, so there is nothing we can do about it.

Evaluate this argument and the determinist response. After you have read Chapter 20, ask: How would the compatibilist respond to it? Discuss your answer.

NOTES

1. Corliss Lamont, *Freedom of Choice Affirmed* (New York: Horizon, 1967), 3.

2. Arthur Eddington, *The Nature of the Physical World* (New York: Macmillan, 1928).

3. Ledger Wood, "The Free Will Controversy," *Philosophy* 16 (1941): 386.

4. Adolf Grunbaum, "Causality and the Science of Human Behavior," reprinted in part in *Philosophical Problems,* ed. Maurice Mandelbaum (New York: Macmillan, 1957), 336.

5. Richard Taylor, *Metaphysics* (Englewood Cliffs, NJ: Prentice Hall, 1974), 54.

6. Roderick Chisholm, "Human Freedom and the Self," in *Free Will,* ed. Gary Watson (Oxford: Clarendon Press, 1982), 32.

7. William James, "The Dilemma of Determinism," in his *Essays on Faith and Morals* (Cleveland: World, 1962).

FOR FURTHER READING

Dennett, Daniel. *Elbow Room: The Varieties of Free Will Worth Wanting.* Cambridge, MA: MIT Press, 1984. A well-argued defense of compatibilism.

Kane, Robert. *The Significance of Free Will.* Oxford: Oxford University Press, 1996.

Lehrer, Keith, and James Cornman. *Philosophical Problems and Argument,* 3d ed. New York: Macmillan, 1982. Lehrer's essay in Chapter 3 is excellent.

Pojman, Louis, ed. *Introduction to Philosophy: Classical and Contemporary Readings,* 2d ed. Belmont, CA: Wadsworth, 2000. Part 5 contains several important readings on free will, responsibility, and the implications for a theory of punishment.

Stace, Walter T. *Religion and the Modern Mind.* Philadelphia: Lippencott, 1952. Contains a lucid account of compatibilism.

Trustead, Jennifer. *Free Will and Responsibility.* Oxford: Oxford University Press, 1984. A clear, accessible introduction to the subject.

van Inwagen, Peter. *An Essay on Free Will.* Oxford: Clarendon Press, 1983. A highly original study, criticizing compatibilism.

Watson, Gary, ed. *Free Will.* Oxford: Clarendon Press, 1982. Contains important articles, especially those by Frankfurt, van Inwagen, and Watson himself.

20

Compatibilism: How to Have Your Cake and Eat It Too

A RECONCILING PROJECT

We have been struggling with the dilemma of free will and determinism. Causal determinism seems to account for all the events in the world. Even if we modify this to include the conclusions of quantum physics, this does not give us evidence for free will but only randomness that yields statistical probability. On the other hand, we have a deep conviction that we can *do otherwise,* act freely. What is more, morality seems to require that we choose freely and thus may be held accountable for our actions. Which theory is right? Are we free or determined? Or a little bit of each?

A third doctrine has been developed to make sense of our dilemma, one going back to David Hume (1711–1776) and Immanuel Kant (1724–1804) but receiving a more thorough defense in the works of Walter Stace, Harry Frankfurt, and Daniel Dennett.[1] It may be called reconciling determinism, soft determinism, or, my choice, **compatibilism.** It argues that although we are determined we still have moral responsibilities, that the basis of the distinction is that between *voluntary* and *involuntary* behavior.

The language of freedom and the language of determinism are but two different ways of talking about certain human or rational events, both necessary for humankind (one is necessary for science, and the other is necessary for morality and personal relationships). The compatibilist argues that the fact that we are determined does not affect our interpersonal relationships. We will still have feelings that we must deal with, using internalist insights. We will still feel resentment when someone hurts us "on purpose." We will still feel grateful for services rendered and hold people responsible for their actions. However, we will still acknowledge that from the external perspective the determinist's account of all of this is valid.

Along these lines, Walter Stace (1886–1967) has argued that the problem of freedom and determinism is really only a semantic one, a dispute about the meanings of words. Freedom has to do with acts done voluntarily, and determinism has to do with the causal processes that underlie all behavior and events. These need not be incompatible. Mahatma Gandhi (1869–1948) fasted because he wanted to free India from colonial rule and so performed a voluntary or free act, whereas a man starving in the desert is not giving up food voluntarily or as a free act. A thief purposefully and voluntarily steals, whereas a kleptomaniac cannot help stealing. In both cases, each act or event has causal antecedents, but the former in each set are free, whereas the latter are unfree: "Acts freely done are those whose immediate causes are psychological states in the agent. Acts not freely done are those whose immediate causes are states of affairs external to the agent."[2]

Sometimes the compatibilist position is put in terms of reasons for actions. The agent is free just in case he or she acted according to reasons rather than from internal neurotic or external coercive pressure. But our reasons are not things we choose but wants and beliefs with which we find ourselves. Since free actions are caused by that which is not a free act, we can see that our free actions are in a sense determined.

The argument for compatibilism can be formulated like this:

1. The reasons R that someone S has for performing act A are not themselves actions.
2. S could not help having R.
3. Act A could nevertheless be free because it was not coerced by external causes.
4. ∴ An action may result from having a reason that one could not help having—that is, a reason that one was not free not to have—and the action might nevertheless be free.
5. ∴ We obtain the collapse of the argument for the incompatibility of free action and determinism.

The compatibilist challenges the libertarian to produce an action that does not fit this formula. Consider the act of raising my hand at time t_1. Why do I do it? Well, if it's a rational (i.e., free) act, it's because I have a reason for raising my hand. For example, at t_1 I wish to vote for Joan to be president of our club. I deliberate on whom to vote for (read: allow the options to present themselves before my mind), decide that Joan is the best candidate, and raise my hand in response to that judgment. It is a free act, but all the features can be accommodated within causal explanatory theory. Reasons function as causes here.

What would a free act be that was not determined by reasons? Consider the situation of coming to a fork in the road with no obvious reason to take either one (or go back, for that matter). If there are no reasons to do one thing more than another, I have no basis for choice. But I may still believe that doing something is better than just standing still, so I flip a coin in order to decide. This belief functions as my reason for flipping the coin. Similarly, I may flip a "mental coin," by letting the internal devices of my subconscious make an arbitrary decision. The alternative to these arbitrary "flips of the coin" is to be in the same position as Buridan's ass who starved to death while he was an equal distance between two luscious bales of hay because there was no more reason to choose one bale over the other! So, the objection runs, all rational action is determined by reason, and libertarianism turns out to be incoherent.

The compatibilist joins with the determinist to the extent that he asserts that all actions have a sufficient causal explanation. Free actions are caused by reasons the person has, and unfree actions are caused by nonrational coercion. What would it mean to act freely without reasons, he asks? What kind of freedom would that be? Would it not turn out to be irrational, hence arbitrary or unconsciously motivated action?

But if our free acts are the acts that we do voluntarily because we have reasons for them, we can be held accountable for them. We identify with the springs of those actions and so may be said to have produced them in a way that we do not produce involuntary actions. We could have avoided those actions, if we had chosen to do so. Hence, we are responsible for them.

One particularly sophisticated version of this position is that of Harry Frankfurt,[3] who argues that what is important about freedom of the will is not any contracausal notions but the manner in which the will is structured. What distinguishes *persons* from other conscious beings (which he calls "wantons") are the second-order desires that they have. All conscious beings have first-order desires, but persons have attitudes about those first-order desires. They either want it to be the case that their first-order desires motivate them to action or that they do not motivate them to action: "Someone has a desire of the second order either when he wants simply to have a certain desire or when he wants a certain desire to be his will. In situations of the latter kind, I shall call his second-order desires 'second-order volitions.' "[4]

A nicotine addict may very well desire that his first-order desire for a cigarette be frustrated or overcome, whereas a wife unable to feel certain sentiments toward her husband may have a second-order desire that she would come to have feelings of affection for her husband.

Nevertheless, we should not confuse free will with free action:

> We do not suppose that animals enjoy freedom of the will, although we recognize that an animal may be free to run in whatever direction it wants. Thus, having the freedom to do what one wants to do is not a sufficient condition of having a free will. It is not a necessary condition either. For to deprive someone of his freedom of action is not necessarily to undermine the freedom of his will. When an agent is aware that there are certain things he is not free to do, this doubtless affects his desires and limits the range of choices he can make. But suppose someone, without being aware of it, has in fact lost or been deprived of his freedom of action. Even though he is no longer free to do what he wants to do, his will may remain as free as it was before. Despite the fact that he is not free to translate his desires into actions or to act according to the determinations of his will, he may still form those desires and make those determinations as freely as if his freedom of action had not been impaired.[5]

Hence, it makes no sense to define free will as the libertarians do, as those actions that originate in ways underdetermined by antecedent causes. A person's will is free just in case she is free to have the will she wants, whether or not she is able to act.

A CRITIQUE OF COMPATIBILISM:
A "QUAGMIRE OF EVASION"?

The compatibilist may be accused of wanting his cake and eating it too. The libertarian does not meet the compatibilist challenge head on, for he admits that we don't have a straightforward argument for libertarianism. Instead, he shows that compatibilism is really simply a wistful sort of determinism. William James (1842–1910) labeled it "a quagmire of evasion" and argues that the compatibilist is simply an inconsistent determinist or a determinist who tries to smuggle in moral responsibility by virtue of an irrelevant dichotomy between voluntary and involuntary action.

The libertarian points out that the distinction between voluntary and involuntary actions is beside the point since we cannot be held accountable for antecedent causes and all the relevant features in any voluntary or involuntary action can be traced to antecedent causes. As Peter van Inwagen has noted,

> If determinism is true, then our acts are the consequences of the laws of nature and events in the remote past. But it is not up to us what went on before we were born, and neither is it up to us what the laws of nature are. Therefore, the consequences of these things (including our present acts) are not up to us.[6]

Since according to the determinist (and the compatibilist as a determinist), all our actions are the results of antecedent causes, the notion of free action in this quarter is simply honorific. It does not establish moral responsibility, so it merely "passes the buck" back to antecedent causes. The distinction between voluntary and involuntary actions is simply the difference between the determinist process that doesn't find assent in the will (which is also determined) and the deterministic process that does find assent in the will (which is also determined). How can we be responsible for that which we do not cause? We cannot. Hence, we are not responsible for any of our actions since they can all be traced back to prior causes.

THE ARGUMENT AGAINST COMPATIBILISM
FROM MORAL RESPONSIBILITY

Determinism, as we noted in Chapter 18, seems to conflict with the thesis that we have moral responsibilities, for responsibility implies that we could have done otherwise than we did. We do not hold rabid dogs responsible for catching rabies because they are not free to choose, but we do hold a twenty-year-old man responsible for shooting a store keeper in cold blood because (we believe) he could have done otherwise. Big fish eat live little fish, and we do not condemn them of cannibalism; but if humans eat their fellows, we do condemn them of cannibalism.

We believe that we do have duties, oughts, over which we feel rational guilt at failure to perform. But there can be no such things as duties, oughts, praise, or blame of rational guilt if we are not actually free. The argument is the following:

1. Since *ought* implies *can,* in order to have a duty to do act A, we must be able to do A and to refrain from doing A.

2. Being morally responsible for doing A entails that I could have done otherwise if I had chosen to do so and that at some previous time I could have chosen to have done otherwise (or chosen some course of action that would have enabled me to do A).

3. But if determinism is true and our actions are merely the product of the laws of nature and antecedent states of affairs, then it is not up to us to choose what we do.

4. But if it is not up to us to choose what we do, we cannot be said to be responsible for what we do.

5. So if determinism is true, we are not responsible for what we do.

6. But our belief in moral responsibility is self-evident and more worthy of acceptance than belief in universal causality.

7. So if we believe that we have moral responsibilities, determinism cannot be accepted.

8. Therefore, since we justifiably believe in moral responsibility, we must reject the notion of determinism even if we cannot give a full explanatory account of how agents choose.

Is this argument sound? Interestingly enough both hard determinists and libertarians believe it is. Together they make up the group known as *incompatibilists,* for they claim that free will and moral responsibility are incompatible with determinism.

Here the determinist surely bites the bullet and admits that we do not have moral responsibilities and that it is just an illusion that we do. But we are determined to have such an illusion, so there is nothing we can do about it. We cannot consciously live as determinists, but why should we think that we can? We are finite and fallible creatures, whose behavior is entirely governed by causal laws, but with self-consciousness that makes us aware of part (but only a part) of the process that governs our behavior.

Let's look more closely at the key premises in the argument. The notion that *ought* implies *can* was first pointed out by Kant. It simply makes no sense to say that I have an obligation to do something that I do not have the power to do. Suppose I have been hypnotized and have been ordered to shake hands with every person in my class. I do so, feeling that I am acting under my own free will, but I am not acting freely and I am not responsible for my behavior. Or suppose through some deep brain defect and poor early upbringing I am a kleptomaniac. I am not able to refrain from stealing, so I am not responsible for my behavior even though I may feel free while doing so. I am excused for my behavior and, hopefully, treated.

But suppose I have acquired my habit of theft through giving in to the temptation to steal over a period of time and now cannot refrain. Even though I cannot refrain, I am responsible for the state in which I now find myself. I am responsible for my character and morally responsible for my thievery. This is what is conveyed by premise 2. "Being morally responsible for doing A entails that I could have done otherwise if I had chosen to do so and that at some previous time I could have chosen to have done otherwise (or chosen some course of action that would have enabled me to do A)."

The compatibilist usually responds at this point that the phrase "could have done otherwise" should be translated hypothetically as "would have done otherwise if I had chosen differently." When pressed and asked whether at the time in question I could have *chosen* otherwise, the compatibilist *qua* determinist must answer no. I could not have chosen differently. But if I could not have chosen differently, then what sense does it make to say that freedom amounts to being able to do differently if one chooses to do so? If I could never choose to do differently than I do, I cannot be said to be able to do any other act but the one that I actually do. The hypothetical interpretation is a red herring, amounting to little more than the truth that if things had been different, they would have been different. That is, if I had been *determined* to choose differently, I would have been *determined* to do differently than I did.

Premise 3 contends that if determinism is true, then we do not have the power to refrain from doing A (if A is what we indeed do). For any time *t*, there is only one act open to us, that which the state of the world plus the laws of nature together cause. But if antecedent states of affairs cause A to happen, then they are responsible for what we "do," and we are not responsible for those acts (premise 4). We are puppets in the hands of nature.

So premise 5, "If Determinism is true, we are not responsible for what we do." If nature is responsible for our actions, then nature should be praised or blamed for what we do, not us. The determinist may argue that in punishing or rewarding us we are really punishing or rewarding nature, but this is hyperbolic persiflage, for the notions of reward and punishment presuppose that the subject in question be conscious and have interests, neither of which apply to nature.

But if we are not responsible for our actions, we are mere objects of nature without selves worthy of respect in their own right. As Nagel says, "The area of genuine agency and therefore of legitimate moral judgment seems to shrink under this scrutiny to an extensionless point."

It is at this point that more sophisticated compatibilists like Harry Frankfurt revise the meaning of free will in terms of identification with one's second-order desire. Humans, unlike other animals, have the ability to deliberate and choose courses of actions. Both animals and humans have basic *first-order* desires (e.g., desires to eat, to be warm, and to copulate), but animals act directly on their wants, whereas humans can weigh them and accept or reject them. For example, you may have the first-order desire to stay in bed rather than come to class today, but you may also have a first-order desire to learn more about the problem of free will and determinism from your teacher. So you compare the two desires and form a *second-order* desire that one of the first-order desires be the one that motivates you, hopefully the one enjoining you to come to class, based on your passionate desire to understand the free-will problem. So you choose to let your second-order desire affect your behavior. Frankfurt calls this your second-order *volition:* "To the extent that a person identifies himself with the springs of his actions, he takes a responsibility for those actions and acquires moral responsibility for them."[7]

Frankfurt may have described the phenomenology of free choice, but he hasn't shown that this saves the compatibilist account of free will. He has given only necessary but not sufficient conditions for free choice. Consider this: Suppose you are deciding whether to get up from bed to go to class. You weigh the alternatives of staying in bed and experiencing the delicious taste of another hour of twilight dreams against the intellectual pleasures of your philosophy class. You decide to get up, make it your second-order volition, "identify yourself with the springs of this action," and so rise.

However, it turns out that a brilliant neurologist has been controlling your decisions through electronic waves that affect your neurons and brain patterns, causing you to choose to get up. Would you want to say that you *freely* got up? It sounds like you weren't free at all. You could not have avoided getting up, for your behavior was caused by the neurologist, and despite making "rising from the bed" your second-order volition, it can be said that you were not free at the moment to do otherwise.

The point is that the compatibilist's notion of second-order volitions turns out to be simply a subtler version of the brilliant neurologist story, for it is nature and antecedent causes that cause you to form the second-order volition to get up and go to class. You could not have done anything else at that moment. The idea that you could was only an illusion.

We turn then to premise 6: the idea that the belief that we are morally responsible is better justified than is our belief in universal causality. If there is one thing we are sure of, it is that we have selves, that we exist with moral obligations. There is nothing more certain than that I ought not kill innocent people, break promises simply for my own advantage, harm others without due cause, or cheat. I have a duty to help my aging parents, to protect my children, and to support my spouse and friends. But if determinism is true, all this is a mere illusion.

And what are determinism's credentials for its horrendous freedom-denying claims? Simply, an atavistic faith in universal causality. Everything in the world must have a cause, so all my behavior and all my mental states are caused.

But this is unduly fideistic. Strange that philosophers should have turned up their noses at simple theists for the lack of evidence for belief in a God and themselves have erected a shrine to the despot omnicausality![8] As Hume pointed out in his *Enquiries,* the notion of causality is not a necessary truth, nor one of which we have a clear idea. We just observe regularities in nature and sum up these constant conjunctions of behavior in law-like statements. It is very difficult to define "causality" (to my mind no one has given an adequate definition) or "natural law," and quantum physics tells us that on the most basic level of physical reality, causal relationships do not operate. Until we can solve these problems in the philosophy of science, it behooves us to be modest about our claiming that all behavior and states of affairs, including the self, are caused.

For my part, if I have to compare the propositions (1) "Every event and state of affairs in the world is caused" and (2) "I have moral responsibilities," I have not the slightest doubt about which I must choose.

At this point, the determinists—both the soft and the hard varieties—object that it is only through having determinate character that we can be said to be good or bad, that actions without determined character are capricious and arbitrary. To quote Sidney Hook,

> The great difficulty with the indeterminist view in most forms is the suggestion it carries that choices and actions, if not determined, are capricious. Caprice and responsibility are more difficult to reconcile than determinism and responsibility, for it seems easier to repudiate a choice or action which does not follow from one's character, or history, or nature, or self, than an act which does follow.[9]

But, as Hook himself recognizes, it is not necessary to equate free will with indeterminism. All that is necessary is to have a self that in deliberation can *weight* desires and values.[10] The self can exercise control, can veto or confirm desires, and can subscribe to reason or reject it in defiance, and this self itself transcends the ordinary laws of nature. C. A. Campbell and Robert Nozick think that this inter-vention of the self happens only on rare and momentous occasions, but I suspect that they are unduly modest. If it happens at all, why can't it happen every time the self deliberates?

Of course, we may not be able to give a convincing explanation of the self or agency, for what will count for an explanation in the determinist's eyes is only a causal explanation, and that is exactly what is in question.

Many philosophers who work in the area of this debate tend to be agnostics, so one explanation of the self-cum-free-will is cut off from them—that is, the idea of a Supreme Self, God. If God is a free agent, self-determined, then if he creates humans in his image, why shouldn't we suppose that humans also are self-determining beings? Indeed, the Judeo-Christian tradition supposes that God did create us as free agents and that we have sinned against God; that is, we have mis-used our freedom for disobedience and wrongdoing. We are responsible for our actions and so can be held accountable for them. The alternative is to make God strongly responsible for the evil in the world (at least the moral evil), which is blas-phemy to any theist. It may be in a weak or indirect sense, *qua* omniscient creator, that God is responsible for *allowing* humans to sin and create evil, but he is not responsible in any direct sense. In this case, we must conclude that either God was not able to create a better world—one with a greater proportion of good over evil—than this one or else God will bring good out of the evil in this world.

Since the theist will typically hold to the free-will defense to account for the evil in the world, he will typically embrace the doctrine of free will. The com-prehensive theory, which stands or falls as a whole, carries the theist past the state of **agnosticism** on this matter. Of course, if it turns out that we are wholly deter-mined by antecedent causes, supposing one understands this fact, then one would have to give up the free-will defense and perhaps theism itself. Much is at stake in this dispute.

In conclusion, I have argued that the compatibilist strategy for saving moral responsibility is an illusion and that only libertarianism has a creditable notion of accountability. I have admitted that the problem of free will and determinism is fraught with paradox but have argued that we have no good reason to distrust our intuitions about having a responsible self with moral obligations. I have also argued that if one is inclined to theism, one has additional reasons for preferring the libertarian position over its deterministic rivals.

THE COMPATIBILIST RESPONSE

Although the determinist may admit with Clarence Darrow that strictly speak-ing there is no moral responsibility and that all punishment and reward function as deterrent and incentive, the compatibilist wants to preserve the validity of the notion of accountability within a deterministic framework. The compatibilist will still try to work out the distinction between voluntary and involuntary actions and between rational and coerced behavior. Perhaps he or she will argue that the distinction is a useful fiction or simply that we need to adhere to the notion of voluntary action as the basis of moral responsibility. Perhaps she should admit the paradoxic nature of the problem, refrain from giving it a solution and merely state that we see things in these two different ways, from the viewpoint of agency (where responsibility holds) and from the viewpoint of determinism (where universal causality holds). Perhaps she needs to question whether we know what universal causality involves, for on closer look it turns out to be a rather fuzzy notion. No one has adequately defined it. It has something to do with a necessary condition for another event, but that is not a clear concept, nor is it clear how this applies to individual actions. It may be a metaphor that is inapplicable to action language.

We make a difference between cases where the agent is compelled or influenced by unusual stress or "neurotic" causes and "normal" cases where the agent could have done differently (better or worse). We can take the objective perspective in the first case, excuse the subject, understand the causal mechanisms, and treat the behavior as impersonally derived events. But we cannot treat normal behavior in this manner without losing something precious, something vital to human interaction. Unless I take your intentions seriously as belonging to you, I lose something that is necessary to a fully human existence. I lose the personal aspect of relationships, for to view others as personal is to take their intentions seriously. Hence, even if determinism cannot be proved to be false, I still will have to take other people's intentions seriously, react to them spontaneously, and hold them accountable. Human existence, in its deepest interpersonal, nonmechanistic sense, cannot go on without the notion of freedom.

This is how the compatibilist argues.

SUMMARY

Let's summarize the last three chapters of our work. We have examined the three main theories regarding free will and determinism—determinism, libertarianism, and compatibilism—and have found each to have virtues and vices.

The notion of the libertarian self, which creates new actions that are themselves underdetermined by antecedent causes, is an unexplained mystery and constitutes a little god standing apart from our normal explanatory schemes.

The theory of evolution tells us that wholly deterministic and physicalistic processes are responsible for whatever we are. But we are self-conscious beings whose inner experiences are not physicalist. They are mental. Hence, the fundamental mystery is how something as physicalistic as evolutionary process could result in something nonphysical—consciousness—from which freedom of the will emerges.

Although the determinist cannot explain consciousness or how the physical results in and causes the mental, the libertarian is no better off, for no one has successfully explained how the mental can affect the physical. How does the mind make contact with the body in order to move it to action? Where are its points of contact, its hooks that pull on our brains and/or limbs?

In the end, perhaps the best we can do is to be aware of the fascinating mystery of the problem of free will and determinism and admit our ignorance about a solution. If we look at ourselves through the eyes of science and neurophysiology, we will no doubt regard ourselves as determined. If we look at ourselves from the perspective of morality as subjective deliberators, we must view ourselves as having free will. As philosophers—which we all are, like it or not—we stand in wonder at the dualism that forces us to take both an objective/determinist and a subjective/libertarian perspective of conscious behavior. This dichotomy seems unsatisfactory, incompatible, and yet inescapable.

Or do you see a way of solving this enigma? It's a worthy challenge for the best minds on Earth.

QUESTIONS FOR DISCUSSION

1. Evaluate the three theories discussed in these last three chapters. Which seem the most plausible to you, and why?

2. The British scientist and philosopher J. S. B. Haldane wrote, "If my mental processes are determined wholly by the motions of atoms in my brain, I have no reason to suppose that my beliefs are true . . . and hence I have no reason for supposing my brain to be composed of atoms."[11] Could the same argument be used against the doctrine of determinism? If the theory of determinism has been caused by nonrational processes, what *reason* is there to believe it? Is determinism self-refuting?

3. Jean Paul Sartre wrote, "We are condemned to freedom." We will examine Sartre's ideas in Part VII (existentialism), but can you understand, from what you've studied thus far, what he might be getting at?

4. Discuss the problem of punishment. How would a determinist, a libertarian, and a compatibilist defend the practice of punishing criminals?

5. Examine the following quotation by Thomas Nagel:

   If one cannot be responsible for consequences of one's acts due to factors beyond one's control, or for antecedents of one's acts that are properties of temperament not subject to one's will, or for the circumstances that pose one's moral choices, then how can one be responsible even for the stripped-down acts of the will itself, if *they* are the product of antecedent circumstances outside of the will's control? The area of genuine agency, and therefore of legitimate moral judgment, seems to shrink under this scrutiny to an extensionless point.[12]

   What is your response to Nagel's argument?

6. David Hume wrote,

   Men are not blamed for such actions as they perform ignorantly and casually, whatever may be the consequences. Why? but because the principles of these actions are only momentary, and terminate in them alone. Men are less blamed for such actions as they perform hastily and unpremeditatedly than for such as proceed from deliberation. For what reason? but because a hasty temper, though a constant cause or principle in the mind, operates only by intervals, and infects not the whole character. Again, repentance wipes off every crime, if attended with a reformation of life and manners. How is this to be accounted for? but by asserting that actions render a person criminal merely as they are proofs of criminal principles in the mind.[13]

Evaluate Hume's notion. Which theory of freedom or determinism does it best fit?

7. I present an argument that without the free-will defense for the existence of God, theism probably collapses. What are my reasons for this conclusion? Is this correct? Note that Augustine (354–430) and most of the Protestant Reformers (e.g., Martin Luther and John Calvin) believed in predestination of souls to heaven and hell, thus denying the idea that humans had free will (at least regarding salvation). How would they defend their position against my argument?

NOTES

1. Walter Stace, *Religion and the Modern Mind* (Philadelphia: Lippencott, 1952); Immanuel Kant, *Critique of Pure Reason* (1787); Harry Frankfurt, "Freedom of the Will and the Concept of a Person," in *Free Will,* ed. Gary Watson (Oxford: Clarendon Press, 1982); Daniel Dennett, *Elbow Room* (Cambridge, MA: MIT Press, 1984). See also Michael Levin, *Philosophy of Mind* (Oxford: Clarendon Press, 1979). See most of the articles in John Martin Fischer, ed., *Moral Responsibility* (Ithaca, NY: Cornell University Press, 1986); Gary Watson, ed., *Free Will* (Oxford: Clarendon Press, 1982); Wright Neely, "Freedom and Desire," *Philosophical Review* 83 (1974); and P. F. Strawson, "Freedom and Resentment," *Proceedings of the British Academy* 48 (1962).

2. Stace, op cit.

3. Frankfurt, op. cit., 81–95.

4. Ibid.

5. Ibid., 90.

6. Peter van Inwagen, *An Essay on Free Will* (Oxford: Clarendon Press, 1983), 16.

7. Harry Frankfurt, "Three Concepts of Free Action," in Fischer, op. cit., 120.

8. *Omnicausality* is the doctrine that every event and state of affairs in the universe is caused by antecedent causes.

9. Sidney Hook, "Moral Responsibility in a Determined World," in his *Quest for Being* (New York: St. Martin's Press, 1961).

10. Robert Nozick, *Philosophical Explorations* (Cambridge, MA: Harvard University Press, 1981), Chapter 4.

11. J. S. B. Haldane, *Possible Worlds* (London: Holden & Stoughton, 1937), 209.

12. Thomas Nagel, *Mortal Questions* (New York: Cambridge University Press, 1979), 35.

13. David Hume, *Enquiry Concerning Human Understanding* (1748).

FOR FURTHER READING

Dennett, Daniel. *Elbow Room: The Varieties of Free Will Worth Wanting.* Cambridge, MA: MIT Press, 1984. A well-argued defense of compatibilism.

Lehrer, Keith, and James Cornman. *Philosophical Problems and Argument,* 3rd ed. New York: Macmillan, 1982. Lehrer's essay in Chapter 3 is excellent.

Stace, Walter T. *Religion and the Modern Mind.* Philadelphia: Lippencott, 1952. Contains a lucid account of compatibilism.

Trustead, Jennifer. *Free Will and Responsibility.* Oxford: Oxford University Press, 1984. A clear, accessible introduction to the subject.

van Inwagen, Peter. *An Essay on Free Will.* Oxford: Clarendon Press, 1983. A highly original study, criticizing compatibilism.

Watson, Gary, ed. *Free Will.* Oxford: Clarendon Press, 1982. Contains important articles, especially those by Frankfurt, van Inwagen, and Watson himself.

PART VI

Ethics

NORMAN ROCKWELL
The Golden Rule

21

What Is Morality?

Can anything be better for a country than to produce men and women of the best type?

—SOCRATES, PARAPHRASED

Suppose you are on an island with a dying millionaire. As he lies dying, he entreats you for one final favor: "I've dedicated my whole life to baseball and have gotten endless pleasure, and some pain, rooting for the New York Yankees for fifty years. Now that I am dying, I want to give all my assets, $2 million, to the Yankees. Would you take this money [he indicates a box containing the money in large bills] back to New York and give it to George Steinbrenner, the owner of the New York Yankees, so he can buy better players?" You agree to carry out his wish, at which point a huge smile of relief and gratitude breaks out on his face and he expires in your arms. After returning to New York, you see a newspaper advertisement placed by the World Hunger Relief Organization (whose integrity you do not doubt) pleading for $2 million to be used to save 100,000 people dying of starvation in East Africa. Not only will the $2 million save their lives, but it will be used to purchase small technology and the kinds of fertilizers necessary to build a sustainable economy. You reconsider your promise to the dying Yankees' fan in light of this information. What should you do with the money?

Or suppose two men are starving to death on a raft floating in the Pacific Ocean. One day they discover some food in an inner compartment of a box on the raft. They have reason to believe that the food will be sufficient to keep one of them alive until the raft reaches a certain island where help is available, but if they share the food both of them will most likely die. One man is a brilliant scientist who has in his mind the cure for cancer; the other man is undistinguished.

Otherwise, there is no relevant difference between the two men. What is the morally right thing to do? Share the food and hope against the odds for a miracle? Flip a coin to see which man gets the food? Give the food to the scientist?

What is the right thing to do in these kinds of situations?

What is it to be a moral person? What is the nature of morality, and why do we need it? What is the good, and how will I know it? Are moral principles **absolute** or simply relative to social groups or individual decisions? Is it in my interest to be moral? Is it sometimes in my best interest to act immorally? How does one justify one's moral beliefs? What is the basis of morality? Which ethical theory provides the best justification for and explanation of the moral life? What is the relationship between morality and religion? These are some of the questions that we will be considering in this part of our book. We want to understand the foundation and structure of morality. We want to know how we should live.

The terms *moral* and *ethics* come from Latin and Greek—respectively, *mores* and *ethos*—deriving their meaning from the idea of custom. Although the terms are often used interchangeably, philosophers sometimes use "morality" to refer to customs and practices and "ethics" to refer to theoretical considerations, to *moral philosophy*. In this sense, ethics refers to the systematic endeavor to understand moral concepts and justify moral principles and theories. It undertakes to analyze such concepts as "right," "wrong," "permissible," "ought," "good," and "evil" in their moral contexts. Ethics seeks to establish principles of right behavior that may serve as action guides for individuals and groups. It investigates which values and virtues are paramount to the worthwhile life or society. It builds and scrutinizes arguments in ethical theories, and it seeks to discover valid principles (e.g., "Never kill innocent human beings") and the relationship between those principles (e.g., does saving a life in some situations constitute a valid reason for breaking a promise?).

The Domain of Morality Many people and some philosophers believe that ethics is concerned entirely with rules of conduct based solely on an evaluation of acts, but the situation is more complicated than this. There are four domains of ethical assessment:

Domain	Evaluative Terms
Actions, the act	Right, wrong, permissible
Consequences	Good, bad, indifferent
Character	Virtuous, vicious
Motive	Good will, evil will

Let's briefly illustrate these concepts. First, the most common distinction may be the classification of right and wrong kinds of *actions*. Consider the act of lying. It is generally seen as a wrong type of act (prohibited), whereas telling the truth is generally seen as a right kind of act (obligatory). But some acts do not seem to be either right or wrong; they are morally indifferent. Whether you decide to take a course in European history or Asian literature, whether you decide to eat an orange or an apple for dessert, or whether you prefer blondes to brunettes is morally indifferent. Each is morally permissible. Whether you decide to marry or remain single is up to you. You are under no obligation to do either (unless you have put yourself

"Obligation" from the Latin "Obligare" = to bind by a moral or legal tie.

© 1996 Paul Audi

under an obligation). Some things, such as deciding whether to marry, are very important but still within the domain of permissibility, not obligation.

Within the structure of moral obligation, we can define these terms as follows:

- The "right act" is an act that is obligatory for you to do. It is your duty. You ought to do that act. It is not permissible to refrain from doing it.
- The "wrong act" is an act that you are forbidden to do. You have a duty to refrain from doing that act. You ought not to do it. It is not permissible to do the act.
- A "permissible act" is an act that it is neither right nor wrong to do. It is neither obligatory nor forbidden.

Within the range of permissible acts is the notion of **supererogatory,** or highly altruistic, acts. These acts are not required, are not obligatory, are not "right" in the way we have defined moral rightness, but they are good. They challenge us to go beyond the call of duty, to walk the "second mile," to quote Jesus. You may have an obligation to give a donation to help people in dire need, but you are probably not obliged to sell your car, let alone become destitute, to help them. Nevertheless, when someone sacrifices his or her welfare for others, we typically praise the person for such altruistic behavior.

Theories that place the emphasis on the nature of the act are called **deontological** (from the Greek *deon,* meaning "duty"). They claim that value inheres in the kind of act it is regardless of incidental consequences. The most famous of these systems is Immanuel Kant's moral theory, which we will study in Chapter 25. In our two thought experiments (in the introduction to this chapter), if you choose (1) to give the $2 million to the New York Yankees because the act involves keeping your promise and not giving it to them would be an act of stealing, or (2) if you decide to flip a coin for or share the food while out at sea, you are choosing as a deontologist.

The second domain is *consequences.* We said that lying is generally wrong and truth telling is right. But consider this situation. You are hiding in your home an innocent woman named Laura, who is fleeing gangsters. Gangland Gus knocks on your door, and when you open it, he asks if Laura is in your house. What should you do? Tell the truth or lie? Those who say that morality has something to do with consequences of actions would prescribe lying as the morally right thing to do. Those who deny that we should look at the consequences when considering what to do when there is a clear and absolute rule of action will say that we should either keep silent or tell the truth. When no other rule is at stake, of course, the rule-oriented ethicist will allow the foreseeable consequences to determine a course of action. Theories that focus primarily on consequences in determining moral rightness and wrongness are called **teleological ethical theories** (from the Greek *teleos,* meaning "goal directed"). The most famous of these theories is utilitarianism, which we will study in Chapter 24.

Referring again to our examples, if you choose (1) to give the $2 million to the World Hunger Relief Organization in order to maximize its utility or (2) give the food on the raft to the scientist because of his greater contribution, you are acting as a utilitarian.

Character is the third domain. Whereas some ethical theories emphasize principles of action in themselves and some emphasize principles involving consequences of action, other theories, such as Aristotle's ethics (**aretaic ethics**), emphasize character. According to Aristotle, it is most important to develop virtuous characters, for if and only if we are good people can we ensure habitual right action. Virtues, good habits, and dispositions to right conduct provide the assurance and drive for moral actions. To paraphrase Kant, "While virtues without principles may be blind, principles without virtues are impotent." Courage, friendliness, kindness, integrity, discretion, self-discipline, and patience are good in themselves and the impetus to good deeds. Different moral systems emphasize different virtues and emphasize them to different degrees.

Finally, virtually all ethical systems, but especially Kant's system, accept the relevance of *motive*. It is important to the full assessment of any action that the intention of the agent be taken into account. Two acts may be identical, but one may be judged morally culpable and the other excusable. Consider John's pushing Joan off a ledge, causing her to break her leg. In situation A, he is angry and intends to harm her; but in situation B, he sees a knife flying in her direction and intends to save her life. In A what he did was clearly wrong, whereas in B he did the right thing. On the other hand, two acts may have opposite results, but the actions may be judged equally good on the basis of intention. For example, two soldiers may try to cross the enemy lines to communicate with an allied force, but one gets captured through no fault of his own and the other succeeds. In a full moral description of any act, motive will be taken into consideration as a relevant factor.

WHY DO WE NEED MORALITY?

A Reflection on *The Lord of the Flies*

Which is better—to have rules and agree, or to hunt and kill?[1]

Why exactly do we need moral codes? What function do they play in our lives and in society in general? Rather than write a discursive essay on the benefits of morality, let me draw your attention to a book every young person has or should have read: William Golding's classic novel *The Lord of the Flies* (1954). This modern moral allegory may provide us with a clue to the nature and purpose of morality.

A group of English private school boys between the ages of six and twelve years are cast adrift on an uninhabited island in the Pacific Ocean, and create their own social system. For a while, the constraints of their upbringing in a civilized society prevent total chaos. All the older boys recognize the necessity of substantive and procedural rules. Only he who has the white conch, the symbol of authority, may speak at an assembly. The leader is chosen democratically and is invested with limited powers. Even the evil Roger, while taunting little Henry by throwing stones near him, manages to keep the stones from harming the child: "Here invisible yet strong, was the taboo of the old life. Round the squatting child was the protection of parents and school and policemen and the law. Roger's arm was conditioned by a civilization that knew nothing of him and was in ruins."[2]

After an initial euphoria at being liberated from the adult world of constraints into an exciting world of fun in the Sun, the children come up against the usual banes of social existence: competition for power and status, neglect of social responsibility, failure of public policy, and escalating violence. Two boys, Ralph and Jack, vie for leadership, and a bitter rivalry emerges between them. As a compromise, a division of labor ensues in which Jack's choirboy hunters refuse to help the others in constructing shelters. Freeloading soon becomes a common phenomenon as the majority of children leave their tasks to play on the beach. Neglect of duty results in failure to be rescued by a passing airplane. The unbridled lust for excitement leads to the great orgiastic pig kills and finally, at its nadir, to the thirst for human blood.

Civilization's power is weak and vulnerable to atavistic, volcanic passions. The sensitive Simon, the symbol of religious consciousness (viz., "Simon Peter," Jesus' first disciple), who prophesies that Ralph will be saved and is the first to discover and fight against the "ancient, inescapable recognition" of the beast in us, is slaughtered by the group in a wild frenzy. Only Piggy and Ralph, mere observers of the orgiastic homicide, feel vicarious pangs of guilt at this atrocity.

The incarnation of philosophy and culture—poor, fat, nearsighted Piggy with his broken spectacles and asthma—becomes ever more pathetic as the chaos increases. The nadir of his ridiculous position is reached after the rebels led by Jack steal his spectacles in order to harness the Sun's rays in starting fires. After Ralph, the emblem of not-too-bright but morally good civilized leadership, fails to persuade Jack to return the glasses, Piggy asserts his moral right to them: ". . . You're stronger than I am and you haven't got asthma. You can see . . . But I don't ask for my glasses back, not as a favour. I don't ask you to be a sport . . . not because you're strong, but because what's right is right. Give me my glasses, . . . you got to."[3]

He might as well have addressed the fire itself, for in this state of moral anarchy, moral discourse is a foreign tongue that only incites the worst elements to greater immorality. Roger, perched on a cliff above, responds to moral reasoning by dislodging a huge rock that hits Piggy and flings him to his death forty feet below.

The Lord of the Flies is a translation of the Greek "Beelzebub," which was a name for the devil. Golding shows that we need no external devil to bring about evil but that we have found the devil and, in the words of Pogo, "he is us." Ubiquitous, ever-waiting for a moment to strike out, he emerges from the depths of the subconscious wherever there is a conflict of interest or a moment of moral lassitude. As E. L. Epstein says, "The tenets of civilization, the moral and social codes, the Ego, the intelligence itself, form only a veneer over this white-hot power, this uncontrollable force, 'the fury and the mire of human veins.'"4

Beelzebub's ascendancy proceeds through fear, hysteria, violence, and death. A delegation starts out hunting pigs for meat. Then they find themselves enjoying the kill. To drown the incipient shame over bloodthirstiness and to take on a persona more compatible with their deed, the children paint themselves with colored mud. Their lusting for the kill takes on all the powerful overtones of an orgiastic sexual ritual, so that being liberated from their social selves they kill without remorse whomever gets in their way. The death of Simon and Piggy (religious and philosophical—the two great fences blocking the descent to hell) and the final orgiastic hunt with the "spear sharpened at both ends" signal for Ralph the depths of evil in the human heart.

Ironically, it is the British navy that finally comes to the rescue and saves Ralph (civilization) just when all seems lost. But the symbol of the navy is a Janus-faced omen. On the one hand, it may symbolize the fact that a military defense is unfortunately sometimes needed to save civilization from the barbarians (Hitler's Nazis or Jack and Roger's allies), but on the other hand, it symbolizes the quest for blood and vengeance latent in contemporary civilization. The children's world is really only a stage lower than the adult world from whence they come, and that shallow civilization could very well regress to tooth and claw if it were scratched too sharply. The children were saved by the adults, but who will save the adults who put so much emphasis on military enterprises and weapons systems—in the euphemistic name of "defense"? To quote Epstein, "The officer, having interrupted a man-hunt, prepares to take the children off the island in a cruiser which will presently be hunting its enemy in the same implacable way. And who will rescue the adult and his cruiser?"5

The fundamental ambiguity of human existence is seen in every section of the book, poignantly mirroring the human condition. Even Piggy's spectacles, the sole example of modern technology on the island, become a bane for the island. Jack uses the spectacles to ignite a forest fire in order to smoke out their prey, Ralph, and the fire ends up burning down the entire forest and destroying the island's animal life. The event is a symbol both of our penchant for misusing technology to vitiate the environment and of our ability to create weapons that will lead to global suicide.

THE PURPOSES OF MORALITY

What is the role of morality in human existence? What are boys and girls and men and women made of that requires ethical consciousness? Ralph answers these questions at the end of the tale: "And in the middle of [the children], with filthy body, matted hair, and unwiped nose, Ralph wept for the end of innocence, the darkness of man's heart, and the fall through the air of the true, wise friend called Piggy."6

In this modern moral allegory, we catch a glimpse of some of the purposes of morality. Rules formed over the ages and internalized within us hold back and, hopefully, defeat "The Lord of the Flies" in society, whether he be inherent in us individually or an emergent property of corporate existence. The moral code restrains the Rogers of society from evil until untoward social conditions open up the sluice gates of sadism. It is the force that enables Piggy and Ralph to maintain a modicum of order within their dwindling society, first motivating them to compromise with Jack and then keeping things in perspective.

In Golding's allegory, morality is honored more in the breach than in the observance, for we see the consequences of not having rules, principles, and virtuous character. If we analyze this further, we see that morality has at least five related purposes:

- To promote the survival of society
- To resolve conflicts of interest justly
- To ameliorate human suffering
- To promote human flourishing
- To assign responsibility, praise, and blame to actions.

Morality, first of all, *promotes the survival of society* and keeps it from falling apart, from sinking to a state of chaos where everyone is the enemy of everyone else, where fear and insecurity dominate the mind and prevent peace and happiness. Thomas Hobbes (1588–1679) described the dismal condition as a "state of nature" wherein there exists a perpetual war of all against all and life is "solitary, poor, nasty, brutish and short." The purpose of moral rules is to help us prevent the state of nature. As a means to prevent this condition, it must have rules of justice *to resolve conflicts of interest* that are mutually agreed on and seen as just. There are scarce resources, be they positions of power and status, wealth, jobs, land, property, opportunities, or whatever, and we need rules to adjudicate conflicts when different people lay claim to these goods. Unless we can satisfactorily resolve these conflicts of interest, we will not be able to reach any other goals. Similarly, morality generally emphasizes "win-win" outcomes, the advancement of cooperation instead of destructive competition.

Related to this is morality's function to *ameliorate or prevent unnecessary suffering.* It establishes social institutions and conventions that aid victims of disease, famine, and violence. Of course, some suffering may be deserved (i.e., punishment) and some may be part of an acceptable process (i.e., the suffering I endure in the dentist's chair, as part of medical treatment, or in being turned down for a job).

But the purpose of morality is not simply negative—to prevent chaos and unjust suffering. The rules also play a positive role in *promoting human flourishing.* They enable people to pursue their goals in peace and freedom, encouraging them to friendship and fidelity, challenging them to excellence and a worthwhile life. Deep morality, as it is ingrained in good character, is a "jewel that shines in its own light." It creates a worthwhile life for its participants and turns a potential hell into something that at its highest point (usually confined to small communities, friendships, and families) approximates a heaven on Earth. In sum, morality tries to promote human flourishing.

We might characterize morality as a set of rules or practices that if almost everyone obeys, almost all of the time, almost everyone will be better off. This allows for free riders, as well as occasional lapses, and it acknowledges the possibility that sometimes it may not be in our best interest to be moral (e.g., when I refrain from stealing a large sum of money even though I know I will not be discovered if I do steal it).

Morality provides criteria for holding people responsible for their actions, as worthy of praise and blame, reward and punishment. We think we are centers of action, and, as such, *deserve* the good or bad that attaches to those actions. In our time, many people overemphasize rights and underemphasize responsibilities. Both are important, but moral responsibility is central to being an autonomous person.

Although these five purposes of morality are related they are not identical, and different moral theories emphasize different purposes in different ways. Utilitarianism fastens on human flourishing and the amelioration of suffering, whereas contractual systems rooted in Hobbesian egoism accent the role of ensuring social survival and resolving conflicts of interest. Kant's deontological theory emphasizes universal rules of justice. As you examine the various theories set forth, you should ask yourself whether it is important to deal with all five purposes satisfactorily. But first, we need to look closely at the status of moral principles. Are they universally valid or simply dependent on individual or cultural approval?

SUMMARY

Morality has to do with how one *ought* to live. It can be assessed from the point of view of the nature of the act, the consequences of the act, the character of the individual, and the agent's motive. It has broad purposes, including the survival of society, the resolution of conflicts of interest, the amelioration of suffering, and the promotion of human flourishing. In general, it promises that if we are moral there is a high probability that we will be benefited. The good is, on the whole, good for you.

QUESTIONS FOR DISCUSSION

1. Read again the two thought experiments discussed at the beginning of this chapter. How would you act, and why?

2. Think of a moral problem, one you've recently had or heard about. Discuss how you might go about resolving it.

3. Suppose you are given too much change at the checkout counter of a large supermarket. You have walked out the door when you realize what has occurred. Should you go back to the checkout counter to return the money? Would you?

4. Can you provide illustrations of how the different aspects of morality (importance of act, consequence, motive, and character) might conflict when one is making moral decisions? Do you ever have to do evil in order to act morally? Explain.

5. If you have read Golding's *The Lord of the Flies,* compare the analysis in this chapter with your understanding of the book. What is the moral significance of the story?

6. Do you agree with the five purposes of morality? Can you think of other purposes morality might have?

7. Should we combine our five purposes? Can we have only some of these traits without others? For example, is unjust human flourishing possible? Why, or why not?

NOTES

1. William Golding, *The Lord of the Flies* (New York: Putnam, 1954), 222.

2. Ibid., 78.

3. Ibid., 211.

4. E. L. Epstein, "Notes on *Lord of the Flies,*" in Golding, op. cit., 252.

5. Ibid.

6. Golding, op. cit., 248.

FOR FURTHER READING

Frankena, William. *Ethics,* 2d. ed. Englewood Cliffs, NJ: Prentice-Hall, 1973. A succinct, clear discussion of the nature of morality.

Louden, Robert B. *Morality and Moral Theory.* New York: Oxford University Press, 1992. An important recent work combining Aristotelian and Kantian ideas and arguing for the need to engage in moral theory.

MacIntyre, Alasdair. *A Short History of Ethics.* New York: Macmillan, 1966. An engaging history of moral philosophy.

Pojman, Louis, ed. *Ethical Theory: Classical and Contemporary Readings,* 3d ed. Belmont, CA: Wadsworth, 1998. A comprehensive anthology.

Pojman, Louis. *Ethics: Discovering Right and Wrong.* Belmont, CA: Wadsworth, 1999.

Rachels, James. *The Elements of Morality.* New York: Random House, 1986. An excellent introduction to the main themes of moral philosophy, especially egoism.

Singer, Peter. *The Expanding Circle: Ethics and Sociobiology.* Oxford: Oxford University Press, 1983. A fascinating attempt to integrate the theory of sociobiology with ethics.

Sommers, Christina Hoff, ed. *Vice and Virtue in Everyday Life.* New York: Harcourt Brace Jovanovich, 1985. A helpful introductory anthology focusing on the virtues, responsibility, the family, and social morality.

Taylor, Richard. *Good and Evil.* Buffalo, NY: Prometheus Books, 1984. A lively, accessible, and highly original work, arguing that the main role of morality is the resolution of conflicts of interest.

Van Wyk, Robert. *Introduction to Ethics.* New York: St. Martin's Press, 1990. A well-thought-out, carefully argued introductory text.

22

Ethical Relativism versus Ethical Objectivism

There is one thing a professor can be absolutely certain of: almost every student
entering the university believes, or says he believes, that truth is relative. If this
belief is put to the test, one can count on the students' reaction: they will be
uncomprehending. That anyone should regard the proposition as not self-evident
astonishes them, as though he were calling into question 2 + 2 = 4. . . . The danger
they have been taught to fear from absolutism is not error but intolerance. Relativism
is necessary to openness; and this is the virtue, the only virtue, which all primary
education for more than fifty years has dedicated itself to inculcating.[1]

—ALAN BLOOM

In the nineteenth century, Christian missionaries sometimes used coercion to
change the customs of pagan tribal people in parts of Africa and the Pacific
islands. Appalled by the customs of public nakedness, polygamy, working on the
Sabbath, and infanticide, they paternalistically went about reforming the "poor
pagans." They clothed them, separated wives from their husbands in order to create monogamous households, made the Sabbath a day of rest, and ended infanticide. In the process, they sometimes created social malaise, causing the estranged
women to despair and their children to be orphaned. The natives often did not
understand the new religion but accepted it in deference to the white man's
power. The white people had guns and medicine.

Since the nineteenth century, we've made progress in understanding cultural
diversity, and we realize that the social dissonance caused by "do-gooders" was a
bad thing. In the last century or so, anthropology has exposed our penchant for
ethnocentrism, the prejudicial view that interprets all of reality through the eyes of

our cultural beliefs and values. We have come to see enormous variety in social practices throughout the world.

Eskimos allow their elderly to die by starvation, whereas we believe that this is morally wrong. The Spartans of ancient Greece and the Dobu of New Guinea believe that stealing is morally right, but we believe it is wrong. Many cultures, past and present, have practiced or still practice infanticide. A tribe in East Africa once threw deformed infants to the hippopotamus, but our society condemns such acts. Sexual practices vary over time and clime. Some cultures permit homosexual behavior, but others condemn it. Some cultures, including Muslim societies, practice polygamy, whereas Christian cultures view it as immoral. Anthropologist Ruth Benedict describes a tribe in Melanesia that views cooperation and kindness as vices, and anthropologist Colin Turnbull has documented that the Ik in northern Uganda have no sense of duty toward their children or parents. There are societies that make it a duty for children to kill (sometimes by strangling) their aging parents.

The ancient Greek historian Herodotus (ca. 485–430 B.C.) tells the story of how Darius, the king of Persia, once brought together some Callatians (Asian tribal people) and some Greeks. He asked the Callatians how they disposed of their deceased parents; they told how they ate the bodies of their dead parents. The Greeks, who cremated their parents, were horrified at such barbarous behavior. No amount of money could tempt them to do such an irreverent thing. Then Darius asked the Callatians, "What should I give them to burn the bodies of their fathers at their decease?" The Callatians were utterly horrified at such barbarous behavior and begged Darius to cease from such irreverent discourse. Herodotus concludes that "custom is the king o'er all."[2]

Today we condemn ethnocentrism, the uncritical belief in the inherent superiority of one's own culture, as a variety of prejudice tantamount to racism and sexism. What is right in one culture may be wrong in another, what is good east of the river may be bad west of the same river, what is a virtue in one nation may be seen as a vice in another, so it behooves us not to judge others but to be tolerant of diversity.

This rejection of ethnocentrism in the West has contributed to a general shift in public opinion about morality, so that for a growing number of Westerners, consciousness raising about the validity of other ways of life has led to a gradual erosion of belief in **moral objectivism,** the view that there are universal moral principles, valid for all people at all times and in all climes. For example, in polls taken in my ethics and introduction to philosophy classes in recent years (in three different universities, in three areas of the country), students, by a 2 to 1 ratio, affirmed a version of *moral relativism* over *moral absolutism,* with barely 3 percent seeing something in between these two polar opposites. Of course, I'm not suggesting that all these students have a clear understanding of what relativism entails, for many of those who say that they are ethical relativists also state on the same questionnaire that "abortion except to save the mother's life is always wrong," that "capital punishment is always morally wrong," or that "suicide is never morally permissible." The apparent contradictions signal an apparent confusion on the matter.

Is ethical relativism true? Is morality dependent for its validity on individual or cultural approval? Or are some principles universally valid, public opinion to the contrary? We turn now to an analysis of ethical relativism.

AN ANALYSIS OF ETHICAL RELATIVISM

Ethical relativism is the theory that there are no universally valid moral principles, that all moral principles are valid relative to *culture* or *individual choice.* That is,
there are two types of relativism: Conventionalism holds that moral principles are
relative to the culture or society, and subjectivism holds that it is the individual
choice that determines the validity of a moral principle. We'll start with conventionalism. Philosopher John Ladd, of Brown University, defines *conventional ethical
relativism* this way:

> Ethical relativism is the doctrine that the moral rightness and wrongness of actions
> varies from society to society and that there are no absolute universal moral stan-
> dards binding on all men at all times. Accordingly, it holds that whether or not it is
> right for an individual to act in a certain way depends on or is relative to the society
> to which he belongs.[3]

According to Ladd, ethical relativism consists of two theses: (1) A *diversity thesis*
specifies that what is considered morally right and wrong varies from society to
society, so that no moral principles are accepted by all societies, and (2) a *dependency thesis* specifies that all moral principles derive their validity from cultural acceptance. From these two ideas, he concludes that there are no universally valid moral
principles, objective standards that apply to all people everywhere and at all times.

The diversity thesis, or what may simply be called **cultural relativism,** is an
anthropological thesis. It registers the fact we noted at the beginning of this chapter, that moral rules differ from society to society. There is enormous variety in
what may count as a moral principle in a given society. The human condition is
malleable in the extreme, allowing any number of folkways or moral codes. As
Benedict has written,

> The cultural pattern of any civilization makes use of a certain segment of the great
> arc of potential human purposes and motivations . . . that any culture makes use of
> certain selected material techniques or cultural traits. The great arc along which all
> the possible human behaviors are distributed is far too immense and too full of con-
> tradictions for any one culture to utilize even any considerable portion of it. Selec-
> tion is the first requirement.[4]

The dependency thesis asserts that individual acts are right or wrong depending on the nature of the society from which they emanate. What is considered
morally right or wrong must be seen in a context, depending on the goals, wants,
beliefs, history, and environment of the society in question. As William Graham
Sumner says,

> We learn the [morals] as unconsciously as we learn to walk and hear and breathe,
> and they never know any reason why the [morals] are what they are. The justifica-
> tion of them is that when we wake to consciousness of life we find them facts
> which already hold us in the bonds of tradition, custom, and habit.[5]

Trying to see things from an independent, noncultural point of view would
be like taking out our eyes to examine their contours and qualities. We are simply culturally determined beings.

In a sense, we all live in radically different worlds. Each person has a different
set of beliefs and experiences, a particular perspective that colors all his or her

perceptions. Do the farmer, the real estate dealer, and the artist, looking at the same spatiotemporal field, see the *same* field? Not likely. Their different orientations, values, and expectations govern their perceptions so that different aspects of the field are highlighted and some features are missed. Even as our individual values arise from personal experience, so social values are grounded in the peculiar history of the community. Morality, then, is just the set of common rules, habits, and customs that have won social approval over time so that they seem part of the nature of things, as facts. There is nothing mysterious or transcendent about these codes of behavior. They are the outcomes of our social history.

The conclusion that no absolute or objective moral standards bind all people follows from the first two propositions. Cultural relativism (the diversity thesis) plus the dependency thesis yield ethical relativism in its classic form. If there are different moral principles from culture to culture and if all morality is rooted in culture, then it follows that no universal moral principles are valid for all cultures and people at all times.

SUBJECTIVE ETHICAL RELATIVISM
(SUBJECTIVISM)

Some people think that even this conclusion is too tame and maintain that morality is not dependent on the society but on the individual himself or herself. As students sometimes maintain, "Morality is in the eye of the beholder." Ernest Hemingway wrote,

> So far, about morals, I know only that what is moral is what you feel good after and what is immoral is what you feel bad after and judged by these moral standards, which I do not defend, the bullfight is very moral to me because I feel very fine while it is going on and have a feeling of life and death and mortality and immortality, and after it is over I feel very sad but very fine.[6]

This form of moral subjectivism has a sorry consequence: It makes morality a useless concept, for, on its premises, little or no interpersonal criticism or judgment is logically possible. Hemingway may feel good about the killing of bulls in a bullfight, but Albert Schweitzer or Mother Teresa would feel the opposite. No argument about the matter is possible. The only basis for judging Hemingway (or anyone else) wrong would be if he failed to live up to his own principles; however, one of Hemingway's principles could be that hypocrisy is morally permissible (he feels good about it), so that it would be impossible for him to do wrong. For Hemingway, hypocrisy and nonhypocrisy are both morally permissible. On the basis of subjectivism, it could very easily turn out that Adolf Hitler was as moral as Mahatma Gandhi, as long as each believed he was living by his chosen principles. Notions of moral good and bad, right or wrong, cease to have interpersonal evaluative meaning.

When students argue vehemently for subjectivism, I sometimes return the next test to them marked F. Some have never seen this letter on an exam and ask me what it means. I explain that it stands for "fail." "But," they loudly protest, "I did very well on the test—I got all the answers right." I explain to them that I am a subjectivist, and it feels very good to me as a sadistic professor to give everyone an F and watch them groan. When the students express outrage at this injustice, I point out that from the perspective of subjectivism the principle of justice has no objective validity.

Absurd consequences follow from subjective ethical relativism. If it is correct, then morality reduces to aesthetic tastes over which there can be no argument nor interpersonal judgment. Although many people say that they hold this position, a conflict often arises between it and some of their other moral views (e.g., that Hitler was really morally bad or that capital punishment is always wrong). There seems to be a contradiction between subjectivism and the very concept of morality, which it is supposed to characterize, for morality has to do with "proper" resolution of interpersonal conflict and the amelioration of the human predicament. Whatever else it does, it has a minimal aim of preventing a state of chaos where life is "solitary, poor, nasty, brutish, and short." But if so, subjectivism is no help at all in doing this, for it doesn't rest on social *agreement* of principle (as the conventionalist maintains) or on an objectively independent set of norms that bind all people for the common good.

Subjectivism treats individuals like billiard balls on a societal pool table where they meet only in radical collisions, each aiming for its own goal and striving to do in the other fellow before he does it to you. This atomistic view of personality is belied by the fact that we develop in families and mutually dependent communities, in which we share a common language, common institutions, and habits, and that we often feel one another's joys and sorrows. As John Donne wrote in his poem *Devotions,* "No man is an *Island,* entire of it self. Every man is a piece of the continent."

Recall the goals of morality discussed in the last chapter: (1) to promote the survival of society, (2) to resolve conflicts of interest justly, (3) to ameliorate human suffering, and (4) to promote human flourishing. Subjectivism either violates or ignores each of these goals. As such, it seems to be misguided and not a candidate for morality at all. Radical individualistic relativism seems incoherent. If so, it follows that the only plausible view of ethical relativism must be one that grounds morality in the group or culture. This form of relativism is called conventionalism, which we looked at earlier and to which we now return.

CONVENTIONAL ETHICAL RELATIVISM
(CONVENTIONALISM)

Conventional ethical relativism, the view that there are no objective moral principles but that all valid moral principles are justified by virtue of their cultural acceptance, recognizes the social nature of morality. That is precisely its power and virtue. It does not seem subject to the same absurd consequences that plague subjectivism. Recognizing the importance of our social environment in generating customs and beliefs, many people suppose that ethical relativism is the correct ethical theory. Furthermore, they are drawn to it for its liberal philosophical stance. It seems to be an enlightened response to the "sin of ethnocentricity," and it seems to entail or strongly imply an attitude of tolerance toward other cultures. As

Benedict says, in recognizing ethical relativity "we shall arrive at a more realistic social faith, accepting as grounds of hope and as new bases for tolerance the coexisting and equally valid patterns of life which mankind has created for itself from the raw materials of existence."[7] The most famous of those holding this position is the anthropologist Melville Herskovits, who argues even more explicitly than Benedict that ethical relativism entails intercultural tolerance.[8]

The view contains a contradiction. If no moral principles are universally valid, how can tolerance be universally valid? Whence comes its validity? If morality is simply relative to each culture and if the culture does not have a principle of tolerance, its members have no obligation to be tolerant. Herskovits seems to be treating the *principle of tolerance* as the one exception to his relativism—as an absolute moral principle. But from a relativistic point of view, there is no more reason to be tolerant than to be intolerant, and neither stance is objectively morally better than the other.

Not only do relativists fail to offer a basis for criticizing those who are intolerant, but they cannot rationally *criticize* anyone who espouses what they might regard as a heinous principle. If, as seems to be the case, valid criticism supposes an objective or impartial standard, relativists cannot morally criticize anyone outside their own culture. Hitler's genocidal actions, as long as they were culturally accepted, were as morally legitimate as Mother Teresa's works of mercy. If conventional relativism is accepted, racism, genocide of unpopular minorities, oppression of the poor, slavery, and even the advocacy of war for its own sake are equally as moral as their opposites. And if a subculture decided that starting a nuclear war was somehow morally acceptable, we could not morally criticize these people. The result would be that any actual moral code, whatever its content, is as valid as every other and more valid than ideal moralities—since the latter aren't adhered to by *any* culture.

Ethical relativism has other disturbing consequences. It seems to entail that reformers are always (morally) wrong because they go against the tide of cultural standards. William Wilberforce was wrong in the eighteenth century to oppose slavery, the British were immoral in opposing suttee in India (the burning of a widow on her husband's funeral pyre, which is now illegal in India), and missionaries and other progressive people are immoral in opposing clitorectomies (female genital mutilation) in Africa. The Jews and early Christians were wrong in refusing to serve in the Roman army or bow down to Caesar since the majority in the Roman Empire believed that these two acts were moral duties. In fact, Jesus himself was immoral in breaking the Jewish law of his day by healing on the Sabbath and by advocating the principles of the Sermon on the Mount since it is clear that few in his time (or in ours) accepted them.

Yet we normally feel just the opposite, that the reformer is the courageous innovator who is right, who has the truth, against the mindless majority. Sometimes the individual must stand alone with the truth, risking social censure and persecution. As Dr. Stockman says in Ibsen's *Enemy of the People,* after he loses the battle to declare his town's profitable, polluted tourist spa unsanitary: "The most dangerous enemy of the truth and freedom among us—is the compact majority. Yes, the damned, compact and liberal majority. The majority has *might*—unfortunately—but *right* it is not. Right—are I and a few others." Yet if relativism is correct, the opposite is necessarily the case. Truth is with the crowd and error with the individual.

An even more basic problem arises with the notion that morality is dependent on cultural acceptance for its validity. The problem is that the notion of a culture or society is notoriously difficult to define. This is especially so in a pluralistic society like our own where the notion seems to be vague, with unclear boundary lines. One person may belong to several societies (subcultures) with different value emphases and arrangements of principles. A person may belong to the nation as a single society with certain values of patriotism, honor, courage, laws (including some that are controversial but have majority acceptance, such as the law on abortion). But he or she may also belong to a church that opposes some of the laws of the state. He may also be an integral member of a socially mixed community where different principles hold sway, or she may belong to clubs and a family that adhere to still other rules. Relativism would seem to tell us that where a person is a member of societies with conflicting moralities, he or she must be judged both wrong and not-wrong, whatever he (she) does. For example, if Mary is a U.S. citizen and a member of the Roman Catholic Church, she is wrong (*qua* Catholic) if she chooses to have an abortion and not-wrong (*qua* citizen of the United States) if she acts against the teaching of the church on abortion. As a member of a racist organization, the Ku Klux Klan, John has no obligation to treat his fellow African-American citizens as equals; but as a member of the university community itself (where the principle of equal rights is accepted), he does have the obligation; but as a member of the surrounding community (which may reject the principle of equal rights), he again has no such obligation; but then again as a member of the nation at large (which accepts the principle), he is obligated to treat his fellow citizens with respect. What is the morally right thing for John or Mary to do? The question no longer makes much sense in this moral Babel. It has lost its action-guiding function.

Perhaps the relativist would adhere to a principle that says in such cases the individual may choose which group to belong to as primary. If Mary chooses to have an abortion, she is choosing to belong to the general society relative to that principle. And John must similarly choose between groups. The trouble with this option is that it seems to lead back to counterintuitive results. If Gangland Gus of Murder, Inc., feels like killing bank president Ortcutt and wants to feel good about it, he identifies with the Murder, Inc., society rather than the general public morality. Does this justify the killing? In fact, couldn't one justify anything simply by forming a small subculture that approved of it? Charles Manson would be morally pure in killing innocents simply by virtue of forming a little coterie. How large must the group be to be a legitimate subculture or society? Does it need ten or fifteen people? How about just three? Come to think about it, why can't my burglary partner and I found our own society with a morality of its own? Of course, if my partner dies, I could still claim that I was acting from an originally social set of norms. But why can't I dispense with the interpersonal agreements altogether and invent my own morality, since morality, in this view, is only an invention anyway? Conventionalist relativism seems to reduce to subjectivism. And subjectivism, as we have seen, leads to the demise of morality altogether.

THE CASE FOR ETHICAL OBJECTIVISM

The discussion heretofore has been largely negative, against moral relativism. Now we must make a case for a positive, objective core morality, a set of principles that serve the five purposes set forth as serving the function of morality in the last chapter.

First, let me make it clear that I am distinguishing moral *absolutism* from moral *objectivism*. The absolutist believes that there are non-overridable moral principles that ought *never* to be violated. Immanuel Kant's system is a good example of this. One ought never break a promise or tell a lie, no matter what. An objectivist need not posit any non-overridable principles, at least not in unqualified general form, and so need not be an absolutist. As Renford Bambrough puts it,

> To suggest that there is a right answer to a moral problem is at once to be accused of or credited with a belief in moral absolutes. But it is no more necessary to believe in moral absolutes in order to believe in moral objectivity than it is to believe in the existence of absolute space or absolute time in order to believe in the objectivity of temporal and spatial relations and of judgments about them.[9]

On the objectivist's account, moral principles are what the Oxford University philosopher William David Ross (1877–1971) refers to as **prima facie** principles, valid rules of action that should generally be adhered to but that may be overridden by another moral principle in cases of moral conflict.[10] For example, a principle of justice may generally outweigh a principle of benevolence, but there are times when enormous good could be done by sacrificing a small amount of justice, so an objectivist would be inclined to act according to the principle of benevolence. There may be some absolute or non-overridable principles (indeed the next principle I mention is probably one), but there need not be any or many for objectivism to be true.[11]

If we can establish or show that it is reasonable to believe that at least one objective moral principle is binding on all people everywhere in some ideal sense, we will have shown that relativism is probably false and that a limited **objectivism** is true. Actually, I believe that many qualified general ethical principles are binding on all rational beings, but one will suffice to refute relativism. The principle I've chosen is the following. Call it principle A:

A: It is morally wrong to torture people for the fun of it.

I claim that this principle is binding on all rational agents, so that if some agent S rejects A, we should not let that affect our intuition that A is a true principle but rather try to explain S's behavior as perverse, ignorant, or irrational instead. For example, suppose Adolf Hitler didn't accept A. Should that affect our confidence in the truth of A? Is it not more reasonable to infer that Hitler was morally deficient, morally blind, ignorant, or irrational than to suppose that his noncompliance was evidence against the truth of A?

Suppose further that there is a tribe of Hitlerites somewhere who enjoy torturing people. The whole culture accepts torturing others for the fun of it. Suppose Mother Teresa tries unsuccessfully to convince them that they should stop torturing people altogether, and they respond by torturing her. Should this affect our confidence in A? Would it not be more reasonable to look for some explanation of Hitlerite behavior? For example, we might hypothesize that this tribe lacked a developed sense of sympathetic imagination that is necessary for the moral life. Or we might theorize that this tribe was on a lower evolutionary level than most *Homo sapiens*. Or we might simply conclude that the tribe was closer to a Hobbesian state of nature than most societies and as such probably would not survive. But we need not know the correct answer as to why the tribe was in such bad shape in order to maintain our confidence in A as a moral principle. If A is a basic or core belief for us, we will be more likely to doubt the Hitlerites' sanity or ability to think morally than to doubt the validity of A.

We can perhaps produce other candidates for membership in our minimally basic objective moral set. For example,

1. Do not kill innocent people.
2. Do not cause unnecessary pain or suffering.
3. Ameliorate pain and suffering where it is feasible.
4. Keep your promises and contracts.
5. Do not deprive another person of his or her freedom.
6. Do justice, treating equals equally and unequals unequally.
7. Show gratitude for services rendered, reciprocate.
8. Tell the truth.
9. Help other people.
10. Obey just laws.

These ten principles are examples of what I call the **Core Morality,** principles necessary for the good life. Fortunately, it isn't as though the ten principles were arbitrary principles, for we can give reasons why we believe that these rules will be necessary to any satisfactory social order. Principles like the Ten Commandments, the Golden Rule, justice (treating equals equally), truth telling, promise keeping, and the like are central to the fluid progression of social interaction and the resolution of conflicts about ethics (at least minimal morality is, even though there may be more to morality than simply these kinds of concerns). For example, language itself depends on a general and implicit commitment to the principle of truth telling. Accuracy of expression is a primitive form of truthfulness. Hence, every time we use words correctly, we are telling the truth. Without this behavior, language wouldn't be possible. Similarly, without the recognition of a rule of promise keeping, contracts would be of no avail, and cooperation less likely to occur. And without the protection of life and liberty, we could not secure our other goals.

A moral code would be adequate if it contained the principles of the core morality, but there could be more than one adequate moral code, each of which *applies* these principles differently. That is, there may be a certain relativity to secondary principles (e.g., whether to opt for monogamy rather than polygamy, whether to include a principle of high altruism in the set of moral duties, whether to allocate more resources to medical care than to environmental concerns, whether to institute a law to drive on the left side of the road or the right side of the road), but in every morality a certain core will remain, although applied somewhat differently because of differences in environment, belief, tradition, and the like.

"You'll find there's no right or wrong here. Just what works for *you.*

The core morality rules are analogous to the vitamins necessary for a healthy diet. We need an adequate amount of each vitamin—for some humans, more of one than another—but in prescribing a nutritional diet, we don't have to set forth recipes, specific foods, place settings, or culinary habits. Gourmets will meet the requirements differently than ascetics and vegetarians, but the basic nutrients may be had by all without rigid regimentation or an absolute set of recipes.

Imagine that you have been miraculously transported to the dark kingdom of hell, and there you get a glimpse of the sufferings of the damned. What is their punishment? Well, they have eternal back itches, which ebb and flow constantly, but they cannot scratch their backs, for their arms are paralyzed in a frontal position. And so they writhe with itchiness through eternity. But just as you are beginning to feel the itch in your own back, you are suddenly transported to heaven. What do you see in the kingdom of the blessed? Well, you see people with eternal back itches, who cannot scratch their own backs. But they are all smiling instead of writhing. Why? Because everyone has his or her arms stretched out to scratch someone else's back, and, so arranged in one big circle, a hell is turned into a heaven of ecstasy.

If we can imagine some states of affairs or cultures that are better than others in a way that depends on human action, we can ask what are those character traits that make them so. In our story, people in heaven, but not in hell, cooperate for the amelioration of suffering and the production of pleasure. These are very primitive goods, not sufficient for a full-blown morality, but they give us a hint as to the objectivity of morality. Moral goodness has something to do with the ameliorating of suffering, the resolution of conflict, and the promotion of human flourishing. If our heaven is really better than the eternal itchiness of hell, then whatever makes it so is constitutively related to moral rightness.

So who's to judge what's morally right and wrong? You and I are—using our best reasons to discover sound moral principles, as well as sympathy and insight to enable us to transform a potential hell into an actual approximation of heaven.

SUMMARY

Ethical relativism, the thesis that moral principles derive their validity from dependence on society or the individual, seems, at first glance, plausible but when scrutinized is seen to have some serious difficulties. Subjectivism seems to boil down to anarchistic individualism, and conventionalism must deal with the problems of the reformer, the question of defining a culture, and the whole enterprise of moral criticism. On the other hand, we have seen that the purposes of morality, promoting human welfare and ameliorating suffering, call for an objective core morality that transcends cultures.

QUESTIONS FOR DISCUSSION

1. Go over Ladd's definition of ethical relativism, discussed toward the beginning of this chapter. Is it a good definition? Can you find a better definition of relativism? Ask your friends what they think ethical relativism is and whether they accept it. You might put the question this way: "Are there any moral absolutes, or is morality completely relative?" Discuss your findings.

2. Sometimes students argue that since there are no universal moral norms, each culture's morality is equal to every other, so we ought not to interfere in their practices. Assess this argument.

3. Can you separate the anthropological claim (the diversity thesis, called cultural relativism)—that different cultures have different moral principles—from the judgment that *therefore* they are all equally good (ethical relativism)?

4. Benedict has written that our culture is "but one entry in a long series of possible adjustments" and that "the very eyes with which we see the problem are conditioned by the long traditional habits of our own society." What are the implications of these statements? Is Benedict correct?

5. My colleague Sandra Visser notes that even people who claim to be subjectivist relativists sometimes feel that in the past they have done morally wrong acts—even though they felt good about them at the time. This seems contradictory, for if one's subjective feeling is the only criterion of rightness and wrongness, what one felt good about at time t must have been the right act. So the subjectivist seems to contradict himself or herself. Evaluate this argument.

6. In Mark Twain's classic novel, Huckleberry Finn develops a deep attachment to Jim, a runaway slave. Huck anguishes over whether he ought to turn in Jim. He finally concludes that he has a moral duty to do so, based on his understanding of his society's values. Nevertheless, Huck cannot bring himself to turn in Jim. He feels guilty but concludes that it is better to deserve hell than betray his friend. Can you apply this problem to the problem of relativism?

7. Read over Bloom's provocative claim at the beginning of this chapter. Do you think he is correct? Explain your answer.

8. Does moral relativism have deleterious effects on society? Here is a paraphrase of a tape-recorded conversation between the serial murderer Ted Bundy and one of his victims in which Bundy attempts to justify the murder of his victims on the basis of the idea that all moral values are subjective:

> Then I learned that all moral judgments are "value judgments," that all value judgments are subjective, and that none can be proved to be either "right" or "wrong." I even read somewhere that the Chief Justice of the United States had written that the American Constitution expressed nothing more than collective value judgments. Believe it or not, I figured out for myself—what apparently the Chief Justice couldn't figure out for himself—that if the rationality of one value judgment was zero, multiplying it by millions would not make it one whit more rational. Nor is there any "reason" to obey the law for anyone, like myself, who has the boldness and daring—the strength of character—to throw off its shackles.
>
> I discovered that to become truly free, truly unfettered, I had to become truly uninhibited. And I quickly discovered that the greatest obstacle to my freedom, the greatest block and limitation to it, consisted in the insupportable "value judgments" that I was bound to respect the rights of others. I asked myself, who were these "others"? Other human beings, with human rights? . . . Surely, you would not, in this age of scientific enlightenment, declare that God or nature has marked some pleasures as "moral" or "good" and others as "immoral" or "bad"? In any case, let me assure you, my dear young lady, that there is absolutely no comparison between the pleasure I might take in eating ham, and the pleasure I anticipate in raping and murdering you. That is the honest conclusion to which my education has led me—after the most conscientious examination of my spontaneous and uninhibited self.[12]

Analyze Bundy's discussion. How would the relativist respond to Bundy's claim that relativism justifies rape and murder? What do you think? Why?

9. Just because there is considerable agreement throughout time and place on the main principles of morality, does this provide evidence for moral truth? Or could it be that human nature simply inclines us or forces us to *believe* that there are moral truths?

10. Explain the differences between moral absolutism and moral objectivism. What are the best arguments for each?

NOTES

1. Alan Bloom, *The Closing of the American Mind* (New York: Simon & Schuster, 1987).

2. *History of Herodotus,* book 3, trans. George Rawlinson (New York: Appleton, 1859), Chapter 38.

3. John Ladd, *Ethical Relativism* (Belmont, CA: Wadsworth, 1973).

4. Ruth Benedict, *Patterns of Culture* (New York: Pelican, 1934), 219.

5. William Graham Sumner, *Folkways* (New York: Athenaeum, 1906), sect. 80. Ruth Benedict indicates the depth of our cultural conditioning this way: "The very eyes with which we see the problem are conditioned by the long traditional habits of our own society." "Anthropology and the Abnormal," *Journal of General Psychology* (1934): 59–82.

6. Ernest Hemingway, *Death in the Afternoon* (New York: Scribner, 1932), 4.

7. Benedict, *Patterns of Culture,* 257.

8. Melville Herskovits, *Cultural Relativism* (New York: Random House, 1972).

9. Renford Bambrough, *Moral Skepticism and Moral Knowledge* (London: Routledge & Kegan Paul, 1979), 33.

10. William David Ross, *The Right and the Good* (Oxford: Oxford University Press, 1931).

11. In a sense, *objective* and *absolute* are not opposites. If we defined a moral principle broadly so as to include all its exceptions, that principle would be an absolute. But since we normally cannot think of all the exceptions, we are on safer ground in holding to objective principles.

12. Paraphrased by Harry V. Jaffa in *Homosexuality and the Natural Law* (Claremont Institute for the Statesmanship and Political Philosophy, 1990), 2–3.

FOR FURTHER READING

Bennett, Jonathan. "The Conscience of Huckleberry Finn." *Philosophy* 49 (1974). A fascinating discussion of the Huckleberry Finn dilemma.

Fishkin, James. *Beyond Subjective Morality.* New Haven, CT: Yale University Press, 1984. A valuable examination of relativism.

Mackie, J. L. *Ethics: Inventing Right and Wrong.* London: Penguin Books, 1976. Probably the best defense of ethical relativism available.

Pojman, Louis, ed. *Ethical Theory: Classical and Contemporary Readings.* Belmont, CA: Wadsworth, 1989. Contains several important readings on the subject.

Taylor, Paul. *Principles of Ethics.* Belmont, CA: Dickenson, 1975. Chapter 2 is a good discussion.

23

Egoism, Self-love, and Altruism

Nice guys finish last.

—LEO DUROCHER

The achievement of his own happiness is man's highest moral purpose.

–AYN RAND

Children are sometimes brought up feeling guilty if they are concerned about their own good. They are taught that self-love is selfishness, a sinful attitude. To do things for yourself is evil. Indeed, I was brought up in a strict religious community in which children were made to feel they were sinful. The proper attitude toward one's self was one of humility ("blessed are the poor in spirit, for theirs is the kingdom of heaven") and self-effacement ("unless a person hate his own life, he cannot enter the kingdom of God").[1] Sometimes such an upbringing results in self-hatred, low self-esteem, masochism, and pervasive, irrational guilt. Let's call this attitude the **morality of self-effacement.**

Lise, in Fyodor Dostoyevsky's *The Brothers Karamazov,* breaks her engagement with the saintly Alyosha, explaining to him that he is too gentle for her needs:

> I was just thinking for the thirtieth time what a good thing it is that I broke off our engagement and decided not to become your wife. You wouldn't be much of a husband, you know. . . . I want someone to marry me, tear me to pieces, betray me, and then desert me. I don't want to be happy.[2]

Shortly afterward we read,

Lise unlocked the door, opened it a little, put her finger in the crack, and slammed the door as hard as she could. Ten seconds later she released her hand, went slowly to her chair, sat down, and looked intently at her blackened, swollen finger and the blood that was oozing out from under the nail. Her lips quivered. "I'm vile, vile, vile, a despicable creature."[3]

At the exact opposite extreme is the morality of self-exaltation, or the morality of **meism.** One is to love one's self first. Ayn Rand's *The Virtue of Selfishness,* Robert Ringer's *Looking Out for Number One,* and David Seabury's *The Art of Selfishness* advise us to love ourselves first even if it means hurting others. Perhaps no one was more candid about the legitimacy of **egoism** than Friedrich Nietzsche (1844—1900), who taught that you should strive to satisfy your own will to power even to the extent of exploiting and dominating others before they dominated you: "What is strong wins. That is the universal law. To speak of right and wrong per se makes no sense at all. No act of violence, rape, exploitation, destruction, is intrinsically 'unjust,' since life itself is violent, rapacious, exploitative, and destructive and cannot be conceived otherwise."[4]

But Nietzsche's version of egoism is an extreme one. A less virulent version is found in Thomas Hobbes's (1588–1679) classic *Leviathan* (1651). Hobbes believes egoism is the proper foundation for the moral and political life. Human nature is basically self-interested, so it makes no sense to ask people to be altruistic. All apparent altruistic acts are, if you look deeply into the heart of people, merely disguised acts of selfishness. Nevertheless, out of enlightened egoism arises objective moral norms and a legitimate political system, the *Leviathan.*

Hobbes's argument goes like this. Suppose we existed outside of any society, without laws or an agreed-on morality, in a "state of nature." There are no common ways of life, no means of settling conflicts of interest except violence, no reliable expectations of how other people will behave—except that, as psychological egoists, they will follow their own inclinations and perceived interests, tending to act and react and overreact in fearful, capricious, and violent ways.

The result of life in the state of nature is chaotic anarchy. Reason advises us not to depend on anyone except ourselves, for others will let us down if it is in their interests to do so. I must always be on my guard, protecting my vital interests. But I see that others are thinking the same thing—perhaps they are ganging up on me. This increases my fear of others and in turn leads to preventive or preemptive aggression, which leads to "a war of all against all":

> During the time men live without a common Power to keep them all in awe they are in that condition called War; and such a war, as is of every man against every other man.... To this war every man against every man, this is consequent; that nothing can be Unjust. The notions of Right and Wrong, Justice and Injustice have no place.[5]

In such a state, life is "solitary, poor, nasty, brutish, and short."

Reason tells us, however, that a war of all against all is really in no one's interest. It would be better for all of us, individually and collectively, if we adopted certain minimal rules that would override immediate self-interests whenever self-interests were a threat to others. Thus, the notion of a **mutually agreed-on moral code** arises from a situation of rational self-interest. Even if the code is not the best one or ideal, so long as it prevents the state of nature, it is better than no code at all.

The moral code will not work, of course, if only some obey it. They will be slaughtered like sheep before waiting wolves. Reason can only support morality when the presumption about other people's behavior is reversed. Hobbes thought that this could only be achieved by the creation of a *Leviathan,* an absolute ruler with absolute power to enforce his laws. But this is incorrect. The minimal moral society can be achieved by a people democratically if common rules or ways of life are taught to all members of the society, inculcated in them early in life, and enforced by the group.

The members must be able to count on one another to obey these rules even when it is not in their immediate self-interest. Nonetheless, violating the rules is still rational whenever two conditions obtain: (1) You calculate that you can get away with it, and (2) your infraction will not seriously threaten the stability of the social system as a whole, sending you back toward the state of nature.

To prevent such violations, Hobbes proposed a strong central government with a powerful police force and a sure and effective system of punishment. The threat of being caught and punished should function as a deterrent to crime. People must believe that offenses against the law are not in their overall interest. Is Hobbes correct in his account of human nature? Is he correct in his view that ethical egoism is the correct moral theory?

What is the place of self-regard, self-interest, or self-love in the moral life? Is everything we do really done out of the motive of self-interest so that morality is necessarily egoistic? Is some form of egoism the best moral theory? Or is egoism really diametrically opposed to true morality? What is the relationship of egoism to morality?

There are two versions of egoism: individual ethical egoism and universal ethical egoism, both of which claim to tell how to live the moral life. *Individual ethical egoism* is the view that everyone ought to serve *my* self-interest. That is, moral rightness is defined solely in terms of what is good for me, whether or not it is good for anyone else. Of course, everyone of us may put his own name in the place of "me." Say, for example, that Aunt Ruth is an individual ethical egoist; thus, all moral rightness consists entirely in what is good for Aunt Ruth. It would follow that whether or not a mother in India loves her child is morally irrelevant, for it has no effect on Aunt Ruth. Now that Aunt Ruth is dead, morality is dead, for it has no object. Interestingly enough, while individual ethical egoism seems implausible, it may be the central position of many religious people who define ethics as that which serves God's interests and pleases him. Be that as it may, as far as mere mortals are concerned, individual ethical egoism seems a partial and absurd theory. What makes you so special that all of us have an obligation to grant your interests as our primary concern?

Universal ethical egoism is the theory that everyone ought to serve his or her own self-interest. That is, everyone ought to do what will maximize one's own expected utility or bring about one's own happiness, even when it means harming others. Brian Medlin defines ethical egoism this way: "Everyone (including the speaker) ought to look after his own interest and to disregard those of other people except insofar as their interests contribute towards his own."[6] And Jesse

Kalin defines it thus: For everyone (x) and for every act (y), "x ought to do y if and only if y is in x's overall self-interest."[7] This has all the earmarks of a legitimate ethical theory. It is a universal theory, applying to everyone equally and without bias, which is not the case with individual egoism. It is not egotistical but prudential and favoring long-term interests over short-term interests. In its most sophisticated form, it urges everyone to *try* to win in the game of life and recognizes that to do this some compromises are necessary. Indeed, the universal egoist will admit that to some extent we must all give up a certain freedom and cooperate with others to achieve our ends.

There are three arguments for universal ethical egoism, which we'll consider: the economist argument, the Ayn Rand argument, and the Hobbesian argument. We want to know whether any of them give us an argument for an adequate moral theory based on egoism.

ARGUMENTS FOR ETHICAL EGOISM

The Economist Argument Economists, following Adam Smith (1723–1790), often argue that individual self-interest in a state of competition in the marketplace produces a state of optimal goodness for society at large because the peculiar nature of self-interested competition causes each competitor to produce a better product and sell it at a lower price than his or her competitors. Enlightened self-interest leads, as by an invisible hand, to the best overall situation.

The *economist argument,* essentially not an argument for ethical egoism, is really an argument for utilitarianism (see Chapter 24), which makes use of self-interest to attain (paradoxically) the good of all. Its goal is social utility, but it places its faith in an invisible hand inherent in the free-enterprise system to use enlightened self-interest to reach that goal. We might say that it is a two-tier system. On the highest level, it is utilitarian; but on a lower level of day-to-day action, it is practical egoism. It tells us not to worry about the social good but only our own good, and in that way we will attain the highest social good possible.

There may be some truth in such a two-tier system, but two objections arise. First, it is, at best, unclear whether you can transpose the methods of economics (which are debatable) into the realm of personal relations. Personal relations may have a different logic than economic relations. The best way to maximize utility in an ethical sense may be to give one's life for others rather than kill another person, as an egoist may enjoin. Second, it is not clear that classical laissez-faire capitalism works. Since the Great Depression of 1929, most economists have altered their faith in classical capitalism, and most Western nations have supplemented capitalism with some government intervention. Similarly, although self-interest may often lead to greater social utility, it may get out of hand and need to be supplemented by a concern for others. Just as classical capitalism has been altered to allow government intervention—resulting in a welfare system for the worst-off people, public education, Social Security, and Medicare—an adequate moral system may need to draw attention to the needs of others and direct us to meeting those needs even where we do not see it to be in our immediate self-interest.

The Ayn Rand Argument In her book *The Virtue of Selfishness*, Ayn Rand (1905–1982), describing her "objectivist ethics" as egoistic, argues that selfishness is a virtue and altruism is a vice, a totally destructive idea that leads to the undermining of individual worth:

> Man's proper values and interests, that *concern with his own interests* is the essence of a moral existence, and that *man must be the beneficiary of his own moral actions*. . . . If a man accepts the ethics of altruism, his first concern is not how to live his life, but how to sacrifice it. . . . Altruism erodes men's capacity to grasp the value of an individual life; it reveals a mind from which the reality of a human being has been wiped out. . . . Altruism holds *death* as its ultimate goal and standard of value—and it is logical that renunciation, resignation, self-denial, and every other form of suffering, including self-destruction, are the virtues it advocates.[8]

In her novel *The Fountainhead,* Rand paints Howard Rourk, her hero, as an egoist who is dedicated to his own happiness, and Ellsworth Toohey, the altruist philanthropist, as a scoundrel. Altruism, in the hands of the likes of Toohey, Rand avers, calls on one to sacrifice his or her life, not to find happiness, which is the highest goal of life.

According to Rand, the perfection of one's abilities in a state of happiness is the highest goal for humans. We have a moral duty to attempt to reach this goal. Because the ethics of altruism prescribes that we sacrifice our interests and lives for the good of others, it is incompatible with the goal of happiness. But ethical egoism prescribes that we seek our own happiness exclusively, and as such it is consistent with the happiness goal. Therefore, ethical egoism is the correct moral theory.

The *Ayn Rand argument* for the virtues of selfishness is flawed by the fallacy of a false dilemma. It simplistically assumes that absolute altruism or absolute egoism are the only alternatives, but this is an extreme view of the matter. There are plenty of options between these two positions. Even a predominant egoist would admit that (analogous to the **hedonistic paradox**) sometimes the best way to reach self-fulfillment is for us to forget about ourselves and strive to live for goals, causes, or other persons. Even if altruism is not required as a duty, it may be permissible in many cases. Furthermore, self-interest may be compatible with concern for others. Even the Second Commandment, "Love your neighbor as yourself," set forth by Moses and Jesus, states not that you must always sacrifice yourself for the other person but that you ought to love your neighbor *as* yourself (Leviticus 19:18; Matthew 22:39). Self-interest and self-love are morally good things, but not at the expense of other people's legitimate interests. When there is a moral conflict of interests, a fair process of adjudication needs to take place.

Actually, Rand slides back and forth between advocating selfishness and self-interest. Most of the time, if I understand her, she is really advocating self-interest, in which case non-egoists can agree with her. Her villain, her paradigmatic altruist Ellsworth Toohey, is not an altruist at all but an insecure, envious ideologue who manipulates others for his causes.

The Hobbesian Argument As we noted earlier, Hobbes thought that we were fundamentally egoistical. We might as well recognize this fact and work it into our moral theory. It is permissible to live self-interested lives since we cannot do otherwise without unreasonable effort. However, enlightened common sense tells us that we should aim at fulfilling our long-term versus our short-term interests, and so we need to refrain from immediate gratification of our senses, from doing those things that would break down the social conditions that help us reach our goals. We should even, perhaps, generally obey the Golden Rule, "Do unto others as you would have them do unto you," for doing good unto others will help ensure that they do good unto us. However, sometimes we should cheat when our doing so will maximize agent utility, and sometimes we should harm others when it is in our overall self-interest to do so.

Sometimes this version of egoism is based on the notion that all values are essentially owned by an agent and that each of us has our own hierarchy and specific set of values, so that each of us has different reasons for acting. There are no agent-neutral values, identical in all persons. Naturally, we will have to cooperate with others in the pursuit of our projects, but ultimately we are alone in the world, the only persons who know exactly what the values are. Sometimes we may have to harm others in order to realize our projects.

Hobbes's argument is flawed by ideological pessimism. It assumes that we cannot do any better than be egoists, so we should be as enlightened about our egoism as possible. But this cynicism about human nature seems extreme. Although there is a tendency toward self-interest, humans are capable of disinterested action, benevolence, and even high altruism. As David Hume (1711–1776) said, "There is some benevolence, however small, infused into our bosom; some spark of friendship for humankind; some particle of the dove kneaded into our frame, along with the elements of the wolf and serpent."[9] There is a great variation in people regarding their ability to act disinterestedly, kindly, and altruistically. Some seem innocently other-regarding, whereas others seem pugnacious Scrooges from birth on. But for most, if not all of us, it may be possible to combine a moderate degree of altruism with self-interest.

ARGUMENTS AGAINST ETHICAL EGOISM

Not only do the arguments for ethical egoism have drawbacks, but there are also four arguments against this doctrine.

The Publicity Argument On the one hand, it seems a necessary condition for something to be a moral theory to publicize one's moral principles. Unless principles are put forth as universal prescriptions that are accessible to the public, they cannot serve as guides to action or as helps in resolving conflicts of interest. On the other hand, it is not in the egoist's self-interest to publicize them. Egoists would rather that the rest of us be altruists. (Why did Nietzsche and Rand write books announcing their positions—were the royalties taken in by announcing ethical egoism worth the price of "letting the cat out of the bag"?)

It would be a bad thing for the egoist to argue for his position and even worse that he should convince others of it! But it is perfectly possible to have a private morality that does not resolve conflicts of interest (for that, the egoist publicizes standard principles of traditional morality). So, if you're willing to pay the price, you can accept the solipsistic-directed norms of egoism.

If the egoist is prepared to pay the price, egoism could be a consistent system but have some limitations. Although the egoist can cooperate with others in limited ways and perhaps even have friends—as long as their interests don't conflict with his—he has to be very careful about preserving his isolation. The egoist can't give advice or argue about his position, not sincerely at least. He must act alone, atomistically or solipsistically, in moral isolation, for to announce one's adherence to the principle of egoism would be dangerous to his project. He can't teach his children or justify himself to others or forgive others.

The Paradox of Egoism The situation, however, may be even worse than the sophisticated, self-conscious egoist supposes. Could the egoist have friends? And if limited friendship is possible, could she ever be in love or experience deep friendship? Suppose the egoist discovers that in the pursuit of the happiness goal, deep friendship is in her best interest. Can she become a friend? What is necessary to deep friendship? A true friend is one who is not always preoccupied with her own interest in the relationship but who forgets about herself altogether, at least sometimes, in order to serve or enhance the other person's interest. "Love seeketh not its own" is an altruistic disposition, the very opposite of egoism. One could go on to argue that friendship is a necessary ingredient for psychological health. Since egoists cannot have true friends, they cannot attain psychological health. Since any theory that undermines psychological health is an inadequate moral theory, ethical egoism must be rejected. So the paradox of egoism is that in order to reach the goal of egoism, one must give up egoism and become (to some extent) an altruist, the very antithesis of egoism.

Does the egoist have a reply to this criticism? Perhaps she can construct a split-level egoism. On the higher level, I am committed to advancing my own good above all else, whatever the effect on others. But I may conclude that, in order to maximize personal utility, I must have friends. Because having friends requires having altruistic dispositions, I must on a *lower* or *practical* level be selectively *altruistic,* rather than egoistic.

I leave it to you to decide whether such split-level egoism is really egoism or whether it is even possible to maintain.

Relevant Difference Argument This argument, based on a concept of universalizability and developed by James Rachels, goes like this.[10] All difference of treatment between people must be justified by some relevant difference in description of the people or their acts. For example, I am justified in paying Mary twice as much as John because she is working twice as long and producing twice as many widgets, but I am not justified in paying Mary twice as much as Sam simply because Mary is an African American and Sam is an Asian American. Race is an irrelevant difference. Racism, sexism, and fanatical nationalism are all prejudices that violate the relevant difference principle. But this principle applies to egoism as well. For the question is, What makes you so different from everyone else that you will allow your preferences to count for more than those of other rational beings? It seems unjust.

Of course, the egoist will reject the relevant difference principle in his behavior and so allow racism and sexism and other forms of discrimination. I've heard egoists deny that they are racists, but the truth is there is no reason to prohibit them from being racists. If it's in my interest to be a racist, I *ought* to be one, and if it's not, then I *ought not* be one. It all depends on whether being thus serves my interest. If it does, the version of egoism set forth above would require we be racists.

The Argument from Counterintuitive Consequences The final argument against ethical egoism is that it leads to consequences that seem abhorrent. If we followed its dictates, we would be prohibited from doing acts that seem obvious- ly good. It is an absolute ethics that not only permits egoistic behavior but also demands it. Helping others at one's own expense is not only not required but also morally wrong. Whenever I do not have good evidence that my helping you will end up to my advantage, I must refrain from helping you. In New York City (Queens) in March 1964, the thirty-eight people who watched Kitty Genovese being beaten and repeatedly stabbed to death not only had *no* obligation to call for help, but it also would have been wrong for them to do so. If I can save the whole of Europe and Africa from destruction by pressing a little button, as long as there is nothing for me to gain by it, it is wrong for me to press that button. The Good Samaritan was, by this logic, a vicious man in helping the injured vic- tim and not collecting on it. It is certainly hard to see why the egoist should be concerned about environmental matters if he or she is profiting from polluting the environment (e.g., if the egoist gains 40 hedons in production P that produces pollution that in turn causes others 1000 dolors—units of suffering—but he only suffers 10 of those dolors himself, by an agent-maximizing calculus, he is moral- ly obligated to produce P). There is certainly no obligation to preserve scarce nat- ural resources for future generations. "Why should I do anything for posterity?" the egoist asks. "What has posterity ever done for me?"

In the above we have taken a strong version of ethical egoism. One could accuse me of attacking a straw man if it weren't for the fact that people like Rand, Kalin, and others defend this strong position, making serving one's self-interest a necessary and sufficient condition for moral obligation. Perhaps a weaker form of ethical egoism states that it is always *permissible* to do whatever is in your (the agent's) self-interest. The problem with this is that it seems either to reduce moral- ity to subjectivism (discussed in Chapter 22) or to eliminate any normativity from ethics altogether. If it's always permissible to do what is in my self-interest, it is permissible to do what is not in my self-interest. Unless we are given supplemen- tary guidance, this seems to leave *every* act as permissible!

EVOLUTION AND ALTRUISM

If sheer unadulterated egoism is an inadequate moral theory, does that mean we ought to aim at complete altruism, total self-effacement for the sake of others? What is the role of self-love in morality? An interesting place to start is with the new field of sociobiology, which posits the theory that social structures and behavioral patterns, including morality, have a biological base, explained by evo- lutionary theory.

In the past, linking ethics to evolution meant justifying exploitation. Social Darwinism justified imperialism and the principle that "might makes right" by saying that the law of nature is the survival of the fittest. This philosophy lent itself to a promotion of ruthless egoism. This is nature's law, "nature red in tooth and claw." Against this view, ethologists like Robert Ardrey and Konrad Lorenz argue for a more benign view of the animal kingdom—reminiscent of Rudyard Kipling—where the animal kingdom survives by cooperation, which is at least as important as competition. In Ardrey and Lorenz's view, it is the group or species, not the individual, that is of primary importance.

With the onset of sociobiology in the work of E. O. Wilson, but particularly with the work of Robert Trivers, J. Maynard Smith, and Richard Dawkins, a theory has come to the fore that combines radical individualism with limited altruism. It is not the group or species that is of evolutionary importance but the gene or, more precisely, the gene type. Genes, the parts of the chromosomes that carry the blueprints for all our natural traits (e.g., height, hair color, skin color, health, and intelligence), copy themselves as they divide and multiply. At conception, they combine with the genes of the member of the opposite sex to form a new individual.

In his fascinating sociobiological study *The Selfish Gene,* Richard Dawkins describes human behavior as determined evolutionarily by stable strategies set to replicate the gene.[11] This is not done consciously, of course, but it's the invisible hand that drives the consciousness. We're essentially Gene Machines, who act as though we are servants of our genes.

Morality—or successful morality—can be seen as an evolutionary strategy for gene replication. Here's an example. Birds are inflicted with life-endangering parasites. Because they cannot use limbs to pick them off their heads, they—like much of the animal world—depend on the ritual of mutual grooming. It turns out that nature has evolved two different basic types of birds in this regard: those who are disposed to groom anyone (the nonprejudiced type?) and those who refuse to groom anyone who presents himself for grooming. The former type of bird Dawkins calls "Suckers" and the latter "Cheaters."

In a geographic area with harmful parasites where there are only Suckers or Cheaters, Suckers will do fairly well but Cheaters will not survive for want of cooperation. But in a Sucker population where a mutant Cheater arises, he will prosper, and his gene type will multiply. As the Suckers are exploited, they will gradually die out. But if and when they become too few to groom the Cheaters, the Cheaters will start to die off too and eventually become extinct.

Why don't birds all die off, then? Well, somehow nature has come up with a third type, call them "Grudgers." Grudgers groom all and only those who **reciprocate** in grooming them. They groom one another and Suckers, but not Cheaters. In fact, once a Cheater is caught, he is marked forever. There is no forgiveness. It turns out then that unless there are a lot of Suckers around, Cheaters have a hard time of it—harder even than Suckers! But it is the Grudgers that prosper. Unlike Suckers, they don't waste their time messing with unappreciative Cheaters, so that they are not exploited and have ample energy to gather food and build better nests for their loved ones.

J. L. Mackie argues that the real name for a Sucker is "Christian," one who believes in complete altruism, even turning the other cheek to one's assailant and loving one's enemy. Though Mackie may be misinterpreting Christianity, surely some people, like Lise, mentioned on the first page of this chapter, do evince this quality. Cheaters are ruthless egoists who can only survive if there are enough naive altruists around. Grudgers are *reciprocal altruists* who have a rational morality based on cooperative self-interest, helping those who cooperate and harming those who don't. Suckers advocate "turning the other cheek and repaying evil with good."[12] Instead of a Rule of Reciprocity, "I'll scratch your back if you'll scratch mine," the extreme altruist substitutes the Lackey Rule, "If you'd like the other fellow to scratch your back, you scratch his—even if he won't reciprocate and scratch yours."

The moral of the story is this: Altruist's morality (so interpreted) is only rational given the payoff of eternal life (with a scorekeeper, as Woody Allen says). Take that away, and it looks like a Sucker system. What replaces the "Christian" vision of submission and saintliness is the reciprocal altruist with his tit-for-tat morality, one who is willing to share with those willing to cooperate.

Mackie may caricature the position of the religious altruist, but he misses the subtleties of wisdom involved (Jesus said, "Be as wise as serpents but as harmless as doves"). Nevertheless, he does remind us that there is a difference between core morality and complete altruism. We have duties to cooperate and reciprocate, but no duty to serve those who manipulate us and no obvious duty to sacrifice ourselves for people outside our domain of special responsibility. We have a special duty of high altruism toward those in the close circle of our concern, namely, our family and friends.

Conclusion   The Protestant Reformer Martin Luther once said that humanity is like a man mounting a horse who always falls off on the opposite side, especially when he tries to overcompensate for his previous exaggerations. So it is with ethical egoism. Trying to compensate for an irrational, guilt-ridden, complete Sucker altruism of the *morality of self-effacement,* it falls off the horse on the other side, embracing a Cheater's preoccupation with selfishness which shuts out one's neighbor and robs the self of the deepest joys in life, love and friendship. Only the person who mounts properly, avoiding both extremes, is likely to ride the horse of happiness to its goal.

SUMMARY

Of the two versions of egoism, individual and universal ethical egoism, the latter is more plausible. Three arguments for ethical egoism were considered: the economist argument, the Ayn Rand argument, and the Hobbesian argument. Then four arguments against egoism were examined: the publicity argument, the paradox of egoism, the relevant difference argument, and the argument from counterintuitive consequences. Finally, we looked at the relationship between evolutionary theory and egoism. I leave it to you to sort out the valid and invalid aspects of this important theory.

QUESTIONS FOR DISCUSSION

1. Distinguish between individual and universal ethical egoism. Which theory appeals to you more? Does either constitute an adequate ethical theory? Explain your answer.

2. Discuss the three arguments in favor of ethical egoism and the four against it. Which side has the best arguments? Why?

3. Examine the discussion (above) of evolution and altruism. What is the relationship between ethics and evolution? How does this relationship throw light on egoism? What is the significance of reciprocity for ethics? Should we be complete altruists or reciprocators?

4. Can an ethical egoist have friends? Some philosophers, beginning with Plato, have argued that ethical egoism is irrational, since it precludes psychological health. Laurence Thomas sets forth the following argument:

   1. A true friend could never, as a matter of course, be disposed to harm or to exploit a friend [definition of a friend].

   2. An egoist could never be a true friend to anyone [for the egoist must be ready to exploit others whenever it is in his or her interest].

   3. Only someone with an unhealthy personality could never be a true friend to anyone [definition of a healthy personality; that is, friendship is a necessary condition for a healthy personality].

   4. Ethical egoism requires that we have a kind of disposition which is incompatible with our having a healthy personality [from 1–3].

      Conclusion: Therefore, from the standpoint of our psychological makeup, ethical egoism is unacceptable as a moral theory.[13]

   Do you agree with Thomas? Explain your answer.

5. In this chapter we have argued against various forms of egoism. Can you think of a version of ethical egoism that can meet the objections presented?

NOTES

1. Luke 14:26 "If any man come to me and hate not his father and his mother and his wife and children and brethren and sisters, yea and his own life also, he cannot be my disciple." Some interpretations of this difficult passage argue that Jesus is saying that in *comparison* to one's devotion to God, which should be absolute, other relationships should be secondary or nonabsolute.

2. Fyodor Dostoevsky, *The Brothers Karamazov,* trans. Andrew MacAndrews (New York: Bantam Books, 1970), 697.

3. Ibid., 703.

4. Friedrich Nietzsche, *Genealogy of Morals,* trans. Walter Kaufmann (New York: Random House, 1966), 208. Some may accuse Nietzsche of *nihilism,* of undermining ethics altogether, but I think that Nietzsche believed in an elitist morality where the "superior" egoists cooperated with one another in their struggle against the herd, the mediocre masses of humanity.

5. Thomas Hobbes, *Leviathan,* Chapter 13.

6. Brian Medlin, "Ultimate Principles and Ethical Egoism," *Australasian Journal of Philosophy* (1957).

7. Jesse Kalin, "In Defense of Ethical Egoism," *Philosophical Review* (1968).

8. Ayn Rand, *The Virtues of Selfishness* (New York: Signet Books, 1964), ix, 27–34, 80ff.

9. David Hume, *An Enquiry Concerning the Principles of Morals* (1751), conclusion.

10. James Rachels, *The Elements of Moral Philosophy* (New York: Random House, 1986), Chapter 6.

11. Richard Dawkins, *The Selfish Gene* (Oxford: Oxford University Press, 1976), Chapter 10.

12. J. L. Mackie, "The Law of the Jungle: Moral Alternatives and Principles of Evolution," *Philosophy* 53 (1978).

13. Laurence Thomas, "Ethical Egoism and Psychological Dispositions," *American Philosophical Quarterly* 17 (1980).

FOR FURTHER READING

Baier, Kurt. *The Moral Point of View.* Ithaca, NY: Cornell University Press, 1958. A good discussion of egoism and related issues.

Gauthier, David. *Morality by Agreement.* Oxford: Clarendon Press, 1986. The best defense in the literature of a contractualist position based on enlightened self-interest.

Pojman, Louis, ed. *Ethical Theory: Classical and Contemporary Readings,* 3d ed. Belmont, CA: Wadsworth, 1998. Contains several important readings in this area.

Rachels, James. *The Elements of Moral Philosophy.* New York: Random House, 1986. Chapters 5 and 6 are two of the best discussions of egoism in the literature.

Rand, Ayn. *The Virtues of Selfishness.* New York: Signet Books, 1964. An example of ethical egoism, wherein altruism is considered a vice.

Singer, Peter. *The Expanding Circle: Ethics and Sociobiology.* Oxford: Oxford University Press, 1983. A good discussion of egoism in the light of sociobiology.

24

Utilitarianism and
the Structure of Ethics

Recall the two thought experiments given in the introduction to this part of the book. In the first example, you are on an island with a dying millionaire, who entreats you to take his entire assets, $2 million, to the owner of the New York Yankees, so that he can buy better baseball players. You promise him that you will carry out his request. But on returning to the United States, you see an advertisement placed by a highly reputable hunger relief organization, pleading for $2 million to be used to save 100,000 people dying of starvation in East Africa. Not only will the $2 million save their lives, but it also will be used to purchase small technology and the kinds of fertilizers necessary to build a sustainable economy. You reconsider your promise to the dying Yankees' fan in the light of this information. I asked you, "What should you do with the money?"

The second example was that of two men who are starving to death on a raft. They discover some food in an inner compartment of a box on the raft and have reason to believe that the food will be sufficient to keep only one of them alive until the raft reaches a certain island where help is available; if they share the food, both of them will most likely die. One man is a brilliant scientist who has in his mind the cure for cancer. The other man is undistinguished. Otherwise, there is no relevant difference between the two men. I asked you, "What is the morally right thing to do? Share the food and hope against the odds for a miracle? Flip a coin to see which man gets the food? Give the food to the scientist?"

What is the right thing to do in these kinds of situations? Consider some traditional moral principles and see if they help you come to a decision. One principle often given to guide action is "Let your conscience be your guide." I recall this principle with fondness, for it was the one my father taught me at an early age, and it still echoes in my mind. But does it help here? No, since conscience is primarily a function of our upbringing, people's consciences will speak to them in different ways according to how they were brought up. Depending on upbringing, some people feel no qualms of conscience about committing terrorist acts, whereas others feel torments of conscience if they step on a gnat. Suppose your conscience tells you to give the money to the Yankees and my conscience tells me to give the money to the World Hunger Relief Organization. How can we ever discuss the matter? If conscience is the end of the matter, we're left mute.

Another principle urged on us is "Do whatever is most loving." St. Augustine (354–430) said, "Love God and do whatever you want." Love is surely a wonderful value, but is it enough to guide our actions where there is a conflict of interest? "Love is blind," it has been said, "but reason, like marriage, is an eye opener." Whom should I love in the case of the disbursement of the millionaire's money? The millionaire or the starving people? How do I apply the principle of love in the case of the two starving men on the raft? Should I take into consideration the needs of the two men, their families, those in need of a cure for cancer, everyone? It's not clear how love alone will settle anything. In fact, it is not obvious that we must always do what is most loving. Should we always treat our enemies in loving ways? Or is it morally acceptable to hate those who have purposefully and unjustly harmed us, our loved ones, and other innocent people? Should the survivors of Auschwitz love Adolph Hitler? We will deal with these questions later. Here we must be content to notice that love alone does not solve difficult moral issues.

A third principle often given to guide us in moral actions is the Golden Rule, "Do unto others as you would have them do unto you." This is also a noble rule of thumb, which works in simple commonsense situations, but it has problems. First of all, it cannot be taken literally. Suppose I love to hear loud rock 'n roll music. I would love you to play it loudly for me, so I reason that I should play it loudly for you—even though I know that you hate it. So the rule must be modified: "Do unto others as you would have them do unto you if you were in their shoes." But this still has problems. If I were in Sirhan Sirhan's (the assassin of Robert Kennedy) shoes, I'd want to be released from the penitentiary, but it's not clear that he should be. If I put myself in a sex-starved person's shoes, I'd want the next available person to have sex with me, but it's not obvious that I need to comply with that want. Similarly, the Golden Rule doesn't tell me to whom to give the millionaire's money or the food on the raft.

Conscience, love, the Golden Rule—all are worthy rules of thumb to help us through life. They work for most of us, most of the time, over ordinary moral situations. However, in more complicated cases, especially where there are legitimate conflicts of interests, they are limited.

A more promising strategy for solving dilemmas is that of following definite moral rules. Suppose you decide to give the millionaire's money to the Yankees in order to keep your promise or because to do otherwise would be stealing. The principle you followed would be "Always keep your promise" and/or "Thou shalt not steal" (the Eighth Commandment). Principles are important in life. All learning involves understanding a set of rules. As Oxford University philosopher R. M. Hare says,

> To learn to do anything is never to learn to do an individual act; it is always to learn to do acts of a certain kind in a certain kind of situation; and this is to learn a principle....Without principles we could not learn anything whatever from our elders.... Every generation would have to start from scratch and teach itself. But . . . self-teaching, like all other teaching, is the teaching of principles.[1]

If you decide to act on the principle of promise keeping or not stealing in the case of the millionaire's money or if you decide to share the food in the case of the two men on the raft on the basis of the principle of fairness or equal justice, then you adhere to a type of moral theory called **deontology,** or **deontological ethics.**

If, on the other hand, you decide to give the money to the World Hunger Relief Organization in order to save an enormous number of lives and restore economic solvency to the region, you side with a theory called **teleology,** or **teleological ethics.** Similarly, if you decide to give the food to the scientist because he would probably do more good with his life, you side with the teleologist.

Traditionally, two major types of ethical systems have dominated the field, one in which the locus of value is the act or kind of act and the other in which the locus of value is the outcome or consequences of the act. The former type of theory is called *deontological* (from the Greek *deon,* meaning "duty," and *logos,* meaning "logic"), and the latter is called *teleological* (from the Greek *teleos,* meaning "having reached one's end" or "finished"). Whereas teleological systems see the ultimate criterion of morality in some nonmoral value that results from acts, deontological systems see certain features in the act itself as having intrinsic value. For example, a teleologist would judge whether lying was morally right or wrong by the consequences it produced, but a deontologist would see something intrinsically wrong in the very act of lying. In this chapter we consider the dominant version of teleological ethics, utilitarianism. In Chapter 25, we'll examine Immanuel Kant's ethics as the major form of deontological ethics. By way of introduction to these theories, let me say a few words about teleological ethics.

As we mentioned earlier, a teleologist is a person whose ethical decision making aims solely at maximizing nonmoral goods such as pleasure, happiness, welfare, and the amelioration of suffering. That is, the standard of right or wrong action for the teleologist is the comparative consequences of the available actions. The act that produces the best consequences is right. Whereas the deontologist is concerned only with the rightness of the act itself, the teleologist asserts that there is no such thing as an act having intrinsic worth. Whereas for the deontologist there is something intrinsically bad about lying, for the teleologist the only thing wrong with lying is the bad consequences it produces. If you can reasonably calculate that a lie will do even slightly more good than telling the truth, you have an obligation to lie.

We have already noticed one type of teleological ethics: ethical egoism, the view that the act producing the most amount of good for the agent is the right act. Egoism is teleological ethics narrowed to the agent himself or herself. Utilitarianism, on the other hand, is a universal teleological system. It calls for the maximization of goodness in society, or the greatest goodness for the greatest number. We will turn to an examination of utilitarianism.

WHAT IS UTILITARIANISM?

The Greatest Happiness for the Greatest Number.

—FRANCIS HUTCHESON

One of the earliest examples of utilitarian reasoning is recorded in the New Testament, where Caiaphas, the High Priest, advised the Council to deliver Jesus to the Romans for execution: "You know nothing at all; you do not understand that it is expedient that one man should die for the people, and that the whole nation should not perish" (John 11:50). Sometimes Jesus himself is interpreted as adhering to utilitarianism, as when he breaks the Sabbath laws in order to do good, saying that "the Sabbath was made for man, not man for the Sabbath" (Mark 2:27).

However, as a moral philosophy, **utilitarianism** begins with the work of Scottish philosophers Francis Hutcheson (1694–1746), David Hume (1711–1776), and Adam Smith (1723–1790) and comes into its classical stage in the persons of English social reformers Jeremy Bentham (1748–1832) and John Stuart Mill (1806–1873). They were the nonreligious ancestors of the twentieth-century secular humanists, optimistic about human nature and our ability to solve our problems without recourse to providential grace. Engaged in a struggle for legal as well as moral reform, they were impatient with the rule-bound character of law and morality in eighteenth and nineteenth-century Great Britain and tried to make the law serve human needs and interests.

Bentham's concerns were mostly practical rather than theoretical. He worked for a thorough reform of what he regarded as an irrational and outmoded legal system. He might well have paraphrased Jesus, making his motto "Morality and Law were made for man, not man for Morality and Law." What good was adherence to outworn deontological rules that served no useful purpose? That kept the poor from enjoying a better life and punitive codes that only served to satisfy a sadistic lust for vengeance?

The changes the utilitarians proposed were not done in the name of justice; rather, even justice must serve the human good. The poor were to be helped, women were to be liberated, and the criminal rehabilitated if possible, not in the name of justice but because by so doing we could bring about more utility: ameliorate suffering and promote more pleasure or happiness.

Their view of punishment is a case in point. Whereas deontologists believe in retribution—that all the guilty should be punished in proportion to the gravity of their crimes—the utilitarians' motto is "Don't cry over spilt milk!" They believe that the guilty should only be punished if the punishment would serve some deterrent (or preventive) purpose. Rather than punish John in exact proportion to the heinousness of his deed, we ought to find the right punishment that will serve as the optimum deterrent.

The proper amount of punishment to be inflicted upon the offender is the amount that will do the most good (or least harm) to all those who will be affected by it. The measure of harm inflicted on John should be preferable to the harm avoided by fixing that penalty rather than one slightly lower. If punishing John will do no good (because John is not likely to commit the crime again and no one will be deterred by the punishment), John should go free.

It is the *threat* of punishment that is the important thing! Every act of punishment is to that extent an admission of the failure of the threat. If the threat were successful, there would be no punishment to justify. Of course, utilitarians believe that, given human failing, punishment is vitally necessary as a deterrent, so that the guilty will seldom if ever be allowed to go free.

There are two main features of utilitarianism: the consequentialist principle (or its teleological aspect) and the utility principle (or its hedonic aspect). The *consequentialist principle* states that the rightness or wrongness of an act is determined by the goodness or badness of the results that flow from it. It is the end, not the means, that counts; the end justifies the means. The *utility principle* states that the only thing that is good in itself is some specific type of state (e.g., pleasure, happiness, welfare). *Hedonistic utilitarianism* views pleasure as the sole good and pain as the only evil. To quote Bentham, the first one to systematize classical utilitarianism, "Nature has placed mankind under the governance of two sovereign masters, pain and pleasure. It is for them alone to point out what we ought to do, as well as what we shall do."[2] An act is right if it promotes a balance of pleasure over pain or prevents pain, and an act is wrong if it brings about more pain than pleasure or prevents pleasure from occurring.

Bentham invented a scheme for measuring pleasure and pain, which he called the *hedonic calculus.* The quantitative score for any pleasure or pain experience comes about by giving sums to seven aspects of an experience in terms of pleasure and pain. The seven aspects of a pleasurable or painful experience are its intensity, duration, certainty, nearness, fruitfulness, purity, and extent. By adding up the sums of each possible act in terms of pleasure and pain and comparing them, we would be able to decide on which act to perform. With regard to our example of deciding between giving the dying man's money to the Yankees or the starvation victims, we should add up the likely pleasures to all involved in terms of these seven qualities. Suppose we find that by giving the money to the East African famine victims we will cause at least 3 million *hedons* (i.e., units of happiness), but by giving the money to the Yankees, we will probably cause less than 1000 hedons. So we would have an obligation to give the money to the famine victims.

There is something appealing about Bentham's utilitarianism. It is simple in that there is only one principle to apply: Maximize pleasure and minimize suffering. It is commonsensical in that we think that morality really is about ameliorating suffering and promoting benevolence. It is scientific: Simply make quantitative measurements and apply the principle impartially, giving no special treatment to yourself or to anyone else because of race, gender, or religion.

However, Bentham's philosophy may be too simplistic in one way and too complicated in another. It may be too simplistic in that there are other values than pleasure, such as freedom and wisdom, and it seems too complicated in that its hedonic calculus is encumbered with too many variables and problems in attempting to give scores to the variables. What score does one give a cool drink on a hot day or a warm shower on a cool day? How do you compare a five-year-old's delight over a new toy with a fifty-year-old's delight with a new lover? Can I take your second car from you and give it to Beggar Bob who does not own a car and would enjoy it more than you? And if it's simply the overall benefits of pleasure that we are measuring, might it not turn out that if Jack or Jill would be "happier" in the Pleasure or Happiness Machine or on drugs than in the real world, then do we have an obligation to see to it that these conditions obtain? Because of these considerations, Bentham's version of utilitarianism was even in his own day referred to as the "pig philosophy" since a pig enjoying his life would constitute a higher moral state than a slightly dissatisfied Socrates.

It was to meet these sorts of objections and save utilitarianism from the charge of being a pig philosophy that Bentham's brilliant successor John Stuart Mill sought to distinguish happiness from mere sensual pleasure. His version of utilitarianism, *eudaimonistic utilitarianism* (from the Greek *eudaimonia,* meaning "happiness"), defines happiness in terms of certain types of higher-order pleasures or satisfactions such as intellectual, aesthetic, and social enjoyments, as well as in terms of minimal suffering. That is, there are two types of pleasures: the lower or elementary (e.g., eating, drinking, sexuality, resting, and sensuous titillation) and the higher (e.g., the intellectual, creative, and spiritual). Although the lower pleasures are perhaps more intensely gratifying, they also lead to pain when one overindulges in them. The spiritual or achieved pleasures tend to be more protracted, continuous, and gradual.

Mill argues that the higher or more refined pleasures are superior to the lower ones. "A being of higher faculties requires more to make him happy, is capable probably of more acute suffering, and certainly accessible to it at more points, than one of an inferior type," but still he is qualitatively better off than the person without these higher faculties. "It is better to be a human being dissatisfied than a pig satisfied; better to be Socrates dissatisfied than a fool satisfied."[3]

Humans are the kind of creatures who require more to be truly happy. We want the lower pleasures but also deep friendship, intellectual ability, culture, ability to create and appreciate art, knowledge, and wisdom. But, one may object, how do we know that it really is better to have these higher pleasures? Here Mill imagines a panel of experts and says that of those who have had wide experience of pleasures of both kinds almost all give a decided preference to the higher type. Since Mill was an empiricist, one who believed all knowledge and justified belief was based in our experience, he had no recourse but to rely on the composite consensus of human history. People who experience both rock music and classical music will, if they appreciate both, prefer Bach and Beethoven to the Rolling Stones or Dancing Demons. We generally move up from appreciating simple things (e.g., nursery rhymes to more complex poetry rather than the other way around).

Mill has been criticized for not giving a better reply, for being an elitist and unduly favoring the intellectual over the sensual. But he has a point. Don't we generally agree, if we have experienced both the lower and the higher types of pleasure, that while a full life would include both, a life with only the former is inadequate for human beings? Isn't it better to be Socrates dissatisfied than the pig satisfied? And better still to be Socrates satisfied?

The point is not merely that humans would not be satisfied with what satisfies a pig but that somehow the quality of these pleasures is *better.* But what does it mean to speak of better pleasure? Is Mill unwittingly assuming some nonhedonic notion of intrinsic value to make this distinction? That is, knowledge, intelligence, freedom, friendship, love, health, and so forth are good things in their own right. Or is Mill simply saying that the lives of humans are generally such that we can predict that they will be happier with the more developed, refined, spiritual values? Which thesis would you be inclined to defend?

THE STRENGTHS AND WEAKNESSES
OF UTILITARIANISM

The Strong Features Utilitarianism has two very positive features. The first attraction or strength is that it is a system with a single absolute principle, with a potential answer for every situation. Do what will promote the most utility! It's good to have a simple action-guiding principle, applicable for every occasion— even if it may be difficult to apply (life is not simple). The second strength is that utilitarianism seems to get to the substance of morality. It is not merely a *formal system,* offering only formal principles (i.e., broad guidelines for choosing substantive principles, such as the Golden Rule, the rule to "Let your conscience be your guide," or "Never do what you cannot will to make a universal law"), but has a *material* core: promoting human (and possibly animal) happiness and ameliorating suffering. The first virtue gives one a clear decision procedure in arriving at our answer about what to do. The second virtue appeals to our sense that morality is made for humans (and other animals?) and that morality is not so much about rules as about helping people and alleviating the suffering in the world.

This seems commonsensical. Utilitarianism gives us clear and reasonable guidance in everyday matters. We should try to make our colleges, our towns, our families, as well as our nation and world, better places than they are. We should help people, ameliorate their suffering whenever it does not cost us unduly. In the case of deciding what to do with the $2 million of the dead millionaire, something in us says that it is absurd to keep a promise to a dead man when it means allowing hundreds of thousands of famine victims to die (how would we like it if we were in their shoes?). Far more good can be accomplished by helping the needy than by giving the money to the Yankees!

The Weak Features However, utilitarianism has problems that need to be addressed before one can give it a clean bill of health.

Problem 1: How Can We Know the Consequences of Actions? Sometimes utilitarians are accused of playing God. They seem to hold to an ethical theory that demands godlike powers, that is, knowledge of the future. Of course, we normally do not know the long-term consequences of our actions, for life is too complex and the consequences go on into the indefinite future. One action causes one state of affairs that, in turn, causes another state of affairs indefinitely, so that calculation becomes impossible. Recall the nursery rhyme:

> For want of a nail, the shoe was lost;
> For want of a shoe, the horse was lost;
> For want of a horse, the rider was lost;
> For want of a rider, the battle was lost;
> For want of a battle, the kingdom was lost;
> And all for the want of a horseshoe nail.

Poor, unfortunate blacksmith! What utilitarian guilt he must bear all the rest of his days.

But it is ridiculous to blame the loss of one's kingdom on the poor unsuccessful blacksmith, and utilitarians are not so foolish as to hold him responsible for the bad situation. Instead, following C. I. Lewis, they distinguish three different kinds of consequences: actual consequences of an act, consequences that could reasonably have been expected to occur, and intended consequences.[4] An act is *absolutely* right if it has the best actual consequences. An act is *objectively* right if it is reasonable to expect that it will have the best consequences. An act is *subjectively* right if its agent intends or actually expects it to have the best consequences. It is the second kind of rightness (*objective rightness*), based on reasonable expectations, that is central here, for only the subsequent observer of the consequences is in a position to determine the actual results. The most that the agent can do is use the best information available and do what a reasonable person would expect to have the best overall results. Suppose, for example, that while Stalin's aunt was carrying little baby Josef up the stairs to her home, she slipped and had to choose between dropping infant Josef, allowing him to be fatally injured, or breaking her arm. According to the formula just given, it would have been absolutely right for her to let him be killed, but it would not have been within her power to know that. She did what any reasonable person would do—save the baby's life at the risk of some injury to herself. She did what was objectively right. The utilitarian theory is that, generally, by doing what reason judges to be the best act based on likely consequences, we will, in general, actually promote the best consequences.

Problem 2: The No-Rest Objection. According to utilitarianism, one should always do the act that promises to promote the most utility. But there are usually an indefinite set of possible acts from which to choose, and even if I can be excused from considering all of them, I can be fairly sure that there is often a preferable act that I could be doing. For example, when I am about to go to the movies with a friend, I should ask myself if helping the homeless in my community wouldn't promote more utility. When I am about to go to sleep, I should ask myself whether I could at this moment be doing something to help save the ozone layer. And why not simply give all my assets (beyond what is absolutely necessary to keep me alive) to the poor in order to promote utility? How would a sophisticated utilitarian respond to this criticism?

Problem 3: The Absurd Implications Objection. W. D. Ross argued that utilitarianism is to be rejected because it is counterintuitive. If we accepted it, we would have to accept an absurd implication. Consider two acts, A and B, that will both result in 100 hedons (units of pleasure of utility). The only difference is that A involves telling a lie and B involves telling the truth. The utilitarian must maintain that the two acts are of equal value, but this seems counterintuitive, at least, at first glance. Most of us think that truth telling is an intrinsically good thing. Who is right here?

Similarly, in Arthur Koestler's *Darkness at Noon,* Rubashov writes of the Communist philosophy in the Soviet Republic:

> History has taught us that often lies serve her better than the truth; for man is sluggish and has to be led through the desert for forty years before each step in his development. And he has to be driven through the desert with threats and promises, by imaginary terrors and imaginary consolations, so that he should not sit down prematurely to rest and divert himself by worshipping golden calves. [5]

According to this interpretation, orthodox Soviet Communism justifies its lies and atrocities by utilitarian ideas. Something in us revolts at this kind of value system. Truth is sacred and must not be sacrificed on the altar of expediency.

Problem 4: The Justice Objection. Suppose that in a racially volatile community a rape and murder is committed. You are the sheriff who has spent a lifetime working for racial harmony. Now, just when your goal is about to be realized, this incident occurs. The crime is thought to be racially motivated, and a riot is about to break out, which will very likely result in the death of several people and create long-lasting racial antagonism. You are able to frame a derelict for the crime, so that a trial will show that he is guilty. He will then be executed. There is every reason to believe that a speedy trial and execution will head off the riot and save the community. Only you (and the real criminal, who will keep quiet about it) will know that an innocent man has been tried and executed. What is the morally right thing to do? The utilitarian seems committed to framing the derelict, but many would find this appalling.

Or consider this hypothetical situation. You are a utilitarian physician who has five patients under your care. One needs to have a heart transplant, one needs two lungs, one needs a liver, and the last two need kidneys. Now into your office comes a healthy bachelor needing a flu shot. You judge him to be a perfect sacrifice for your five patients. Doing a utility calculus, there is no doubt in your mind that you could do more good by injecting the healthy man with a sleep-inducing drug and using his organs to save your five patients.[6]

This cavalier view of justice offends us. The very fact that utilitarians even countenance such actions, that they would misuse the legal system or the medical system to carry out their schemes, seems frightening. It reminds us of the medieval Roman Catholic bishop's justification for heresy hunts, inquisitions, and religious wars:

> When the existence of the Church is threatened, she is released from the commandments of morality. With unity as the end, the use of every means is sanctified, even cunning, treachery, violence, simony, prison, death. For all order is for the sake of the community, and the individual must be sacrificed to the common good.[7]

UTILITARIAN RESPONSES
TO THE STANDARD OBJECTIONS

These objections are weighty and too complicated to attempt to refute here, but we can allow the utilitarian to make an initial defense. What sorts of responses are open to utilitarians? Well, it seems to be that a sophisticated version of utilitarianism can offset at least some of the force of these criticisms. He or she can use the *multilevel strategy*, which goes like this. We must split considerations of utility into two levels, the lower level dealing with a set of rules that we judge to be most likely to bring about the best consequences most of the time. We'll call this the *rule-utility* feature of utilitarianism. Normally, we have to live by the best rules our system can devise, and rules of honesty, promise keeping, and justice will be among them.

But sometimes the rules conflict or clearly will not yield the best consequences. In these infrequent cases, we will need to suspend or override the rule in favor of the better consequences. We call this the *act-utility* feature of utilitarianism. It constitutes the second level of consideration and is referred to only when there is dissatisfaction with the rule–utility feature. An example of this might be the rule against breaking a promise. Normally, the most utility will occur through keeping one's promises, but consider this situation: I have promised to meet you at the movies tonight at seven o'clock. Unbeknown to you, on the way to our rendezvous I come across an accident and am able to render great service to the injured parties. Unfortunately, I cannot contact you, and you are inconvenienced as you wait patiently in front of the theater for an hour. I have broken a utility rule in order to maximize utility and am justified in so doing.

Here is another example set forth by Judith Jarvis Thomson. You are a trolley car driver who sees five workers on the track before you. You suddenly realize that the brakes have failed. Fortunately, the track has a spur leading off to the right, and you can turn the trolley onto it. Unfortunately, there is one person on the right-hand track. You can turn the trolley to the right, killing one person, or you can refrain from turning the trolley, in which case five people will die.[8] Under traditional views, a distinction exists between killing and letting die, between actively killing and passively allowing death, but the utilitarian rejects this distinction. You should turn the trolley, causing the lesser evil, for the only relevant issue is expected utility. So the normal rule against actively causing an innocent to die is suspended in favor of the utility principle.

This is the kind of defense the sophisticated utilitarian is likely to lodge against all of the preceding criticisms. The utilitarian responds to Problem 2, the no-rest objection, by insisting that a rule prescribing rest and entertainment is actually the kind of rule that would have a place in a utility-maximizing set of rules. The agent should aim at maximizing his or her own happiness as well as other people's happiness. For the same reason, it is best not to worry overly much about the needs of those not in one's primary circle. Although one should be concerned about the needs of future and distant people, it actually would promote disutility for the average person to become preoccupied with these concerns. But, the utilitarian would remind us, we can surely do a lot more for suffering humanity than we now are doing.

With regard to Problem 3, Ross's absurd implications objection, the utilitarian can agree that there is something counterintuitive in the calculus of equating an act with a lie with one with honesty; but, he argues, we must be ready to change our culture-induced moral biases. What is so important about truth telling or so bad about lying? If it turned out that lying really promoted human welfare, we'd have to accept it. But that's not likely. Our happiness is tied up with a need for reliable information (i.e., truth) on how to achieve our ends. So truthfulness will be a member of the rule–utility set. But where lying will clearly promote utility without undermining the general adherence to the rule, we simply ought to lie. Don't we already accept lying to a gangster or telling "white" lies to spare people's feelings?

With regard to Rubashov's utilitarian defense of Communism and its inhumanity or the medieval defense of the Inquisition, the utilitarian replies that this abuse of utilitarianism only illustrates how dangerous the doctrine can be in the hands of self-serving bureaucrats. Any theory can be misused in this way.

We turn to the most difficult objection, the claim that utilitarianism permits injustice, as seen in the example of the sheriff framing the innocent derelict. The utilitarian counters that justice is not an absolute—mercy, benevolence, and the good of the whole society sometimes should override it; but, the sophisticated utilitarian insists, it makes good utilitarian sense to have a principle of justice that is generally obeyed. It is not clear what the sheriff should do in the racially torn community. More needs to be said, but if we could be certain that it would not start a precedent of sacrificing innocent people, it may be right to sacrifice one person for the good of the whole. Wouldn't we all agree, the utilitarian continues, it is sometimes the case to harm an innocent person in order to prevent great evil. The trolley car case is one example. Here is another.

Virtually all standard moral systems have a rule against torturing innocent people. But suppose a maniac is about to set off a nuclear bomb that will destroy New York City. He is scheduled to detonate the bomb in one hour. His psychiatrist knows the lunatic well and tells us that there is only one way to stop him: Torture his ten-year-old daughter and show it on television. Suppose, for the sake of the argument, there is no way to simulate the torture. Would you not consider torturing the child in this situation? (Just in case you don't think New York City is worth saving, imagine that the lunatic has a lethal gas that will spread throughout the globe and wipe out *all* life within a few weeks.)

Is it not right to sacrifice one innocent person to stop a war or save the human race from destruction? We seem to proceed on this assumption in wartime, in every bombing raid, especially in the dropping of atomic bombs on Hiroshima and Nagasaki. We seem to be following this rule in our decision to drive automobiles and trucks even though we are fairly certain that the practice will result in the death of thousands of innocent people each year.

On the other hand, the sophisticated utilitarian may argue that in the case of the sheriff framing the innocent derelict, justice should not be overridden by current utility concerns, for human rights themselves are outcomes of utility consideration and should not lightly be violated. That is, because we tend to subconsciously favor our own interests and biases, we institute the principle of rights to protect ourselves and others from capricious and biased acts that would in the long run have great disutility. Thus, we must not undermine institutional rights too easily—we should not kill the bachelor in order to provide a heart, two lungs, a liver, and two kidneys to the five patients—at least not at this present time, given people's expectations of what will happen to them when they enter hospitals. But neither should we worship rights! They are to be taken seriously but not given ultimate authority. The utilitarian cannot foreclose the possibility of sacrificing innocent people for the greater good of humanity. If slavery could be humane and resulted in great overall utility, utilitarians would accept it.

We see then that sophisticated, multileveled utilitarianism has responses to all the criticisms leveled on it. For most people most of the time, the ordinary moral principles should be followed, for they actually maximize utility in the long run. But we should not be tied down to this rule. To paraphrase Jesus, "Morality was made for man, not man for morality." The purpose of morality is to promote flourishing and ameliorate suffering, and where these can be done by sacrificing a rule, we should do them. Whether this is an adequate defense, I leave for you to decide.

SUMMARY

We have examined Bentham's and Mill's versions of utilitarianism and have found Mill's version stronger. Utilitarianism has the virtue of focusing on some of the essential purposes of morality, but several questions must be answered regarding it: How can we know the consequences of actions? Can we ever be at rest if we are always to maximize utility? Does it not lead us to absurd consequences? Does it even promote injustice? We saw how utilitarians respond to each of these objections and left the final decision up to you.

QUESTIONS FOR DISCUSSION

1. Consider Bentham's and Mill's versions of utilitarianism. Evaluate the strengths and weaknesses of each. Then evaluate the main criticism of utilitarianism.

2. One criticism of utilitarianism is that it fails to protect people's rights. Consider five excitable sadists getting a total of 100 hedons while torturing an innocent victim who is suffering 10 dolors (units of pain). On a utilitarian calculus, this would result in a total of 90 hedons. If no other act would result in as many or more hedons, the utilitarian would have to endorse this act and argue that the victim has a duty to submit to the torture and that the sadists have a duty to torture the victim. What do you think of this sort of reasoning? How much does it count against utilitarianism?

3. Consider the case, discussed in the text, of the doctor needing organs for five needy patients, all of whom are in danger of dying unless you get suitable organs within the day. One needs a heart transplant, two need kidneys, one needs lungs, and another needs a liver. A homeless man who has no family walks into the hospital for minor emergency care (he cut his finger). By killing him and using his organs for the five, you could save five persons, restoring them to health. If you don't kill the man, are you negatively responsible for the death of the five patients? Explain your answer.

4. Rawls's false-analogy argument: John Rawls argues that utilitarianism errs in applying to society the principle of personal choice. That is, we all would agree that an individual has a right to forgo a present pleasure for a future good. I have a right to go without a new suit so that I can save the money for my college education or so that I can give it to my favorite charity. Utilitarianism, however, prescribes that we demand that you forgo a new suit for someone else's college education or for the overall good of the community—whether or not you like it or agree to it. That is, it takes the futuristic notion of agent-utility maximization and extends it to cover society in a way that violates the individual's rights. Is this a fair criticism?

5. Earlier in the chapter, we quoted Francis Hutcheson: "The Greatest Happiness to the Greatest Number." Do you find anything puzzling about this motto? Notice that it has two superlatives and that sometimes two superlatives can conflict with each other. Suppose I tell you that I am going to give a $1000 prize to the person who runs the farthest distance in the least amount of time. Three people sign up and run. Here are the results:

Runner	Distance	Time
John	7 miles	50 minutes
Joe	5 miles	31 minutes
Jack	1 mile	6 minutes

Who should get the prize? Can you see how this could become a problem for utilitarian calculus? How does the utilitarian go about deciding how to distribute goods to different groups of people?

6. Suppose we have a situation involving three social policies that will divide welfare between three equal groups of people. In policy I, group A will receive 75 units; group B, 45 units; and group C, 25 units of welfare—for a total of 145 units. In policy II, A will receive 50 units, and B and C will receive 45 units each—for a total of 140 units. In policy III, A will receive 100 units, and B and C will receive 25 each—for a total of 150 units (see the accompanying figure). Suppose it is agreed that 30 units are necessary for a minimally acceptable social existence. Which policy should the utilitarian choose?

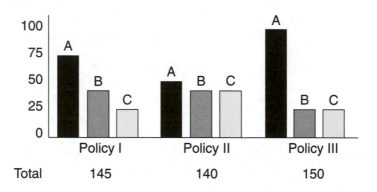

NOTES

1. R. M. Hare, *Language of Morals* (Oxford: Oxford University Press, 1952), 60.

2. Jeremy Bentham, *An Introduction to the Principles of Morals and Legislation* (1789), Chapter 1.

3. John Stuart Mill, *Utilitarianism* (1863), Chapter 2.

4. See Anthony Quinton, *Utilitarian Ethics* (listed in "For Further Reading"), 49f., for a good discussion of this and other similar points. My discussion is indebted to Quinton.

5. Arthur Koestler, *Darkness at Noon* (New York: Macmillan, 1941), 80.

6. This example and the trolley car example are found in Judith Jarvis Thomson's "The Trolley Problem," in her *Rights, Restitution and Risk* (Cambridge, MA: Harvard University Press, 1986), 94–116.

7. Dietrich von Nieheim, Bishop of Verden, *De Schismate Librii,* iii, ad 1411, quoted in Koestler, op. cit., 76.

8. Thomson, op. cit.

FOR FURTHER READING

On Ethical Theory

Becker, Lawrence, and Charlotte Becker, eds. *A History of Western Ethics.* New York: Garland, 1992. A collection of essays offering a succinct history of the subject.

Brandt, Richard. *Ethical Theory.* Englewood Cliffs, NJ: Prentice-Hall, 1959. Although a little old, this is still one of the best discussions of ethical theory available.

Harris, C. E. *Applying Moral Theories,* 2d ed. Belmont, CA: Wadsworth, 1992. Accessible, well-balanced, and well-argued on the subject of ethical theories.

Pojman, Louis, ed. *Ethical Theory: Classical and Contemporary Readings,* 3d ed. Belmont, CA: Wadsworth, 1998. Several important essays on ethical theory are included.

Sterba, James. *How to Make People Just.* Totowa, NJ: Rowman and Littlefield, 1988. A brilliant attempt to reconcile various moral theories.

Sterba, James, ed. *Contemporary Ethics: Selected Readings.* Englewood Cliffs, NJ: Prentice-Hall, 1989. A good selection of contemporary work in ethical theory.

On Utilitarianism

Bentham, Jeremy. *Introduction to the Principles of Morals and Legislation,* ed. W. Harrison. Oxford: Oxford University Press, 1948. A classic work. Part of it is reprinted in Pojman (see below).

Brandt, Richard. "In Search of a Credible Form of Rule-Utilitarianism." In *Morality and the Language of Conduct,* ed.

H. N. Castaneda and George Nakhnikian. Detroit: Wayne State University Press, 1953. This often anthologized article is one of the most sophisticated defenses of utilitarianism.

Brock, Dan. "Recent Work in Utilitarianism." *American Philosophical Quarterly* 10 (1973). A good survey of the literature.

Hare, R. M. *Moral Thinking: Its Levels, Method and Point.* Oxford: Oxford University Press, 1981. Provides an extended development of a multilevel utilitarianism.

Mill, John Stuart. *Utilitarianism.* Indianapolis: Bobbs-Merrill, 1957. A classic.

Parfit, Derik. *Reasons and Persons.* Oxford: Oxford University Press, 1984. Somewhat advanced but worth the effort.

Pojman, Louis, ed. *Ethical Theory: Classical and Contemporary Readings,* 3d ed. Belmont, CA: Wadsworth, 1998. Contains classic and contemporary readings on utilitarianism.

Quinton, Anthony. *Utilitarian Ethics.* London: Macmillan, 1973. A clear exposition of classical utilitarianism.

Smart, J. J. C., and Bernard Williams. *Utilitarianism For and Against.* Cambridge, Eng.: Cambridge University Press, 1973. A sharp and insightful debate on the subject.

Taylor, Paul. *Principles of Ethics.* Encino, CA: Dickenson, 1975. Contains a good chapter on utilitarianism.

25

Kantian Deontological Ethics

Hour by hour resolve to do the task of the hour carefully, with unaffected
dignity, affectionately, freely and justly. You can avoid distraction that might
interfere with such performance if every act is done as though it were the last act
of your life. Free yourself from random aims and curb any tendency to let the passions
of emotion, hypocrisy, self-love and dissatisfaction with your allotted
share cause you to ignore the commands of reasons.

—MARCUS AURELIUS (A.D. 121–180)

Act only on that maxim whereby thou canst at the same time will
that it would become a universal law.

—IMMANUEL KANT

What makes a right act right? The teleological answer to this question is
that it is the good consequences that make it right. Moral rightness and
wrongness are determined by nonmoral values (e.g., happiness or utility). To this extent, the end justifies the means. The deontological answer to this
question is quite the opposite. The end *never* justifies the means. Indeed, you must
do your duty whatever the consequences, simply because it is your duty. As the
quotation from the stoic emperor Marcus Aurelius indicates, you must do your
duty disinterestedly, as though it was the last act of your life, simply because it is
your duty. Similarly, the Danish philosopher Søren Kierkegaard (1813–1855)
described his childhood experience of sensing his duty to learn his first-grade
grammar lesson thusly: "It was as if heaven and earth might collapse if I did not
learn my lesson, and on the other hand as if, even if heaven and earth were to collapse, this would not exempt me from doing what was assigned to me."[1]

It is not the consequences that determine the rightness or wrongness of an act but certain features in the act itself. For example, there is something right about truth telling and promise keeping even when acting thusly may bring about some harm, and there is something wrong about lying and promise breaking even when acting thusly may bring about good consequences. Acting unjustly is wrong even if it will maximize expected utility. Referring to our examples in the introduction to this part of the book, as a deontologist you would very likely keep your promise and give the $2 million to the Yankees and share or flip a coin for the food on the raft.

IMMANUEL KANT'S
RATIONALIST DEONTOLOGICAL SYSTEM

Immanuel Kant (1724–1804), the greatest philosopher of the German Enlightenment and one of the most important philosophers of all time, was both an *absolutist* and a *deontological rationalist*. He believed that we could use reason to work out an absolute (i.e., nonoverridable) consistent set of moral principles.

To understand Kant's moral philosophy, it is helpful to understand a little about his life. Kant was born in Königsberg, Germany, in 1724 and died there in 1804, never having left the surroundings of the city. His father was a saddle maker. His parents were Pietists in the Lutheran church. The Pietists were a sect in the church, much like present-day Quakers, who emphasized sincerity, deep feeling, and the moral life rather than theological doctrine or orthodox belief. Pietism is a religion of the heart, not the head, of the spirit rather than ritual. However, Kant, as an intellectual, emphasized the head as much as the heart, but it was a head that was concerned about the moral life, especially goodwill.

Kant, a short quiet man, was so methodical that tradition has it that the citizens of Königsberg set their watches by his daily three o'clock walks. He never married but devoted his life to the study and teaching of philosophy at the University of Königsberg. His magnum opus, *The Critique of Pure Reason* (1781), was heralded in his own day as a monumental work, and his *The Fundamental Principles of the Metaphysic of Morals* (1785) is generally regarded as one of the two or three most important books in the history of ethics.

There were three strong influences on Kant's ethical thinking. The first is Pietism, already mentioned, which set a tone of deep sincerity to his views. It is not correct beliefs or results that really matter but inner goodness. The idea is that if we live within our lights we will be given more light and that God judges us not on how lucky or successful we are in accomplishing our tasks but on how earnestly we have lived according to our principles. It is this influence that informs his notion of the goodwill as the sole intrinsic good in life.

The second influence was the work of Jean Jacques Rousseau (1712–1778) on human freedom, especially his *Social Contract,* and it was said that the only time Kant ever missed his three o'clock walk was the day on which he read that tome. Rousseau taught him the meaning and importance of human dignity, the primacy of freedom and autonomy, and that human beings had intrinsic worth apart from any functions they might perform.

Finally, Kant was influenced by the debate between rationalism and empiricism, which took place in the seventeenth and eighteenth centuries. Rationalists, such as René Descartes, Baruch Spinoza, Gottfried Leibniz, and Christian Wolff, claimed that pure reason could tell us how the world is, independent of experience. We can know metaphysical truth such as the existence of God, the immortality of the soul, freedom of the will, and the universality of causal relations apart from experience (experience may be necessary to open our minds to these ideas, but essentially they are innate ideas, synthetic a priori truths). Empiricists, led by John Locke and David Hume, on the other hand, denied that we had any innate ideas and argued that all knowledge came from experience. Our minds were a *tabula rasa,* an empty slate, upon which experience wrote her lessons.

The rationalists and empiricists carried their debate into the area of moral knowledge. The rationalists claimed that our knowledge of moral principles was a type of metaphysical knowledge, implanted in us by God, and discoverable by reason as it deduces general principles about human nature. The Scottish empiricists, especially Francis Hutcheson, David Hume, and Adam Smith, on the other hand, argued that morality is founded entirely on the contingencies of human nature and based on desire. Morality has to do with making people happy, fulfilling their reflected desires, and reason is just a practical means of helping us obtain our desires. There is nothing of special importance in reason in its own right. It is mainly a rationalizer and servant of the passions ("a pimp of the passions"). As Hume said, "Reason is and ought only to be a slave of the passions and can never pretend to any other office than to serve and obey them." Morality is founded on our feeling of sympathy with other people's sufferings, on fellow feeling. For such empiricists then, morality is contingent upon human nature:

Human Nature ⟶ Feelings and Desires ⟶ Moral Principles

If we had a different nature, we would have different feelings and desires, and hence we would have different moral principles.

Kant rejected the ideas of Hutcheson, Hume, and Smith. He was outraged by the thought that morality should depend on human nature and be subject to the fortunes of change and the luck of empirical discovery. Morality is not contingent but necessary. It would be no less binding on us if our feelings were different than they are:

> Every empirical element is not only quite incapable of being an aid to the principle of morality, but is even highly prejudicial to the purity of morals; for the proper and inestimable worth of an absolutely good will consists just in this, that the principle of action is free from all influence of contingent grounds, which alone experience can furnish. We cannot too much or too often repeat our warning against this lax and even mean habit of thought which seeks for its principle amongst empirical motives and laws; for human reason in its weariness is glad to rest on this pillow, and in a dream of sweet illusions it substitutes for morality a bastard patched up from limbs of various derivation, which looks like anything one chooses to see in it; only not like virtue to one who has once beheld her in her true form.[2]

No, said Kant, it is not our desires that ground morality but our rational will. Reason is sufficient for establishing the moral law as something transcendent and universally binding on all rational creatures.

THE GOODWILL

The only thing that is intrinsically good, good in itself and without qualification, is the goodwill. All other virtues, both intellectual and moral, can serve the vicious will and thus contribute to evil. None of these are good in themselves but good only for a further purpose. They can be united in themselves but only for further purposes. They are only valuable if accompanied by goodwill. Even success and happiness are not good in themselves. Honor can lead to pride. Happiness without goodwill is not worthwhile. Is honor with deceit worth attaining? No. Nor is utilitarianism plausible, for if we have a quantity of happiness to distribute, is it just to distribute it equally regardless of virtue? Should we not distribute it discriminately, according to moral goodness? Happiness should be distributed in proportion to one's moral worth, and happiness without moral worth is not inherently valuable.

How good is Kant's argument for the goodwill? Could we imagine a world where nonmoral virtues were always and necessarily put to good use, where it was simply impossible to use a virtue like intelligence for evil? Is happiness any less good simply because it can be distributed incorrectly? Can't the goodwill itself be put to bad use, as with the misguided do-gooder? As the aphorism goes, "The road to hell is paved with good intentions." Could Adolf Hitler have had good intentions in carrying out his dastardly programs? Can't the goodwill have bad effects?

We may agree that the goodwill is a great good, but it is not obvious on Kant's account that it is the *only* inherently good thing, for even as intelligence, courage, and happiness can be put to bad uses, so can the goodwill; and even as it does not seem to count against the goodwill that it can be put to a bad use, so it shouldn't count against the other virtues that they can be put to bad uses. The goodwill may be a necessary element to any morally good action, but it's another question whether it is also a *sufficient* condition to moral goodness.

But perhaps we can reinterpret Kant in such a way as to preserve his central insight. There does seem to be something morally valuable about the goodwill apart from any consequences. Consider this illustration. Two soldiers volunteer to cross the enemy lines to make contact with their allies on the other side. They both start off and do their best to make their way through the enemy's area. One succeeds, but the other doesn't and is captured. But aren't they both morally praiseworthy? The success of one in no way detracts from the goodness of the other. Judged from a commonsense moral point of view, their actions are equally good; judged from a utilitarian or consequentialist view, the successful act is far more valuable than the unsuccessful one. Here one can distinguish the agent's worth from the value of the consequences and make two separate, nonconflicting judgments.

DUTY AND THE MORAL LAW

As we noted earlier, Kant wants to remove moral truth from the zone of contingency and empirical observation and place it securely in the area of **necessary truth,** that is, truth that is absolute and universal. Morality's value is not based on the fact that it has instrumental value, that it often secures nonmoral goods such as happiness, but it is valuable in its own right:

Even if it should happen that, owing to special disfavour of fortune, or the niggardly provision of a step-motherly nature, this [Good] will should wholly lack power to accomplish its purpose, if with its greatest efforts it should yet achieve nothing, and there should remain only the goodwill . . . then, like a jewel, it would still shine by its own light, as a thing which has its whole value in itself. Its usefulness or fruitfulness can neither add to nor take away anything from this value.[3]

All mention of duties (or obligations) can be translated into the language of imperatives or commands. As such, moral duties can be said to have imperative force. Kant distinguishes two kinds of imperatives: hypothetical and categorical. The formula for a hypothetical injunction is

If you want to A, then do B.

Two examples are "If you want to get a good job, get a good education," and "If you want to be happy, stay sober and live a balanced life." The formula for a categorical injunction is simply

Do B!

That is, do what reason discloses to be the intrinsically right thing to do; for example, "Tell the truth!" **Hypothetical imperatives,** or means-ends, are not the kind of imperatives that characterize moral actions. Categorical or unqualified imperatives are the right kind of imperatives, for they show proper recognition of the imperial status of moral obligations. This imperative is an intuitive, immediate, and absolute injunction that all rational agents understand by virtue of their rationality.

Moral duty must be done solely for its own sake ("duty for duty's sake"). Some people conform to the moral law because they deem it in their own enlightened self-interest to be moral, but they are not moral because they do not act for the sake of the moral law. For example, a businessman may believe that "honesty is the best policy." That is, he may judge that it is conducive to good business to give his customers correct change and good-quality products; but unless he does these acts *because* they are his duty, he is not acting morally, even though his acts are the same ones that they would be if he were acting morally.

The kind of imperative that fits Kant's scheme as a product of reason is one that universalizes principles of conduct. He names it the **categorical imperative:** "Act only on that maxim whereby thou canst at the same time will that it would become a universal law." This is given as the criterion (or second-order principle) by which to judge all other principles.

By *maxim,* Kant means the general rule in accordance with which the agent intends to act; by *law,* he means an objective principle, a maxim that passes the test of universalization. The categorical imperative is the way to apply the universalization test. It helps us stand outside our personal maxims and impartially and impersonally estimate whether they are suitable as principles for all of us to live by. If you could consistently will that everyone would do some type of action, then there is an application of the categorical imperative enjoining that type of action. If you cannot consistently will that everyone would do some type of action, then that type of action is morally wrong. The maxim must be rejected as self-defeated. The formula looks like this:

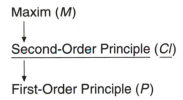

To take one of Kant's examples, suppose I need some money and consider whether it would be moral to borrow the money from you and promise to repay it without intending ever to do so.

M: Whenever I need money, I should make a lying promise while borrowing the money.

Can I universalize the maxim of my act?

P: Whenever anyone needs money, that person should make a lying promise while borrowing the money.

But something has gone wrong, for if I universalize this principle of making promises without intending to keep them, I would be involved in a contradiction. The resulting state of affairs would be self-defeating, for no one in his right mind would take promises as promises unless there was the expectation of fulfillment. So the maxim of the lying promise fails the **universalizability** criterion. Hence, it is immoral. Now I universalize the opposite:

M_1: Whenever I need money, I should make a sincere promise while borrowing it.

Can I universalize this maxim?

P_1: Whenever anyone needs money, he or she should make a sincere promise while borrowing it.

Yes, I can universalize M_1, for there is nothing self-defeating or contradictory in this. So, it follows, making sincere promises is moral. We can make the maxim of promise keeping into a universal law.

Some of Kant's illustrations do not fare as well as the duty to promise keeping. For instance, he argues that the categorical imperative would prohibit suicide, for the principle

P: Whenever it looks like one will experience more pain than pleasure, one ought to kill oneself.

is, according to Kant, a self-contradiction in that it would go against the very *principle of survival* on which it is based. However, whatever the merit of the form of this argument, we could modify the principle to read

P_1: Whenever the pain or suffering of existence erodes the quality of life in such a way as to make nonexistence a preference to suffering existence, one is permitted to commit suicide.

Why couldn't this (or something close to it) be universalized? It would not oppose the general principle of survival itself but cover rare instances where no hope is in sight for terminally ill patients and victims of torture or deep depression. It would not cover the normal kinds of suffering and depression that most of us experience in the normal course of life. Kant seems unduly absolutist in his prohibition of suicide.

Kant's other two examples of the application of the categorical imperative are also questionable. In his third example, he claims that we cannot universalize a maxim to refrain from developing our talents. But again, could we not qualify this and stipulate that under certain circumstances it was permissible not to develop our talents? Perhaps, Kant is correct: If everyone refrained from developing any talent, society would soon degenerate into anarchy. But couldn't one universalize the following maxim?

M_2: Whenever I am not inclined to develop a talent and this refraining will not seriously undermine the social order, I may so refrain.

Kant's fourth example of the way the categorical imperative functions regards the situation of not coming to the aid of others whenever I am secure and independent. He claims that I cannot universalize this maxim because I never know whether I will need the help of others in some future time. It seems that Kant is wrong again. I could universalize that people who are completely independent never help those who are less well off just as long as their own independence is not threatened by the less well-off. Perhaps it would be selfish and cruel to make this into a universal law, but I don't see anything contradictory or self-defeating in the principle itself. The problems with universalizing selfishness are the same ones that we encountered in analyzing egoism, but it's dubious whether Kant's categorical imperative captures what is wrong with egoism. Perhaps he has other weapons that do capture what is wrong with egoism. We will return to this later.

Kant thought that he could generate an entire moral law from his categorical imperative. It seems to work with such principles as promise keeping and truth telling and a few other maxims, but it doesn't seem to give us all that Kant wanted. It has been objected that Kant's categorical imperative is both *too wide* and *too unqualified,* leading to horrendous possibilities.

The charge that it is too wide is based on the perception that it seems to justify some actions that we would think to be trivial and even immoral. Consider, for example, principle *P:*

P: Everyone should always tie one's right shoe before one's left shoe.

Can we universalize *P* without contradiction? Why not? Just as we universalize that people should drive cars on the right side of the street rather than the left, we could make it a law that everyone would tie the right shoe before the left shoe. It seems obvious that there would be no point to such a law; it would be trivial. It is justified, however, by the categorical imperative.

It may be objected that all this counterexample shows is that it may be permissible to live by the principle of tying the right shoe before the left, for we could also universalize the opposite maxim (tying the left before the right) without contradiction. That seems correct.

A more serious objection is the charge that the categorical imperative seems to justify acts that we judge to be horrendously immoral. Consider P_1:

P_1: Always kill blue-eyed children.

Is there anything contradictory in this injunction? Could we make it into a universal law? Why not? Blue-eyed children might not like it (and might even be required to cooperate or commit suicide), but there is no logical contradiction involved in such a principle. Had I been a blue-eyed child when this command was in effect, I would not be around to write this book, but the world would have survived my loss without too much inconvenience.

Of course, it would be possible to universalize the opposite: No one should kill innocent people, but that only shows that either type of action is permissible.

It may be objected that Kant presupposed that only rational acts could be universalized, but this won't work, for the categorical imperative is supposed to be the criterion for rational action. It may be that when we come to Kant's second formulation of the categorical imperative, he will have more ammunition with which to defeat P_1.

Finally, Kant thought that the categorical imperative yielded unqualified **absolutes.** The rules that the categorical imperative generates are universal and exceptionless. He illustrates this point with regard to truth telling. Suppose an innocent man comes to your door, begging for asylum, for a group of gangsters is hunting him down in order to kill him. You take the man in and hide him in your third-floor attic. Moments later the gangsters arrive and inquire after the innocent man. "Is he in your house?" they inquire. What should you do? Kant's advice is to tell them the truth: "Yes, he's in my house."[4]

What is Kant's reasoning here? It is simply that the moral law is sacrosanct and exceptionless. It is your duty to obey its commands, not to reason about the likely consequences. You have done your duty: hidden an innocent man and told the truth when asked a straightforward question. You are absolved of any responsibility for the harm that comes to the innocent man. It's not your fault that there are gangsters in the world.

To many of us, this kind of absolutism seems counterintuitive. There are two ways in which we might alter Kant here. First, simply write in qualifications to the universal principles, changing the sweeping generalization "Never lie" to the more modest "Never lie except to save an innocent person's life." The trouble with this way of solving the problem is that there seem to be no limits on the qualifications that would need to be attached to the original generalization: for example, "Never lie *except* to save an innocent person's life (except when trying to save the innocent person's life will undermine the entire social fabric)" or when lying will spare people great anguish (e.g., telling a cancer patient the truth about her condition). And so on. The process seems infinite and time-consuming and thus impractical.

A second way of qualifying the counterintuitive results of the Kantian program is to follow W. D. Ross and distinguish between actual and **prima facie** duties. The prima facie duty that wins out in the comparison is called the *actual duty* or the *all-things-considered duty.* We can apply this distinction to Kant's innocent man example. First, we have the principle

L: Never lie.

Next, we ask whether any other principle is relevant in this situation, and we discover that principle

P: Always protect innocent life

also applies. But we cannot obey both *L* and *P* (we assume for the moment that silence will be a giveaway). We have two general principles, but neither is to be seen as absolute or nonoverridable, but rather as prima facie. We have to decide which of the two overrides the other, which has greater moral force. This is left up to our considered judgment (or the considered judgment of the reflective moral community). Presumably, we will opt for *P* over *L,* so lying to the gangsters becomes our actual duty.

Will this maneuver save the Kantian system? Well, it changes it in a way that Kant might not have liked, but it seems to make sense. It transforms Kant's absolutism into an objectivist system. But now we need to have a separate criterion to adjudicate the conflict between two objective principles.

I conclude then that the categorical imperative is an important criterion for evaluating moral principles, but it needs supplementation. In itself it is purely formal and leaves out any understanding about the content or material aspect of morality. The categorical imperative with its universalizability test constitutes a necessary condition for being a valid moral principle, but it does not provide us with a sufficiency criterion. That is, any principle, if it is to count as rational or moral, must be universalizable. It must apply to everyone and every case that is relevantly similar. If I believe that it's wrong for others to cheat on exams, then unless I can find a reason to believe that I am relevantly different from others, it is also wrong for me to cheat on exams. If premarital heterosexual sex is prohibited for women, then it must also be prohibited for men. (Otherwise, with whom would the unmarried men have sex? Other men's wives?) But this formal consistency does not tell us whether cheating itself is right or wrong or whether premarital sex is right or wrong. That has to do with the substantive content of morality, on which other considerations must help us decide.

KANT'S SECOND FORMULATION
OF THE CATEGORICAL IMPERATIVE

Kant offered a second formulation of the categorical imperative, which has been referred to as the *principle of ends:* "So act as to treat humanity, whether in your own person or in that of any other, in every case as an end and never as merely a means only." Each person *qua* rational being has dignity and profound worth entailing that he or she must never be exploited or manipulated or merely used as a means to our idea of what is for the general good or to any other end.

What is Kant's argument for viewing rational beings as having ultimate value? It goes like this: In valuing anything, I endow it with value. It has no value apart from someone's valuing it. As a valued object, it has *conditional* worth, derived from my valuation. On the other hand, the person who values the object is the ultimate source of the object's value and, as such, belongs to a different sphere of beings. We, as valuers, must conceive of ourselves as having *unconditional* worth. We cannot think of our personhood as a mere thing, for then we would have to judge it to be without any value except that given to it by the estimation of other people. But then that person would be the source of value, and there is no reason to suppose that one person should have unconditional worth and not another who is relevantly similar. Therefore, we are not mere objects. We have unconditional worth and so must treat all such value givers as valuable in themselves, as ends, not merely means. I leave it to you to evaluate the validity of this argument, but most of us do hold that there is something exceedingly valuable about human life.

Kant thought that this formulation, the principle of ends, was substantively identical with his first formulation of the categorical imperative, but most scholars disagree with him. It seems better to treat this principle as a supplement to the first, adding content to the purely formal categorical imperative. In this way, Kant would limit the kinds of maxims that could be universalized. Egoism and the principle P_1, enjoining killing blue-eyed children, would be ruled out at the very outset since they involve a violation of the dignity of rational persons. The process would be as follows:

1. Maxim (M) formulated.
2. Ends test (does the maxim involve violating the dignity of rational beings?).
3. Categorical imperative (can the maxim be universalized?).
4. Successful moral principles survive both tests.

Does the principle of treating persons as ends in themselves fare better than the original version of the categorical imperative? Three problems soon emerge. The first problem has to do with Kant's setting such a high value on rationality. Why does reason and only reason have intrinsic worth? Who gives this value to rational beings, and how do we know that they have this value? What if we believe that reason has only instrumental value?

Kant's notion of the high inherent value of reason will be more plausible to those who believe that humans are made in the image of God and interpret that, as the mainstream of the Judeo-Christian tradition has, as entailing that our rational capabilities are the essence of being created in God's image. We have value because God created us with worth, that is, with reason. Kant doesn't use such an argument. Instead, he thinks that we must necessarily value rational nature, since we, *qua* rational beings, must value ourselves—and so, by the principle of consistency, anyone rational like us.

Kant seems to many to be correct in valuing rationality (the essence of our rational nature). It does enable us to engage in deliberate and moral reasoning and lifts us above lower animals. Where he is more controversial is in neglecting other values or states of being that may have moral significance. For example, he believed that we have no obligations to animals since they are not rational. Many of us believe (with Jeremy Bentham and Peter Singer) that the fact that animals can suffer should constrain us in our behavior toward them. We ought not cause unnecessary harm. Perhaps Kantians can supplement their system to accommodate this objection.

This brings us to our second problem with Kant's formulation. If we agree that reason (or rational nature) is an intrinsic value, then does it not follow that those who have more of this quality should be respected and honored more than those who have less? Doesn't more mean better here?

Following Kant's logic, we should treat people in exact proportion to their ability to reason. Thus, geniuses and intellectuals should be given privileged status in society (as Plato and Aristotle might argue). Kant could deny the second premise and argue that rationality is a threshold quality, that anyone having a sufficient quantity of it grants one equal worth. The question is whether Kant or Kantians have good (nonreligious) reasons to accept the egalitarian premise that all those who have rational nature have equal worth. I leave this question for you to discuss and come to your own conclusion.

There is a third problem with Kant's view of the dignity of rational beings. Even if we should respect them and treat them as ends, this does not tell us very much. It may tell us not to enslave them or act cruelly toward them without a good reason, but it doesn't tell us what to do in conflict situations. For example, what does it tell us to do about a terminally ill patient who wants us to help her die? What does it tell us to do in a war when we are about to aim our gun at an enemy soldier? Aren't we treating the soldier merely as a means?

Furthermore, what does it mean to treat this rational being as an end? What does it tell us to do with regard to the innocent victim and the gangsters who have just asked us about the whereabouts of the victim? What does it tell us about whether we should steal from the pharmacy in order to procure medicine that we can't afford to buy in order to bring healing to a loved one?

THE PRINCIPLE OF AUTONOMY

The final formulation of the categorical imperative invokes the principle of **autonomy:** Every rational being is able to regard himself as a maker of universal law; that is, one does not need an external authority, be it God, the state, one's culture, or anyone else to determine the nature of the moral law. One can discover this for oneself, and, the Kantian faith proclaims, everyone who is ideally rational will legislate exactly the same universal moral principles.

The opposite of autonomy is **heteronomy.** The heteronomous person is one whose actions are motivated by the authority of others, whether it be religion, the state, one's parents, or peer group. The following illustration may serve as an example of the difference between these two states of being.

In the early 1960s, Stanley Milgram of Yale University conducted a series of experiments in social psychology in order to determine the degree to which the ordinary citizen was obedient to authority. Volunteers from all walks of life were recruited to participate in "a study of memory and learning." Two people were taken into the laboratory. One was to play the role of the teacher, and the other was to play the role of the learner. The experimenter explained the process to both. The "teacher" was put in a separate room where he or she could see the "learner" through a window. He was instructed to ask the "learner" to choose the correct correlate to a given word, and the learner was to choose from a set of options. If the "learner" got the word correct, fine, they moved on to the next word. But if the learner chose the wrong word, he or she was punished with an electric shock. The "teacher" was given a sample shock of 45 volts just to get the feeling of the game. Each time the "learner" made a mistake the shocks were increased by 15 volts (starting with 15 volts and continuing to 450 volts). The meter was marked with verbal designators: slight shock, moderate shock, strong shock, very strong shock, intense shock, extreme intensity shock, danger: severe shock and XXX.

As the experiment proceeded, the "learner" would generally be heard grunting at the 75-volt shock, crying out at 120 volts, begging for release at 150 volts, and screaming in agony at 270 volts. Around 300 volts there was usually dead silence. Now unbeknown to the "teacher," the "learner" was not actually experiencing the voltage shocks. The "learners" were really trained actors who were simulating agony.

The results of the experiment were astounding. Whereas Milgram and associates expected that only a small proportion of "teachers" would comply with the instructions, actually 60 percent were completely obedient to their authority and carried out the experiment to the very end. Only a handful refused to participate in the experiment at all once they discovered what it involved. Some 35 percent left at various stages of the experiment. Milgram's experiments were later replicated in Munich, Germany, where 85 percent of the subjects were found to be completely "obedient to authority."

There are two ways in which the problem of autonomy and heteronomy are illustrated by this example. First, the experiment seems to show that the average person acts less autonomously than we might have suspected. People are basically heteronomous, herd followers. Second, there is the question about whether Milgram should have subjected people to these experiments. Was he violating their autonomy and treating them as means (rather than ends) in deceiving them in the way he did? Perhaps a utilitarian would have an easier time justifying these experiments than a Kantian.

In any case, for Kant it is our ability to use reason in universalizing the maxims of our actions that sets rational beings apart from nonrational beings. As such, rational beings belong to a kingdom of ends. Kant thought that as fully rational, autonomous legislators, each of us would be able to reason to exactly the same set of moral principles, the ideal moral law.

SUMMARY

Deontological theories place the locus of moral value in the act itself, regardless of the actual consequences. The end never justifies the means. The greatest of the deontologists was Kant, whose moral theory is centered in the categorical imperative: "Act only on that maxim whereby thou canst at the same time will that it would become a universal law." His second principle was "So act as to treat humanity, whether in your own person or in that of any other, in every case as an end and never merely as a means only." Finally, we noted the importance of autonomy for Kant's ethics. The strengths and weaknesses of Kant's system were examined.

QUESTIONS FOR DISCUSSION

1. Do you think that the Kantian argument that combines the categorical imperative with the notion of the kingdom of ends is successful? Is the notion of treating persons as ends clear enough to be a significant guiding action? Does it cover some intelligent animals but not severely retarded people? What about fetuses and infants? Are they included in it? Why, or why not?

2. Note the comments of the anti-Kantian Richard Taylor:

   > If I were ever to find, as I luckily never have, a man who assured me that he really *believed* Kant's metaphysical morals, and that he modeled his own conduct and his relations with others after those principles, then my incredulity and distrust of him as a human being could not be greater than if he told me he regularly drowned children just to see them squirm.[5]

   He and others have criticized Kant for being too rigid. Many people use the idea of moral duty to keep themselves and others from enjoying life and showing mercy. Do you think that there is a basis for this criticism?

3. Kant has been criticized for stifling spontaneous moral feelings in favor of the deliberate will, so that the person who successfully exercises the will in overcoming a temptation is superior to the person who isn't tempted at all but acts rightly spontaneously. For example, the person who just barely resists the temptation to shoplift through a strenuous act of the will would be, on this criterion, morally superior to the person who isn't tempted to shoplift at all. Based on your analysis of Kant, do you think that this is a fair interpretation of Kant, and if so, does it undermine his ethics?

4. Here is a question similar to the above. Kant holds that we must act from a motive centered on doing the morally right act simply because it is right and not because we simply are altruistic or benevolent or have good moral habits. He has been criticized for emphasizing the will too much and for rejecting the place of character and feelings in moral actions. Are these criticisms valid?

5. Many people besides Taylor have a negative reaction to Kant's moral theory. Evaluate the following quotation from Oliver Wendell Holmes, Jr.:

   > From this it is easy to proceed to the Kantian injunction to regard every human being as an end in himself and not as a means. I confess that I rebel at once. If we want conscripts, we march them up to the front with bayonets in their rear to die for a cause in which perhaps they do not believe. The enemy we treat not even as a means but as an obstacle to be abolished, if so it may be. I feel no pangs of conscience over either step, and naturally am slow to accept a theory that seems to be contradicted by practices that I approve.[6]

6. Does Kant's moral theory depend on a libertarian view of freedom of the will? Can the rational nature of humanity have the dignity or high worth it does without the notion of radical free will?

NOTES

1. Søren Kierkegaard, *Either/Or,* vol. II, trans. Walter Lowrie (New York: Anchor Books, 1959), 271.

2. Immanuel Kant, *Fundamental Principles of the Metaphysics of Morals,* trans. T. K. Abbott (1873), preface.

3. Ibid., Section 1.

4. Immanuel Kant, *On a Supposed Right to Lie from Altruistic Motives* (1797), in *Immanuel Kant: Critique of Practical Reason and Other Writings in Moral Philosophy,* ed. Lewis White Beck (New York: Garland, 1976).

5. Richard Taylor, *Good and Evil* (Buffalo, NY: Prometheus, Books, 1984), xii.

6. Oliver Wendell Holmes, Jr., *Collected Legal Papers* (New York: Harcourt Brace Jovanovich, 1920), 340.

FOR FURTHER READING

Acton, Harry. *Kant's Moral Philosophy.* London: Macmillan, 1970. A succinct, clearly written introduction to Kant's thought.

Donagan, Alan. *The Theory of Morality.* Chicago: University of Chicago Press, 1977. A contemporary version of a deontological theory.

Feldman, Fred. *Introductory Ethics.* Englewood Cliffs, NJ: Prentice-Hall, 1978. Chapters 7 and 8 present a clear and critical exposition of Kant's theory.

Gewirth, Alan. *Reason and Morality.* Chicago: University of Chicago Press, 1978. An important but advanced version of a deontological theory.

Harris, C. E. *Applying Moral Theories.* Belmont, CA: Wadsworth, 1992. Chapters 6 and 7 give an excellent exposition of contemporary deontological theories, especially of Gewirth's work.

Hill, Thomas E. *Dignity and Practical Reason in Kant's Moral Theory.* Ithaca, NY: Cornell University Press, 1992. A helpful interpretation of difficult issues in Kant.

Kant, Immanuel. *Foundations of the Metaphysics of Morals,* translated by Lewis White Beck. Indianapolis: Bobbs–Merrill, 1959. The classic treatise.

Wolff, Robert P. *The Autonomy of Reason: A Commentary on Kant's "Groundwork of the Metaphysics of Morals."* New York: Harper & Row, 1973. A useful commentary on Kant's work.

26

Religion and Ethics

Does God love goodness because it is good, or is it good because God loves it?

—SOCRATES, PARAPHRASED

The attempts to found a morality apart from religion are like the attempts of children who, wishing to transplant a flower that pleases them, pluck it from the roots that seem to them unpleasing and superfluous, and stick it rootless into the ground. Without religion there can be no real, sincere morality, just as without roots there can be no real flower.[1]

—LEO TOLSTOY

Adam and Eve disobeying God in the Garden of Eden and bringing suffering and death upon themselves and all people for all time; Moses receiving the Ten Commandments from the hand of God and delivering them to the people of Israel as laws to be obeyed on pain of death; the prophets Amos, Hosea, Isaiah, and Jeremiah warning the people that to disobey God's laws is to ensure doom and destruction; Jesus' Sermon on the Mount, Golden Rule, and Parable of the Good Samaritan, his teachings that we should not only love God with all our hearts, our neighbor as ourselves, but also our enemy; visions in the Apocalypse of the Last Judgment, wherein God shall reward every man and woman according to his or her deeds on earth; the hope of heaven and the fear of hell—all these events and teachings have profoundly influenced conscious life and moral behavior for two millennia. For the majority of humanity throughout the ages, morality has been identified with adherence to religion, immorality with sin, and the moral law with the command of God. Even Plato, Locke, and Rousseau advocated banishing professed atheists from the State, since they would lack sufficient incentive for being moral, especially under strong temptation. The moral life in most cultures in human history has been viewed as a personal relationship between the individual or the community and a heavenly parent. David, after committing adultery with Bathsheba and arranging for the death of her husband, Uriah, can say to God without being misunderstood, "Against Thee only have I sinned" (Psalm 51).

Whether it be the poor Calcutta harijan (untouchable) accepting his degradation as his karma, the Shiite Muslim fighting a jihad in the name of Allah, the Jew circumspectly striving to keep kosher, or the Christian giving to charity in the name of Christ, religion has so dominated the moral landscape as to be virtually indistinguishable from it. There have been exceptions to be sure: Confucianism in China is essentially a secular system, there are nontheist versions of Buddhism; and the philosophers of Greece contemplated morality independently of religion. But for the most part, throughout most of our history, most people have identified morality with religion, with the commands of God.

The question is whether the equation is a valid one. Is morality essentially tied to religion so that the term *secular ethic* is an oxymoron, a contradiction in terms? Can morality survive without religion? Is it the case, as Tolstoy declares in the quotation at the beginning of this chapter, that to separate morality from religion is like cutting a flower from its roots and transplanting it rootless into the ground? Is Dostoevsky's character Ivan Karamazov correct when he proclaims that "If God doesn't exist, everything is permissible"?

Essentially, our inquiry comes down to two questions: (1) Does morality depend on religion? (2) Is religious ethics essentially different from secular ethics?

DOES MORALITY DEPEND ON RELIGION?

The first question is whether moral standards themselves depend on God for their validity, or whether there is an autonomy of ethics, so that even God is subject to the moral order. The question first arises in Plato's dialogue in the *Euthyphro,* in which Socrates asks the pious Euthyphro, "Do the gods love holiness because it is holy, or is it holy because the gods love it?"[2] Changing the terms but still preserving the meaning, we want to know whether God commands what is good because it is good, or whether the good is good because God commands it. According to one theory, called the *Divine Command Theory (DCT),* ethical principles are simply the commands of God. They derive their validity from God's commanding them, and they *mean* "commanded by God." Without God, there would be no universally valid morality. Here is how the theologian Carl F. H. Henry states this view:

> Biblical ethics discredits an autonomous morality. It gives theonomous ethics its classic form—the identification of the moral law with the Divine will. In Hebrew-Christian revelation, distinctions in ethics reduce to what is good or what is pleasing, and to what is wicked or displeasing to the Creator-God alone. The biblical view maintains always a dynamic statement of values, refusing to sever the elements of morality from the will of God. . . . The good is what the Creator-Lord does and commands. He is the creator of the moral law, and defines its very nature.[3]

If we analyze the Divine Command Theory, we find three separate theses:

1. Morality (i.e., rightness and wrongness) originates with God.
2. *Moral rightness* simply means "willed by God," and *moral wrongness* means "being against the will of God."
3. Since morality is based essentially on divine will, not on independently existing reasons for action, no further reasons for action are necessary.

There are modified versions of the Divine Command Theory that drop or qualify one or more of these three theses, but the strongest form includes all three. We may characterize that position as follows:

> Necessarily, for any person S and for all acts A, if A is forbidden of S, then God commands that not-A for S. Likewise, if A is permitted for S, then God has commanded neither A nor not-A for S.

Bringing out the implications of this theory, we can list four propositions:

1. Act A is wrong if and only if it is contrary to the command of God.
2. Act A is right (required) if and only if it is commanded by God.
3. Act A is morally permissible if and only if it is permitted by the command of God.
4. If there is no God, then nothing is ethically wrong or required. Rather, everything is permitted.

We may summarize the Divine Command Theory this way: Morality not only originates with God, but *moral rightness* simply means "willed by God" and *moral wrongness* means "being against the will of God." That is, an act is right *in virtue* of being permitted by the will of God, and an act is wrong *in virtue* of being against the will of God. Since morality is essentially based on divine will, not on independently existing reasons for action, no further reasons for action are necessary. As Ivan Karamazov asserts, "If God doesn't exist, everything is permissible." Nothing is forbidden or required. Without God we have moral nihilism. If there is no God, then nothing is ethically wrong or required. Everything is permitted.

The opposing viewpoint, call it the *autonomy thesis* (standing for the independence of ethics), denies the theses of the Divine Command Theory, asserting, to the contrary, the following:

1. Morality does not originate with God (though the way God created us may affect the specific nature of morality).
2. Rightness and wrongness are not based simply on God's will.
3. Essentially, there are reasons for acting one way or the other, which may be known independently of God's will.

In sum, ethics are autonomous, and even God must obey the moral law, which exists independently of himself—as the laws of mathematics and logic do. Just as even God cannot make a three-sided square or make it the case that he never existed, so even God cannot make what is intrinsically evil good or make what is good evil.

Theists who espouse the autonomy thesis may well admit some epistemological advantage to God: God knows what is right—better than we do. And since he is good, we can always learn from consulting him. But in principle we act morally for the same reasons that God does: We both follow moral reasons that are independent of God. We are against torturing the innocent because it is cruel and unjust, just as God is against torturing the innocent because it is cruel and unjust. By this account, if there is no God, then nothing is changed; morality is left intact, and both theists and nontheists have the very same moral duties.

The attractiveness of the Divine Command Theory lies in the fact that it seems to do justice to the omnipotence or sovereignty of God. God somehow is thought to be less sovereign or necessary to our lives if he is not the source of morality. It seems inconceivable to many believers that anything having to do with goodness or duty could be "higher" than or independent of God, for he is the supreme Lord of the believer's life, and what the believer means by *morally right* is that "the Lord commands it—even if I don't fully understand it." When the believer asks what the will of God is, it is a direct appeal to a personal will, not to an independently existing rule.

Two problems with the Divine Command Theory need to be faced by those who hold it. One problem is that the Divine Command Theory would seem to make the attribution of "goodness" to God redundant. When we say "God is good," we think that we are ascribing a property to God; but if *good* simply means "what God commands or wills," then we are not attributing any property to God. Our statement "God is good" merely means "God does whatever he wills to do" or "God practices what he preaches," and the statement "God commands us to do what is good" merely is the tautology "God commands us to do what God commands us to do."

A second problem with the Divine Command Theory is that it seems to make morality into something arbitrary. If God's fiat is the sole arbiter of right and wrong, it would seem to be logically possible for such heinous acts as rape, killing of the innocent for the fun of it, and gratuitous cruelty to become morally good actions—if God suddenly decided to command us to do these things. The radicality of the Divine Command Theory is set forth in a classic statement by William of Occam:

> The hatred of God, theft, adultery, and actions similar to these actions according to common law, may have an evil quality annexed, in so far as they are done by a divine command to perform the opposite act. But as far as the sheer being in the actions is concerned, they can be performed by God without any evil condition annexed; and they can even be performed meritoriously by an earthly pilgrim if they should come under divine precepts, just as now the opposite of these in fact fall under the divine command.[4]

The implications of this sort of reasoning seem far reaching. If there are no constraints on what God can command, no independent measure or reason for moral action, then anything can become a moral duty, and our moral duties can change from moment to moment. Could there be any moral stability? The proponent of the Divine Command Theory may object that God has revealed his will in his word, the sacred scriptures. But the fitting response is, How do you know that God isn't lying? For if there is no independent criterion of right and wrong except what God happens to will, how do we know God isn't willing to make lying into a duty (in which case, believers have no reason to believe the Bible)?

When I was a teenager I read in the newspaper of a missionary in Africa who put a knife through the hearts of his wife and five children. Upon his arrest for murder, he claimed God had commanded him to kill his family and he was only obeying God.

The missionary might also say, "Didn't God command Abraham to kill his son Isaac in Genesis 22?" How do we know that God didn't command the missionary to do this horrible deed? He would only be sending his family to heaven a bit sooner than normal. Insane asylums are filled with people who have heard the voice of God commanding them to do what we normally regard as immoral: rape, steal, embezzle, and kill. If the divine command theory is correct, we could be treating these people as insane simply for obeying God.

If God could make what seems morally heinous morally good simply by willing it, wouldn't morality be reduced to the right of the powerful—Nietzsche's "Might makes Right"? Indeed, what would be the difference between the devil and God if morality were simply an arbitrary command? Suppose we had two sets of commands, one from the devil and one from God. How would we know which set was which? Could they be identical? What would make them different? If there is no independent criterion by which to judge right and wrong, it's difficult to see how we could know which was which. The only basis for comparison would be who won. God is simply the biggest bully on the block (granted it is a pretty big block—covering the entire universe).

Furthermore, the scriptures speak of God being love. "Beloved, let us love one another, for love is of God, and he who loves is born of God and knows God. He who does not love does not know God; for God is love (I John 4:7, 8). Could you truly love people and at the same time rape, kill, or torture them? Could a loving God command you to torture them? If so, then I suppose that Auschwitz could be considered God's loving act to the Jews.

The opponent of the Divine Command Theory (i.e., the proponent of the autonomy thesis) denies that God's omnipotence includes his being able to make evil actions good. Even as God's power does not include being able to override the laws of logic (e.g., he cannot make a contradiction true or make $2 + 2 = 5$), so likewise God cannot make rape, injustice, cruelty, and the torturing or killing of innocents good deeds. The objective moral law, which may be internal to God's nature, is a law that even God must follow, if he is to be a good God.

Some philosophers and theologians acknowledge that God cannot change the moral law any more than he can change the laws of logic, but claim that he is, nevertheless, the source of the moral law. I recently heard the Christian philosopher William Lane Craig set forth the following argument.[5]

1. If there is no God, no moral absolute values exist.
2. Evil exists (which is a negative absolute value and implies that the Good exists as an absolute positive value).
3. ∴ God exists.

Craig assumes that unless God is the ultimate source and authority of morality, morality cannot have absolute or objective status. But if the autonomy thesis is correct, objective moral principles exist whether or not God exists. They are the principles that enable human beings to flourish, to make life more nearly a heaven than a hell. Rational beings can discover these principles independently of God or revelation—using reason and experience alone.[6]

Are Religious Ethics Essentially Different from Secular Ethics? The second problem related to the matter of religion and morality has to do with the relationship between religion and secular morality. Are they essentially compatible or incompatible? We can divide this question into two subquestions: (1) Does religion actually do moral harm and detract from deep morality? (2) Does religion provide, and secular systems fail to provide, ethics with the necessary motivation to be deeply moral?

Immanuel Kant (1724–1804), who held to the autonomy thesis, thought that there could be no difference between valid religious ethics and valid philosophical ethics. God and humanity both have to obey the same rational principles, and reason is sufficient to guide us to these principles:

> [Christianity] has enriched philosophy with far more definite and purer concepts than it had been able to furnish before; but which, once they are there, are freely assented to by Reason and are assumed as concepts to which it could well have come of itself and which it could and should have introduced. . . . Even the Holy One of the Gospels must first be compared with our ideal of moral perfection, before we can recognize him as such.[7]

Kant's system exalts ethics to an intrinsic good; indeed, doing one's duty for no other reason but that it is one's duty is the highest good there is. As such it is related to religion; it is our duty to God. God loves the virtuous, and finally will reward them with happiness in proportion to their virtue. In fact, God and immortality are necessary postulates of ethics. Immortality is necessary in this way: According to Kant, we are commanded by the moral law to be morally perfect. Since *ought* implies *can,* we must be *able* to reach moral perfection. But we cannot attain perfection in this life, for the task is an infinite one. So there must be an afterlife in which we continue to make progress toward this ideal.

God is a necessary postulate in that there must be someone to enforce the moral law. That is, in order for the moral law to be completely justified, there must finally be a just recompense of happiness in accordance to virtue. The good must be rewarded by happiness in proportion to their virtue, and the evil punished in proportion to their vice. This harmonious correlation of virtue and happiness does not happen in this life, so it must happen in the next life. Thus there must be a God, acting as judge and enforcer of the moral law, without which the moral law would be unjustified.

Kant is not saying that we can *prove* that God exists or that we ought to be moral *in order* to be happy. Rather, the idea of God serves as a completion of our ordinary ideas of ethics. Is Kant right about this?

IS RELIGION IRRELEVANT
OR EVEN INIMICAL TO MORALITY?

Many secularists, such as Bertrand Russell and Kai Nielsen, have argued against both the stronger claim of the Divine Command Theory (that religion is the basis of ethics) and the weaker, Kantian claim (that religion completes ethics). They contend that morality has no need of God: One can be moral and, within the

limits of thoughtful, stoic resignation, even happy. The world may well be a product of blind evolutionary striving, ultimately absurd, but this doesn't remove our
duty to fill our lives with meaning and goodness. As Russell put it:

> Nature, omnipotent but blind, in the revolutions of her secular hurryings through
> the abysses of space, has brought forth at last a child, subject still to her power, but
> gifted with sight, with knowledge of good and evil, with the capacity of judging all
> the works of his unthinking Mother.[8]

It is this conscious power of moral evaluation that makes the child superior to his
omnipotent Mother. He is free to think, evaluate, create, and live committed to
ideals. So in spite of suffering, despair, and death, humans are free. Life has the
meaning that we give it, and morality will be part of any meaningful life.

Theists may counter that secularists like Russell are "whistling in the dark."
Christian philosopher George Mavrodes has criticized Russell's secular view as
puzzling.[9] If there is no God, then doesn't secular ethics suffer from a certain
inadequacy? Mavrodes argues that the Russellian world of secular morality can't
satisfactorily answer the question, "Why should I be moral?" For, on its account,
the common goods, at which morality in general aims, are often just those that
we sacrifice in carrying out our moral obligations. Why should we sacrifice our
welfare or self-interest for our moral duty?

The second oddity about secular ethics, according to Mavrodes, is that it is
superficial and not deeply rooted. It seems to lack the necessary metaphysical basis
afforded by a Platonic worldview (i.e., the view that reality and value essentially
exist in a transcendent realm) or a Judeo-Christian worldview:

> Values and obligations cannot be deep in such a [secular] world. What is deep in a
> Russellian world must be such things as matter and energy, or perhaps natural law,
> chance, or chaos. If it really were a fact that one had obligations in a Russellian
> world, then something would be laid upon man that might cost a man everything
> but that went no further than man. And that difference from a Platonic world seems
> to make all the difference.[10]

Of course, the secularist will continue the debate. If what morality seeks is the
good, as I have argued, then secular morality based on a notion of the good life is
inspiring in itself, for it promotes human flourishing and can be shown to be in all
of our interests, whether or not a God exists. A religious or Platonic metaphysical
orientation may not be necessary for a rational, secular, commonsense morality. To
be sure, there will be differences in the exact nature of the ethical codes—religious
ethics will be more likely to advocate strong altruism, whereas secular codes will
emphasize reciprocal altruism—but the core morality will be the same.

Some secularists—call them antireligious secularists—go even further than
Russell or Nielsen, claiming that not only are religious and secular morality dis-
similar but that religious morality is an inferior brand of morality that actually
prevents deep moral development. Both P. H. Nowell-Smith and James Rachels
have argued that religion is (or gives rise to) an inferior morality.[11] Both base
their contention on the notion of autonomy. Nowell-Smith's argument is based
on child psychologist Jean Piaget's research in child development. Very small
children have to be taught to value rules. When they do, they tend to hold tenaciously to those rules, even when games or activities would seem to call for a

suspension of the rules. For example, suppose ten children are to play baseball on a rectangular lot that lacks a right field. Some children might object to playing with only five on a side and no right field, because that violates the official rules. Religious morality, in being deontologically rule-governed, is analogous to children who have not understood the wider purposes of the rules of games. It is an infantile morality.

Rachels's argument alleges that believers relinquish their autonomy in worship and so are immoral. Using Kant's dictum that "kneeling down or groveling on the ground, even to express your reverence for heavenly things, is contrary to human dignity," he argues that since we have inherent dignity, no one deserves our worship. But since the notion of *God* implies "being worthy of worship," God cannot exist. Rachel writes:

1. If any being is God, he must be a fitting object of worship.
2. No being could possibly be a fitting object of worship, since worship requires the abandonment of one's role as an autonomous moral agent.
3. ∴ There cannot be any being who is God.[12]

Are Nowell-Smith's and Rachels's arguments sound? They seem to have problems. Consider Nowell-Smith's contention that religious morality is infantile. Perhaps some religious people, and some secularists as well, are rigidly and unreasonably rule-bound, but not all religious people are. Indeed, Jesus himself broke the rule regarding not working on the Sabbath day, to heal and do good, admonishing his critics, the Pharisees, saying, "The Sabbath was made for man, not man for the Sabbath." Does not the strong love motif in New Testament religious morality indicate that the rules are seen as serving a purpose—the human good?

With regard to Rachels's argument, premise 2 seems false. In worshipping God, you need not give up your reason, your essential autonomy. Doesn't a rational believer need to use reason to distinguish the good from the bad, the holy from what is not holy? A mature believer does not (or need not) sacrifice his or her reason or autonomy in worship; rather, these traits are part and parcel of what worship entails. The command to love God is for one to love him with one's whole *mind* as well as one's heart and strength. If there is a God, he must surely want us to be intelligent and discriminating and sensitive in all of our deliberations. Being a religious worshipper in no way entails or condones intellectual suicide.

Of course, a believer may submit his or her judgment to God's, when there is good evidence that God has given a judgment. If this is sacrificing one's autonomy, then it only shows that autonomy is not an absolute value but a significant prima facie value. If I am working in the physics laboratory with Albert Einstein, whom I have learned to trust as a competent authority, and he advises me to do something different from what my amateur calculations dictate, I am likely to defer to his authority. But I don't thereby give up my autonomy. I freely and rationally decide that in this particular matter I ought to defer to Einstein's judgment on the grounds that it is more likely to be correct. Functioning autonomously is not to be equated with deciding each case from scratch; nor does it require self-sufficiency in decision-making. Autonomy is *higher-order* reflective control over one's life; a considered judgment that in certain cases, someone else's opinion is more likely to be correct than one's own in an *exercise* of autonomy rather than an abdication of it.[13] Similarly, the believer may submit to God whenever he or she judges God's authority to override his or her own finite judgment. It seems eminently rational to give up that kind of autonomy. To do otherwise would be to make autonomy a foolhardy fetish.

DOES RELIGION ENHANCE
THE MORAL LIFE?

Contrary to philosophers like Nowell-Smith and Rachels (and even Russell and Nielsen), there may be some morally relevant advantages to theism. Theists argue that there are at least five ways in which morality may be enriched by religion.

1. If there is a God, good will win out over evil. We're not fighting alone—God is on our side in the battle. Neither are we fighting in vain—we'll win eventually. As William James (1842–1910) said,

> If religion be true and the evidence for it be still insufficient, I do not wish, by putting your extinguisher upon my nature, to forfeit my sole chance in life of getting upon the winning side—that chance depending, of course, on my willingness to run the risk of acting as if my passional need of taking the world religiously might be prophetic and right.[14]

This thought of the ultimate Victory of Goodness gives us confidence to go on in the fight against injustice and cruelty when others calculate that the odds against righteousness are too great to oppose. While the secularist may embrace a noble stoicism, resigned to fate, as Bertrand Russell claims, the believer lives in faith, confident of the final triumph of the kingdom of God on earth. For the believer life is not a mad, chaotic joke, a product of chance and necessity. God's *Grand Design* holds sway over the seemingly random happenstance.

2. If God exists, then cosmic justice reigns in the universe. The scales are perfectly balanced so that everyone will eventually get what he or she deserves, according to their moral merit. It is true that in most religious traditions God forgives the repentant sinner his or her sins—in which case divine grace goes beyond what is strictly deserved. It's as though a merciful God will never give us *less* reward than we deserve, but if we have a good will, will give us more than we deserve. Nonetheless, the idea that "whatsoever a man sows, that will he also reap" (Gal. 6:7) is emphasized in Judaism, Islam, Christianity, and most other world religions. In Hinduism it is carried out with a rigorous logic of karma (that is, what you are now is a direct result of what you did in a previous life, and what you do with your life now will determine what kind of life you inherit in the next life).

The question that haunts secular ethics—"Why should I be moral, when I can get away with being immoral?" (for often, it seems we can profit by being immoral)—has a ready answer: I will not get away with immorality. God is the perfect judge who will bring my works to judgment, so that my good works will be rewarded and my bad works punished.

Allied to this point is the idea that each person will be judged on his or her own merit, by how well the person has lived within the light he or she has had. It may turn out that only a religious view of human nature preserves the notion of free will and moral responsibility, which may be necessary for a deep sense of personal worth and accountability. It is hard to see that materialism or even bio-logical naturalism has the resources to support a libertarian notion of free will.

3. If theism is true, moral reasons always override nonmoral reasons. Let me illustrate this controversy: I once had an argument with my teacher Philippa Foot, of Oxford University, over the Gauguin case. Paul Gauguin aban-doned his family and moved to Paris and then to Tahiti in order to fulfill his artis-tic dream. I argued that Gauguin did wrong, all things considered, to abandon his family. Foot, however, to my utter amazement, argued that although Gauguin did what was morally wrong, he did what was right, all things considered, for some-times nonmoral reasons override moral ones. From a secular perspective, Foot's argument seems plausible: Why should moral reasons always override nonmoral ones? It is true that philosophers like R. M. Hare build overridingness into the definition of a moral principle but then stipulate that we are *free to choose* our prin-ciples. Here is the dilemma for secular ethics: *either* overridingness *or* objectivity but not both. If you believe in moral realism, the idea that moral principles are universally valid whether or not anyone recognizes them, then the secularist is faced with the question, "Why should I adhere to a given moral principle when I can get away with violating it?" If you hold to overridingness, that is, if you believe that moral reasons are always the highest motivating reasons, the best rea-sons all things considered, then it seems likely that we will adopt some sort of agent-relativity with regard to morals. From a religious perspective, however, the world is so ordered that the question "Why be moral?" can hardly be taken seri-ously: To be moral is to function properly, the way God intended us to live, and he will see that the good are ultimately rewarded and the wicked punished. God ensures the supremacy of morality.[15] Moral reasons always override other reasons. We preserve both overridingness and objectivity.

4. If theism is true, then there is a God who loves and cares for us—his love inspires us. A sense of gratitude pervades the life of the believer so that he or she is ready to make greater sacrifices for the good of others. That is, the believer has an *added reason* to be moral, beyond the ones a secular person already has, beyond even rewards and punishments: He or she wants to please a perfect God. A religious person is never alone. God is always caring for him and will at least ensure his or her immortality in a divine paradise.

5. If there is a God who created us in his image, all persons are of equal worth. Theism claims that God values us all equally. If we are all his chil-dren, then we are all brothers and sisters; we are family and ought to treat each other benevolently, as we would family members of equal worth. Indeed, modern secular moral and political systems often assume the equal worth of the individ-ual without justifying it. But without the parenthood of God it makes no sense to say that all persons are innately of positive equal value. What gives us animals, the products of a process of the survival of the fittest, any value at all, let alone equal value? From a perspective of intelligence and utility, Aristotle and Nietzsche seem to be right; there are enormous inequalities, and why shouldn't the superi-or persons use the baser types to their advantage? In this regard, secularism, in rejecting inegalitarianism, seems to be living off the interest of a religious capital that it has relinquished.

In sum, if theism is false, then it may be doubtful whether all humans have free will, and equal worth, or any worth at all, and it may be more difficult to provide an equivocal response to the question "Why be moral even when it is not in my best interest?" If there is no sense of harmony and objective purpose in the universe, many of us will conclude that we are sadder and poorer because of it.

Add to this the fact that theism doesn't deprive us of any of the autonomy that we have in nontheistic systems. If we are equally free to choose the good or the evil whether or not God exists (assuming that the notions of good and evil make sense in a nontheistic universe), then it seems plausible to assert that in some ways, the world of the theist is better and more satisfying than one in which God does not exist. It could also be the case that via revelation, the theist has access to deeper moral truths that are not available to the secularist.

Of course, two important points may be made on the other side: First, a lot of evil has been done by religious people in the name of religion. We have only to look at our sordid history of heresy hunts, religious bigotry, and religious wars, some of which are still being fought. Religion may be used as a powerful weapon with which to harm others. Second, we don't know for sure whether a benevolent God exists. The arguments for the existence of God are not obviously compelling. Furthermore, even if a divine being exists, we don't have the kind of compelling evidence needed to prove that our interpretation of God's will and ways is the right one. Religion is based largely on faith rather than on hard evidence, so that it behooves believers to be modest about their policies. It would seem that most of us are more certain about the core of our morality than about the central doctrines of theology. So it is ill-advised to require society to give up a morality based on reason for some injunctions based on revelation. Sometimes a religious authority claims to put forth a command that conflicts with our best rational judgments, giving rise to the kind of confrontation that can rip society apart.

The Medieval Crusades and Inquisition; the religious wars of the Reformation period; the present religious conflict in Northern Ireland between Roman Catholics and Protestants; the current devastation of the former Yugoslavia, where Christians and Muslims are killing each other; the Hindu-Muslim massacres in India; and the Ayatollah Khoumeni's order to kill author Salmon Rushdie for writing his allegedly blasphemous book *The Satanic Verses* rightly cause apprehension in many fair-minded people. Religion can be a force for good or for evil, but dogmatic and intolerant religion deeply and rightly worries the secularist, who sees religion as a threat to society.

Our hope in solving such problems rests in working out an adequate morality on which theists and nontheists alike can agree. If there is, as I have argued elsewhere, an ethics of belief, then we can apply rational scrutiny to our religious beliefs, as well as to all our other beliefs, and work toward a better understanding of the status of our belief system.[16] It is a challenge that should inspire the best minds, for it may turn out that it is not science or technology, but rather deep, comprehensive ethical theory and moral living that will not only save our world but solve its perennial problems and produce a state of flourishing.[17]

QUESTIONS FOR DISCUSSION

1. Evaluate Leo Tolstoy's statement quoted at the beginning of this chapter:

   The attempts to found a morality apart from religion are like the attempts of children, who, wishing to transplant a flower that pleases them, pluck it from the roots that seem to them unpleasing and superfluous, and stick it rootless into the ground. Without religion there can be no real, sincere morality, just as without roots there can be no real flower.

2. In your judgment, how important is religion for a meaningful moral life? How would a secularist respond to the five claims made in favor of religion's ability to give added meaning to morality? Do you think that religion really does enhance the moral life?

3. Karl Marx said that religion was the opium of the people. (Today, the metaphor might better be changed to "cocaine" or "crack.") It deludes them into thinking that all will be well with the world, leading to passive acceptance of evil and injustice. Is there some truth in Marx's dictum? How would a theist respond to this?

4. Imagine that a superior being appears to you and says, "I am God and I am good; therefore, obey me when I tell you to torture your mother." (In case you don't think that a religious tradition would set forth such a message, read Gen. 22, in which God commands Abraham to kill his son Isaac, offering him as a sacrifice to God.) How would a proponent of the divine command theory deal with this problem?

5. Discuss the problems connected with religious revelation and rational morality. What if one's religion prohibits certain types of speech and requires the death penalty for those who disobey, such as was the case when the Ayatollah Khomeni condemned author Salman Rushdie to death for blasphemous words in his novel *The Satanic Verses*? Some religious people believe that abortion or homosexual behavior is morally wrong based on religious authority. How should a secular ethicist who believes that these practices are not morally wrong argue with the believer? Can there be rational dialogue?

NOTES

1. "Religion and Morality," in *Leo Tolstoy: Selected Essays,* trans. Aylmer Maude (New York: Random House, 1964), 31.

2. Plato, *Euthyphro,* trans. William Jowett (New York: Scribner, 1889).

3. Carl F. Henry, *Christian Personal Ethics* (Grand Rapids, MI: Eerdmans, 1957), 210.

4. William of Occam, quoted in *Divine Command Morality,* ed. J. M. Idziak (Lewiston, NY: Mellon, 1979).

5. William Lane Craig set forth this argument in a debate with Paul Draper at the United States Military Academy, Sept. 30, 1997.

6. More sophisticated versions of the Divine Command Theory exist. See Robert Adams, "A Modified Divine Command Theory of Ethical Wrongness," in *Virtue and Faith* (Oxford: Oxford University Press, 1987). See also my critique, "Analysis of

the Modified Divine Command
Theory," in *Ethics: Discovering Right and
Wrong* (Belmont, CA: Wadsworth,
1999).

7. Immanuel Kant, *Critique of Judgment,*
trans. J. Bernard (Haefner, 1951), 410;
and *Fundamental Principles of the
Metaphysics of Ethics,* trans. T. K. Abbott
(Longmans, Green, 1898).

8. Bertrand Russell, "A Free Man's
Worship," in *Ethical Theory: Classical and
Contemporary Readings,* 3d ed. Louis
Pojman (Belmont, CA: Wadsworth,
1998). Note also the comment of my
former student Laura Burrell
(University of Mississippi):

God is like a cosmic gardener—he
tends and protects individual morality,
he nourishes it and helps it bloom.
Some people, like a hothouse orchid
or a fancy rose, do seem to need religion for their morality to have a purpose or justification. Others are like
the Queen Anne's Lace (QAL)—able
to withstand almost anything on their
own. And many are borderline QAL,
who need just that extra bit of fertil-
izer to break into bloom—and God
provides it. But mankind could do as
well. The relationship between God
and morality is as simple as that—
God is a parent, gardener, etc. He
strengthens and cushions individual
morality, he gives motivation (in the
form of the outcomes: heaven or hell)
and justice and order in a sometimes
extremely chaotic world. But morality exists apart from God, and as hard
as it is for some to accept it, could
survive and even flourish in a world
without God.

9. George Mavrodes, "Religion and the
Queerness of Morality," in *Ethical Theory:
Classical and Contemporary Readings,* 3d ed.
Louis Pojman (Belmont, CA: Wadsworth,
1998).

10. Ibid., 539.

11. Patrick Nowell-Smith, "Morality:
Religious and Secular," in *Philosophy of
Religion: Classical and Contemporary Readings,*
3d ed. Louis Pojman (Belmont, CA:
Wadsworth, 1998).

12. James Rachels, "God and Human
Attitudes," in *Religious Studies* 7 (1971).
Reprinted, with a reply by Philip Quinn, in
Paul Helm, ed., *Divine Commands and
Morality* (Oxford: Oxford University Press,
1979).

13. For a fuller defense of this thesis, see
Arthur Kuflik, "The Inalienability of
Autonomy," *Philosophy & Public Affairs* (Fall
1984). My ideas have been influenced by
Kuflik's work here.

14. William James, *The Will to Believe* (New
York: Longmans, Green, 1897).

15. For a fuller account of the differences
between religious and secular morality, see
Louis Pojman, "Ethics: Religious and
Secular," *The Modern Schoolman* LXX
(November 1992), 1–30.

16. See Louis P. Pojman, "Belief, Will and
the Ethics of Belief," in *The Theory of
Knowledge,* 2d ed. (Belmont, CA: Wadsworth, 1999), 525–543. Samuel Scheffler in
Human Morality (Oxford: Oxford University
Press, 1992), like Foot, rejects the Over-
ridability Thesis.

17. I am indebted to Michael Beaty and
Arthur Kuflik for criticisms of an earlier
draft of this chapter.

FOR FURTHER READING

Adams, Robert M. "A Modified Divine
Command Theory of Ethical
Wrongness," in *The Virtue of Faith.*
Oxford: Oxford University Press, 1987.

Hare, John. *The Moral Gap.* Oxford: Oxford
University Press, 1996.

Helm, Paul, ed. *The Divine Command Theory
of Ethics.* Oxford: Oxford University
Press, 1979. Contains valuable articles
by Frankena, Rachels, Quinn, Adams,
and Young.

Kant, Immanuel. *Religion Within the Bounds of Reason Alone,* translated by T. M. Greene and H. H. Hudson. New York: Harper & Row, 1960.

Kierkegaard, Søren. *Fear and Trembling,* translated by Howard Hong and Edna Hong. Princeton, NJ: Princeton University Press, 1983.

Mitchell, Basil. *Morality: Religious and Secular.* Oxford: Oxford University Press, 1980.

Mouw, Richard. *The God Who Commands.* Notre Dame, IN: University of Notre Dame Press, 1990.

Nielsen, Kai. *Ethics Without God.* Buffalo, NY: Prometheus Books, 1973. A very accessible defense of secular morality.

Outka, Gene, and J. P. Reeder, eds. *Religion and Morality: A Collection of Essays.* New York: Anchor Books, 1973. Contains Robert M. Adams's "A Modified Divine Command Theory of Ethical Wrongness."

Pojman, Louis. "Ethics: Religious and Secular." *The Modern Schoolman* LXX (November 1992), 1–30.

Pojman, Louis, ed. *Ethical Theory: Classical and Contemporary Readings.* Belmont, CA: Wadsworth, 1989. Part XI contains important essays by Immanuel Kant, Bertrand Russell, George Mavrodes, and Kai Nielsen.

Quinn, Philip. *Divine Commands and Moral Requirements.* Oxford: Clarendon Press, 1978.

Robinson, Richard. *An Atheist's Values.* Oxford: Clarendon Press, 1964.

Ward, Keith. *Ethics and Christianity.* London: Allen & Unwin, 1970.

PART VII

Existentialism and
the Meaning of Life

THOMAS COLE
The Voyage of Life: Manhood

—Asia Mellon Bruce Fund, © 1993
National Gallery of Art, Washington, DC

27

Existentialism

WHAT IS EXISTENTIALISM?

There was once a young student of philosophy and theology who mastered
all the philosophical positions of his time, who patiently worked through
one system of knowledge after another, memorizing, analyzing, refuting,
revising, and amalgamating the theses of learned men. His one aim was to find the
Truth, but not simply empirical truth, factual knowledge, but a truth for which
there wasn't yet a name, a sort of inner truth, a spiritual ideal for which he could
live and die, an ideology that either proceeded from the heart or found a resounding echo of affirmation in the heart. The student wrote in his diary:

> What I really lack is to be clear in my mind what *I am to do,* not what I must
> know—except that a certain amount of knowledge is presupposed in every action. I
> need to understand my purpose in life, to see what God wants me to do, and this
> means that I must find a truth which is true for me, that I must find *that idea for
> which I can live and die.*[1]

He then criticizes his whole academic career as largely superfluous:

> What would be the use of discovering so called "objective" truth, of working
> through all the systems of philosophy and of being able to review them all and show
> up the inconsistencies within each system? What good would it do me to be able to
> develop a political theory and combine all the intricate details of politics into a
> complete system, and so construct a world for the exhibition of others but in which
> I did not live; what would it profit me if I developed the correct interpretation of
> Christianity in which I resolved all the internal problems, if it had no deeper signifi-
> cance *for me and for my life;* what would it profit me if truth stood before me cold

and naked, indifferent to whether I recognized her, creating in me paroxysms of anxiety rather than trusting devotion?[2]

He then asks, "What is truth but to live for an idea? Ultimately everything must rest on a hypothesis but the moment it is no longer outside him, but he lives in it, then and only then does it cease to be merely a hypothesis for him." It becomes the *lived truth,* subjective truth.

The student graduated from the university with honors but was unable to obtain a teaching position. So he began to write, developing the sort of thoughts expressed in the sentences you have just read—only he didn't write in the usual philosophical jargon. Instead, he told stories and wrote witty aphorisms and essays about literature, music, the aesthetic life, morality, and religion in which the flow of the discourse was arranged so as to awaken the conscience, compelling the reader to ask questions about the meaning and purpose of life. His first books were best-sellers—only no one knew who this mysterious author was, for he didn't sign his name to his books. Instead, he used pseudonyms: Victor Eremita, Johannes de Silentio, Vigilius Haufniensis, Nicolas Notabene, Constantine Constantius, Johannes Climacus, and so forth. All these Latin pseudonyms had symbolic meaning. Translated they read, "The Victorious Hermit," "John Who Is Silent," "The Vigilant Watchman of the Harbor" (he lived in a harbor town), "Nicolas Note Well," "Constant Constantine" (who is not fickle as you suppose, my beloved), and "John Who Is Trying to Climb" to heaven. The author's reasons for not including his own name were complex, but the main reason was his desire to draw attention to the ideas contained in his books and to the reader's personal relationship with these ideas, often written on several levels: an innocent story, a message to his ex-fianceé, a philosophical discourse, a call to "subjective truth." He was prolific, producing eighteen books in five years, publishing completely at his own expense and losing money in the venture.

His life was filled with constant and intense suffering. He was frustrated in love, frustrated in his vocational aspirations, frustrated by his physical liabilities—especially by his severe back ailment that eventually led to a premature death. He opposed the journalistic corruption of his day, incurring the wrath of the avant-garde press, which mocked him almost daily. One cartoon depicts him standing in the center of the universe with the Sun, Moon, stars, and all else revolving around him—as though to suggest that he was an egomaniac. Eventually, his reputation was ruined, and he became undeservedly the laughingstock of his community. He felt a mission to teach the common folk but was rejected even by them. They began to name their dogs after him. He was deeply religious, devoutly Christian, but in his quest for integrity he felt compelled to reject the established church of his land as anti-Christian and joined the Atheist Society in protest to the spiritual deadness of the church. The established church responded in kind, hurling abuse his way. An intense controversy erupted between him and the church. He wrote of the church,

> As a religion [organized Christianity], as it is now practiced, is just about as genuine as tea made from a bit of paper which once lay in a drawer beside another bit of paper which once had been used to wrap up a few dried tea leaves from which tea had already been made three times.

In the midst of his battle with the church, he collapsed one October day on the main street of his city, Copenhagen. He was taken to the hospital. Some days later, a priest came to administer last rites, the Eucharist (Holy Communion), advising him that he was dying. Our subject brushed the priest aside, exclaiming, "No, I will not accept the body and blood of my Lord and Savior from the hands of a lackey of the state! Send an unpaid layman and I will partake." A few days later, without having received the Eucharist, he died at the age of forty-two. Thus ended the life of the father of existentialism, Søren Aabye Kierkegaard (May 5, 1813–November 11, 1855).

SØREN AABYE KIERKEGAARD

Søren Aabye Kierkegaard was born in Copenhagen on May 5, 1813, the youngest of seven children. His mother was in her early forties, and his father was fifty-five years old when he was born. A retiring, lonely child, Kierkegaard largely spent his youth in the presence of his brilliant father, who retired from a successful business in order to devote himself to theology and philosophy. He was held back from the university for a year, being judged immature. On entering the University of Copenhagen in 1831, he became involved in the social life of a group of aesthetes, talented but somewhat dissolute students, among whom was the writer Hans Christian Andersen.

Inattention to studies, partying, and high living delayed his academic progress, led to quarrels, and severed the relationship with his father. Kierkegaard left home and ceased church attendance. However, in 1838, having spent seven years at the university doing other things besides studying, his life hit bottom. In the depths of despair, he had a conversion experience, was reconciled to his aged and frail father, and dedicated himself to the Christian ministry. He then proceeded to finish his studies in two years and write a doctoral thesis in one year.

Around the time of his conversion, Kierkegaard fell deeply in love with a beautiful fifteen-year-old girl, Regina Olsen. A few years later, he began courting her and in September of 1840 he and the seventeen-year-old Regina were engaged. For a moment, Søren was the happiest man in the world, but the moment he walked out of Regina's home, he realized that it was a mistake, that he could never enter into a normal marital relationship, especially with such a lighthearted young woman as Regina. So believing God had called him to be an exception, a celibate, he spent the next year of his life trying to get Regina to break the engagement. Unsuccessful in this endeavor, he finally broke the engagement and went off to Berlin, where he wrote his first two-volume work *Either/Or*. Regina, in the meantime, recovered from the shock of the ruptured engagement and soon accepted the hand of a former friend. Kierkegaard, who never ceased to love Regina, had hoped that she too would remain single so that they might still maintain an intimate Platonic relationship.

Kierkegaard's relationship with Regina provided the impetus for his early writings. In many of the books, Regina was the unnamed audience, addressed obliquely and in poignant disappointed love.

Such a work is *Fear and Trembling*, written under the pseudonym Johannes de Silento (John the Silent, i.e., he cannot speak directly of his love or his reasons for breaking the engagement). The book is halfway between poetry and philosophy, combining passionate feeling with careful philosophical analysis. The central problem is "What is faith?" The underlying but carefully disguised situation is his problematic relationship with Regina, but the ostensive protagonist is Abraham, who was ready to sacrifice his only child, his most beloved, Isaac, to God. Kierkegaard saw his giving up of Regina as analogous to Abraham's offering, and he believed that he, too, would be recompensed by God "by virtue of the absurd" with the return of the beloved.

However, along with the veiled amorous wall to Regina was a complex philosophical disquisition on the relationship between religion and morality. Can God rightly command a person to suspend the moral law and do something normally considered immoral, such as kill an innocent person like Isaac (or break a promise or engagement to his beloved)? It is reported that Regina didn't understand the work.

"If I had had faith," Kierkegaard later wrote, "I would have married Regina."

This was the beginning of **existentialism** as a philosophical movement. For about fifty years, Kierkegaard's name, as well as his ideas, was almost entirely forgotten in the intellectual world. His books were long out of print and his private papers stowed away in a dusky closet, awaiting the sanitation department. Then suddenly, early in the twentieth century, his ideas exploded like a time bomb. Discovered first in Germany, his thoughts were initially linked with those of Friedrich Nietzsche (1844–1900).

Nietzsche held that the fundamental creative force that motivates all creation is the *will to power*. We all seek to affirm ourselves, to flourish and dominate. Since we are essentially unequal in ability, it follows that the fittest will survive and be victorious in the contest with the weaker and baser. There is great aesthetic beauty in the noble spirit coming to fruition, but this process is hampered by Judeo-Christian morality, which Nietzsche labeled "slave morality." Slave morality, which is the invention of jealous priests, envious and resentful of the power of the noble, prescribes that we give up the will to power and excellence and become meek and mild, that we believe the lie of all humans having equal worth. Of course, the herd really subscribes to the will to power as much as anyone—railing against it is a symptom of the will to power. Nietzsche also referred to this as the ethics of resentment. There is an age-old platitude, going at least as far back as the Roman historian Livy, which says "the tallest blades of grass get cut first."

Nietzsche's ideas of inegalitarian ethics are based on his notion of the death of God. God plays no vital role in our culture—except as a protector of the slave morality, including the idea of equal worth of all persons. If we recognize that

FRIEDRICH NIETZSCHE

Friedrich Nietzsche (1844–1900), a German existentialist, has played a major role in contemporary intellectual development. Descending through both of his parents from Christian ministers, Nietzsche was brought up in a pious German Lutheran home and was known as "the little Jesus" by his schoolmates. He studied theology at the University of Bonn and philology at Leipzig, becoming an atheist in the process. At the age of twenty-four, he was appointed professor of classical philology at the University of Basel in Switzerland where he taught for ten years until forced by ill health to retire. Eventually, he became mentally ill and spent the last ten years of his life in a mental institution. He died on August 25, 1900.

Thoughts on the Meaning of Life
Man would sooner have the Void for his purpose than be void of Purpose.

Hegel says, "That at the bottom of history, and particularly of world history, there is a final aim, and that this has actually been realized in it and is being realized—the plan of Providence—that there is reason in history: that is to be shown philosophically and this as altogether necessary." (This is balderdash.) My life has no aim and this is evident even from the accidental nature of its origin. That I can posit an aim for myself is another matter. But a state has no aim; we alone give it an aim.

Whatever does not kill me makes me stronger.

Truth and Untruth
A belief, however necessary it may be for the preservation of a species, has nothing to do with truth.

The falseness of a judgment is not for us necessarily an objection to a judgment. The question is to what extent it is life-promoting, life-preserving, species preserving, perhaps even species cultivating. To recognize untruth as a condition of life—that certainly means resisting accustomed value feelings in a dangerous way; and a philosophy that risks that would by that token alone place itself beyond good and evil. (*Beyond Good and Evil,* p. 4)

Beyond Good and Evil
To speak of right and wrong per se makes no sense at all. No act of violence, rape, exploitation, destruction, is intrinsically unjust, since life itself is violent, rapacious, exploitative, and destructive and cannot be conceived otherwise. (*Genealogy of Morals,* p. 208)

Will to Power
What is good? All that enhances the feeling of power, the Will to Power, and the power itself in man. What is bad?—All that proceeds from weakness. What is happiness?—The feeling that power is increasing—that resistance has been overcome.

Not contentment, but more power; not peace at any price but war; not virtue, but competence (virtue in the Renaissance sense, virtue, free from moralistic acid). The first principle of our humanism: The weak and the failures shall perish. They ought even to be helped to perish.

What is more harmful than any vice?—Practical sympathy and pity for all the failures and all the weak: Christianity.

Style and Character
One thing is needed—To give style to one's character—a great and rare art! It is practiced by those who survey all the strengths and weaknesses of their nature and then fit them into an artist plan until every one of them appears as art and reason and even weaknesses delight the eye. Here a large mass of second nature has been added; there a piece of original nature has been removed—both times through long practice and daily work at it. Here the ugly that could not be removed is concealed; there it has been reinterpreted and made sublime. Much that is vague and resisted shaping has been saved and exploited for distant views. . . . In the end, when the work is finished, it becomes evident how the constraint of a single taste governed and formed everything large and small. Whether this taste was good or bad is less important than one might suppose, if only it was a single taste!

The Übermensch (Superman)
We immoralists make it a point of honor to be affirmers. More and more our eyes have opened to that economy which needs and knows how to utilize all that the holy witlessness of the priest, of the diseased reason of the priest, rejects—that economy in the law of life which finds an advantage even in the disgusting species of the prigs, the priests, the virtuous. What advantage? But we ourselves, we immoralists, are the answer.

The Madman and the Death of God

Have you ever heard of the madman who on a bright morning lighted a lantern and ran to the market-place calling out unceasingly: "I seek God! I seek God"—As there were many people standing about who did not believe in God, he caused a great deal of amusement. Why! is he lost? said one. Has he strayed away like a child? said another. Or does he keep himself hidden? Is he afraid of us? Has he taken a sea-voyage? Has he emigrated?—the people cried out laughingly, all in a hubbub. The insane man jumped into their midst and transfixed them with his glances. "Where is God gone?" he called out. "I mean to tell you! *We have killed him,*—you and I! We are all his murderers! But how have we done it? How were we able to drink up the sea? Who gave us the sponge to wipe away the whole horizon? What did we do when we loosened this earth from its sun? Whither does it now move? Whither do we move? Away from all suns? Do we not dash on unceasingly? Backwards, sideways, forwards, in all directions: Is there still an above and below? Do we not stray, as through infinite nothingness? Does not empty space breathe upon us? Has it not become colder? Does not night come on continually, darker and darker? Shall we not have to light lanterns in the morning? Do we not hear the noise of the grave-diggers who are burying God? Do we not smell the divine putrefaction?—for even Gods putrefy! God is dead! God remains dead! And we have killed him! How shall we console ourselves, the most murderous of all murderers? The holiest and the mightiest that the world has hitherto possessed, has bled to death under our knife,—who will wipe the blood from us? With what water could we cleanse ourselves? What lustrums, what sacred games shall we have to devise? Is not the magnitude of this deed too great for us? Shall we not ourselves have to become Gods, merely to seem worthy of it? There never was a greater event,—and on account of it, all who are born after us belong to a higher history than any history hitherto!"—Here the madman was silent and looked again at his hearers; they also were silent and looked at him in surprise. At last he threw his lantern on the ground, so that it broke in pieces and was extinguished. "I come too early," he then said, "I am not yet at the right time. This prodigious event is still on its way, and is travelling,—it has not yet reached men's ears. Lightning and thunder need time, the light of the stars needs time, deeds need time, even after they are done, to be seen and heard. This deed is as yet further from them than the furthest star,—*and yet they have done it!*"—it is further stated that the madman made his way into different churches on the same day, and there intoned his *Requiem aeternam deo.* When led out and called to account, he always gave the reply: "What are these churches now, if they are not the tombs and monuments of God?"

there is no rational basis for believing in God, we will see that the whole edifice of slave morality must crumble and with it the notion of equal worth. In its place will arise the morality of noble persons, Supermen, based on the virtues of the high courage, discipline, and intelligence, in the pursuit of self-affirmation and excellence.

Thus, existentialism, as a Christian and an atheist's thought were linked together, entered the world as a two-pronged fork, disturbing the intellectual soil throughout Europe. First, it was the theologians, such as Karl Barth, Rudolf Bultmann, Paul Tillich, and Reinhold Niebuhr, who welcomed Kierkegaard's thoughts. Soon novelists and poets became infected with these new ideas: Fyodor Dostoevsky, Franz Kafka, Hermann Hesse, T. S. Eliot, and W. H. Auden and later Saul Bellow, Norman Mailer, John Barth, Walker Percy, and John Updike. A new breed of philosophers began to spring up, the existentialists, among whom are

Martin Buber, Martin Heidegger, Jean-Paul Sartre, and José Ortega y Gassett. Before long, existentialism had permeated the intellectual world everywhere. It was at first condemned by both the Communist Soviet Union as bourgeois sub-jectivism and by the Roman Catholic Church as dangerous individualism, though before long Catholics had appropriated many of its ideas.

What exactly is this new philosophy? What is its purpose and mission? Well, to touch the spirit of Kierkegaard's and existentialism's ideas, let me tell a story.

There was once a man who discovered his shadow. Watching its lithe motion, he assumed that it was alive. Because it followed him so faithfully, he decided that he was its master and that it was his servant. But gradually he began to believe that it was the shadow that was initiating the action and that the shadow was his irre-placeable guide and companion. He took increasing account of its comfort and welfare. He awkwardly maneuvered himself in order that it might sit in a chair or lie in bed. The importance of the shadow to the man grew to such an extent that finally the man became, in effect, "the shadow of his shadow"!

Existentialism is a call to look inward, to develop one's own personal phi-losophy of life, to get one's priorities right. Kierkegaard and Nietzsche deplored the tendency of humanity to become slaves of their technologies, "shadows of their shadows." Both decried the herd mentality of modern people, their sus-ceptibility to peer pressure, what others think. Kierkegaard warned in his jour-nals in the 1840s, long before the advent of television, that there would come a time when people would stare mesmerized into a box that would inform them on what to believe. The true individual must stand alone, deriving his or her ideals from within, not from without. The eternity that dwells within the heart is a neglected treasure by most people. Each of us has a duty to work out his or her own salvation with fear and trembling, to find a personal truth for which you can live and die.

THREE THESES OF EXISTENTIALISM

If we analyze existential writings, three theses stand out, embraced in one way or another by virtually all members of this movement. Let me identify and briefly comment on each one.

Existence Precedes Essence   In classical philosophy, notably that of Plato and Aristotle, the concept of essence preceded existence. Truth is eternal, unchange-able, absolute, and the central goal of philosophy. For Plato, as we saw in Part 3, the forms or essences exist in a transcendent dimension, and our job is to discover them through philosophical contemplation, through reason. Human beings have a common eternal ("essentialist") nature defined by reason ("Humans are ration-al animals"). As Aristotle said,

> Reason is the true self of every person, since it is the supreme and better part. It
> will be strange, then, if he should choose not his own life, but some other's. . . .
> What is naturally proper to every creature is the highest and pleasantest for him.
> And so, to man, this will be the life of Reason, since Reason is, in the highest
> sense, a man's self.

In one way or another, all the major philosophical systems from Plato through the Middle Ages down to René Descartes and Immanuel Kant carried on this essentialist tradition. Truth is outside of us, and our job is to use reason to discover it.

Existentialism denies the *priority* of objective Truth. What is important is what we do about ourselves, how we live within the light we have, the decisions we make. We find ourselves "thrown" into existence, afloat over 70,000 fathoms of ocean water, and we must somehow keep afloat (or drown). A key question becomes, Why not drown? But the urgency of finding a purpose to life radically transforms the relationship between objective truth and subjective apprehension. For Kierkegaard this thesis is set forth in his dictum that "subjectivity is Truth."

All existential problems are passionate problems, for when existence is interpreted with reflection it generates passion. To think about existential problems without passion is tantamount to not thinking about them at all, since it is to forget the point—that the thinker is himself an existing individual. Passion is the way to Truth, and the way may be more valuable than the end.

A precursor of existentialism, the German philosopher Gotthold Lessing (1729–1781), said, "If God set forth before me the Eternal, unchangeable Truth in his right hand and the eternal quest for Truth in his left hand and said, 'Choose,' I would point to the left hand and say, 'Father, give me this, for the eternal unchangeable Truth belongs to you alone.'" The quest for Truth is appropriate to the dynamics of people still growing, still in need of spiritual development. The reason that God can truly possess absolute Truth is that he is pure Subjectivity (pure Love), but we are sinful, selfish, ignorant, and alienated from the ground of our being; the way to overcome this alienation (for Kierkegaard it is equivalent to sin) is to delve deep and act from our inner resources, listening to the still small voice within rather than the roar of the crowd or the imperious voice of authority.

In this regard, the existentialists follow Blaise Pascal (1623–1662): "The heart has reasons which the mind knows nothing of." Kierkegaard disagreed with Aristotle about the divinity of reason within us: "In existence rational thought is by no means higher than imagination and feeling, but coordinate. In existence all factors must be co-present." The passions, feelings, intuitions, and imagination have been neglected by philosophers, but they are just as valuable as reason and also define our being:

> When the question of truth is put forward in an objective manner, reflection is directed objectively to the truth as an object to which the knower is related. The reflection is not on the relationship but on whether he is related to the truth. If that which he is related to is the truth, the subject is in the truth. When the question of truth is put forward in a subjective manner, the reflection is directed subjectively to the individual's relationship. If the relation's HOW is in truth, the individual is in truth, even if the WHAT to which he is related is not true.
>
> We may illustrate this by examining the knowledge of God. Objectively, the reflection is on whether the object is the true God; subjectively, the reflection is on whether the individual is related to a *what* in such a way that his relationship is a God-relationship.
>
> If one who lives in a Christian culture goes up to God's house, the house of the true God, with a true conception of God, with knowledge of God and prays—but prays in a false spirit; and one who lives in an idolatrous land prays with the total passion of the infinite, although his eyes rest on the image of an idol; where is there

most truth? The one prays in truth to God, although he worships an idol. The other prays in untruth to the true God and therefore really worships an idol.

Here is a definition of Truth: An objective uncertainty held fast in an approximation process of the most passionate inwardness is the truth, the highest truth attainable for an existing individual. . . . The above definition is an equivalent expression for faith. Without risk there is no faith. Faith is precisely the contradiction between the infinite passion of the individual's inwardness and the objective uncertainty. If I am capable of grasping God objectively, I do not believe, but precisely because I cannot do this I must believe . . . , so as to remain out upon the deep, over seventy fathoms of water, still preserving my faith.[3]

We find ourselves thrown out into a sea of unknowing:

Sitting quietly in a ship while the weather is calm is not a picture of faith; but when the ship has sprung a leak, enthusiastically to keep the ship afloat by pumping while yet not seeking the harbor; this is the picture. And if the picture involves an impossibility in the long run, that is but the imperfection of the picture.[4]

Existence is a task filled with paradoxes and never completed. It demands our passionate interest, and reason must take its proper place as a servant of the inner promptings of a passionate heart.

The Absurdity of Existence In his autobiography, Count Leo Tolstoy (1828–1910) tells the story of a traveler fleeing an infuriated animal. Attempting to save himself from the beast, the man runs toward a well and begins to climb down, when to his distress he spies a dragon at the bottom of the well. The dragon is waiting with open jaws, ready to eat him. The poor fellow is caught in a dilemma. He dares not drop into the well for fear of the dragon, but he dares not climb out of the well for fear of the beast. So he clutches a branch of a bush growing in the cleft of the well and hangs onto it for dear life. His hands grow weak, and he feels that soon he will have to give in to his grim fate, but he still holds on desperately. As he grasps the branch for his salvation, he notices that two mice, one white and one black, are nibbling away at the main trunk of the branch onto which he is clinging. Soon they will dislodge the branch.

The traveler is you and I, and his plight is yours and mine, the danger of our demise on every hand. The white mouse represents our days and the black our nights. Together they are nibbling away at the three-score years and ten, which make up our branch of life. Inevitably all will be over, and what have we to show for it? Is this all there is? Can this brief moment in the history of the universe have significance? What gives life value or importance?

The certainty of death heightens the question of the meaning of life. Like a prisoner sentenced to death or a patient with a terminal illness, we know that, in a sense, we are all sentenced to death and are terminally ill, but we flee the thought in a thousand ways. What is the purpose of life?

Albert Camus (1913–1960) compares our existence to that of Sisyphus in Greek mythology. Sisyphus was condemned by the gods for disobedience. His punishment consisted in rolling a huge boulder up the side of a mountain until it reaches the top, whereupon the boulder rolls down to the bottom and Sisyphus must follow its course and retrieve it. He goes through this process again and again for all eternity. Tedious, boring, meaningless, such is the process of our never-ending toil. Consider the average person in our society. One Monday morning, a man or woman gets up early in the morning, washes, dresses, goes to the toilet, and eats breakfast. Another hour or so is spent mindlessly commuting to a job whose work, when looked at with a lucid eye, is ultimately purposeless. If it weren't for the grim need to earn a livelihood, sane people would laugh at such behavior. Then, return: a mindless commute to a mindless evening before a mindless entertainment box and then to a mindless sleep. The sorry saga is repeated Tuesday, Wednesday, Thursday, and Friday for over forty years until the person retires, too old to discover the vacuity of his or her existence. Saturday, he or she spends recovering from the exhaustion of the first five mindless days, and on Sunday he or she is bored at the home of relatives or else enjoys the inconsequential gossip about others, wrings his or her hands at the downward course of the world (especially the young), or mindlessly watches a football game on TV. Occasionally, to relieve the pain of existence, the person gets drunk, takes drugs, or soothes his or her raging hormones in an act that any animal can perform. And what is the goal of such mortals? To generate and rear children so that they can perpetuate this farce.

Is this what life is all about? No wonder Camus says the "one truly philosophical problem" is, Why not commit suicide?

Kierkegaard, being religious, agrees with such sentiments to the extent that life for most people is **absurd,** but he argues that our very alienation from what we inwardly sense to be a higher self is a hint of God's voice, a holy hypochondria, calling us back, inwardly, to God. Not rational demonstration, not the philosophical proofs of God's existence, but the inner turmoil of the soul in the absurdity of existence lead us to make a leap of faith into a religious mode of existence. Absurdity is not an objective but a subjective problem that calls for a subjective response, a decision in passion, a leap of faith into the religious way of life.

Only those who have felt the contradictions of life, the inner alienation, the dread and despair connected with self-realization can appreciate religion, but to have experienced the absurd in life is to be a candidate for the religious quest:

> In this manner God certainly becomes a hypothesis, but not in the useless, passionless way this word is generally used. The only way that an individual can come into a relation with God is when the dialectical contradiction brings his passion to the point of despair, and helps him to embrace God with the "category of despair"—faith. Then the hypothesis that God exists becomes far from arbitrary or detached but a life-necessity. It is not so much that God becomes a hypothesis as that the individual's hypothesis of God becomes necessary.[5]

Ultimately, Kierkegaard believes that Christianity, with its doctrine of the Incarnation, wherein God becomes man in Christ, is the proper fit for the passions of the heart:

> Subjectivity culminates in passion, Christianity [through the doctrine of the Incarnation] is the paradox, paradox and passion are a mutual fit, and the paradox is altogether suited to one whose situation is, to be in the extremity of existence. Aye, never in all the world could there be found two lovers so wholly suited to one another as paradox and passion.[6]

Freedom Jean-Paul Sartre (1905–1980) has emphasized this aspect of our being more than anyone. We "are condemned to freedom." Sartre connects the notion of freedom with the idea that existence precedes essence. Imagine an idea of the most magnificent house in the world, your dream house. You decide to build it and call an architect to design the plans. Then you hire a builder who constructs the house according to your plans. Now you have an existing house to serve your purpose. The essence (or idea) precedes the existence of the house.

Traditionally, this is how humans have viewed the relation between essence and existence. There was a God who had an idea of man and woman and who created them in his image. They, like the house, had a definite nature and a purpose. Their being was defined as rational immortal souls. Existence was merely the living out of this essence.

But take away God. For the atheist (like Sartre or Camus), there is no ideal mind that defines our being. We are not like the house that has been designed for a purpose with a definite nature. We are just born. We find ourselves conscious beings without definite nature or purpose but completely free to determine our nature. We must create our essence:

> The child takes his parents for gods. Their actions like their judgments are absolute. They are the incarnation of universal Reason, law, the meaning and purpose of the world. When the eye of these divine beings is turned on him, their look is enough to justify him at once to the very roots of his existence. It confers on him a definite, sacred character. Since they are infallible, it follows that they see him as he really is. There is no room in his mind for hesitation or doubt. True, all that he sees of himself is the vague success of his moods, but the gods have made themselves the guardians of his eternal essence. He knows that it exists. Even though he can have no direct experience of it, he realizes that his truth does not consist in what he can know of himself, but that it is hidden in the large, terrible yet gentle eyes which are turned towards him. He is a real essence among other real essences; he has his place in the world—an absolute place in an absolute world.[7]

JEAN-PAUL SARTRE

Jean-Paul Sartre was born in 1905 into the home of a historic Swiss-French Protestant family, the Schweitzers. He was the second cousin of Albert Schweitzer. His father died when he was one year old, so he was brought up by his young mother Anne Marie, who was more like his playmate and worshiper than parent, and his maternal grandfather in Alsace. Of his childhood he wrote, "I had no rights because I was overwhelmed with love. I had no duties because I did everything through love." His godlike grandfather spoke to him once about being a writer. Sartre mistook it for a divine command and spent the rest of his life in obedience. He sometimes wrote 10,000 words a day.

That is what the historian of ideas, Paul Johnson, has to say about Sartre:

> October 29, 1945 is the turning point in French culture. Shortly after the end of World War II a beleaguered and exhausted France is trying to recover from defeat and four years of German occupation. A lecture was to be given at the Club Maintenant. Everyone came, fights broke out, people went hysterical trying to get into the hall, which was packed to capacity. Frenchmen and women fought each other for chairs and with chairs, smashing 30 of them before the lecture. Men and women fainted in the fray, as they were crushed against one another. When the celebrated speaker arrived, the mob in the street was so

large, he thought that he was witnessing a demonstration organized by the Communist Party. His friends had to force an entrance for him. Meanwhile, the theaters in Paris were deserted. A leading speaker addressed an all but empty hall. All Paris had gone to hear a short (5'2"), squinty, bespectacled mole of a man give a lecture entitled "Existentialism Is a Humanism." Who was this man and what caused this astonishing spectacle?

A new literary and philosophical hero had emerged from the war with a new philosophy in tune with the times, which accepted the dark tragedy of defeat and war and the absurdity of the human condition. A secular priest was offering a secular gospel, Existentialism, which was neither Christian or Communist, to make sense of a senseless world. Jean-Paul Sartre had just launched his new literary review, *Les Temps Modernes* (named after Charlie Chaplin's famous film) and was about to give one of the most famous speeches in modern cultural history. This editor, philosopher, novelist, and playwright, who would soon be referred to as the "Eiffel Tower of French Culture," would dominate the intellectual life of Europe for the next 25 years. At his funeral April 19, 1980, 50,000 French people would converge in procession on the Montparnasse Cemetery. Sartre's press coverage defied the wildest dreams. Several newspapers carried every word of the long lecture. The Catholic daily *La Croix* called Sartre's existentialism "a greater danger than eighteenth-century rationalism or nineteenth-century positivism." Soon all his books were placed on the Roman Catholic Index (list of censored books), which greatly increased their sales. The Communist *L'Humanite* called Sartre an enemy of society, and Stalin's cultural commissar, Alexander Fadayev, called him "a Jackal with a typewriter, a hyena with a fountain pen." It was the greatest intellectual promotion scheme of the century. "Existentialism as a Humanism" sold over 1/2 million copies in the first month alone. (From Paul Johnson, *Modern Times* [New York: Harper & Row, 1983].)

As the child grows, he or she discovers that his parents are fallible, that they are neither gods nor viceroys of God, that the whole phenomenon of the essence-granting process is a charade. There is no God, no essence, no absolute place in the universe for us, no absolute determinants whatsoever. We are free to create our own essence; we are condemned to **absolute freedom.**

Sartre tells a story to illustrate how even our morality is relative to our free, creative invention. During World War II, a student came to Sartre in order to ask for advice. Should he fight for his country by fleeing France and crossing the channel to England where DeGaulle's Free French Army was preparing for a battle with the Vichy government? Or should he stay home and care for his ailing mother? What does morality require of me? he asked Sartre. Sartre told him that he couldn't give advice, that morality didn't *require* anything as such, but that he, the student, must create his own morality. He must decide which principle to live by and universalize it for all people. Even morality is a function of our freedom.

For Kierkegaard even faith itself is a function of freedom. Reason is a whore who pays the highest bidder: "If I really have reason and am in the situation in which I must act decisively, my reason will put forth as many possibilities *pro* and *contra*, exactly as many." Reason always leads to skepticism, leaving all important issues in doubt; so faith must take over where reason leaves off. Through freedom the leap of faith comes into play. You are responsible even for what you believe!

We usually think of freedom as a very positive, salutary trait, one that all adolescents crave. But it is, according to the existentialists, at least as negative as it is positive. It is a dreadful freedom, imposing a heavy burden of responsibility on us, for with it we cannot get off the hook of existence. We are totally responsible for our actions, for what we become.

The experience of freedom is not that of fear. It's inappropriate to say that we fear freedom. We dread it. It causes deep anxiety within.

Imagine that you are walking along a narrow ridge overlooking two precipices on either side, with no guard rail to hold onto. You might have fear that you will slip on a stone and be hurled over into the abyss or that the earth will give way beneath you. But you might also experience anguish at the vertigo, or dizziness, of looking over the cliff, which could result in your falling into the abyss. You might be numbly aware of a certain attraction for the abyss, which calls to you from below, to which you might respond by casting yourself into its deep bosom. Fear is caused by the world, by an external object that we would avoid. But dread or anxiety is not caused by the world but by ourselves. We would like to ensure our beings against the contingency of freedom, but we can't. No guarantee is given against our destructive use of freedom. It is ominous, pervading our entire being, pushing us at every moment. In dreadful freedom we shape our essence. We said before that, for the existentialists, humans lack an essence, but we could say that freedom is our essence.

In Sartre's most famous play, *No Exit,* three people sit in hell, torturing one another, each believing that fate has conspired against them and that they are damned to torment one another for eternity. "Hell is other people." But at the end of the play, we see that the door next to them has always been unlocked. They endure damnation by their own volition. Similarly, you are responsible for what you do and what you become. You are free to change just as soon as you decide to do so.

ASSESSMENT

Existentialism has served, at least, as an important corrective for an overly rationalistic philosophy that would tend to leave out an appreciation of the arts, the imagination, the passions, and emotions. Perhaps certain classical and medieval systems were guilty of that. Kierkegaard thought that the German idealist George F. W. Hegel (1770–1831) was the major villain of his day. Hegel, Kierkegaard contended, erected marvelous castles in the ethereal heavens of thought while he himself lived in an existential doghouse. Take care, philosopher, how you live!

Each of us must come to terms with his or her personal existence. Kierkegaard is correct. Philosophy must become personal. We must work out the meaning of our lives, not once but continually. Actually, I think many philosophers before Kierkegaard, Nietzsche, and Sartre said as much. Socrates sought to make philosophy practical and personal. St. Augustine recognized the inward element of philosophical endeavor. René Descartes threw off all previous authority in order to work out a new and vibrant system of thought. David Hume recognized the role of the passions and emotions, stating that "reason is and ought only to be a slave of the passions, and can never pretend to any other office than to serve them."[8]

Perhaps it is mainly in its emphasis on the subjective, on freedom, that existentialists tend to distinguish themselves. But this is just where the criticism of existentialism starts. Does it not overemphasize the role and reality of freedom and undermine the reality of determinate structures and the role of reason? I think so.

Sartre, in his passion for freedom, goes so far as to reject the reality of the unconscious! Apparently, even our dreams are freely chosen. But psychologists, if not the Bible and common sense, have taught us that we are not always aware of our deepest motives, that we deceive ourselves, that early experiences, long buried in our subconscious, incline our behavior. Indeed, whether and to what extent we are free is itself a deeply philosophical problem, as we saw in Part 5. Reason is the means by which we discover whether and to what extent we are free.

The emphasis on subjectivity and freedom easily slides into an overemphasis on *individualism*, tending toward a solipsism where the self becomes a world entire to itself, cut off from other selves. But, to quote John Donne, "No man is an island." Men and women are social beings, connected to one another in interpersonal relations, through such institutions as family, school, club, business, community, city, and state. We are all in one another's debt so that we must come out of ourselves, communicate with others, reason together, and strive for an interpersonal moral code.

For Kierkegaard no moral rule was fully binding. God could at any moment call on people to sacrifice their loved ones as he once called Abraham to do. Notice Sartre's description of his student's dilemma over whether to leave his mother and join the Free French Forces or remain with her. Isn't this a dilemma just because two recognizably valid values are at stake: loyalty to family and devotion to justice? What if the student had come to Sartre and said, "I have a dilemma. I want to know whether I should rape my mother or take care of her?" Would Sartre have nothing more to say than, "Morality requires nothing. You must choose your own morality and universalize it for all others!" If so, then we can only say that he misunderstands the social function of morality, which in part is to procure human flourishing and the resolution of conflicts of interest. The mistake of existentialism is to suppose that every moral decision has the same status as a genuine dilemma; but if everything is a dilemma, then nothing is, for nothing matters. It is only because morality has a rational structure wherein universal values inhere that we can rightly realize that sometimes we are placed in situations where two values compete or where whatever we do will be an evil of sorts and so choose the lesser of evils.

So what I recommend is a rationalized, socialized, moral existentialism or, what comes to much the same thing, an analytic philosophy that recognizes the need for autonomy and subjective depth. Reason is a higher value than existentialists sometimes allow, but the passions, imagination, and personal adaptation of ideas are also important, more so than traditional philosophy has sometimes recognized. We are by nature feeling creatures, but so are other animals. What sets us apart is largely our ability to reason and deliberate on our desires and emotions and to act on those deliberations. And then, of course, we can reason about the reasoning that went into the earlier reasons and deliberations. We can judge, compare, and communicate our reasons to others in argument, revise our conclusions in the light of their rational critiques, and generally make progress toward being wiser, more understanding persons.

SUMMARY

Existentialism is a type of philosophy that is rooted in lived experience, concerned with human freedom and purpose in the midst of apparent absurdity. Both religious and secular versions emphasize the need for personal decision, freedom, and the contingent. Kierkegaard, the father of existentialism, thought that the quest for meaning would lead to religion, but secular existentialists—Nietzsche, Sartre, and Camus—reject religion as a viable option and call on humans to live without objective meaning or religion. We noted the criticisms of existentialism—that it tends to be overly individualistic and may become irrational. It may seem as a corrective to more purely abstract (*essentialist*) philosophies.

QUESTIONS FOR DISCUSSION

1. Do you agree with Sartre that there is no objective purpose in life but that each of us must give our lives a purpose? Or are there objective purposes already present that we need only discover? Explain.

2. Some people say that life is made meaningful by ameliorating the suffering in society and/or by bringing revolutionary changes into being. As a youth, the English philosopher John Stuart Mill had such a view. In his *Autobiography,* Mill describes the crisis of meaning that took place in his twenty-second year of life. Following the English utilitarian reformer Jeremy Bentham, his whole life had been dedicated to social reform, and as long as he could see the world improving, he felt satisfaction and even happiness. But a crisis arose in 1826. He was in "a dull state of nerves, such as everybody is occasionally liable to," when the following question occurred to him:

   > Suppose that all your objects in life were realized; that all the changes in institutions and opinions which you are looking forward to, could be completely effected at this very instant: would this be a great joy and happiness to you? An irrepressible self-consciousness distinctly answered, "No!" At this my heart sank within me: the whole foundation on which my life was constructed fell down. All my happiness was to have been founded in the continual pursuit of this end. The end had ceased to charm, and how could there ever again be any interest in the means? I seemed to have nothing left to live for.[9]

   Mill went through a deep depression that lasted several months, in which he came close to suicide. Ask yourself the same question as he did. What would your answer be? What is the significance of your answer?

3. What gives you meaning in life? Kierkegaard defined *subjective truth* as that for which you are willing to live and die. What are you willing to live and die for?

4. Some people argue that only something eternal like God or religious ideals can satisfy the human heart. "Thou hast made us for Thyself, O Lord, and our hearts are restless until they rest in Thee," wrote St. Augustine. Do you agree with this? Explain your answer.

5. Do you agree with the existentialists, especially Sartre, that we are "condemned to freedom"? Are we responsible for what we do with our lives, or
do chance and circumstances have a lot more to do with what we become
than the existentialists assert?

NOTES

1. Søren Kierkegaard, *Papirer,* vol. 1, ed. P A.
Heiberg and Victor Kuhr (Copenhagen:
Gyldendals, 1909); my translation.

2. Ibid.

3. Søren Kierkegaard, *Samlede Vaerker,*
vol. 7, ed. A. B. Drachmann, J. L. Heiberg,
and H. O. Lange (Copenhagen: Gyldendals,
1901); my translation.

4. Ibid.

5. Ibid.

6. Ibid.

7. Jean-Paul Sartre, *Words,* trans. Bernard
Frechtman (New York: Braziller, 1964).

8. David Hume, *Treatise on Human Nature*
(1739), 415.

9. J. S. Mill, *Autobiography* (1873).

FOR FURTHER READING

Barrett, William. *Irrational Man.* New York:
Doubleday, 1958. Still the best introduction to existentialism.

Bretall, Robert, ed. *A Kierkegaard Anthology.*
Princeton, NJ: Princeton University
Press, 1946. A good collection.

Camus, Albert. *The Myth of Sisyphus and
Other Essays,* translated by J. O.
O'Brien. New York: Random House,
1955. Camus's youthful, brilliant essay.

Camus, Albert. *The Plague.* New York: Random House, 1948. Deals poignantly with
existentialism and the problem of evil.

Frankl, Victor. *Man's Search for Meaning.*
Boston: Beacon Press, 1963. An important work in existential psychology.

Kaufmann, Walter, ed. and trans. *A Portable
Nietzsche.* New York: Viking Press, 1954.
A good collection.

Kaufmann, Walter, ed. *Existentialism from
Dostoevsky to Sartre.* New York: New
American Library, 1975. A good
anthology.

Kierkegaard, Søren. *Fear and Trembling,* translated by Walter Lowrie. Princeton, NJ:
Princeton University Press, 1954. One
of Kierkegaard's most important works.

Klemke, E. D. *The Meaning of Life.* New
York: Oxford University Press, 1981. A
good collection.

Nietzsche, Friedrich. *Beyond Good and Evil,*
translated by Walter Kaufmann. New
York: Random House, 1966. A classic.

Oaklander, Nathan, ed. *Existentialist
Philosophy.* Englewood Cliffs, NJ:
Prentice Hall, 1992. An excellent anthol-
ogy with important introductory essays.

Pojman, Louis. *Kierkegaard's Philosophy of
Religion.* San Francisco: International
Scholars Press, 1999. A critical examina-
tion of Kierkegaard's thought.

Sartre, Jean-Paul. *Existentialism and Human
Emotions.* New York: Philosophical
Library, 1948. A classic in modern
existentialism.

How to Read and Write a Philosophy Paper

The styles and methods of philosophy are different from other subjects you have been acquainted with since grammar school: English, history, psychology, and science. Of course, there are many methods, and some writings (e.g., the existentialists—Søren Kierkegaard, Friedrich Nietzsche, Albert Camus, and Jean-Paul Sartre) do resemble what we encounter in literature more than the typical essays in philosophical analysis. In some ways, philosophy resembles mathematics since it usually strives to develop a deductive argument much like a mathematical proof; the premises of the argument, however, are usually in need of much discussion and objections need to be considered. Sometimes I think of arguing about a philosophical problem as a kind of legal reasoning before a civil court. Both sides present their evidence and give reasons for accepting their conclusion rather than the opponent's. For example, suppose you believe in freedom of the will and I believe in determinism. We each set forth the best reasons we have for accepting our respective conclusions. The difference between philosophical argument and the court case is that we are also the jury. We can change our minds on hearing the evidence and even change sides by hearing our opponent make a persuasive case.

Suggestions on Writing a Philosophy Paper Talking about philosophy and writing philosophy are excellent ways to improve your understanding of the content and process of the subject, as well as to improve your skill of philosophical reasoning. Writing an essay on a philosophical issue focuses your mind and forces you to concentrate on the essential arguments connected with the issue. The process is harder than it may seem to some, but it's amazing how much progress one can make. Some writers are faster than others, but in my experience some of those who have the hardest time of it at first end up doing the deepest, most thorough work.

First, you must identify a *problem* that you want to shed light on or solve or a *thesis* that you want to defend. As a preliminary to writing your paper, be sure that you have read at least a few good articles on different sides of the issue and can put the arguments found in these articles in your own words. Now you are ready to begin to write. Here are some suggestions, which may help you:

1. Identify the problem that you want to analyze. For example, you might want to show that W. T. Stace has put forth an unsound argument for the thesis that freedom and determinism can be reconciled (discussed in Chapter 20).

2. State the problem and what you intend to show as clearly as possible (e.g., "I intend to analyze Stace's argument for compatibilism and show that he has misconstrued the issue. His argument for compatibilism is unsound.").

3. Set forth your argument in logical order, supporting your own premises with reasons. It may help to illustrate your points with examples or to point out counterexamples to the opposing points of view.

4. Consider alternative points of view from your own and objections to your position. Try to meet these charges and show why your position is more plausible.

5. End your paper with a summary. Review your argument and show its implications for other issues.

6. You probably will need at least two drafts before you have a working copy. It helps to get another philosophy student to go over the preliminary draft before you write a final draft. Make sure that your argument is well constructed and that your paper as a whole has coherence.

7. Regarding style, write *clearly* in an active voice, put other people's ideas in your own words as much as possible, and use footnotes wherever you have used someone else's idea.

8. Include a bibliography at the end of your paper, listing all sources used for your paper.

When you have a serious problem, do not hesitate to contact your teacher. That is why he or she is there: to help you make progress in doing philosophical reasoning.

Good luck, and I hope you come to enjoy the philosophical quest for truth and wisdom as much as I have.

Glossary*

abduction A form of nondeductive reasoning. Sometimes referred to as inference to the best explanation in which the proponent argues that this explanation beats all its rivals as a plausible account of the events in question. (See Chapter 2.)

absolute A moral absolute is a principle that is universally binding. It can never be overridden by another principle. *Utilitarianism** is a type of system that has only one ethical absolute principle: Do that action that maximizes utility. Immanuel Kant's system has several absolutes, whereas other deontological systems may have only a few broad absolutes, such as "Never cause unnecessary harm." Sometimes ethical absolutism refers to the notion that there is only one correct answer to every moral problem. Diametrically opposed to ethical absolutism is ethical *relativism:* The validity of ethical principles is dependent on social acceptance. In between these polar opposites is ethical *objectivism.*

absolute freedom A concept found in Jean-Paul Sartre's writings to indicate that we are always free to choose and are entirely responsible for our actions.

absurd Irrational, paradoxical, or contradictory. Søren Kierkegaard used the term in two ways: (1) to indicate the apparent contradictions in existence and (2) to signify the Christian doctrine of the Incarnation in which God becomes man in Jesus Christ. This is the absurd, yet, for the passionate believer, the truth. Albert Camus, following Kierkegaard's first meaning, uses the concept to refer to "the confrontation of the reasonable man and an indifferent universe."

ad hoc A *proposition* added to a theory in order to save it from being considered logically impossible or implausible. As ad hoc, the proposition itself may have little or no support itself but simply serve to stave off rejection of the original theory.

agnosticism The view that we do not know whether God exists. It is contrasted with *theism,* the belief in God, and *atheism,* the belief that there is no such being. Although the term is used loosely, a popular way of describing agnostics versus believers and

*__*Note:__ Italicized terms within a definition are defined in this glossary.

atheists is to say that the believer in God holds that the probability of God's existence
is greater than 50 percent, the atheist holds that it is less than 50 percent, and the
agnostic holds that it is right at 50 percent. T. H. Huxley coined the phrase to point to
a less dogmatic attitude from either *theism* or *atheism.*

anthropomorphism From the Greek, meaning "form of humanity." The tendency to
see the divine as having human properties. David Hume argued that when theists view
God as a superhuman being, rather than as something infinitely beyond humanity, they
sacrifice the essence of God's transcendence. (See Chapter 5.)

a posteriori From the Latin, meaning "the later." Knowledge that is obtained only from
experience, such as sense perceptions or pain sensations.

a priori From the Latin, meaning "preceding." Knowledge that is not based on sense
experience but is innate or known simply by the meaning of words or definitions.
David Hume limited the term to "relations of ideas," referring to analytic truths and
mathematics.

aretaic ethics From the Greek, meaning "virtue." The theory, first presented by
Aristotle, that the basis of ethical assessment is character. Rather than seeing the heart
of ethics in actions or duties, it focuses on the character and dispositions of the agent.
Whereas *deontological* and *teleological ethics* emphasize "doing," aretaic or virtue ethics
emphasize "being," being a certain type of person who will no doubt manifest his or
her being in appropriate actions.

argument A process of reasoning from a set of statements, or premises, to a conclusion.
Arguments are either valid or invalid. They are valid if they have proper logical form
and invalid if they do not. (See also *deductive argument* and *inductive argument.*)

assumption A principle or *proposition* that is taken for granted in an argument.

atheism The view that there is no such being as God. (See also *agnosticism* and *theism.*)

autonomy Self-rule, independence. Immanuel Kant uses the term to mean freedom from
external authority (*heteronomy*). It is the ability of the rational person to choose for
himself or herself. Truly autonomous selves, Kant thought, would arrive at common
judgments on moral issues. (See Chapter 25.)

behaviorism The view that no mental events exist or that they are unimportant for science. Statements about mental events are really about dispositions to behave. "She's
angry with me" really means that she is disposed to do nasty things to me and say nasty
things about me. The most important recent behaviorist was B. F. Skinner. (See
Chapters 13 and 14).

biological naturalism The view championed by John Searle and others that consciousness is an emergent property that arises from neurophysiological processes in the brain.
(See Chapter 15.)

categorical imperative The categorical imperative commands actions that are necessary
of themselves without reference to other ends. This is contrasted with the *hypothetical
imperative,* which commands actions not for their own sakes but for some other good.
For Immanuel Kant, moral duties command categorically. They represent the injunctions of reason, which endows them with universal validity and objective necessity.
(See Chapter 25.)

coherence theory of truth The theory that a *proposition* is true only if it coheres with
a system of propositions that mutually entail and support each other. (See Chapter 10.)

compatibilism The view that an act may be entirely determined and yet be free in the
sense that it was done voluntarily and not under external coercion. It is sometimes
referred to as "soft determinism." However, whereas soft determinism positively holds
to *determinism,* compatibilism may be agnostic on the truth of determinism, holding
only that if we are determined, we could still be said to act freely under some conditions. (See Chapter 20.)

contingent A *proposition* is contingent if its denial is logically possible and is not contradictory. A being is contingent if it is not logically necessary. (See Chapter 6.)

contradiction When one statement denies another, both of which cannot be true. For example, "God exists" and "God does not exist."

correspondence theory of truth The theory that a *proposition* is true just in case it corresponds with the facts or states of affairs in reality. The theory goes back to Plato and, especially, Aristotle, who said, "To say of what is that it is not, or of what is not that it is, is false, while to say of what is that it is, or of what is not that it is not, is true."

cultural relativism See *relativism*.

deductive argument An *argument* is a sound deductive argument if it follows a valid form and has true premises. In that case, the truth of its conclusion is guaranteed. A deductive argument is valid (but not necessarily sound) if it follows an approved form that would guarantee the truth of the conclusion if the premises were true. (See Chapter 2.)

deism The view that God exists but takes no interest in human affairs. He wound up the world like a clock and then left it to run itself down.

deontological ethics From the Greek, meaning "duty." Deontological ethical systems see certain features in the moral act itself as having intrinsic value. These are contrasted with *teleological ethics,* which see the ultimate criterion of morality in some non-moral value that results from actions. For example, for the deontologist, there is something right about truth telling even when it may cause pain or harm, and there is something wrong about lying even when it may produce good consequences. (See Chapter 25.)

deontology See *deontological ethics.*

determinism The theory that every event and state of affairs in the world, including human actions, are caused. There are two versions of determinism: hard determinism, which states that because every event is caused, no one is responsible for his or her actions; and soft determinism, or *compatibilism,* which states that rational creatures can still be held accountable for their actions insofar as they acted voluntarily. (See Chapter 18.)

dualism or dualistic interactionism The view that there are two types of substances or realities in conscious beings, mind and matter, and that these interact with each other, the body producing mental events and the mind leading to physical action.

egoism There are two types of egoism. Psychological egoism is a descriptive theory about human motivation and holds that people always act to satisfy their perceived best interests. Ethical egoism is a prescriptive, or normative, theory about how people ought to act. They ought to act according to their perceived best interests. (See Chapter 23.)

eliminative materialism The view that *folk psychology* (commonsense language about mental states, including beliefs, emotions, desires, and intentions) will eventually be replaced in favor of a neurologically accurate language reporting brain states. For example, instead of saying "I have a pain in my forehead," we might be led to say, "My C5 fiber is firing at such and such a rate." (See Chapter 14.)

empiricism The school of philosophy that asserts that the source of all knowledge is experience. John Locke stated that our minds were like blank slates (*tabula rasa*) on which experience writes her messages. There are no *innate ideas*. Empiricism is contrasted with *rationalism,* which holds that there are innate ideas so that the mind can discover important metaphysical truth through reason alone. In our readings, David Hume and Bertrand Russell are empiricists.

epiphenomenalism A version of *dualism* that holds that bodily events cause mental events, but mental events do not cause bodily events. The action is one-way only, from body to mind. (See Chapter 13.)

epistemology The study of the nature, origin, and validity of knowledge and belief. (See Chapter 10.)

ethical relativism See *relativism*.

eudaimonia Aristotle's word for "happiness."

existentialism The philosophical method that studies human existence from the inside of the subject's experience rather than the outside. It takes a first-person, or subjective, approach to the ultimate questions rather than a third-person, or objective, approach. Examples of this view are the Danish philosopher Søren Kierkegaard, the German philosopher Friedrich Nietzsche, and the French philosophers Jean-Paul Sartre and Albert Camus. (See Chapter 27.)

externalism The epistemological view that knowledge is not to be understood in terms of reasons justifying a true belief but as beliefs produced by reliable processes, such as perception or deductive reasoning. (See Chapter 10 and *internalism*.)

fideism The doctrine that one does not need evidence for one's religious faith. Reason is inappropriate for religious belief. (See Chapter 9.)

folk psychology Our commonsense view about mental events (e.g., pains, beliefs, desires, emotions, and intentions) that sees them as of a different nature from physical events and substance. (See Chapter 14.)

functionalism The theory that denies there need be a type–type relationship between mental events and mental states. Although mental events may be identical to certain processes in one brain, they may be identical to a different process in a different brain, and they may eventually be produced in robots without brains like ours. (See Chapter 15.)

hedonic From the Greek *hedon,* meaning "pleasure." Possessing a pleasurable or painful quality. Sometimes "hedon" is used to stand for a quantity of pleasure.

hedonism Psychological hedonism is the theory that motivation is to be explained exclusively in terms of desire for pleasure and aversion from pain. Ethical hedonism is the theory that pleasure is the only intrinsic positive value and pain, or "unpleasant consciousness," the only thing that has negative intrinsic value or intrinsic disvalue. All other values are derived from these two.

hedonistic paradox This is the apparent contradiction arising from the doctrine that pleasure is the only thing worth seeking and the fact that whenever one seeks pleasure, it is not found. Pleasure normally arises as an accompaniment of satisfaction of desire whenever one reaches one's goal. (See Chapter 23.)

heteronomy This is Immanuel Kant's term for the determination of the will on non-rational grounds. It is contrasted with *autonomy* of the will where the will is guided by reason. (See Chapter 25.)

hypothetical imperative Hypothetical imperatives command actions because they are useful for the attainment of some end that one may or may not desire to obtain. Ethicists who view moral duties to be dependent on consequences would view moral principles as hypothetical imperatives. They have the following form: If you want *X*, do action *A* (e.g., if you want to live in peace, do all in your power to prevent violence). This is contrasted with the *categorical imperative*. (See Chapter 25.)

indeterminism The view that some events are uncaused. Some versions state that some events are uncaused because they happen by chance. Others hold the minimal thesis that some events or states of being (e.g., the self) are uncaused, so that free will is consistent with the position. This view is contrasted with *determinism*.

inductive argument An *argument* in which the premises support the truth of the conclusion but do not guarantee it (as a valid *deductive argument* would). (See Chapter 2.)

innate ideas The theory that we first read of in Plato's *Meno* (see Chapter 10) and later in René Descartes that states all humans are born with certain knowledge.

intentionality (from Latin *intendo,* "to aim at" or "point at") refers to the directedness (or *aboutness*) of mental states. Consciousness is often directed at an object, its content—objects of desires, fear, belief, and appearances. Intentions are bidirectional: (1) from Mind to World; and (2) from World to Mind. An example of (1) from Mind to World is our desire to change the world or an aspect in it, such as when I kick the soccer ball, aiming at scoring a goal or when one invests money in stocks, hoping to improve one's financial situation. An example of (2) from World to Mind is an accurate belief that is formed about the makeup of this room when I open my eyes to perceive its content. When intentional acts are successful, they accomplish their task—fulfill a desire or obtain a true belief. (See Chapter 15.)

internalism The theory that knowledge is true belief that is justified in the appropriate manner, as opposed to *externalism,* where no reasons for belief are necessary for knowledge. (See Chapter 10.)

libertarianism The theory that humans have free will in the sense that given the same antecedent conditions, one can do otherwise. That is, the self is underdetermined by causes and is itself the determining cause of action. This view is represented by William James. (See Chapter 19.) This view is contrasted with *compatibilism* and *determinism.*

logic The study of rational *arguments,* the rules of valid inference, and inductive generalization. (See Chapter 2.)

materialism The metaphysical view that only physical matter and its properties exist. What appears to be nonmaterial (e.g., consciousness) is really either physical or a property of what is physical. (See Chapters 3, 13, and 14.)

metaphysics "Beyond physics." The study of ultimate reality, that which is not readily accessible through ordinary empirical experience. Metaphysics includes within its domain such topics as free will, causality, the nature of matter, immortality, and the existence of God.

monism The theory that reality is all of one substance, rather than two or more. Examples are materialist monism, which holds that matter is the single substance that makes up all there is, and idealism, which holds that all reality is spiritual or made up of ideas. Lucretius, Democritus, Bertrand Russell, and Richard Taylor all hold to materialistic monism. Baruch Spinoza, George Berkeley, and Hinduism are examples of proponents of idealism. (See Chapters 3 and 13.)

naturalism The theory that ethical terms are defined through factual terms in that ethical terms refer to natural properties. Ethical *hedonism* is one version of ethical naturalism, for it states that the good that is at the basis of all ethical judgment refers to the experience of pleasure. Other naturalists like Geoffrey Warnock speak of the content of morality in terms of promoting human flourishing or ameliorating the human predicament. The term also has a broader metaphysical meaning: as opposed to supernaturalism, explanations that appeal only to the natural, physical order of things. (See Chapter 1.)

natural theology The view that knowledge of God can be obtained through the use of reason. Strong versions hold that we can prove the existence of God. It is contrasted with revealed theology, which holds that all knowledge of God must come from a revelation of God.

necessary truth A truth that cannot be false, such as an analytic *proposition* (e.g., "All bachelors are male").

neutral monism The view held by Baruch Spinoza and William James that reality was made up of one substance, neither matter nor mind, but something common to both of these. (See Chapter 14.)

objectivism The view that moral principles have objective validity whether or not people recognize them as such; that is, moral rightness or wrongness does not depend on social approval but on independent considerations. Objectivism differs from absolutism in that it allows that all or many of its principles are overridable in given situations. (See Chapter 22.)

Occam's razor Named after William of Occam (1290–1349). Sometimes called the principle of parsimony, states that "entities are not to be multiplied beyond necessity." The razor metaphor connotes that useless or unnecessary material should be cut away from any explanation and the simplest hypothesis accepted. (See Chapter 16.)

ontology The study of the essence of things and of what there is. What kinds of things are there in the universe? For example, the mind–body problem is in part a debate over whether mental events are of a separate substance or property from physical events or things. René Descartes thought there were three different kinds of things: God, created souls, and created material things.

panpsychism The view that everything—that is, every object in the world (stones, blades of grass, molecules) as well as living beings—has a soul. (See Chapter 13.)

pantheism The view that God is everything and everything is God.

parallelism The view first put forth by Gottfried Leibniz that there is no causal interaction between bodies and minds. Each proceeds on its own, parallel to but independent of the other. (See Chapter 13.)

pragmatic theory of truth The theory set forth by C. S. Peirce and William James that interprets the meaning of a statement in terms of its practical consequences. They usually go on, as James does in Chapter 10, to say that a *proposition* is true or false according to its results.

prima facie From the Latin, meaning "at first glance." It signifies an initial status of an idea or principle. In ethics, beginning with W. D. Ross, it stands for a duty that has a presumption in its favor but may be overridden by another duty. Prima facie duties are contrasted with actual duties or all-things-considered duties. (See Chapter 22.)

proposition A sentence or statement that must either be true or false. Every statement that describes the world is a proposition. Questions and imperatives are not propositions. "Would you open the door?" and "Please, open the door" are not propositions, but "The door is open" is, since it claims to describe a situation. (See Chapter 2.)

rationalism The school of philosophy that holds there are important truths that can be known by the mind even though we have never experienced them. The rationalist generally believes in *innate knowledge* (or ideas), so that we can have certainty about metaphysical truth. Plato and René Descartes are two classic examples of rationalists. (See Chapter 2.)

reductive materialism The view that all mental states can be identified with states in the brain. (See Chapter 14.)

relativism There are two main types of relativism: cultural and ethical. Cultural relativism is a descriptive thesis, stating that there is enormous variety of moral beliefs across cultures. It is neutral as to whether this is the way things ought to be. Ethical relativism, on the other hand, is an evaluative thesis stating that the truth of a moral judgment depends on whether a culture recognizes the principle in question. (See Chapter 22.)

skepticism The view that we can have no knowledge. Universal skepticism holds that we cannot know anything at all, whereas local, or particular, skepticism holds that there are important realms in which we are ignorant (e.g., David Hume, regarding *metaphysics*). (See Chapter 11.)

supererogatory From the Latin, meaning "beyond the call of duty." An act that is not required by moral principles but contains enormous value. Supererogatory acts are those that are beyond the call of duty, such as risking one's life to save a stranger.

Although most moral systems allow for the possibility of supererogatory acts, some theories (most versions of classical *utilitarianism*) deny that there can be such acts.

teleological ethics Teleological ethical theories place the ultimate criterion of morality in some nonmoral value (e.g., happiness or welfare) that results from acts. Whereas *deontological ethics* ascribe intrinsic value to features of the acts themselves, teleological theories see only instrumental value in the acts but intrinsic value in the consequences of those acts. Both ethical *egoism* and *utilitarianism* are teleological theories. (See Chapter 24.)

teleology See *teleological ethics.* (See Chapter 24.)

theism The belief that a personal God exists and is providentially involved in human affairs. It is to be contrasted with *atheism,* which believes that no such being exists, and *deism,* which holds that God exists but he is not providentially concerned with human affairs.

theodicy The view that evil can be explained in the light of an overall plan of God and that, rightly understood, this world is the best of all possible worlds. John Hick holds to a version of this doctrine in Chapter 8.

universalizability This principle, which is found explicitly in Immanuel Kant's and R. M. Hare's philosophy and implicitly in most ethicists' work, states that if some act is right (or wrong) for one person in a situation, it is right (or wrong) for any relevantly similar person in that kind of a situation. It is a principle of consistency, which aims to eliminate irrelevant considerations from ethical assessment. (See Chapter 21.)

utilitarianism The theory that the right action is one that maximizes utility. Sometimes "utility" is defined in terms of pleasure (Jeremy Bentham), happiness (J. S. Mill), ideals (G. E. Moore and H. Rashdall), or interests (R. B. Perry). Its motto, which characterizes one version of utilitarianism, is "The Greatest Happiness for the Greatest Number." Utilitarians further divide into act and rule utilitarians. Act utilitarians hold that the right act in a situation is that which results (or is most likely to result) in the best consequences, whereas rule utilitarians hold that the right act is that which conforms to the set of rules that, in turn, will result in the best consequences (relative to other sets of rules). (See Chapter 24.)

Index